CABLE & DEADPOOL

THE HUMAN RACE

writer
FABIAN NICIEZA
pencils
PATRICK ZIRCHER
inks
M3TH & ROB ROSS @UDON
colors
GOTHAM
letters
VIRTUAL CALLIGRAPHY'S CORY PETIT
covers by
**PATRICK ZIRCHER, MARK BROOKS,
M3TH, FRANK D'ARMATA & PAUL MOUNTS**

editor
NICOLE WILEY
consulting editors
JOHN BARBER & RALPH MACCHIO

cable created by
ROB LIEFELD & LOUISE SIMONSON
deadpool created by
ROB LIEFELD & FABIAN NICIEZA

collection editor
JENNIFER GRÜNWALD
assistant editor
MICHAEL SHORT
senior editor, special projects
JEFF YOUNGQUIST
director of sales
DAVID GABRIEL
production
JERRY KALINOWSKI
book designer
CARRIE BEADLE
creative director
TOM MARVELLI

editor in chief
JOE QUESADA
publisher
DAN BUCKLEY

P9-CBJ-856

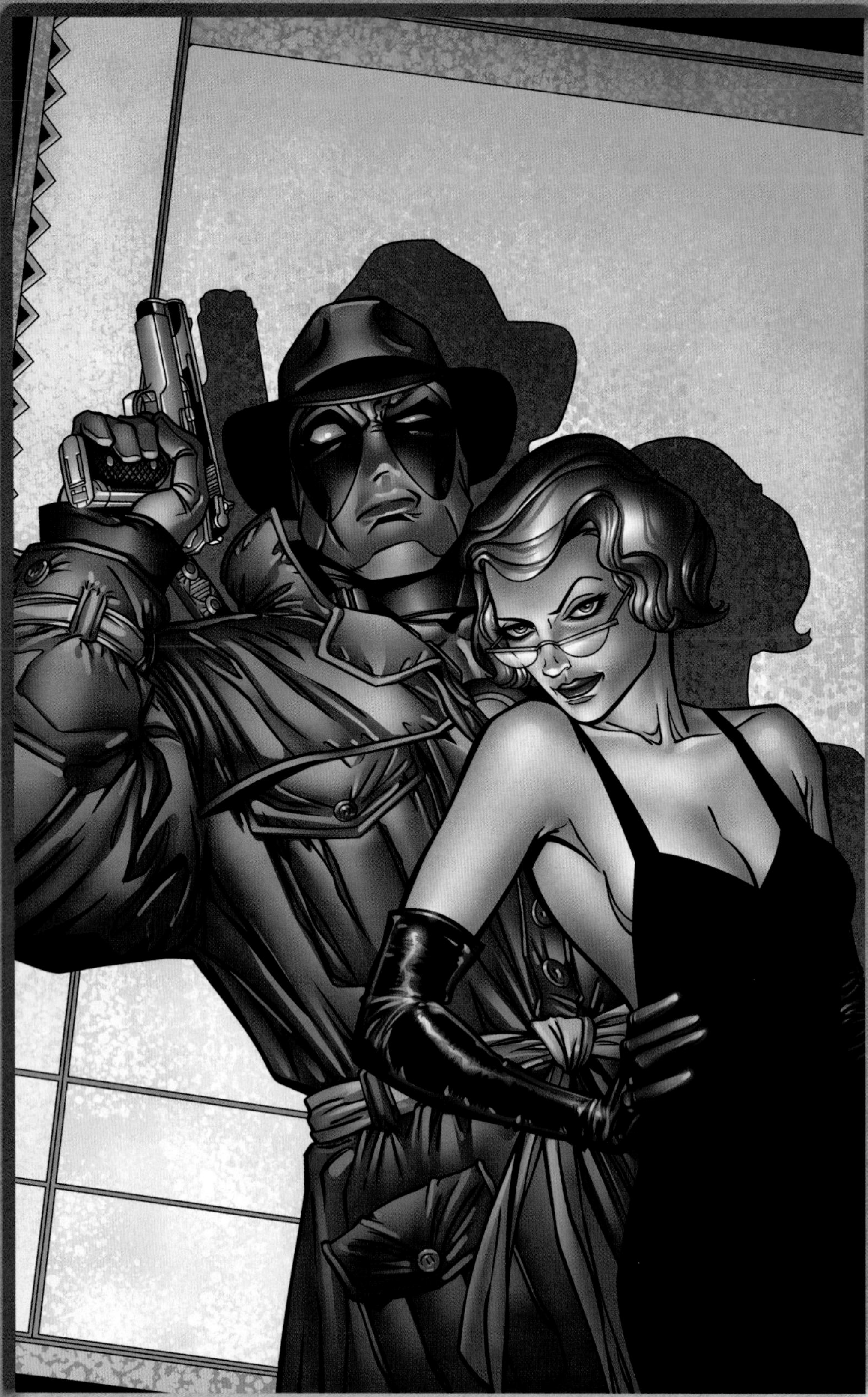

#13

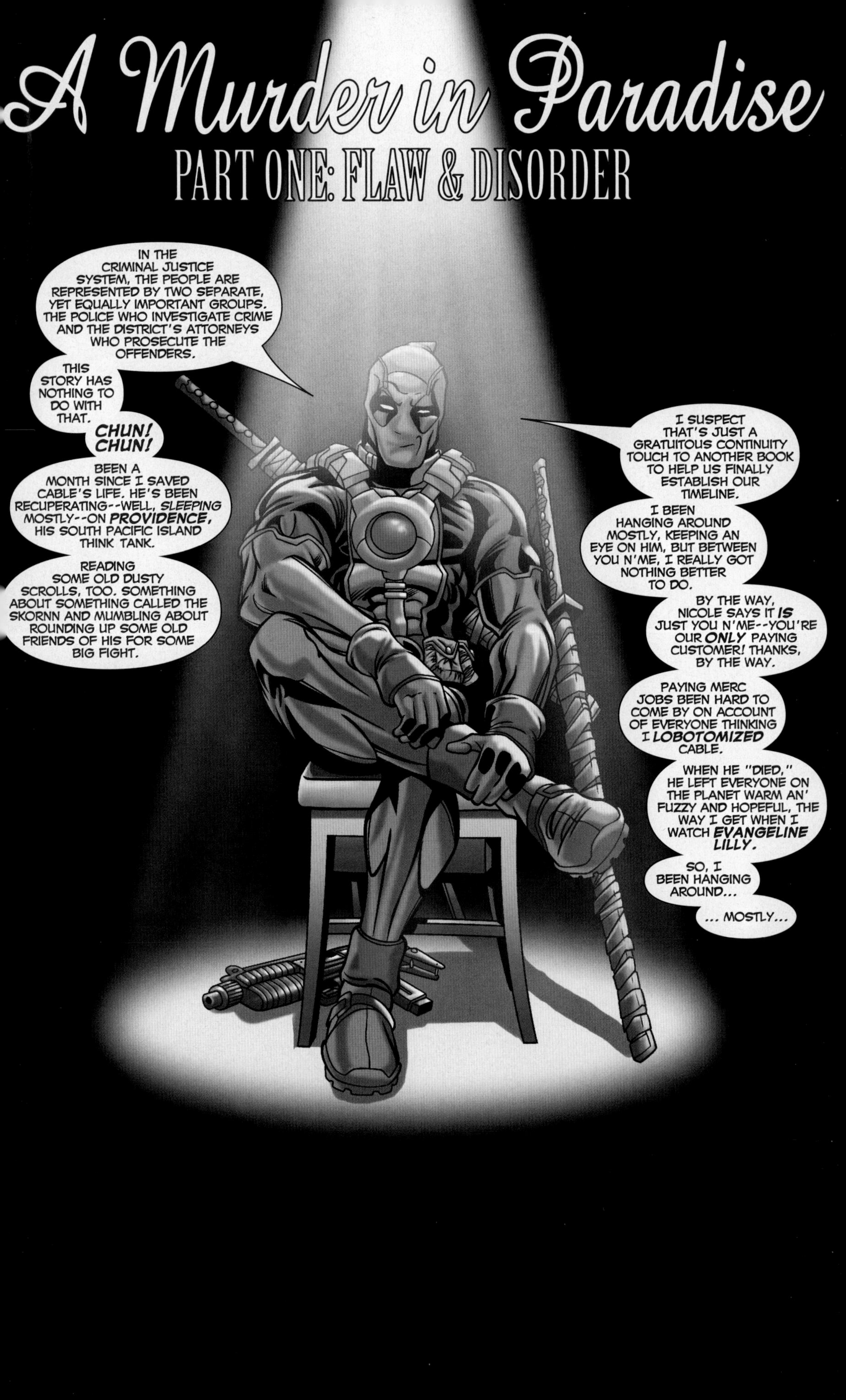
A Murder in Paradise
PART ONE: FLAW & DISORDER
IN THE CRIMINAL JUSTICE SYSTEM, THE PEOPLE ARE REPRESENTED BY TWO SEPARATE, YET EQUALLY IMPORTANT GROUPS. THE POLICE WHO INVESTIGATE CRIME AND THE DISTRICT'S ATTORNEYS WHO PROSECUTE THE OFFENDERS.
THIS STORY HAS NOTHING TO DO WITH THAT.
CHUN! CHUN!
BEEN A MONTH SINCE I SAVED CABLE'S LIFE. HE'S BEEN RECUPERATING--WELL, SLEEPING MOSTLY--ON PROVIDENCE, HIS SOUTH PACIFIC ISLAND THINK TANK.
READING SOME OLD DUSTY SCROLLS, TOO. SOMETHING ABOUT SOMETHING CALLED THE SKORNN AND MUMBLING ABOUT ROUNDING UP SOME OLD FRIENDS OF HIS FOR SOME BIG FIGHT.
I SUSPECT THAT'S JUST A GRATUITOUS CONTINUITY TOUCH TO ANOTHER BOOK TO HELP US FINALLY ESTABLISH OUR TIMELINE.
I BEEN HANGING AROUND MOSTLY, KEEPING AN EYE ON HIM, BUT BETWEEN YOU N'ME, I REALLY GOT NOTHING BETTER TO DO.
BY THE WAY, NICOLE SAYS IT IS JUST YOU N'ME--YOU'RE OUR ONLY PAYING CUSTOMER! THANKS, BY THE WAY.
PAYING MERC JOBS BEEN HARD TO COME BY ON ACCOUNT OF EVERYONE THINKING I LOBOTOMIZED CABLE.
WHEN HE "DIED," HE LEFT EVERYONE ON THE PLANET WARM AN' FUZZY AND HOPEFUL, THE WAY I GET WHEN I WATCH EVANGELINE LILLY.
SO, I BEEN HANGING AROUND...
... MOSTLY...

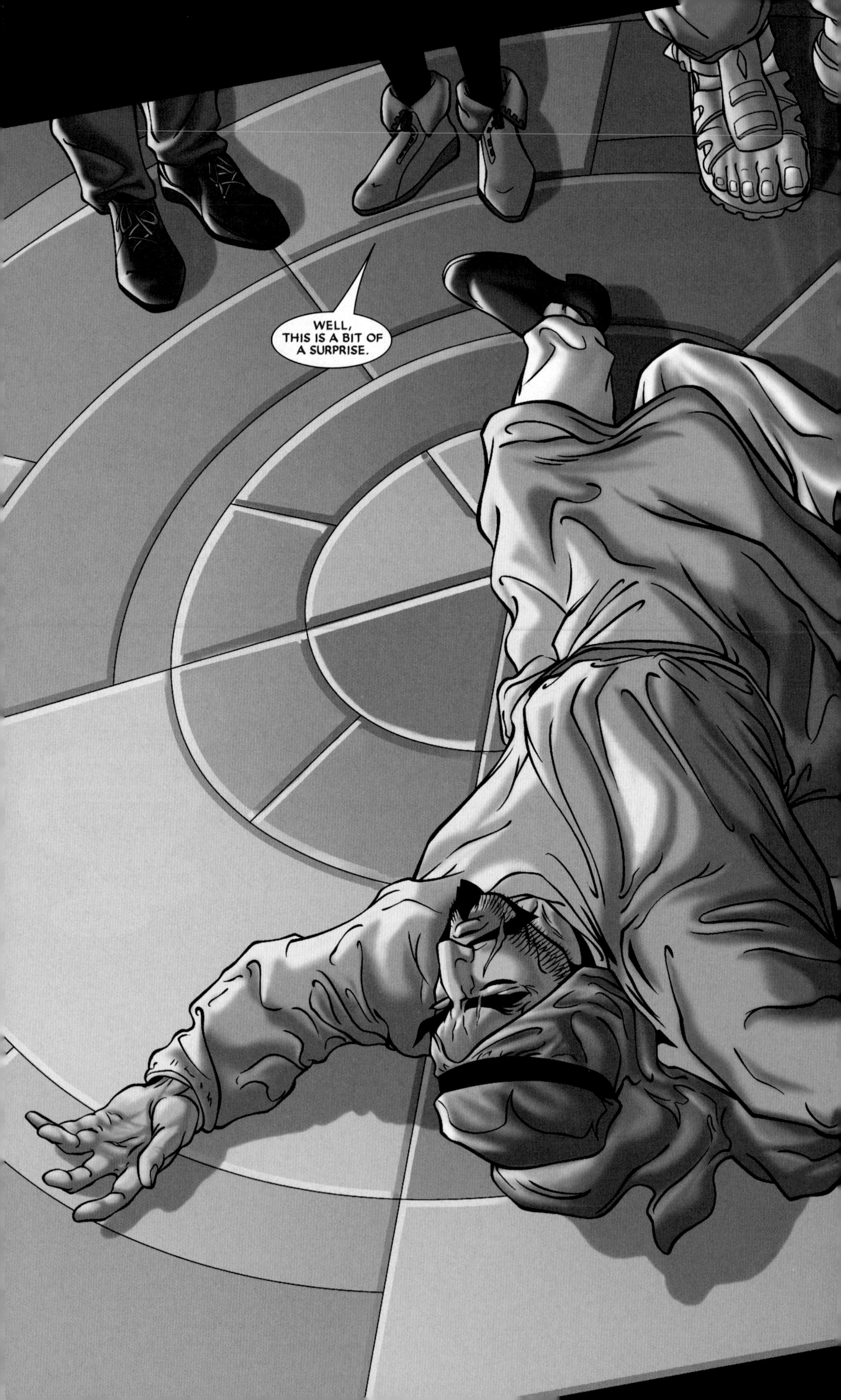
WELL, THIS IS A BIT OF A SURPRISE.

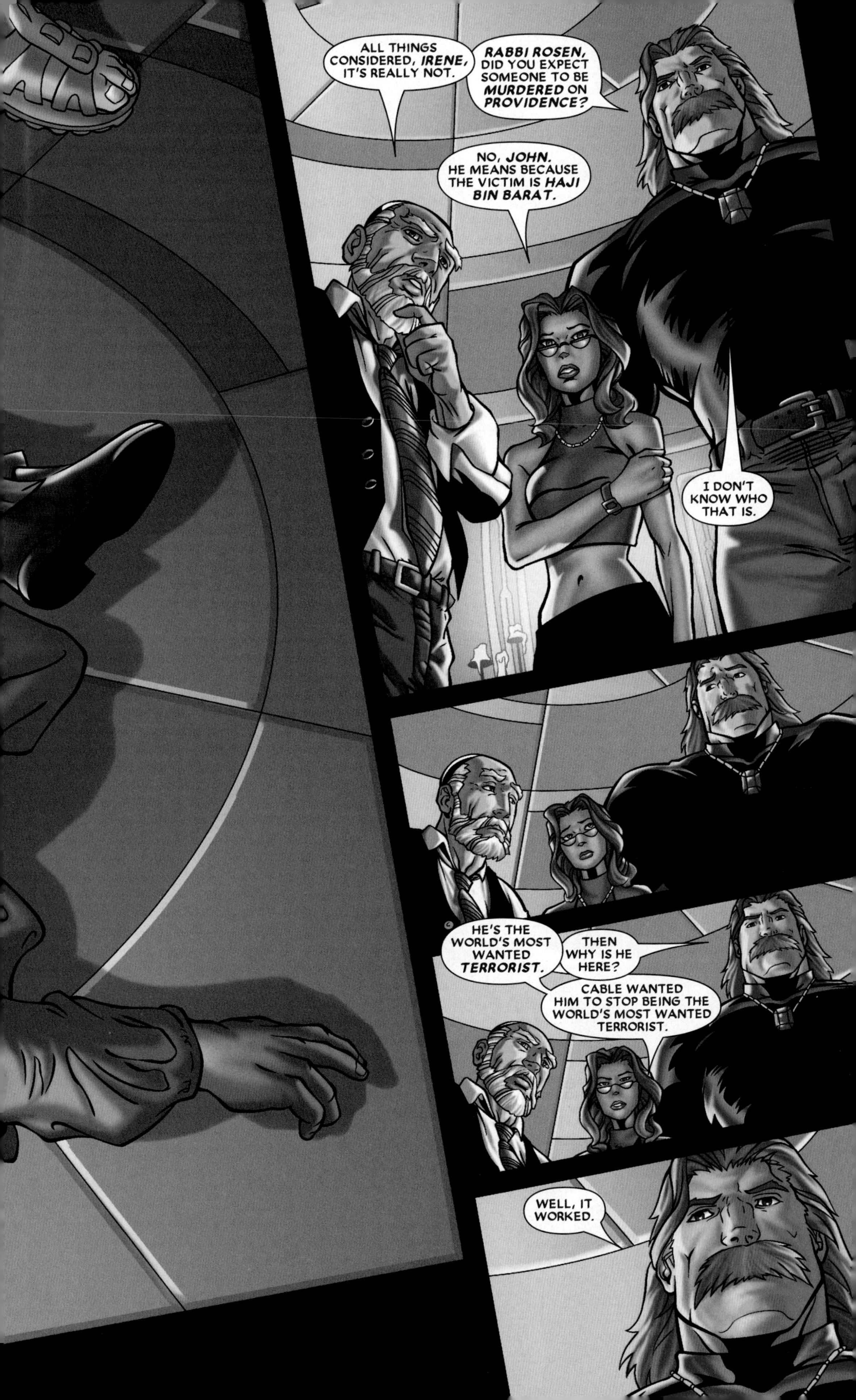
ALL THINGS CONSIDERED, IRENE, IT'S REALLY NOT.
RABBI ROSEN, DID YOU EXPECT SOMEONE TO BE MURDERED ON PROVIDENCE?
NO, JOHN. HE MEANS BECAUSE THE VICTIM IS HAJI BIN BARAT.
I DON'T KNOW WHO THAT IS.
HE'S THE WORLD'S MOST WANTED TERRORIST.
THEN WHY IS HE HERE?
CABLE WANTED HIM TO STOP BEING THE WORLD'S MOST WANTED TERRORIST.
WELL, IT WORKED.

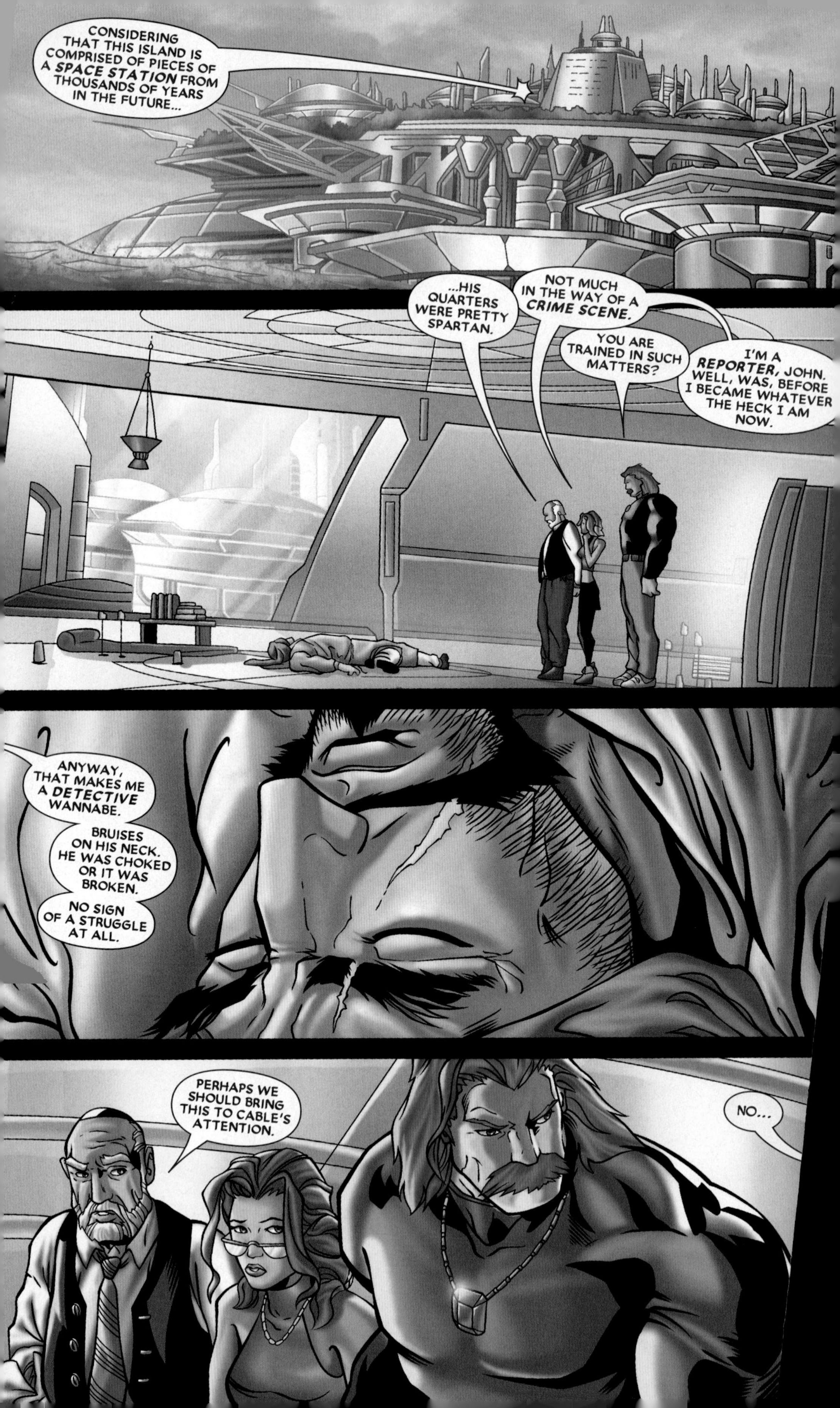
CONSIDERING THAT THIS ISLAND IS COMPRISED OF PIECES OF A SPACE STATION FROM THOUSANDS OF YEARS IN THE FUTURE...
...HIS QUARTERS WERE PRETTY SPARTAN.
NOT MUCH IN THE WAY OF A CRIME SCENE.
YOU ARE TRAINED IN SUCH MATTERS?
I'M A REPORTER, JOHN. WELL, WAS, BEFORE I BECAME WHATEVER THE HECK I AM NOW.
ANYWAY, THAT MAKES ME A DETECTIVE WANNABE.
BRUISES ON HIS NECK. HE WAS CHOKED OR IT WAS BROKEN.
NO SIGN OF A STRUGGLE AT ALL.
PERHAPS WE SHOULD BRING THIS TO CABLE'S ATTENTION.
NO...

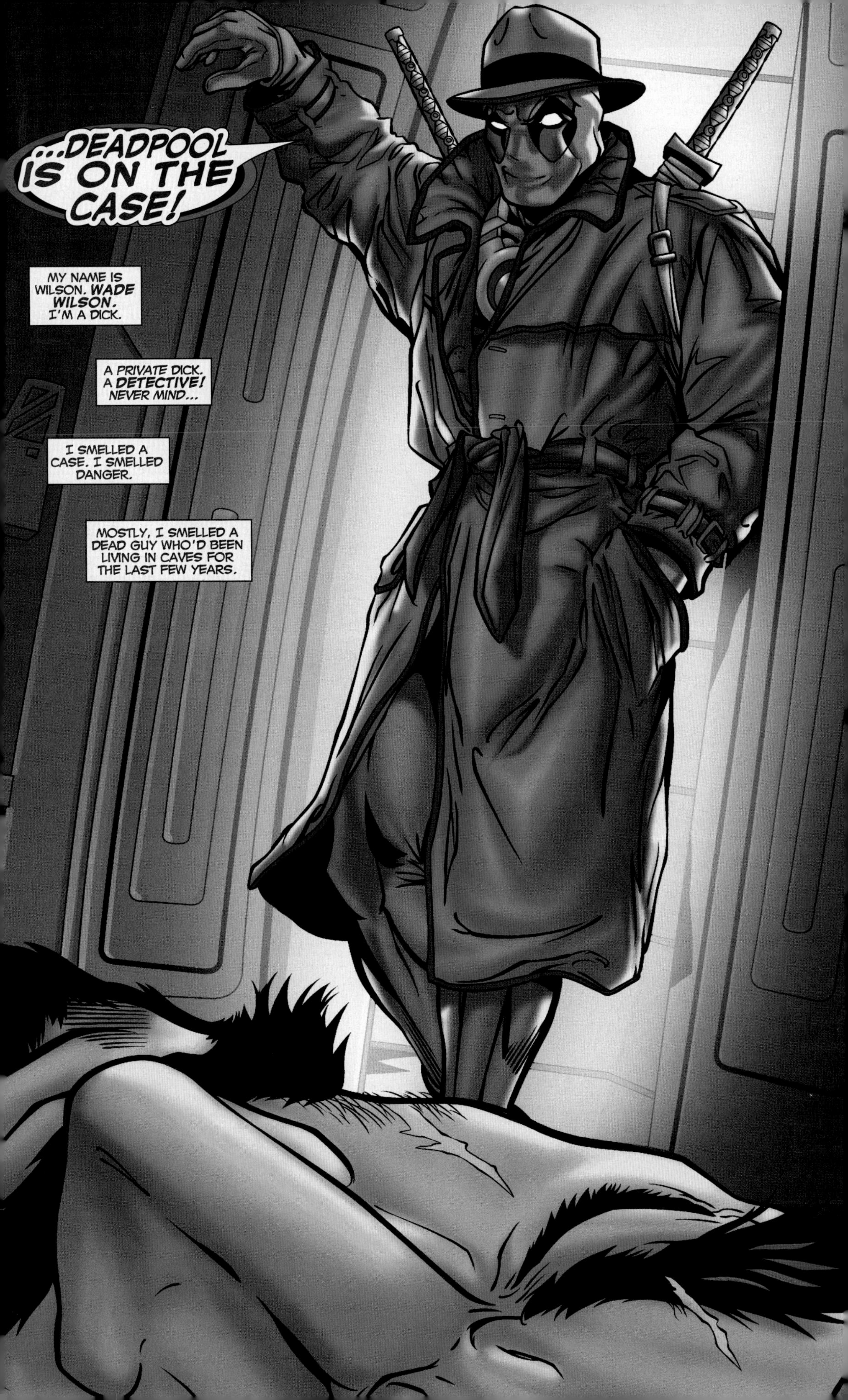
...DEADPOOL IS ON THE CASE!
MY NAME IS WILSON. WADE WILSON. I'M A DICK.
A PRIVATE DICK. A DETECTIVE! NEVER MIND...
I SMELLED A CASE. I SMELLED DANGER.
MOSTLY, I SMELLED A DEAD GUY WHO'D BEEN LIVING IN CAVES FOR THE LAST FEW YEARS.

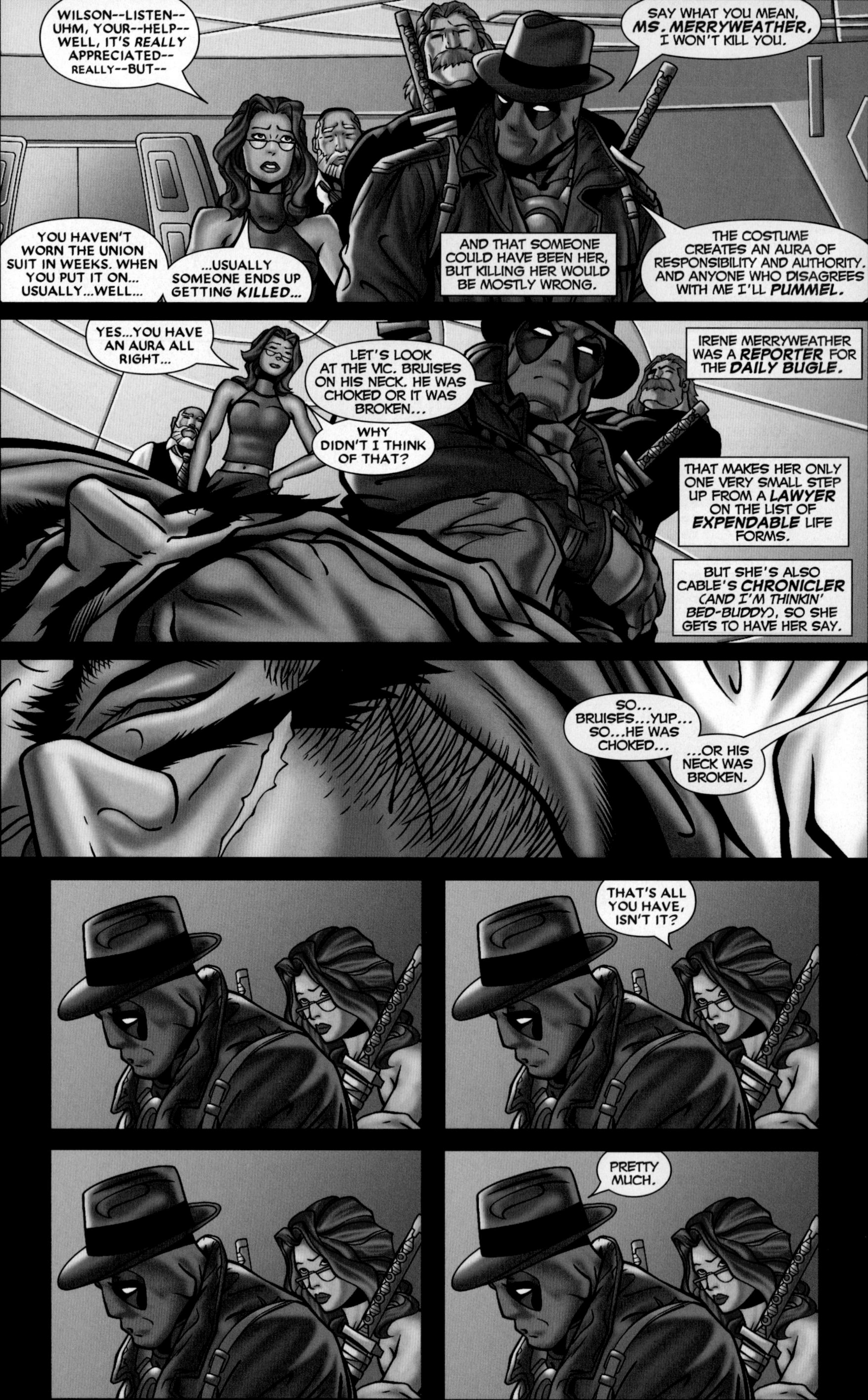
WILSON--LISTEN--UHM, YOUR--HELP--WELL, IT'S *REALLY* APPRECIATED--REALLY--BUT--
SAY WHAT YOU MEAN, ***MS. MERRYWEATHER,*** I WON'T KILL YOU.
YOU HAVEN'T WORN THE UNION SUIT IN WEEKS. WHEN YOU PUT IT ON... USUALLY...WELL...
...USUALLY SOMEONE ENDS UP GETTING ***KILLED...***
AND THAT SOMEONE COULD HAVE BEEN HER, BUT KILLING HER WOULD BE MOSTLY WRONG.
THE COSTUME CREATES AN AURA OF RESPONSIBILITY AND AUTHORITY. AND ANYONE WHO DISAGREES WITH ME I'LL ***PUMMEL.***
YES...YOU HAVE AN AURA ALL RIGHT...
LET'S LOOK AT THE VIC. BRUISES ON HIS NECK. HE WAS CHOKED OR IT WAS BROKEN...
WHY DIDN'T I THINK OF THAT?
IRENE MERRYWEATHER WAS A ***REPORTER*** FOR THE ***DAILY BUGLE.***
THAT MAKES HER ONLY ONE VERY SMALL STEP UP FROM A ***LAWYER*** ON THE LIST OF ***EXPENDABLE*** LIFE FORMS.
BUT SHE'S ALSO CABLE'S ***CHRONICLER*** *(AND I'M THINKIN' BED-BUDDY)*, SO SHE GETS TO HAVE HER SAY.
SO... BRUISES...YUP... SO...HE WAS CHOKED...
...OR HIS NECK WAS BROKEN.
THAT'S ALL YOU HAVE, ISN'T IT?
PRETTY MUCH.

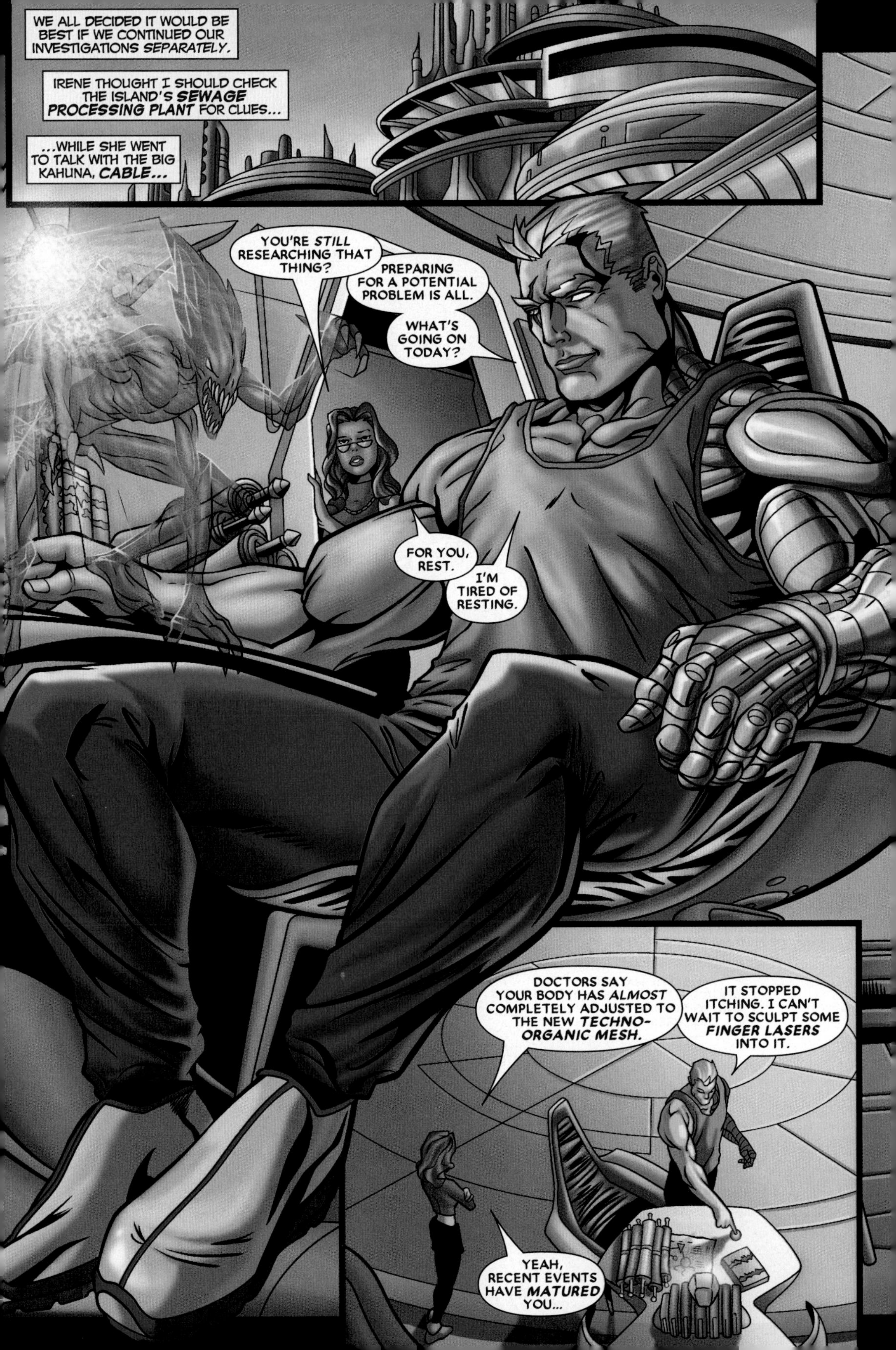
WE ALL DECIDED IT WOULD BE BEST IF WE CONTINUED OUR INVESTIGATIONS SEPARATELY.
IRENE THOUGHT I SHOULD CHECK THE ISLAND'S SEWAGE PROCESSING PLANT FOR CLUES...
...WHILE SHE WENT TO TALK WITH THE BIG KAHUNA, CABLE...
YOU'RE STILL RESEARCHING THAT THING?
PREPARING FOR A POTENTIAL PROBLEM IS ALL.
WHAT'S GOING ON TODAY?
FOR YOU, REST.
I'M TIRED OF RESTING.
DOCTORS SAY YOUR BODY HAS ALMOST COMPLETELY ADJUSTED TO THE NEW TECHNO-ORGANIC MESH.
IT STOPPED ITCHING. I CAN'T WAIT TO SCULPT SOME FINGER LASERS INTO IT.
YEAH, RECENT EVENTS HAVE MATURED YOU...

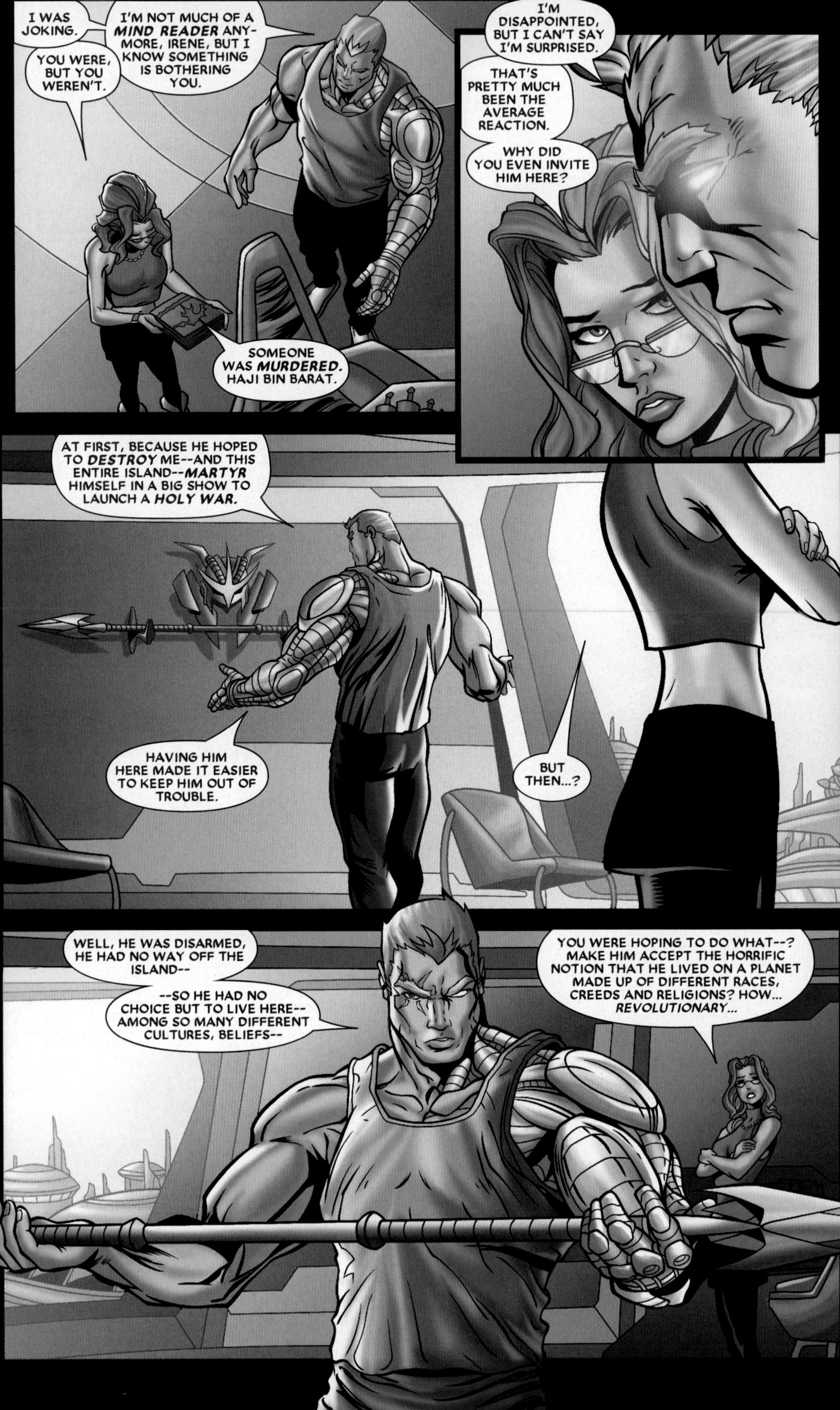
I WAS JOKING.
I'M NOT MUCH OF A MIND READER ANYMORE, IRENE, BUT I KNOW SOMETHING IS BOTHERING YOU.
YOU WERE, BUT YOU WEREN'T.
SOMEONE WAS MURDERED. HAJI BIN BARAT.
I'M DISAPPOINTED, BUT I CAN'T SAY I'M SURPRISED.
THAT'S PRETTY MUCH BEEN THE AVERAGE REACTION.
WHY DID YOU EVEN INVITE HIM HERE?
AT FIRST, BECAUSE HE HOPED TO DESTROY ME--AND THIS ENTIRE ISLAND--MARTYR HIMSELF IN A BIG SHOW TO LAUNCH A HOLY WAR.
HAVING HIM HERE MADE IT EASIER TO KEEP HIM OUT OF TROUBLE.
BUT THEN...?
WELL, HE WAS DISARMED, HE HAD NO WAY OFF THE ISLAND--
--SO HE HAD NO CHOICE BUT TO LIVE HERE--AMONG SO MANY DIFFERENT CULTURES, BELIEFS--
YOU WERE HOPING TO DO WHAT--? MAKE HIM ACCEPT THE HORRIFIC NOTION THAT HE LIVED ON A PLANET MADE UP OF DIFFERENT RACES, CREEDS AND RELIGIONS? HOW... REVOLUTIONARY...

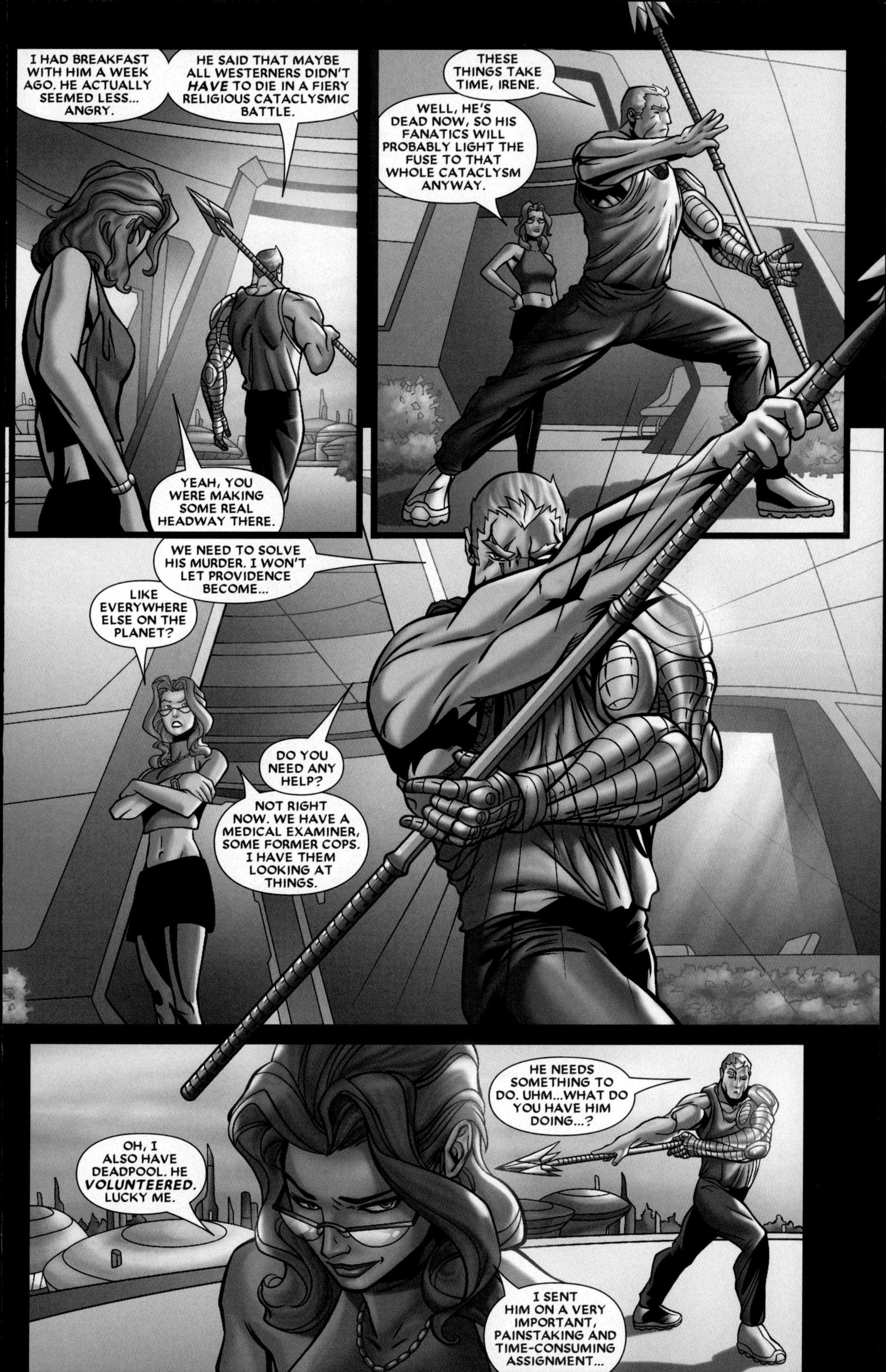

I HAD BREAKFAST WITH HIM A WEEK AGO. HE ACTUALLY SEEMED LESS... ANGRY.
HE SAID THAT MAYBE ALL WESTERNERS DIDN'T *HAVE* TO DIE IN A FIERY RELIGIOUS CATACLYSMIC BATTLE.
YEAH, YOU WERE MAKING SOME REAL HEADWAY THERE.
THESE THINGS TAKE TIME, IRENE.
WELL, HE'S DEAD NOW, SO HIS FANATICS WILL PROBABLY LIGHT THE FUSE TO THAT WHOLE CATACLYSM ANYWAY.
WE NEED TO SOLVE HIS MURDER. I WON'T LET PROVIDENCE BECOME...
LIKE EVERYWHERE ELSE ON THE PLANET?
DO YOU NEED ANY HELP?
NOT RIGHT NOW. WE HAVE A MEDICAL EXAMINER, SOME FORMER COPS. I HAVE THEM LOOKING AT THINGS.
OH, I ALSO HAVE DEADPOOL. HE ***VOLUNTEERED.*** LUCKY ME.
HE NEEDS SOMETHING TO DO. UHM...WHAT DO YOU HAVE HIM DOING...?
I SENT HIM ON A VERY IMPORTANT, PAINSTAKING AND TIME-CONSUMING ASSIGNMENT...

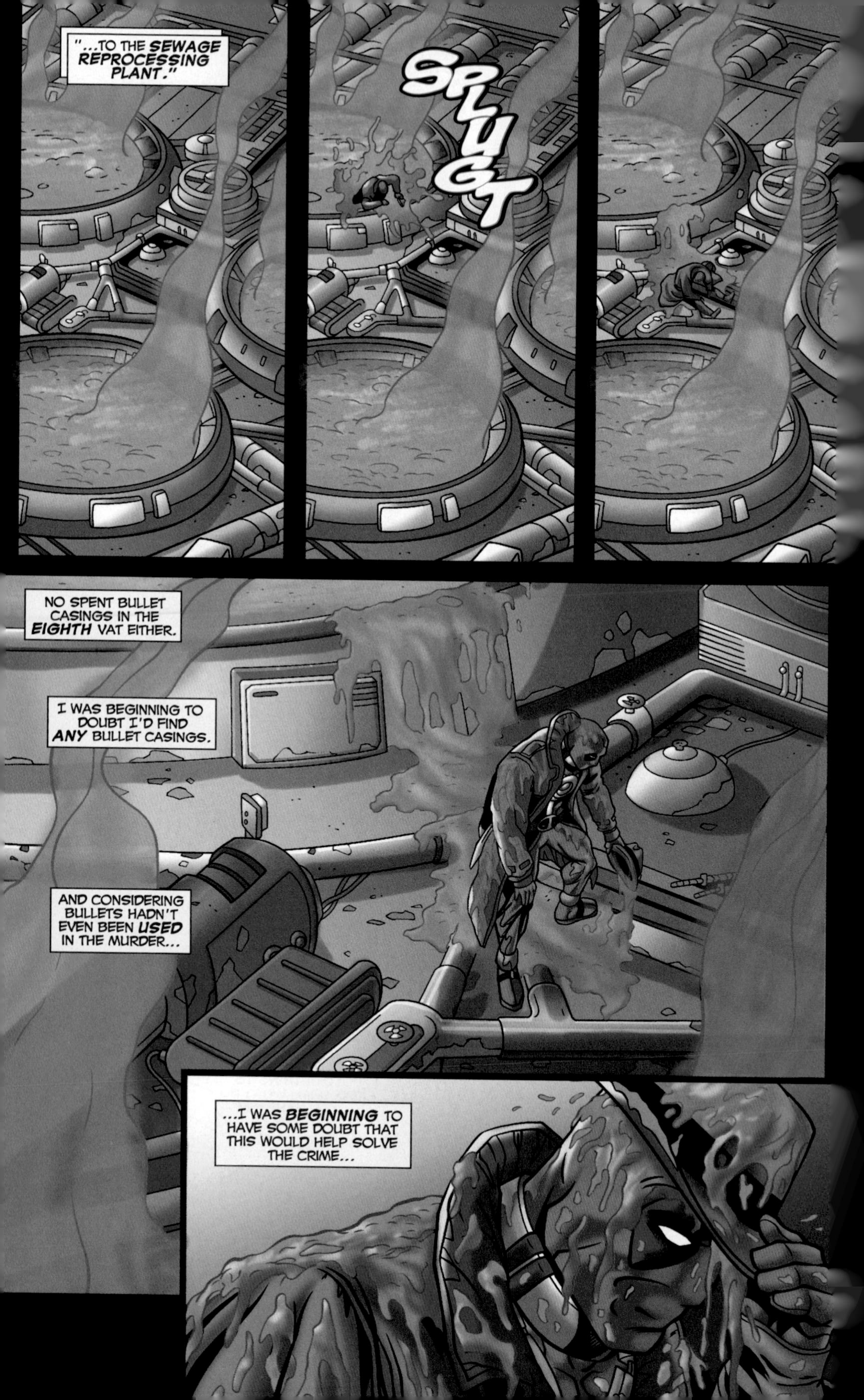
"...TO THE SEWAGE REPROCESSING PLANT."
SPLUGT
NO SPENT BULLET CASINGS IN THE EIGHTH VAT EITHER.
I WAS BEGINNING TO DOUBT I'D FIND ANY BULLET CASINGS.
AND CONSIDERING BULLETS HADN'T EVEN BEEN USED IN THE MURDER...
...I WAS BEGINNING TO HAVE SOME DOUBT THAT THIS WOULD HELP SOLVE THE CRIME...

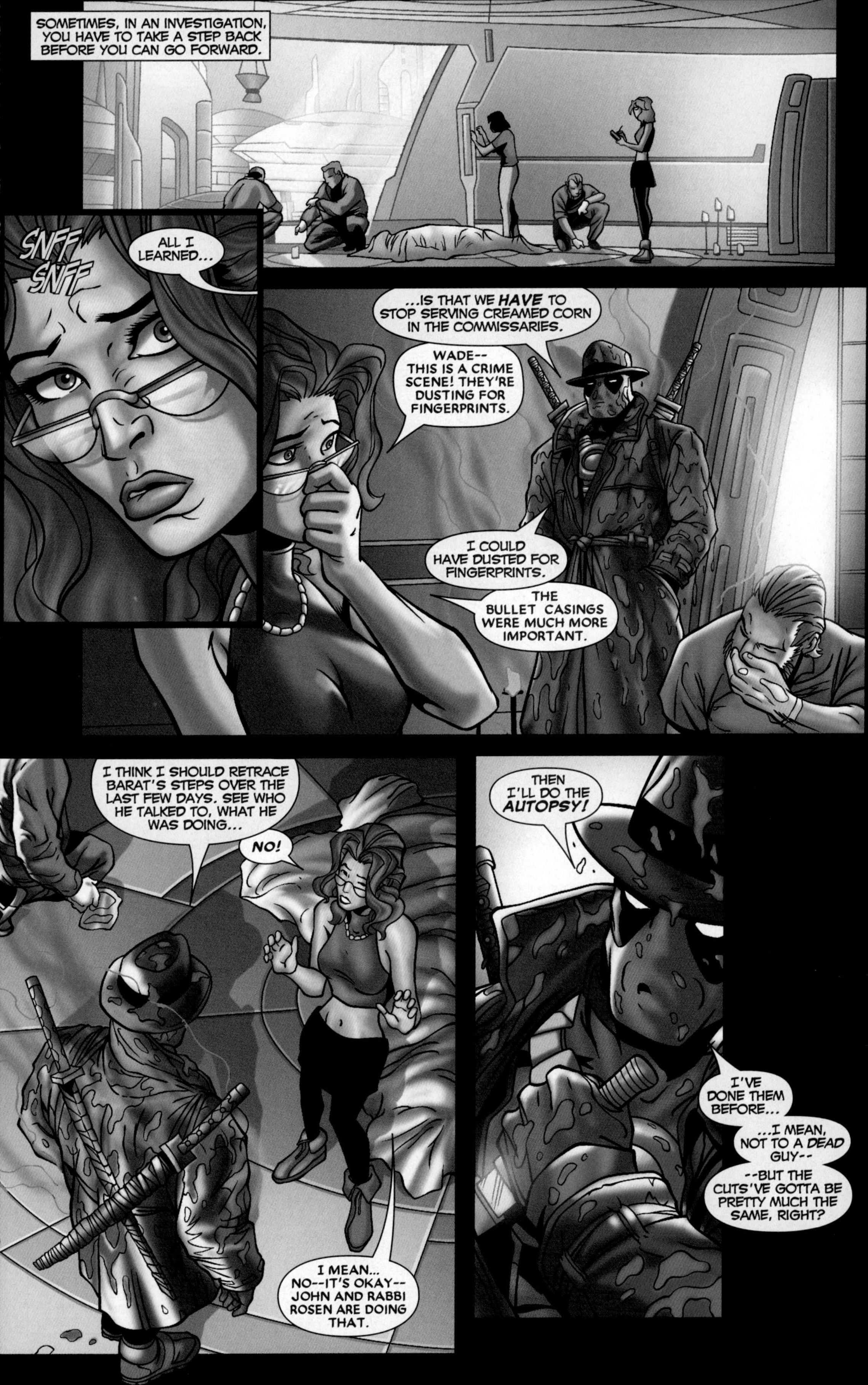
SOMETIMES, IN AN INVESTIGATION, YOU HAVE TO TAKE A STEP BACK BEFORE YOU CAN GO FORWARD.
SNFF SNFF
ALL I LEARNED...
...IS THAT WE HAVE TO STOP SERVING CREAMED CORN IN THE COMMISSARIES.
WADE-- THIS IS A CRIME SCENE! THEY'RE DUSTING FOR FINGERPRINTS.
I COULD HAVE DUSTED FOR FINGERPRINTS.
THE BULLET CASINGS WERE MUCH MORE IMPORTANT.
I THINK I SHOULD RETRACE BARAT'S STEPS OVER THE LAST FEW DAYS. SEE WHO HE TALKED TO, WHAT HE WAS DOING...
NO!
I MEAN... NO--IT'S OKAY-- JOHN AND RABBI ROSEN ARE DOING THAT.
THEN I'LL DO THE AUTOPSY!
I'VE DONE THEM BEFORE...
...I MEAN, NOT TO A DEAD GUY--
--BUT THE CUTS'VE GOTTA BE PRETTY MUCH THE SAME, RIGHT?

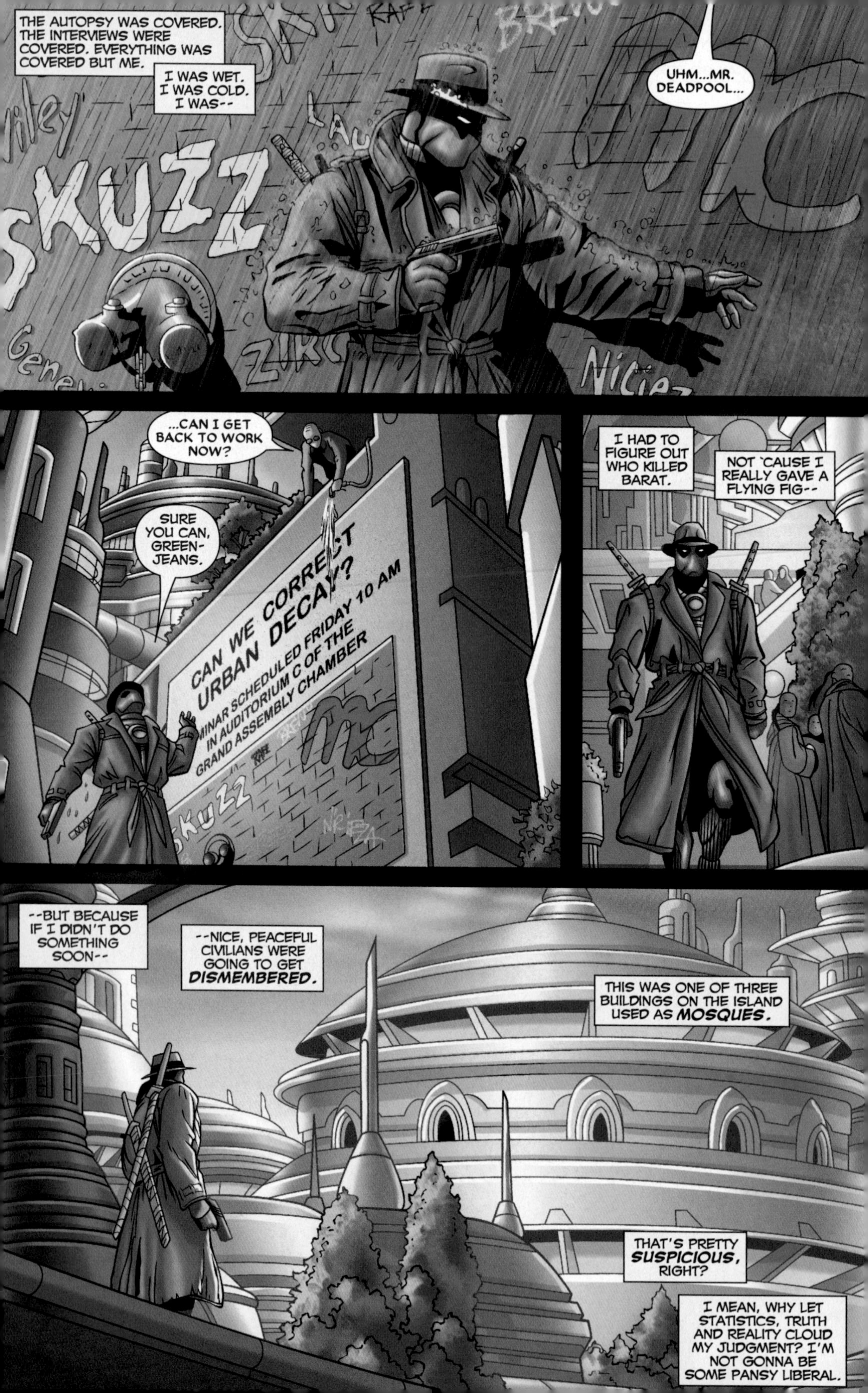
THE AUTOPSY WAS COVERED. THE INTERVIEWS WERE COVERED. EVERYTHING WAS COVERED BUT ME.
I WAS WET. I WAS COLD. I WAS--
UHM...MR. DEADPOOL...
SKUZZ
...CAN I GET BACK TO WORK NOW?
SURE YOU CAN, GREEN-JEANS.
CAN WE CORRECT URBAN DECAY?
MINAR SCHEDULED FRIDAY 10 AM
IN AUDITORIUM C OF THE
GRAND ASSEMBLY CHAMBER
I HAD TO FIGURE OUT WHO KILLED BARAT.
NOT 'CAUSE I REALLY GAVE A FLYING FIG--
--BUT BECAUSE IF I DIDN'T DO SOMETHING SOON--
--NICE, PEACEFUL CIVILIANS WERE GOING TO GET ***DISMEMBERED.***
THIS WAS ONE OF THREE BUILDINGS ON THE ISLAND USED AS ***MOSQUES.***
THAT'S PRETTY ***SUSPICIOUS,*** RIGHT?
I MEAN, WHY LET STATISTICS, TRUTH AND REALITY CLOUD MY JUDGMENT? I'M NOT GONNA BE SOME PANSY LIBERAL.

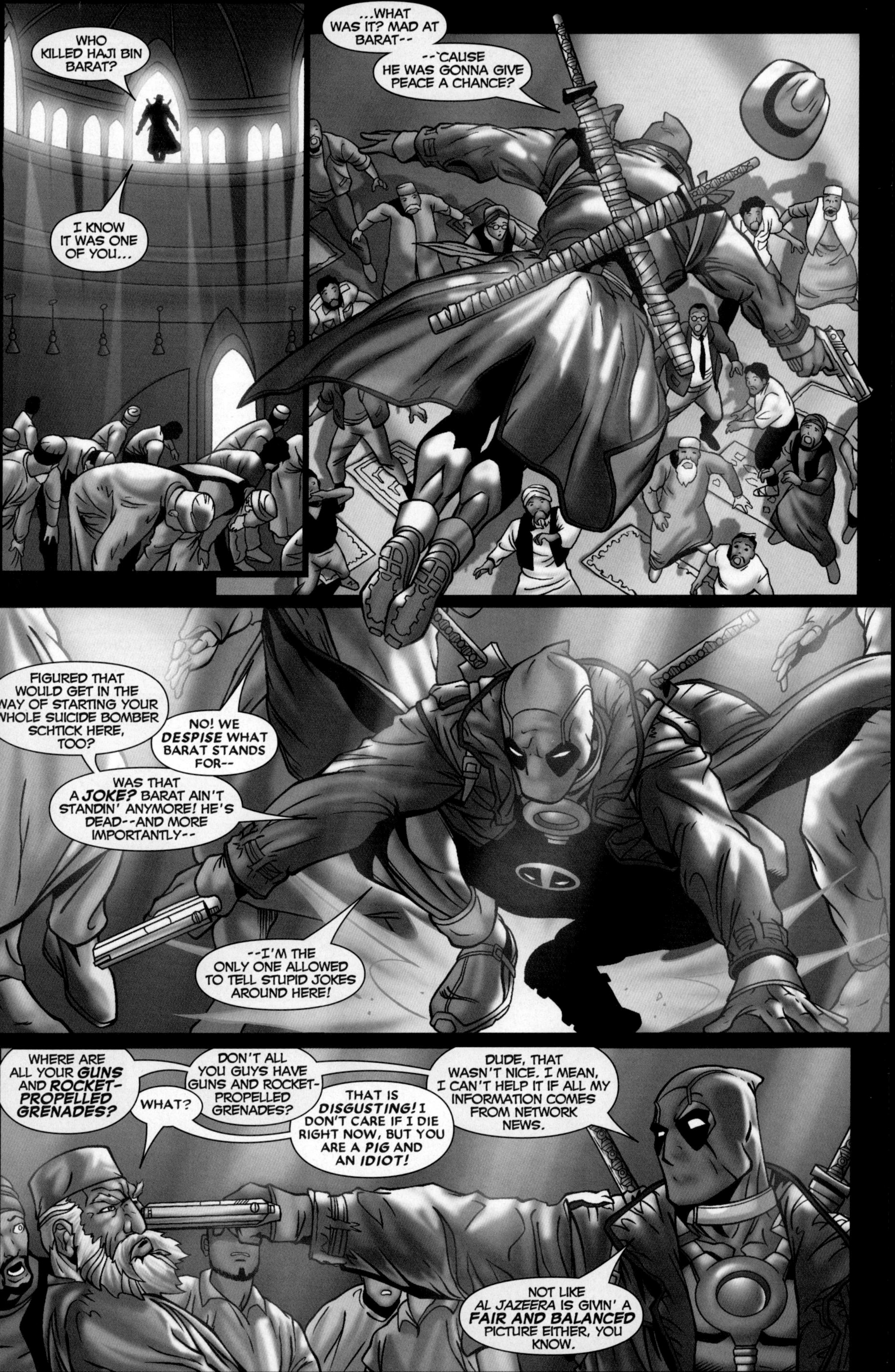

WHO KILLED HAJI BIN BARAT?
I KNOW IT WAS ONE OF YOU...
...WHAT WAS IT? MAD AT BARAT--
--`CAUSE HE WAS GONNA GIVE PEACE A CHANCE?
FIGURED THAT WOULD GET IN THE WAY OF STARTING YOUR WHOLE SUICIDE BOMBER SCHTICK HERE, TOO?
NO! WE DESPISE WHAT BARAT STANDS FOR--
WAS THAT A JOKE? BARAT AIN'T STANDIN' ANYMORE! HE'S DEAD--AND MORE IMPORTANTLY--
--I'M THE ONLY ONE ALLOWED TO TELL STUPID JOKES AROUND HERE!
WHERE ARE ALL YOUR GUNS AND ROCKET-PROPELLED GRENADES?
WHAT?
DON'T ALL YOU GUYS HAVE GUNS AND ROCKET-PROPELLED GRENADES?
THAT IS DISGUSTING! I DON'T CARE IF I DIE RIGHT NOW, BUT YOU ARE A PIG AND AN IDIOT!
DUDE, THAT WASN'T NICE. I MEAN, I CAN'T HELP IT IF ALL MY INFORMATION COMES FROM NETWORK NEWS.
NOT LIKE AL JAZEERA IS GIVIN' A FAIR AND BALANCED PICTURE EITHER, YOU KNOW.

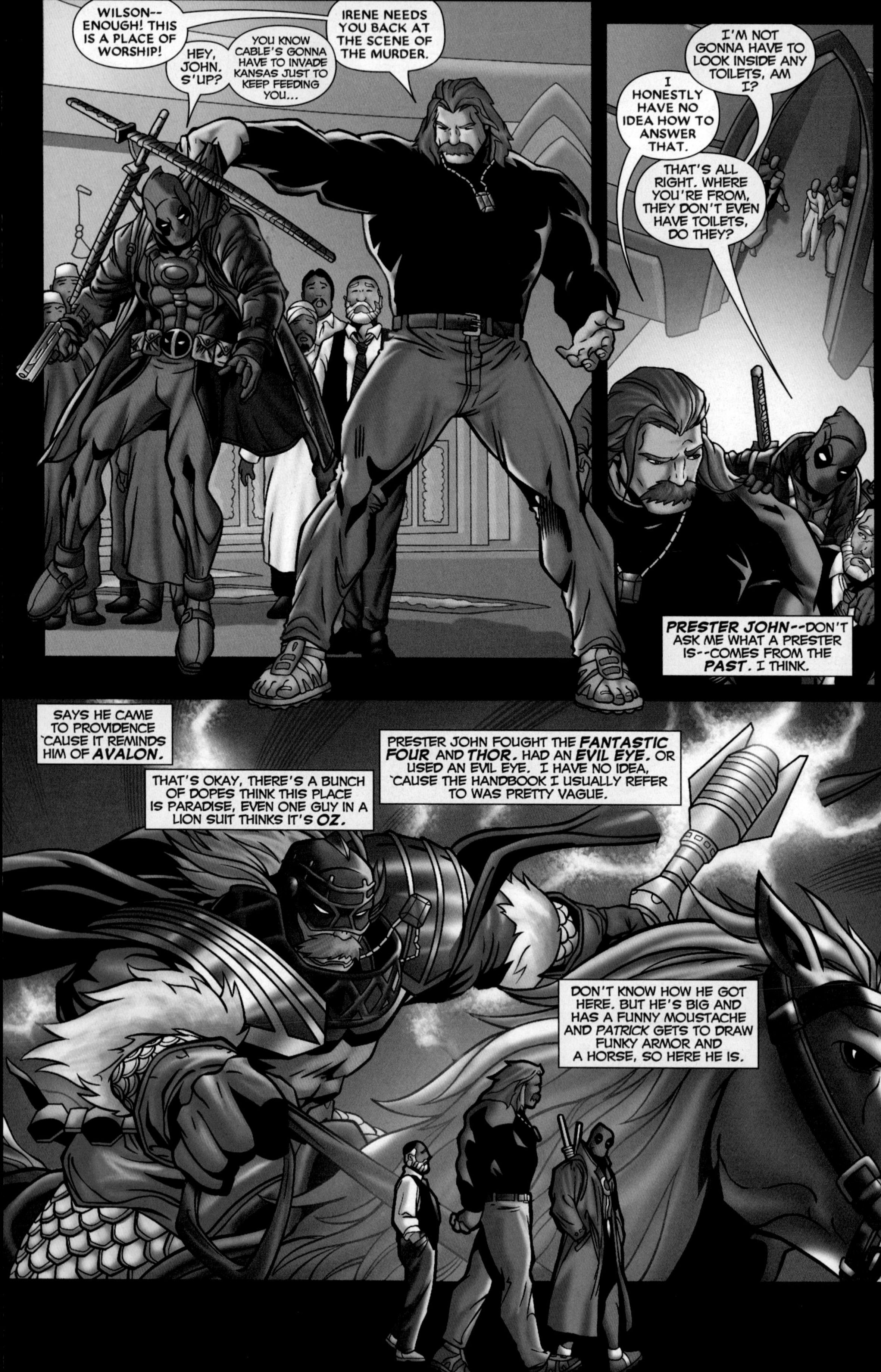

WILSON-- ENOUGH! THIS IS A PLACE OF WORSHIP!
HEY, JOHN. S'UP?
YOU KNOW CABLE'S GONNA HAVE TO INVADE KANSAS JUST TO KEEP FEEDING YOU...
IRENE NEEDS YOU BACK AT THE SCENE OF THE MURDER.
I'M NOT GONNA HAVE TO LOOK INSIDE ANY TOILETS, AM I?
I HONESTLY HAVE NO IDEA HOW TO ANSWER THAT.
THAT'S ALL RIGHT. WHERE YOU'RE FROM, THEY DON'T EVEN HAVE TOILETS, DO THEY?
PRESTER JOHN--DON'T ASK ME WHAT A PRESTER IS--COMES FROM THE PAST. I THINK.
SAYS HE CAME TO PROVIDENCE 'CAUSE IT REMINDS HIM OF AVALON.
THAT'S OKAY, THERE'S A BUNCH OF DOPES THINK THIS PLACE IS PARADISE, EVEN ONE GUY IN A LION SUIT THINKS IT'S OZ.
PRESTER JOHN FOUGHT THE FANTASTIC FOUR AND THOR. HAD AN EVIL EYE. OR USED AN EVIL EYE. I HAVE NO IDEA, 'CAUSE THE HANDBOOK I USUALLY REFER TO WAS PRETTY VAGUE.
DON'T KNOW HOW HE GOT HERE. BUT HE'S BIG AND HAS A FUNNY MOUSTACHE AND PATRICK GETS TO DRAW FUNKY ARMOR AND A HORSE, SO HERE HE IS.

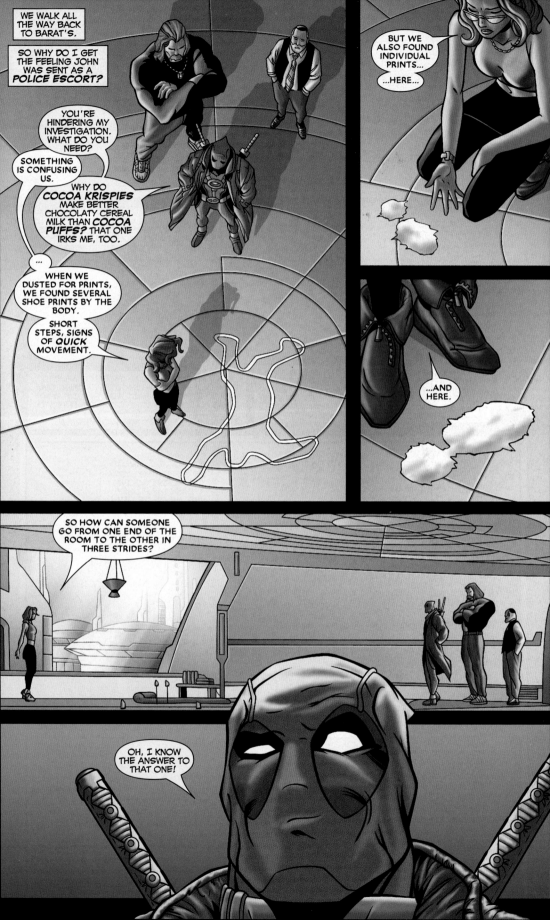

WE WALK ALL THE WAY BACK TO BARAT'S.

SO WHY DO I GET THE FEELING JOHN WAS SENT AS A POLICE ESCORT?

YOU'RE HINDERING MY INVESTIGATION. WHAT DO YOU NEED?

SOMETHING IS CONFUSING US.

WHY DO COCOA KRISPIES MAKE BETTER CHOCOLATY CEREAL MILK THAN COCOA PUFFS? THAT ONE IRKS ME, TOO.

...

WHEN WE DUSTED FOR PRINTS, WE FOUND SEVERAL SHOE PRINTS BY THE BODY.

SHORT STEPS, SIGNS OF QUICK MOVEMENT.

BUT WE ALSO FOUND INDIVIDUAL PRINTS...

...HERE...

...AND HERE.

SO HOW CAN SOMEONE GO FROM ONE END OF THE ROOM TO THE OTHER IN THREE STRIDES?

OH, I KNOW THE ANSWER TO THAT ONE!

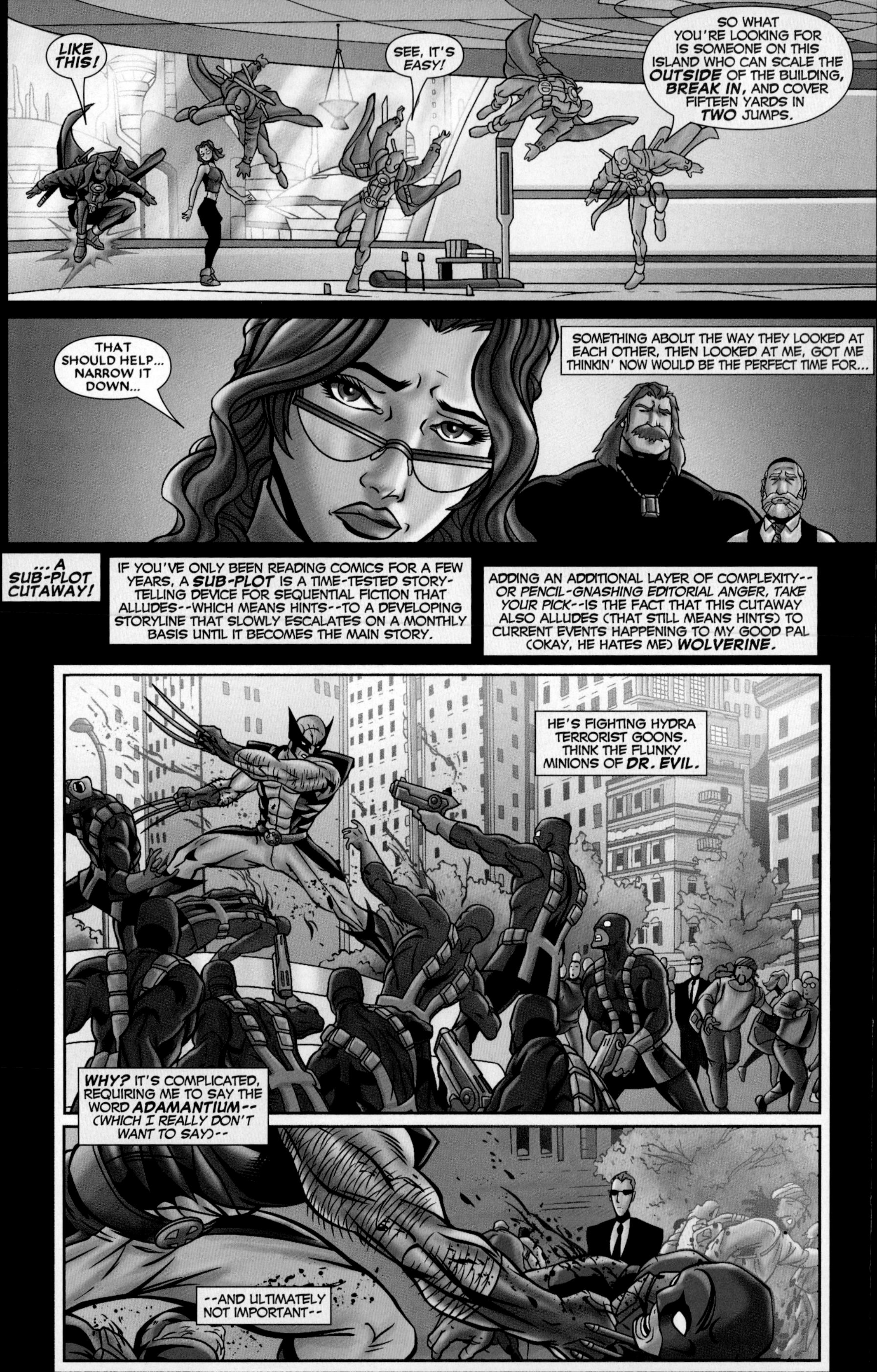
LIKE THIS!
SEE, IT'S EASY!
SO WHAT YOU'RE LOOKING FOR IS SOMEONE ON THIS ISLAND WHO CAN SCALE THE OUTSIDE OF THE BUILDING, BREAK IN, AND COVER FIFTEEN YARDS IN TWO JUMPS.
THAT SHOULD HELP... NARROW IT DOWN...
SOMETHING ABOUT THE WAY THEY LOOKED AT EACH OTHER, THEN LOOKED AT ME, GOT ME THINKIN' NOW WOULD BE THE PERFECT TIME FOR...
...A SUB-PLOT CUTAWAY!
IF YOU'VE ONLY BEEN READING COMICS FOR A FEW YEARS, A SUB-PLOT IS A TIME-TESTED STORY-TELLING DEVICE FOR SEQUENTIAL FICTION THAT ALLUDES--WHICH MEANS HINTS--TO A DEVELOPING STORYLINE THAT SLOWLY ESCALATES ON A MONTHLY BASIS UNTIL IT BECOMES THE MAIN STORY.
ADDING AN ADDITIONAL LAYER OF COMPLEXITY--OR PENCIL-GNASHING EDITORIAL ANGER, TAKE YOUR PICK--IS THE FACT THAT THIS CUTAWAY ALSO ALLUDES (THAT STILL MEANS HINTS) TO CURRENT EVENTS HAPPENING TO MY GOOD PAL (OKAY, HE HATES ME) WOLVERINE.
HE'S FIGHTING HYDRA TERRORIST GOONS. THINK THE FLUNKY MINIONS OF DR. EVIL.
WHY? IT'S COMPLICATED, REQUIRING ME TO SAY THE WORD ADAMANTIUM--(WHICH I REALLY DON'T WANT TO SAY)--
--AND ULTIMATELY NOT IMPORTANT--

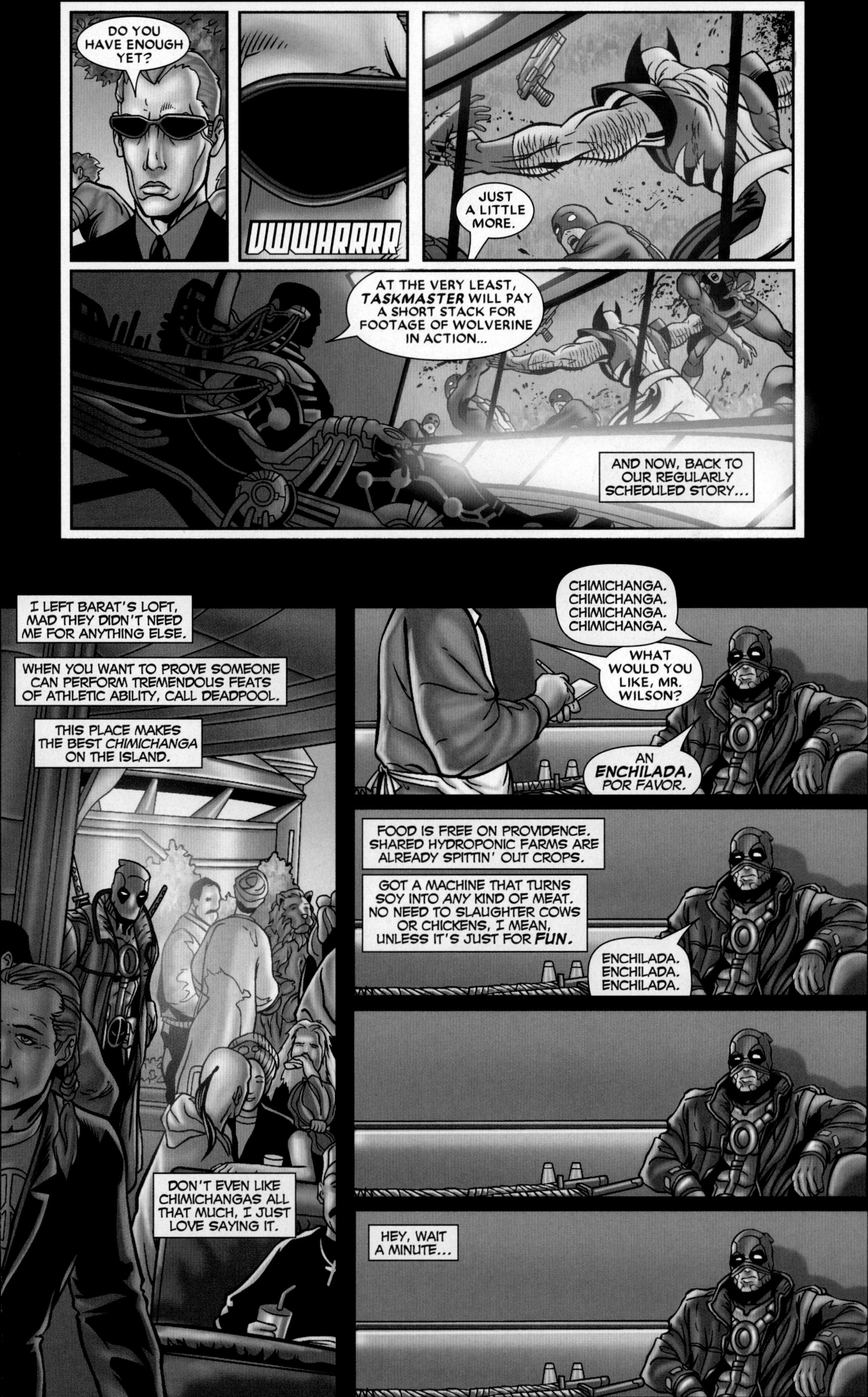
DO YOU HAVE ENOUGH YET?
VWWHRRRR
JUST A LITTLE MORE.
AT THE VERY LEAST, TASKMASTER WILL PAY A SHORT STACK FOR FOOTAGE OF WOLVERINE IN ACTION...
AND NOW, BACK TO OUR REGULARLY SCHEDULED STORY...
I LEFT BARAT'S LOFT, MAD THEY DIDN'T NEED ME FOR ANYTHING ELSE.
WHEN YOU WANT TO PROVE SOMEONE CAN PERFORM TREMENDOUS FEATS OF ATHLETIC ABILITY, CALL DEADPOOL.
THIS PLACE MAKES THE BEST CHIMICHANGA ON THE ISLAND.
DON'T EVEN LIKE CHIMICHANGAS ALL THAT MUCH, I JUST LOVE SAYING IT.
CHIMICHANGA. CHIMICHANGA. CHIMICHANGA. CHIMICHANGA.
WHAT WOULD YOU LIKE, MR. WILSON?
AN ENCHILADA, POR FAVOR.
FOOD IS FREE ON PROVIDENCE. SHARED HYDROPONIC FARMS ARE ALREADY SPITTIN' OUT CROPS.
GOT A MACHINE THAT TURNS SOY INTO ANY KIND OF MEAT. NO NEED TO SLAUGHTER COWS OR CHICKENS, I MEAN, UNLESS IT'S JUST FOR FUN.
ENCHILADA. ENCHILADA. ENCHILADA.
HEY, WAIT A MINUTE...

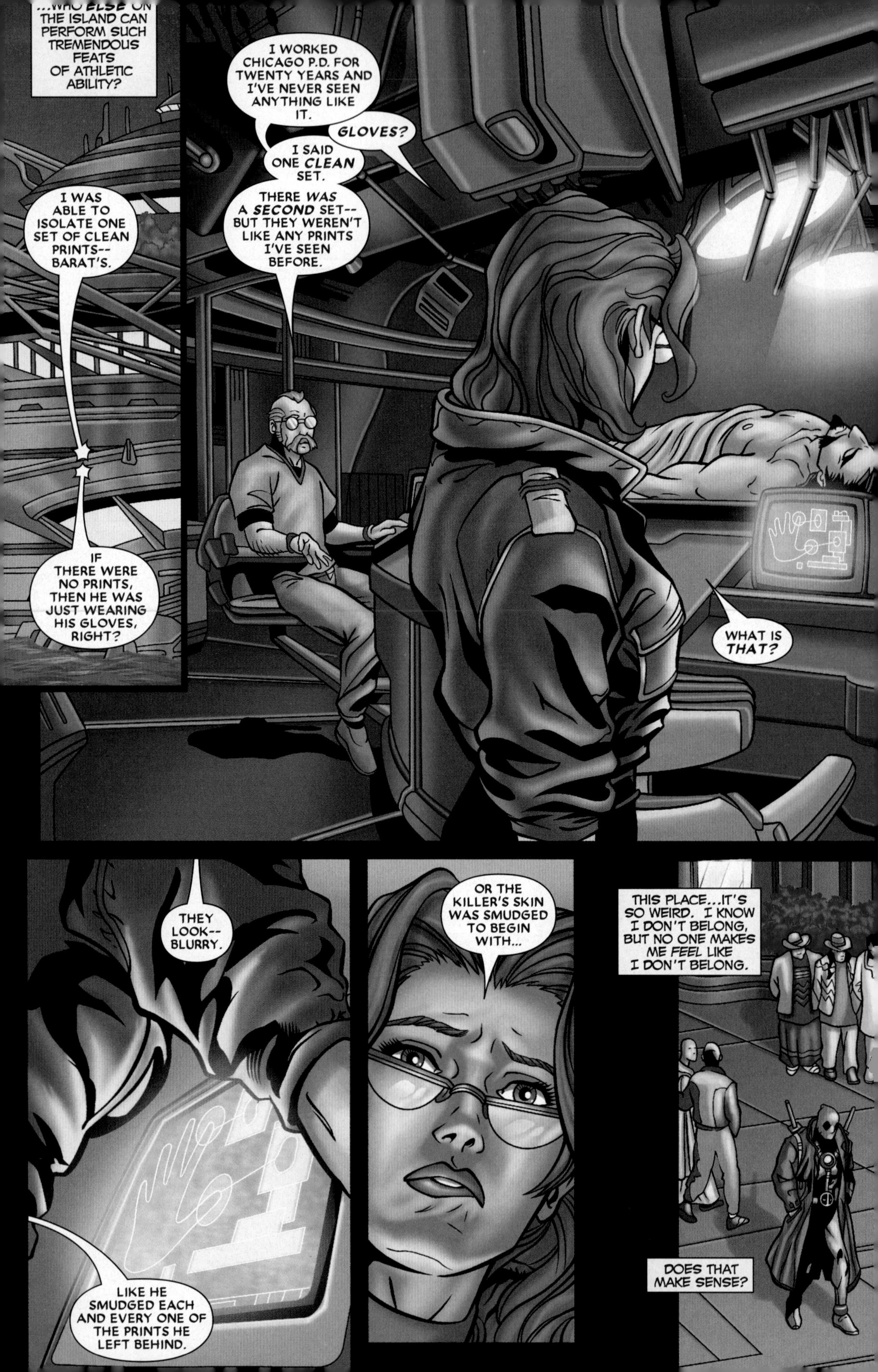
...WHO ELSE ON THE ISLAND CAN PERFORM SUCH TREMENDOUS FEATS OF ATHLETIC ABILITY?
I WAS ABLE TO ISOLATE ONE SET OF CLEAN PRINTS-- BARAT'S.
IF THERE WERE NO PRINTS, THEN HE WAS JUST WEARING HIS GLOVES, RIGHT?
I WORKED CHICAGO P.D. FOR TWENTY YEARS AND I'VE NEVER SEEN ANYTHING LIKE IT.
GLOVES?
I SAID ONE CLEAN SET.
THERE WAS A SECOND SET-- BUT THEY WEREN'T LIKE ANY PRINTS I'VE SEEN BEFORE.
WHAT IS THAT?
THEY LOOK-- BLURRY.
LIKE HE SMUDGED EACH AND EVERY ONE OF THE PRINTS HE LEFT BEHIND.
OR THE KILLER'S SKIN WAS SMUDGED TO BEGIN WITH...
THIS PLACE...IT'S SO WEIRD. I KNOW I DON'T BELONG, BUT NO ONE MAKES ME FEEL LIKE I DON'T BELONG.
DOES THAT MAKE SENSE?

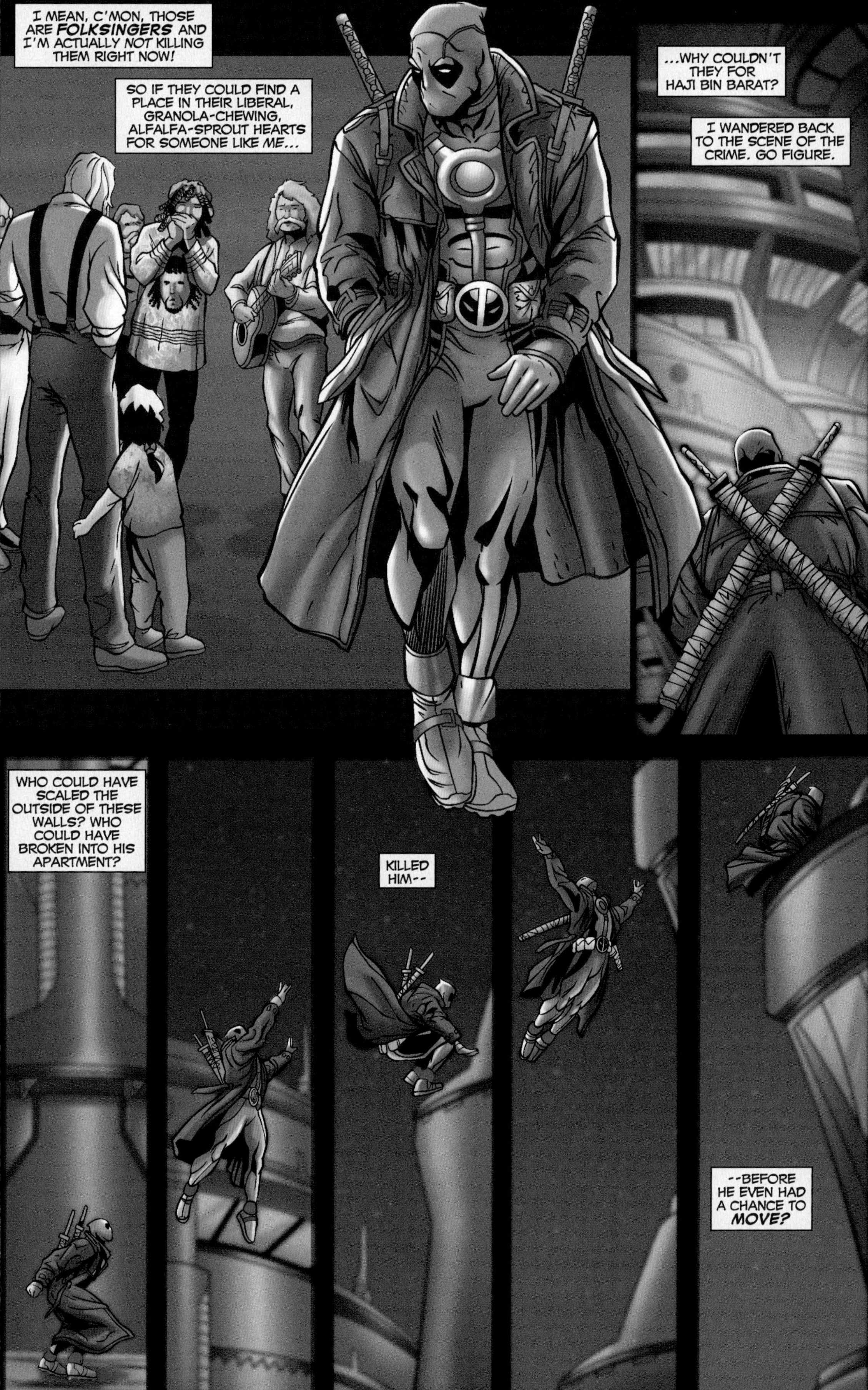
I MEAN, C'MON, THOSE ARE FOLKSINGERS AND I'M ACTUALLY NOT KILLING THEM RIGHT NOW!
SO IF THEY COULD FIND A PLACE IN THEIR LIBERAL, GRANOLA-CHEWING, ALFALFA-SPROUT HEARTS FOR SOMEONE LIKE ME...
...WHY COULDN'T THEY FOR HAJI BIN BARAT?
I WANDERED BACK TO THE SCENE OF THE CRIME. GO FIGURE.
WHO COULD HAVE SCALED THE OUTSIDE OF THESE WALLS? WHO COULD HAVE BROKEN INTO HIS APARTMENT?
KILLED HIM--
--BEFORE HE EVEN HAD A CHANCE TO MOVE?

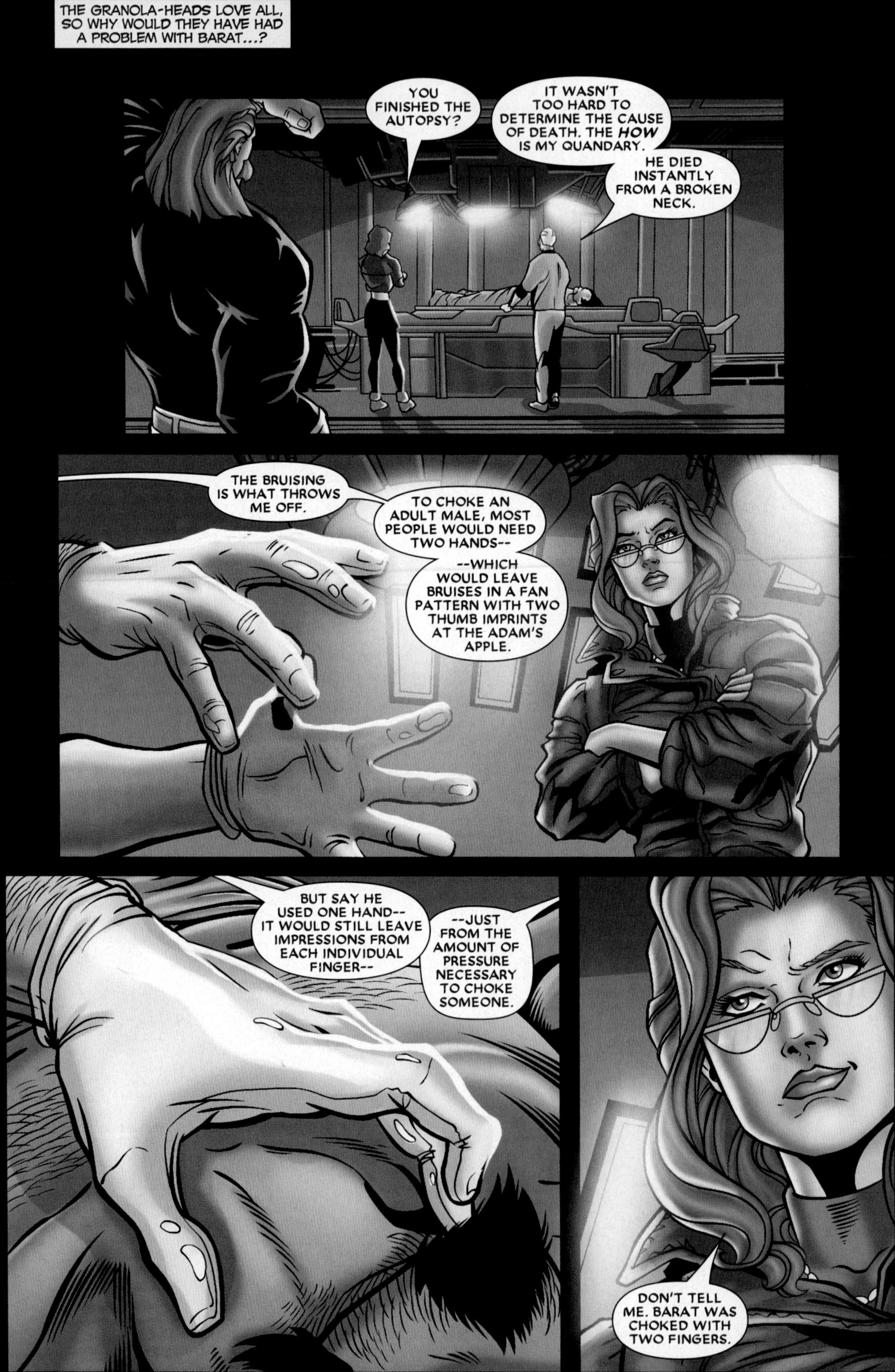
THE GRANOLA-HEADS LOVE ALL, SO WHY WOULD THEY HAVE HAD A PROBLEM WITH BARAT...?
YOU FINISHED THE AUTOPSY?
IT WASN'T TOO HARD TO DETERMINE THE CAUSE OF DEATH. THE *HOW* IS MY QUANDARY.
HE DIED INSTANTLY FROM A BROKEN NECK.
THE BRUISING IS WHAT THROWS ME OFF.
TO CHOKE AN ADULT MALE, MOST PEOPLE WOULD NEED TWO HANDS--
--WHICH WOULD LEAVE BRUISES IN A FAN PATTERN WITH TWO THUMB IMPRINTS AT THE ADAM'S APPLE.
BUT SAY HE USED ONE HAND-- IT WOULD STILL LEAVE IMPRESSIONS FROM EACH INDIVIDUAL FINGER--
--JUST FROM THE AMOUNT OF PRESSURE NECESSARY TO CHOKE SOMEONE.
DON'T TELL ME. BARAT WAS CHOKED WITH TWO FINGERS.

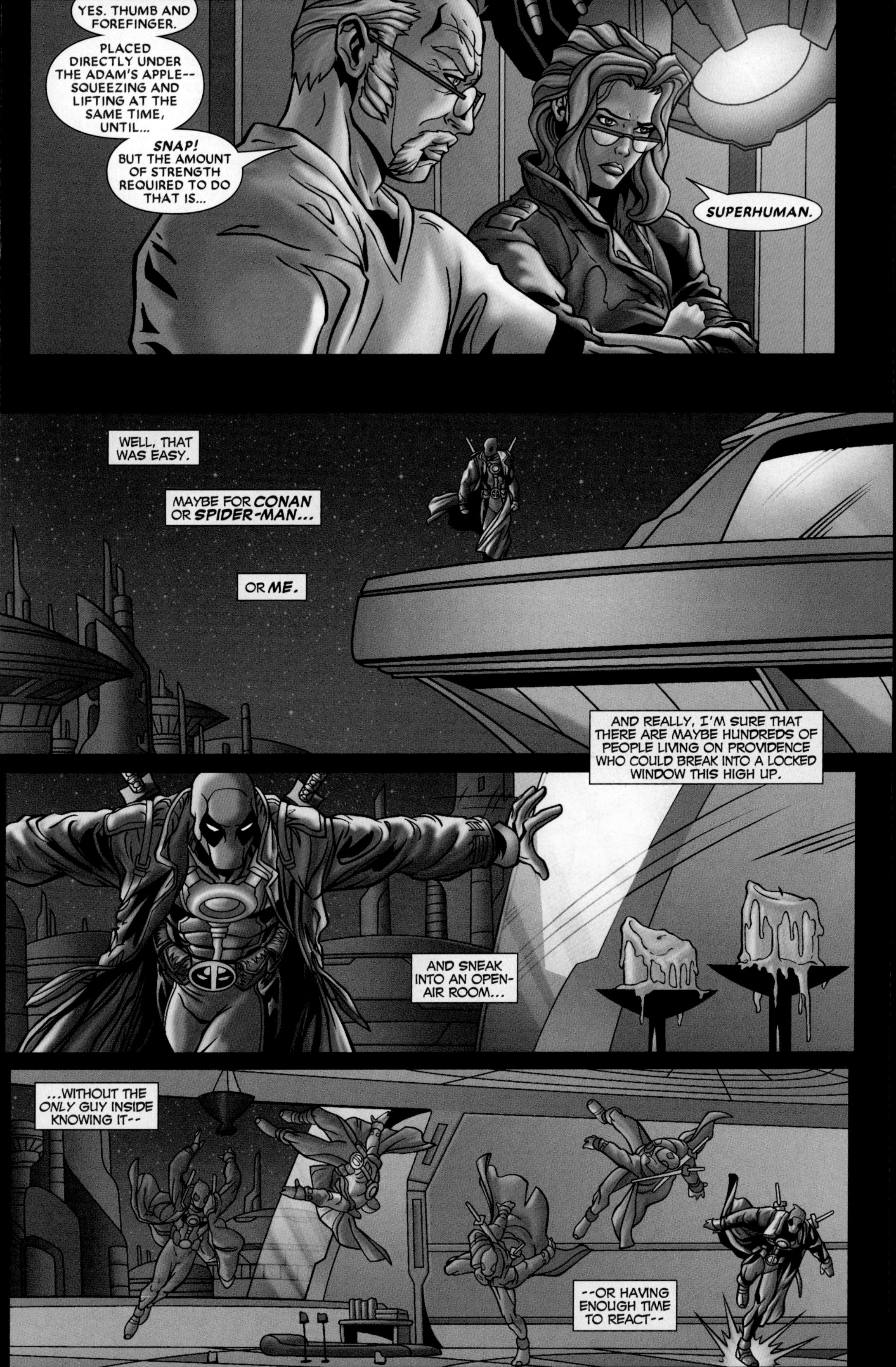
YES. THUMB AND FOREFINGER.
PLACED DIRECTLY UNDER THE ADAM'S APPLE-- SQUEEZING AND LIFTING AT THE SAME TIME, UNTIL...
SNAP! BUT THE AMOUNT OF STRENGTH REQUIRED TO DO THAT IS...
SUPERHUMAN.
WELL, THAT WAS EASY.
MAYBE FOR CONAN OR SPIDER-MAN...
OR ME.
AND REALLY, I'M SURE THAT THERE ARE MAYBE HUNDREDS OF PEOPLE LIVING ON PROVIDENCE WHO COULD BREAK INTO A LOCKED WINDOW THIS HIGH UP.
AND SNEAK INTO AN OPEN-AIR ROOM...
...WITHOUT THE ONLY GUY INSIDE KNOWING IT--
--OR HAVING ENOUGH TIME TO REACT--

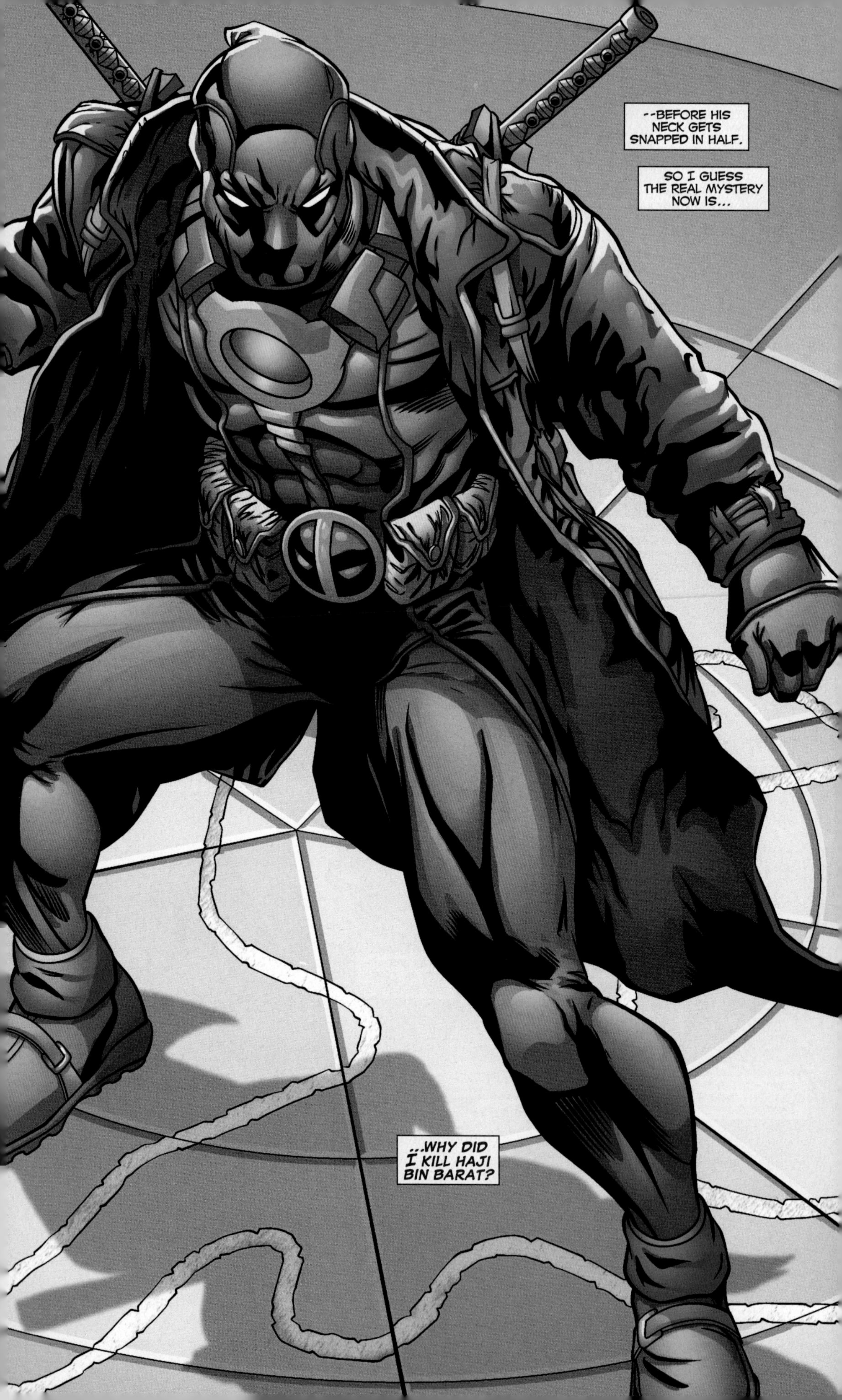
--BEFORE HIS NECK GETS SNAPPED IN HALF.
SO I GUESS THE REAL MYSTERY NOW IS...
...WHY DID I KILL HAJI BIN BARAT?

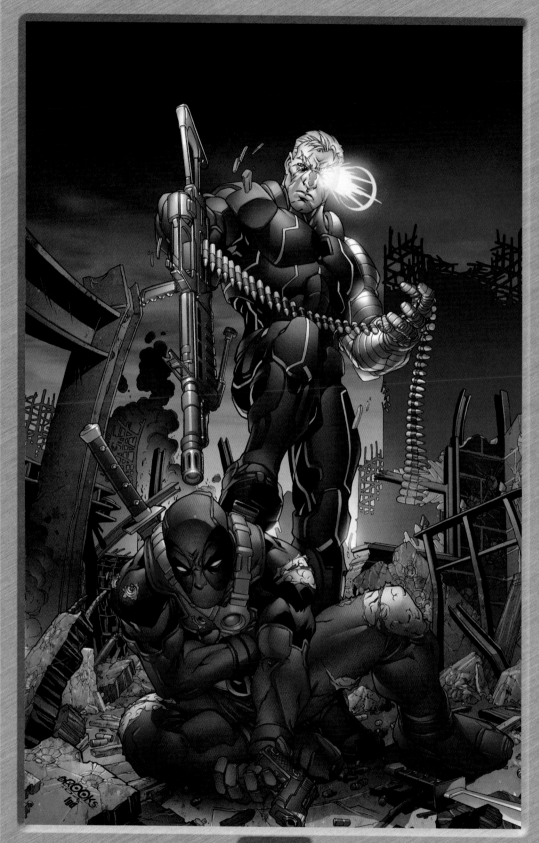

#14

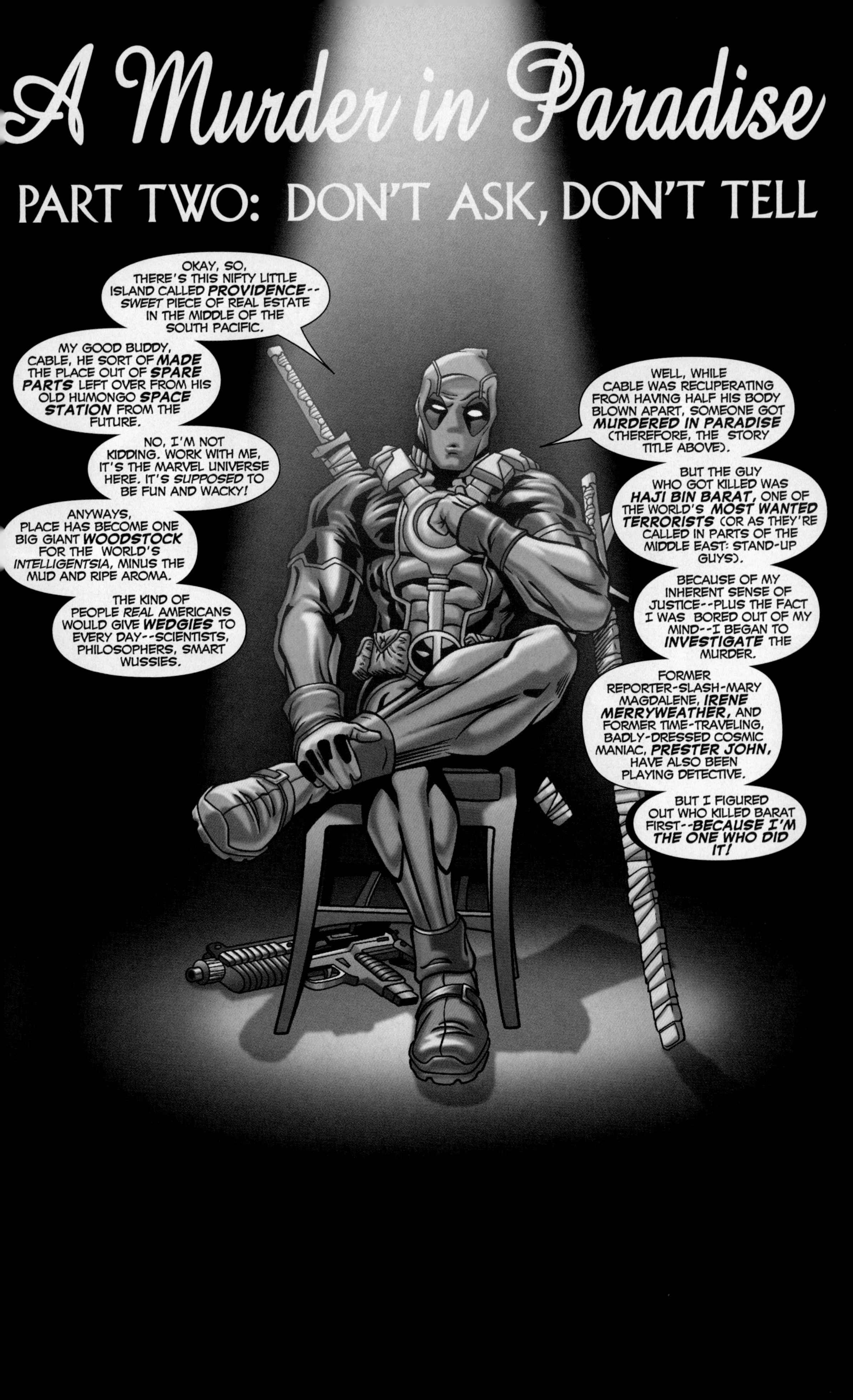

A Murder in Paradise
PART TWO: DON'T ASK, DON'T TELL
OKAY, SO, THERE'S THIS NIFTY LITTLE ISLAND CALLED PROVIDENCE--SWEET PIECE OF REAL ESTATE IN THE MIDDLE OF THE SOUTH PACIFIC.
MY GOOD BUDDY, CABLE, HE SORT OF MADE THE PLACE OUT OF SPARE PARTS LEFT OVER FROM HIS OLD HUMONGO SPACE STATION FROM THE FUTURE.
NO, I'M NOT KIDDING. WORK WITH ME, IT'S THE MARVEL UNIVERSE HERE. IT'S SUPPOSED TO BE FUN AND WACKY!
ANYWAYS, PLACE HAS BECOME ONE BIG GIANT WOODSTOCK FOR THE WORLD'S INTELLIGENTSIA, MINUS THE MUD AND RIPE AROMA.
THE KIND OF PEOPLE REAL AMERICANS WOULD GIVE WEDGIES TO EVERY DAY--SCIENTISTS, PHILOSOPHERS, SMART WUSSIES.
WELL, WHILE CABLE WAS RECUPERATING FROM HAVING HALF HIS BODY BLOWN APART, SOMEONE GOT MURDERED IN PARADISE (THEREFORE, THE STORY TITLE ABOVE).
BUT THE GUY WHO GOT KILLED WAS HAJI BIN BARAT, ONE OF THE WORLD'S MOST WANTED TERRORISTS (OR AS THEY'RE CALLED IN PARTS OF THE MIDDLE EAST: STAND-UP GUYS).
BECAUSE OF MY INHERENT SENSE OF JUSTICE--PLUS THE FACT I WAS BORED OUT OF MY MIND--I BEGAN TO INVESTIGATE THE MURDER.
FORMER REPORTER-SLASH-MARY MAGDALENE, IRENE MERRYWEATHER, AND FORMER TIME-TRAVELING, BADLY-DRESSED COSMIC MANIAC, PRESTER JOHN, HAVE ALSO BEEN PLAYING DETECTIVE.
BUT I FIGURED OUT WHO KILLED BARAT FIRST--BECAUSE I'M THE ONE WHO DID IT!

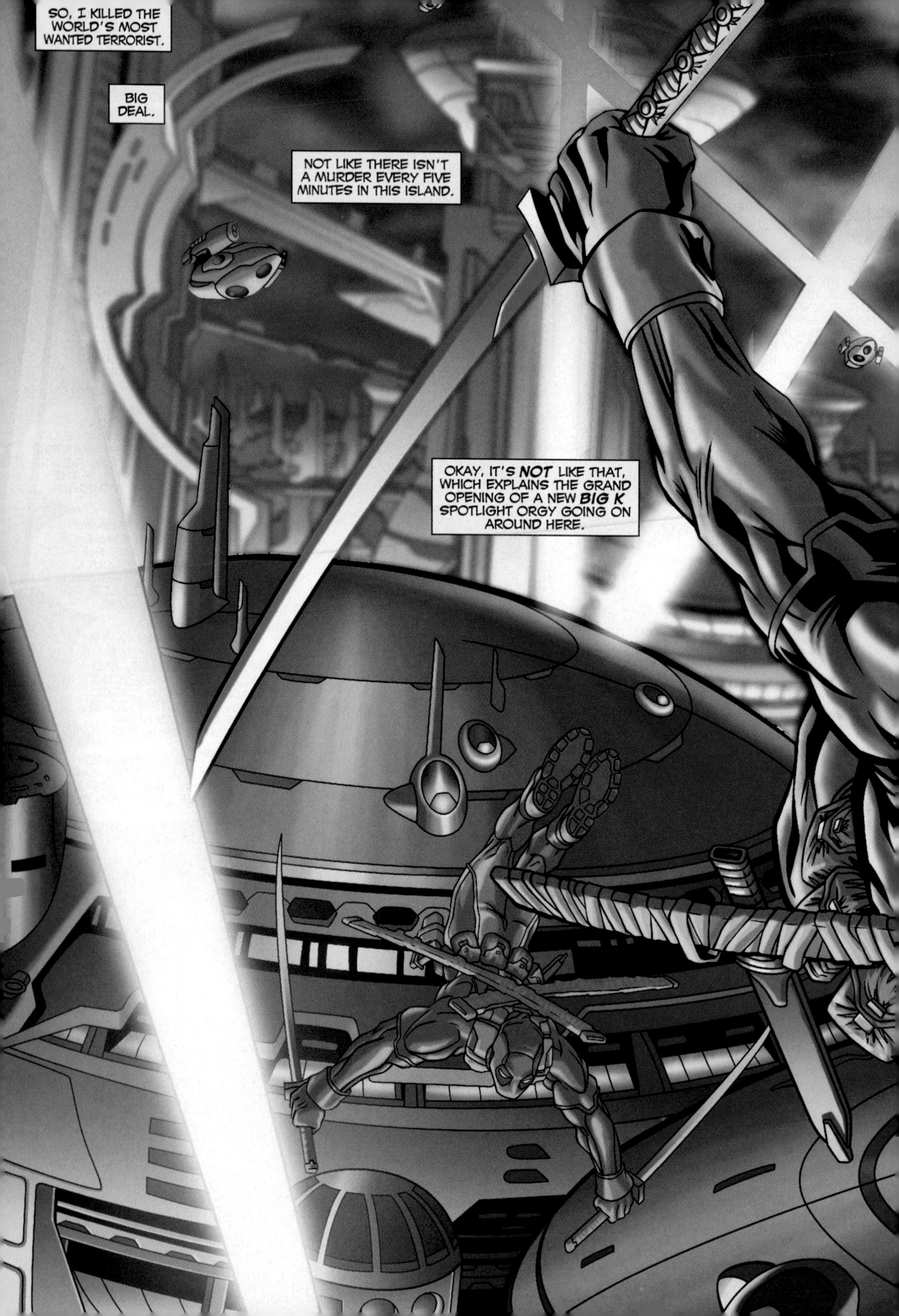
SO, I KILLED THE WORLD'S MOST WANTED TERRORIST.
BIG DEAL.
NOT LIKE THERE ISN'T A MURDER EVERY FIVE MINUTES IN THIS ISLAND.
OKAY, IT'S **NOT** LIKE THAT, WHICH EXPLAINS THE GRAND OPENING OF A NEW **BIG K** SPOTLIGHT ORGY GOING ON AROUND HERE.

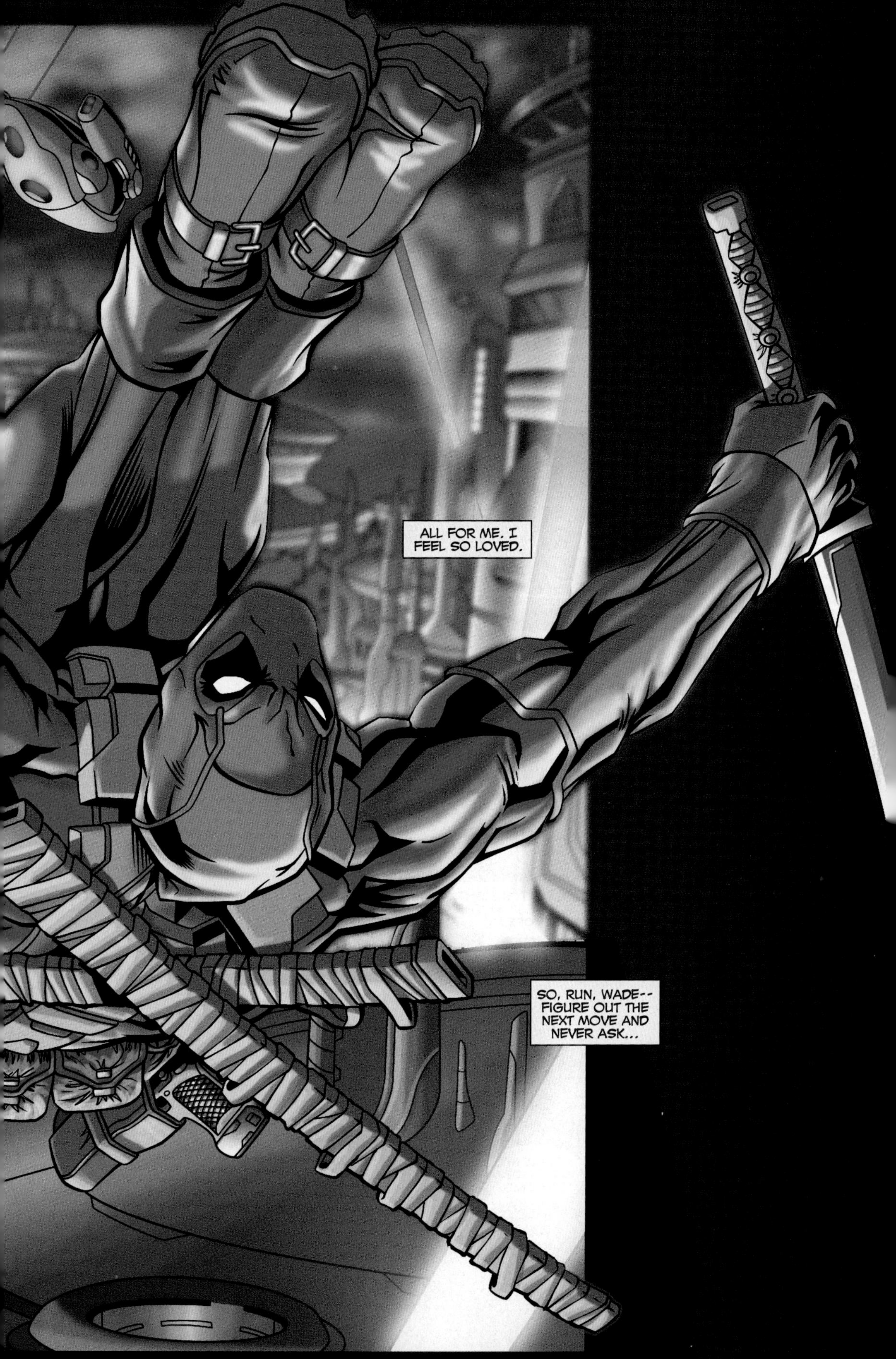
ALL FOR ME. I FEEL SO LOVED.
SO, RUN, WADE--FIGURE OUT THE NEXT MOVE AND NEVER ASK...

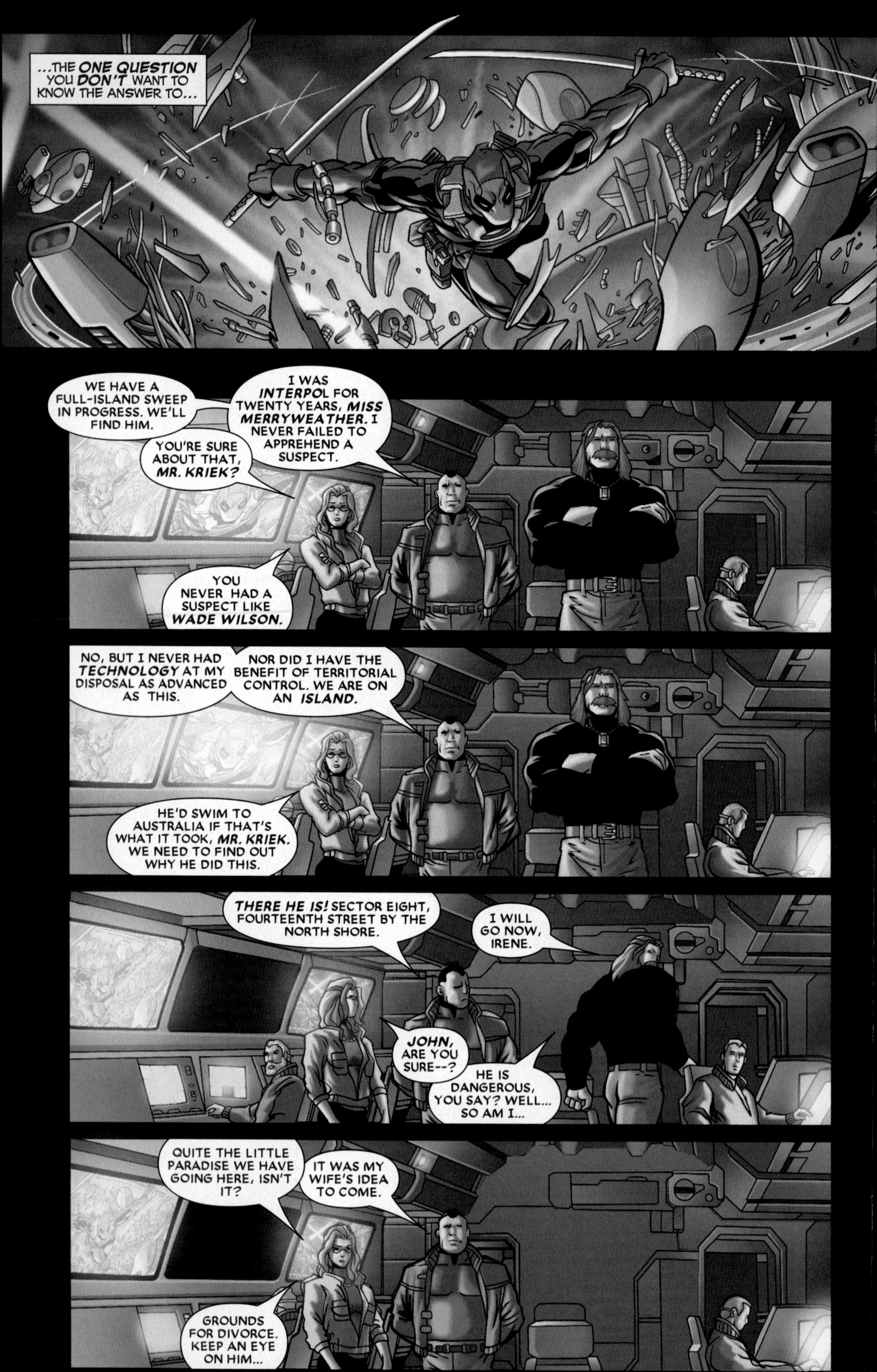
...THE ONE QUESTION YOU DON'T WANT TO KNOW THE ANSWER TO...
WE HAVE A FULL-ISLAND SWEEP IN PROGRESS. WE'LL FIND HIM.
YOU'RE SURE ABOUT THAT, MR. KRIEK?
I WAS INTERPOL FOR TWENTY YEARS, MISS MERRYWEATHER. I NEVER FAILED TO APPREHEND A SUSPECT.
YOU NEVER HAD A SUSPECT LIKE WADE WILSON.
NO, BUT I NEVER HAD TECHNOLOGY AT MY DISPOSAL AS ADVANCED AS THIS.
NOR DID I HAVE THE BENEFIT OF TERRITORIAL CONTROL. WE ARE ON AN ISLAND.
HE'D SWIM TO AUSTRALIA IF THAT'S WHAT IT TOOK, MR. KRIEK. WE NEED TO FIND OUT WHY HE DID THIS.
THERE HE IS! SECTOR EIGHT, FOURTEENTH STREET BY THE NORTH SHORE.
I WILL GO NOW, IRENE.
JOHN, ARE YOU SURE--?
HE IS DANGEROUS, YOU SAY? WELL... SO AM I...
QUITE THE LITTLE PARADISE WE HAVE GOING HERE, ISN'T IT?
IT WAS MY WIFE'S IDEA TO COME.
GROUNDS FOR DIVORCE. KEEP AN EYE ON HIM...

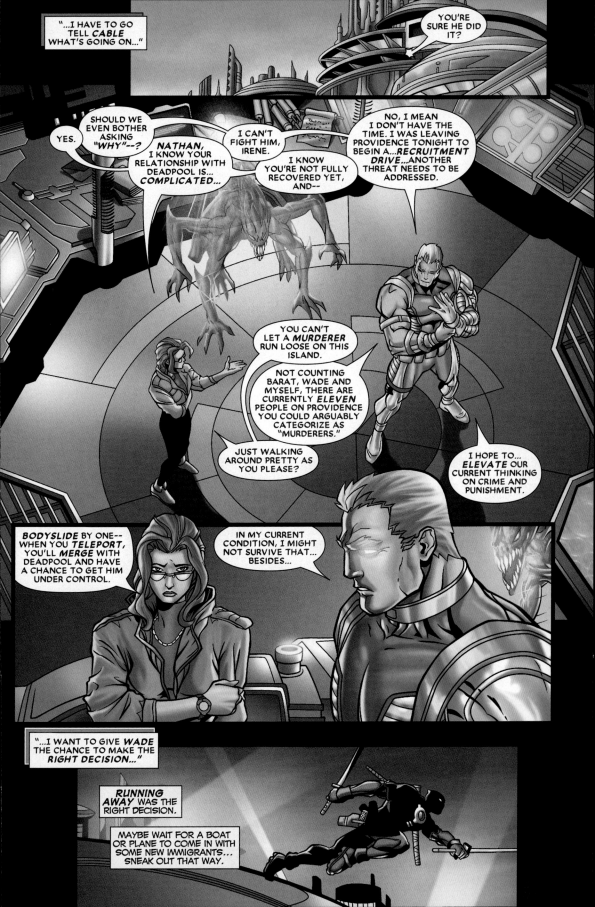

"...I HAVE TO GO TELL *CABLE* WHAT'S GOING ON..."

YOU'RE SURE HE DID IT?

YES.

SHOULD WE EVEN BOTHER ASKING "WHY"--?

NATHAN, I KNOW YOUR RELATIONSHIP WITH DEADPOOL IS... *COMPLICATED*...

I CAN'T FIGHT HIM, IRENE.

I KNOW YOU'RE NOT FULLY RECOVERED YET, AND--

NO, I MEAN I DON'T HAVE THE TIME. I WAS LEAVING PROVIDENCE TONIGHT TO BEGIN A...*RECRUITMENT DRIVE*...ANOTHER THREAT NEEDS TO BE ADDRESSED.

YOU CAN'T LET A *MURDERER* RUN LOOSE ON THIS ISLAND.

NOT COUNTING BARAT, WADE AND MYSELF, THERE ARE CURRENTLY *ELEVEN* PEOPLE ON PROVIDENCE YOU COULD ARGUABLY CATEGORIZE AS "MURDERERS."

JUST WALKING AROUND PRETTY AS YOU PLEASE?

I HOPE TO... *ELEVATE* OUR CURRENT THINKING ON CRIME AND PUNISHMENT.

BODYSLIDE BY ONE-- WHEN YOU *TELEPORT*, YOU'LL *MERGE* WITH DEADPOOL AND HAVE A CHANCE TO GET HIM UNDER CONTROL.

IN MY CURRENT CONDITION, I MIGHT NOT SURVIVE THAT... BESIDES...

"...I WANT TO GIVE *WADE* THE CHANCE TO MAKE THE *RIGHT DECISION*..."

RUNNING AWAY WAS THE RIGHT DECISION.

MAYBE WAIT FOR A BOAT OR PLANE TO COME IN WITH SOME NEW IMMIGRANTS... SNEAK OUT THAT WAY.

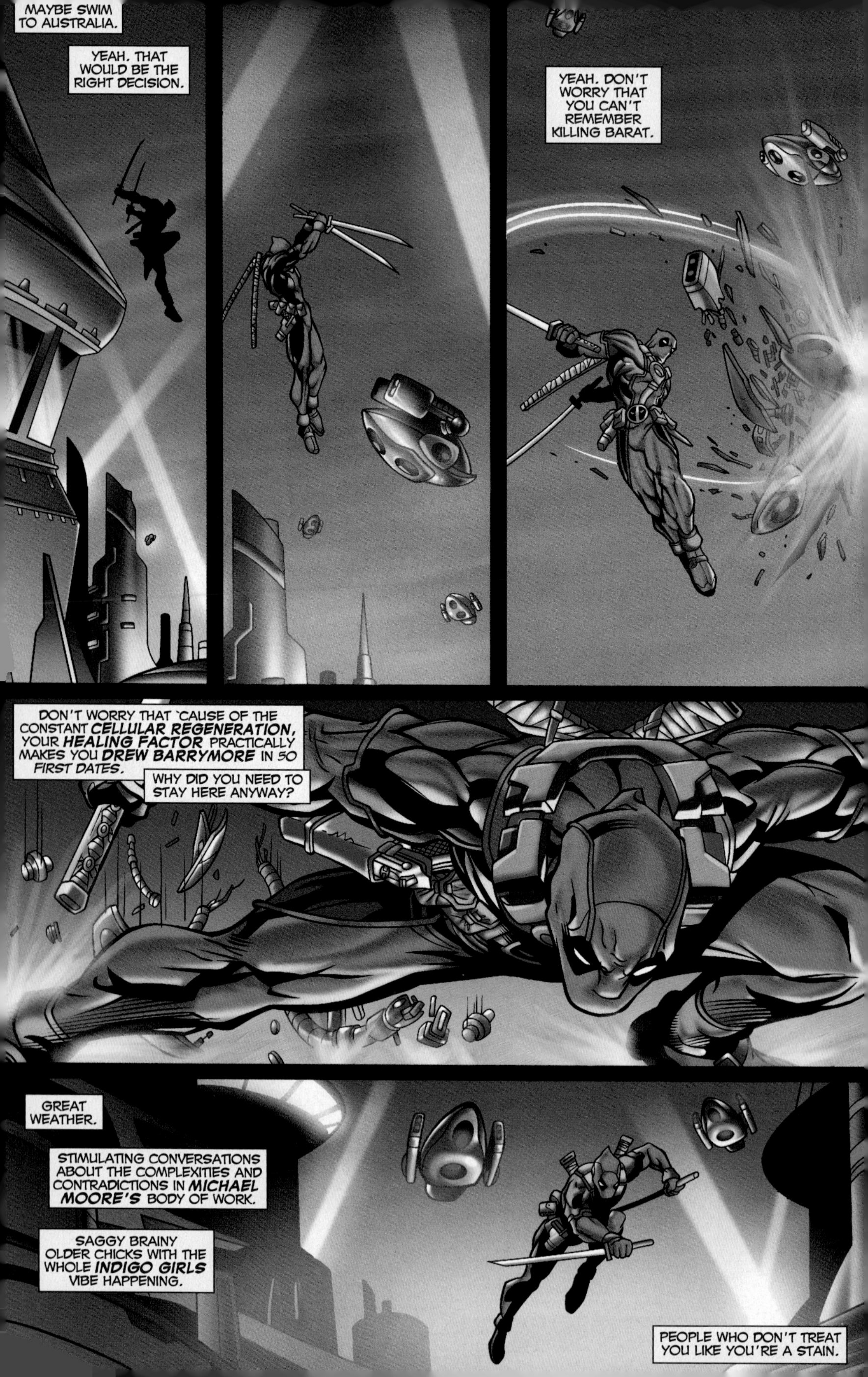
MAYBE SWIM TO AUSTRALIA.
YEAH. THAT WOULD BE THE RIGHT DECISION.
YEAH. DON'T WORRY THAT YOU CAN'T REMEMBER KILLING BARAT.
DON'T WORRY THAT `CAUSE OF THE CONSTANT CELLULAR REGENERATION, YOUR HEALING FACTOR PRACTICALLY MAKES YOU DREW BARRYMORE IN 50 FIRST DATES.
WHY DID YOU NEED TO STAY HERE ANYWAY?
GREAT WEATHER.
STIMULATING CONVERSATIONS ABOUT THE COMPLEXITIES AND CONTRADICTIONS IN MICHAEL MOORE'S BODY OF WORK.
SAGGY BRAINY OLDER CHICKS WITH THE WHOLE INDIGO GIRLS VIBE HAPPENING.
PEOPLE WHO DON'T TREAT YOU LIKE YOU'RE A STAIN.

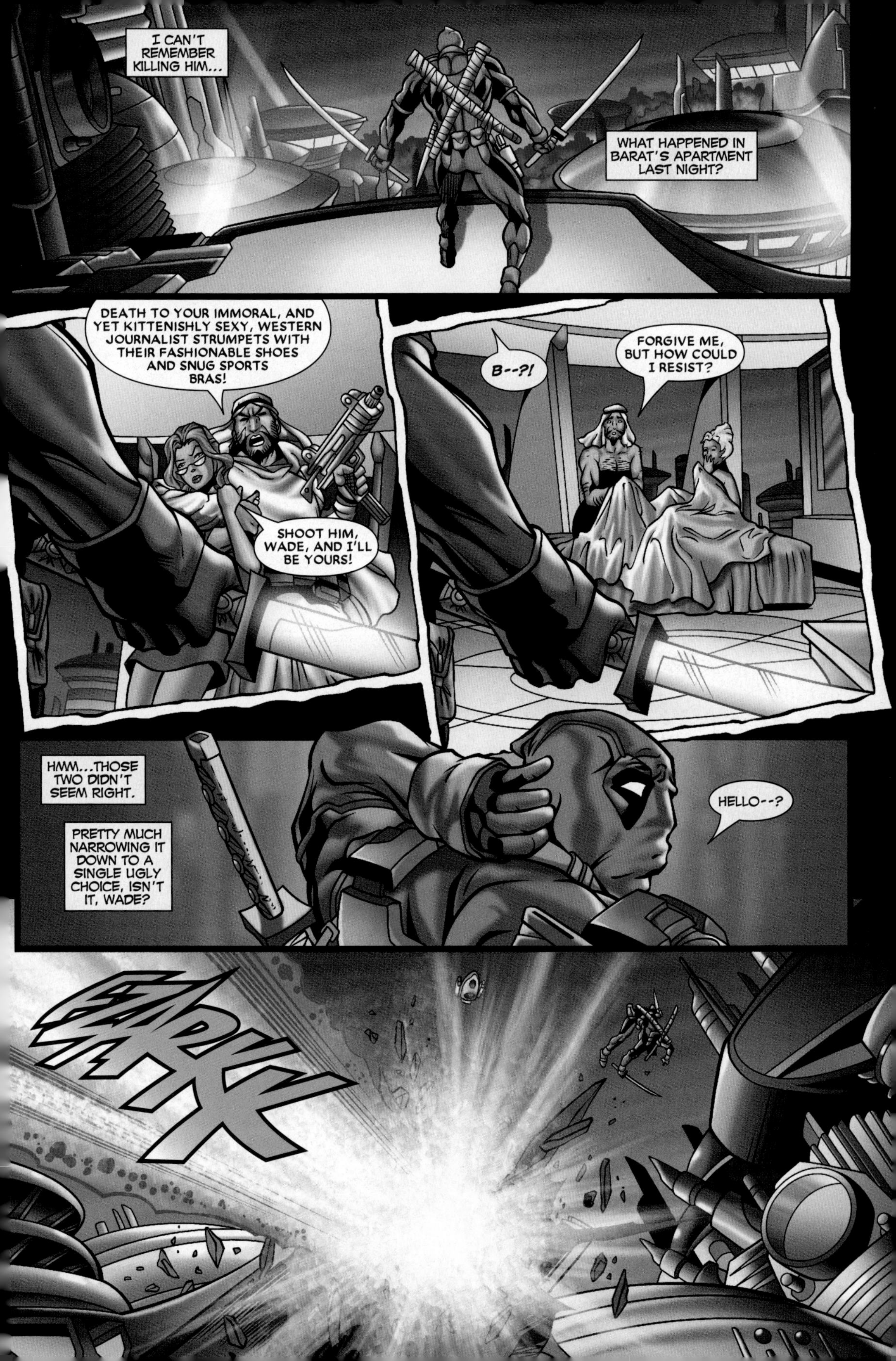
I CAN'T REMEMBER KILLING HIM...
WHAT HAPPENED IN BARAT'S APARTMENT LAST NIGHT?
DEATH TO YOUR IMMORAL, AND YET KITTENISHLY SEXY, WESTERN JOURNALIST STRUMPETS WITH THEIR FASHIONABLE SHOES AND SNUG SPORTS BRAS!
SHOOT HIM, WADE, AND I'LL BE YOURS!
B--?!
FORGIVE ME, BUT HOW COULD I RESIST?
HMM...THOSE TWO DIDN'T SEEM RIGHT.
PRETTY MUCH NARROWING IT DOWN TO A SINGLE UGLY CHOICE, ISN'T IT, WADE?
HELLO--?

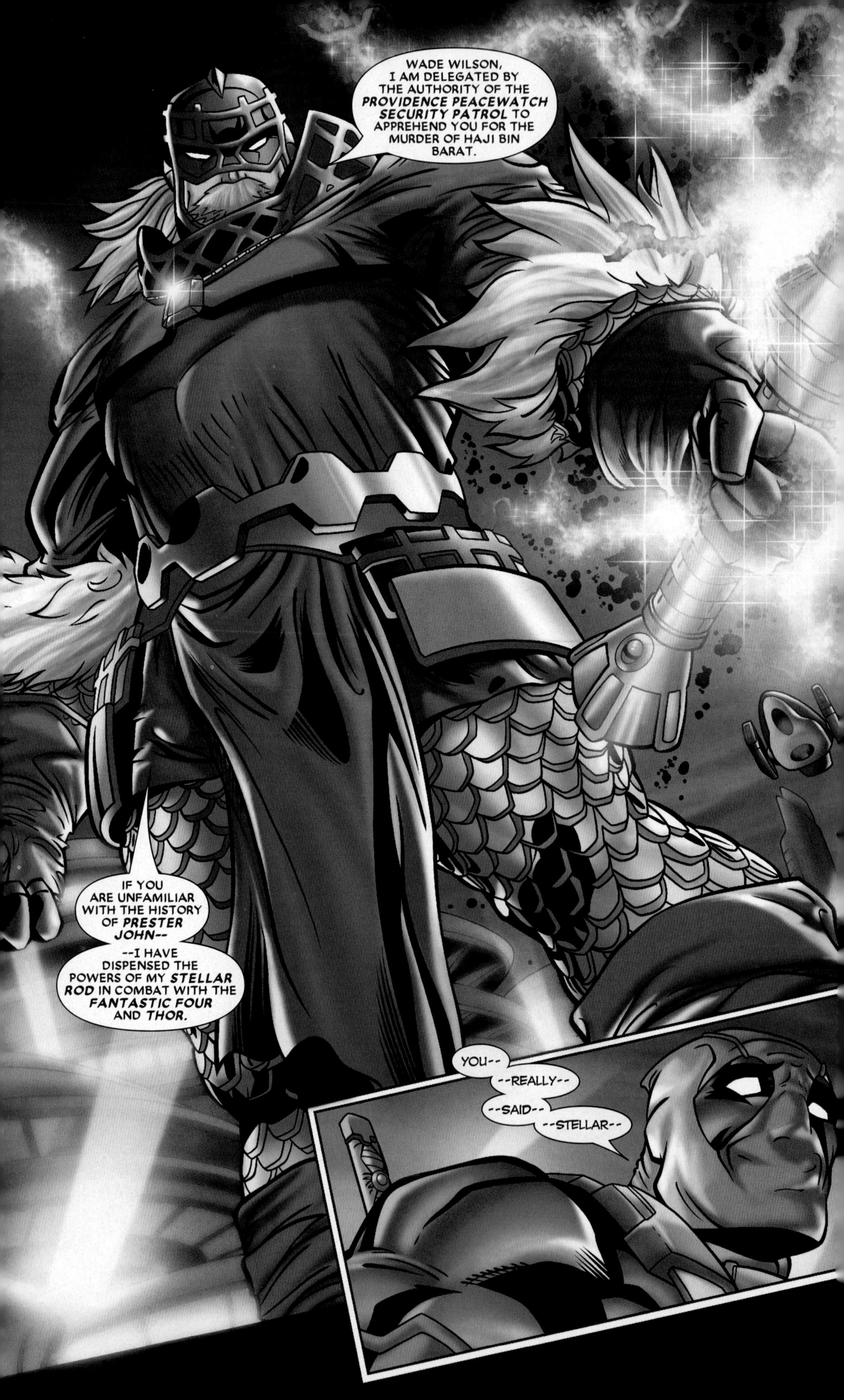
WADE WILSON, I AM DELEGATED BY THE AUTHORITY OF THE *PROVIDENCE PEACEWATCH SECURITY PATROL* TO APPREHEND YOU FOR THE MURDER OF HAJI BIN BARAT.
IF YOU ARE UNFAMILIAR WITH THE HISTORY OF *PRESTER JOHN*--
--I HAVE DISPENSED THE POWERS OF MY *STELLAR ROD* IN COMBAT WITH THE *FANTASTIC FOUR* AND *THOR.*
YOU--
--REALLY--
--SAID--
--STELLAR--

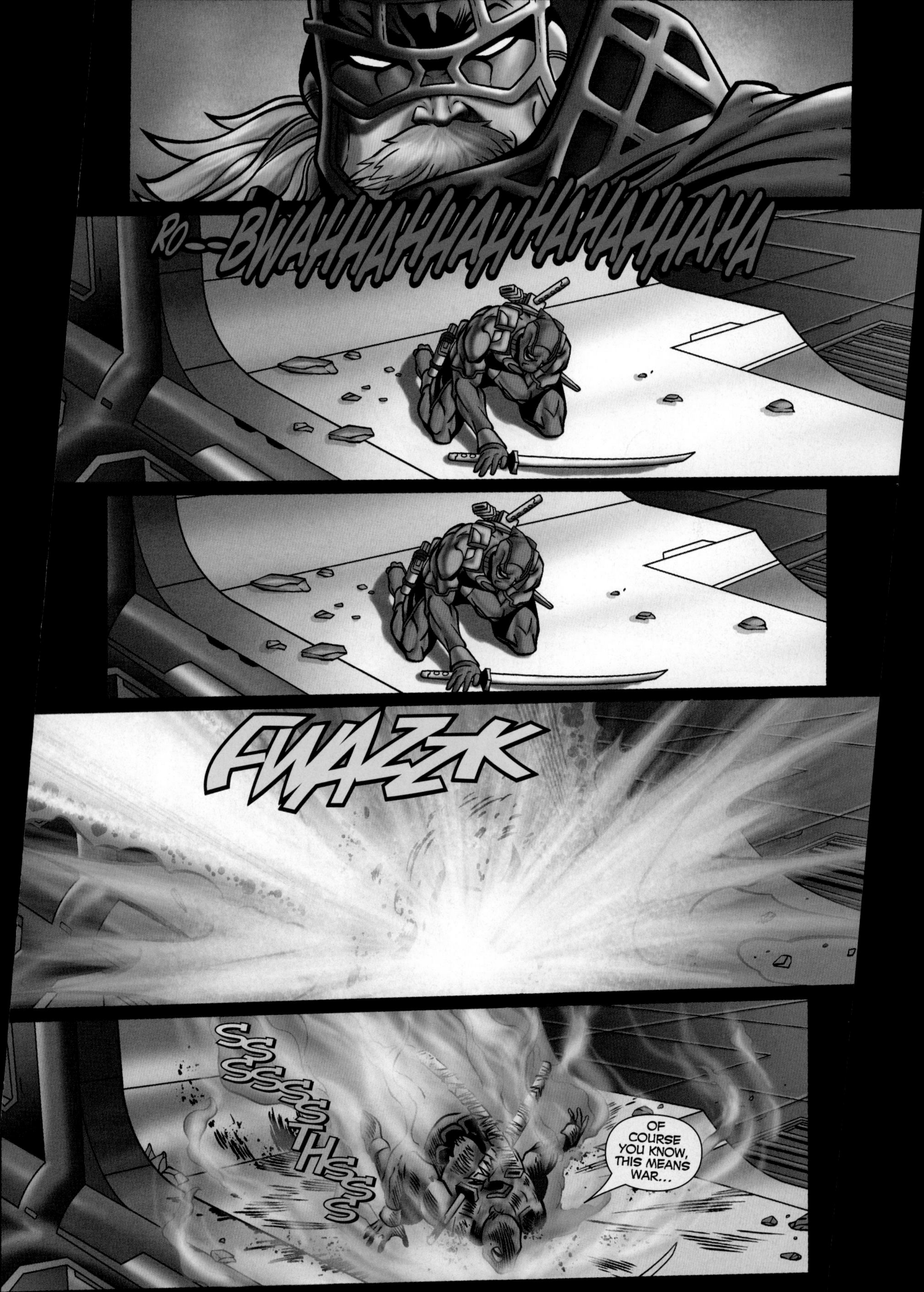
RO--BWAHHAHHAHAH HAHAHHHAHA
FWAZZK
SSSSSSTHSSS
OF COURSE YOU KNOW, THIS MEANS WAR...

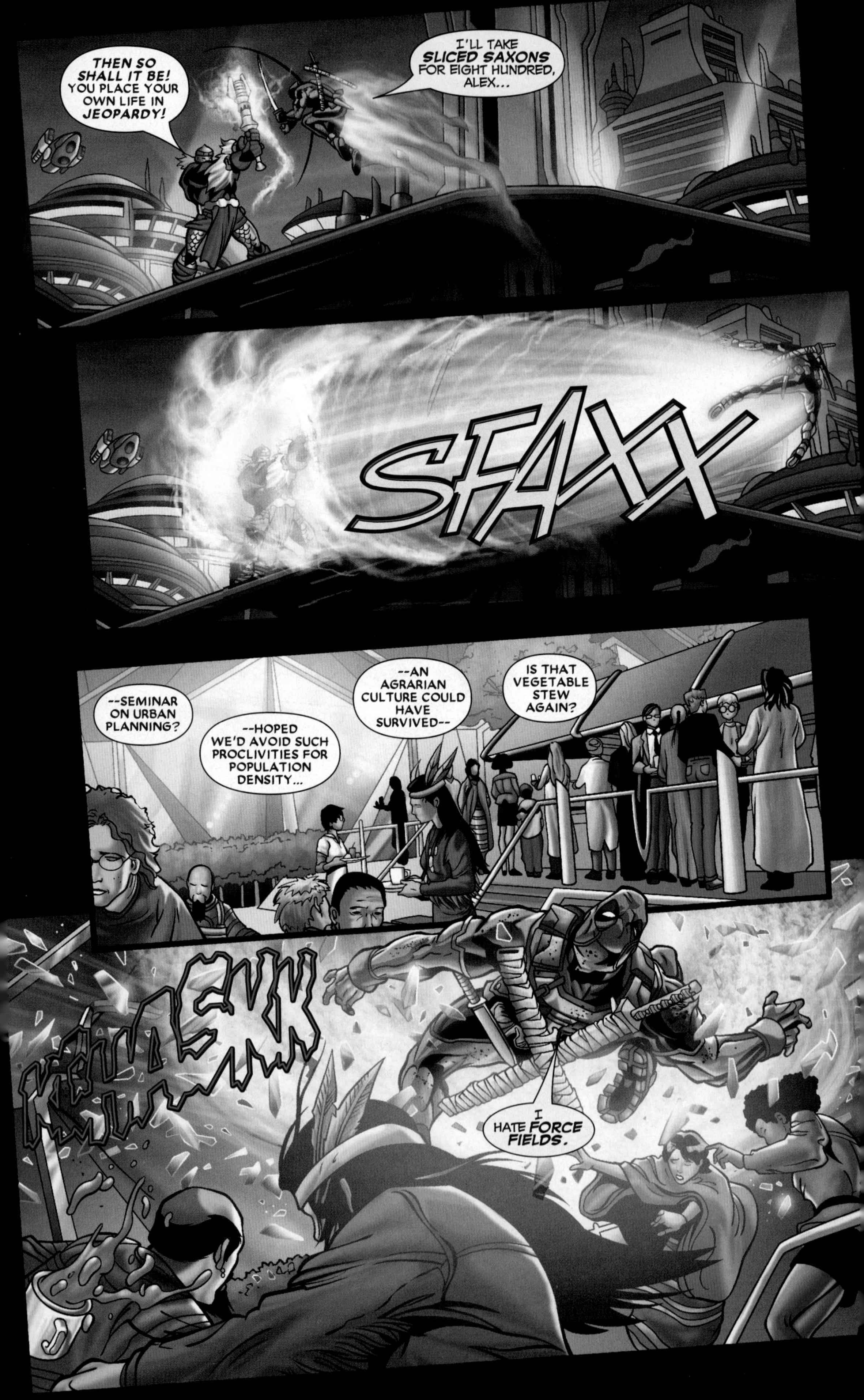

THEN SO SHALL IT BE! YOU PLACE YOUR OWN LIFE IN JEOPARDY!
I'LL TAKE SLICED SAXONS FOR EIGHT HUNDRED, ALEX...
SFAXX
--SEMINAR ON URBAN PLANNING?
--HOPED WE'D AVOID SUCH PROCLIVITIES FOR POPULATION DENSITY...
--AN AGRARIAN CULTURE COULD HAVE SURVIVED--
IS THAT VEGETABLE STEW AGAIN?
I HATE FORCE FIELDS.

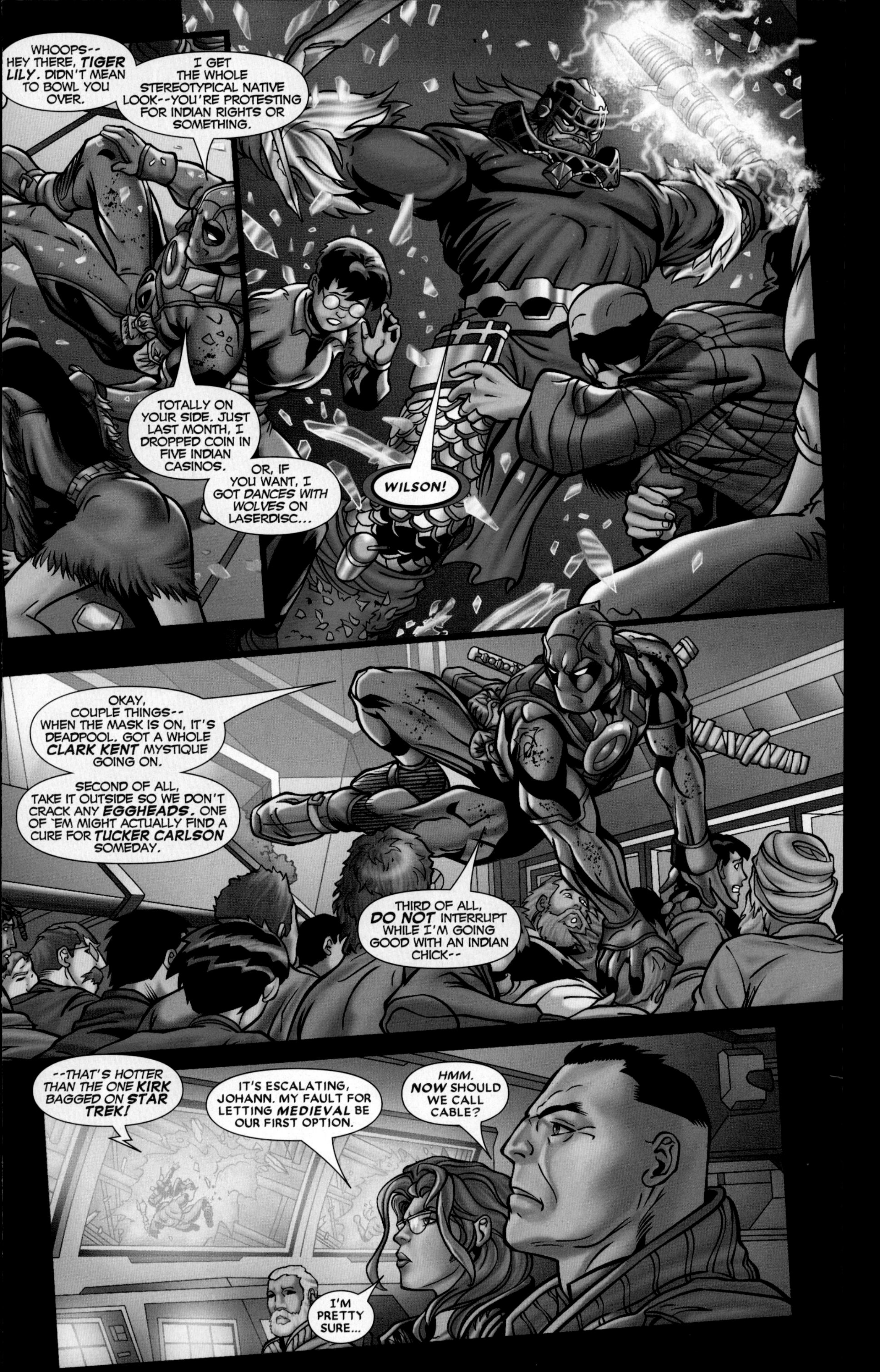
WHOOPS--
HEY THERE, TIGER LILY. DIDN'T MEAN TO BOWL YOU OVER.
I GET THE WHOLE STEREOTYPICAL NATIVE LOOK--YOU'RE PROTESTING FOR INDIAN RIGHTS OR SOMETHING.
TOTALLY ON YOUR SIDE. JUST LAST MONTH, I DROPPED COIN IN FIVE INDIAN CASINOS.
OR, IF YOU WANT, I GOT DANCES WITH WOLVES ON LASERDISC...
WILSON!
OKAY, COUPLE THINGS-- WHEN THE MASK IS ON, IT'S DEADPOOL. GOT A WHOLE CLARK KENT MYSTIQUE GOING ON.
SECOND OF ALL, TAKE IT OUTSIDE SO WE DON'T CRACK ANY EGGHEADS. ONE OF 'EM MIGHT ACTUALLY FIND A CURE FOR TUCKER CARLSON SOMEDAY.
THIRD OF ALL, DO NOT INTERRUPT WHILE I'M GOING GOOD WITH AN INDIAN CHICK--
--THAT'S HOTTER THAN THE ONE KIRK BAGGED ON STAR TREK!
IT'S ESCALATING, JOHANN. MY FAULT FOR LETTING MEDIEVAL BE OUR FIRST OPTION.
HMM. NOW SHOULD WE CALL CABLE?
I'M PRETTY SURE...

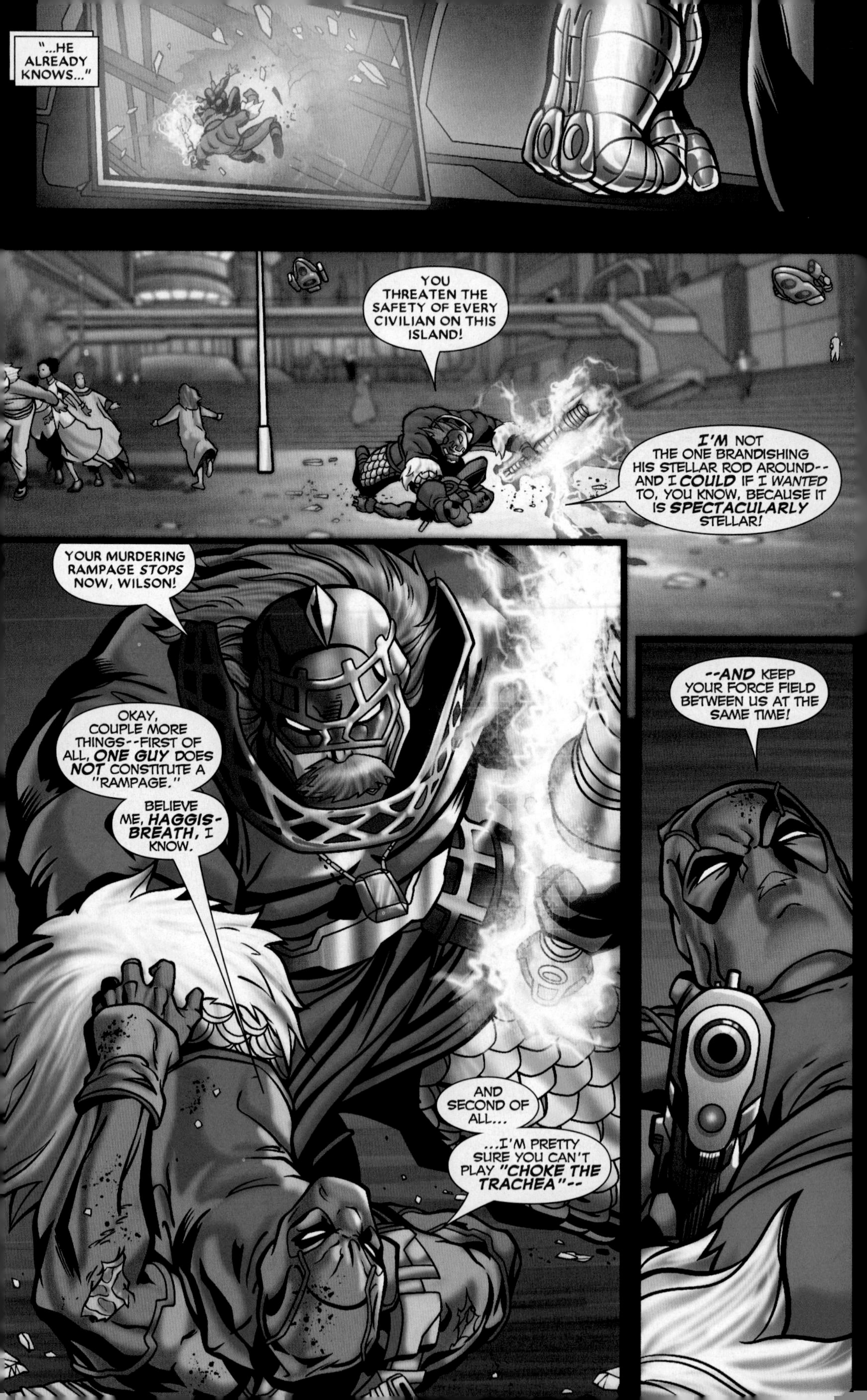
"...HE ALREADY KNOWS..."
YOU THREATEN THE SAFETY OF EVERY CIVILIAN ON THIS ISLAND!
I'M NOT THE ONE BRANDISHING HIS STELLAR ROD AROUND--AND I COULD IF I WANTED TO, YOU KNOW, BECAUSE IT IS SPECTACULARLY STELLAR!
YOUR MURDERING RAMPAGE STOPS NOW, WILSON!
OKAY, COUPLE MORE THINGS--FIRST OF ALL, ONE GUY DOES NOT CONSTITUTE A "RAMPAGE."
BELIEVE ME, HAGGIS-BREATH, I KNOW.
AND SECOND OF ALL...
...I'M PRETTY SURE YOU CAN'T PLAY "CHOKE THE TRACHEA"--
--AND KEEP YOUR FORCE FIELD BETWEEN US AT THE SAME TIME!

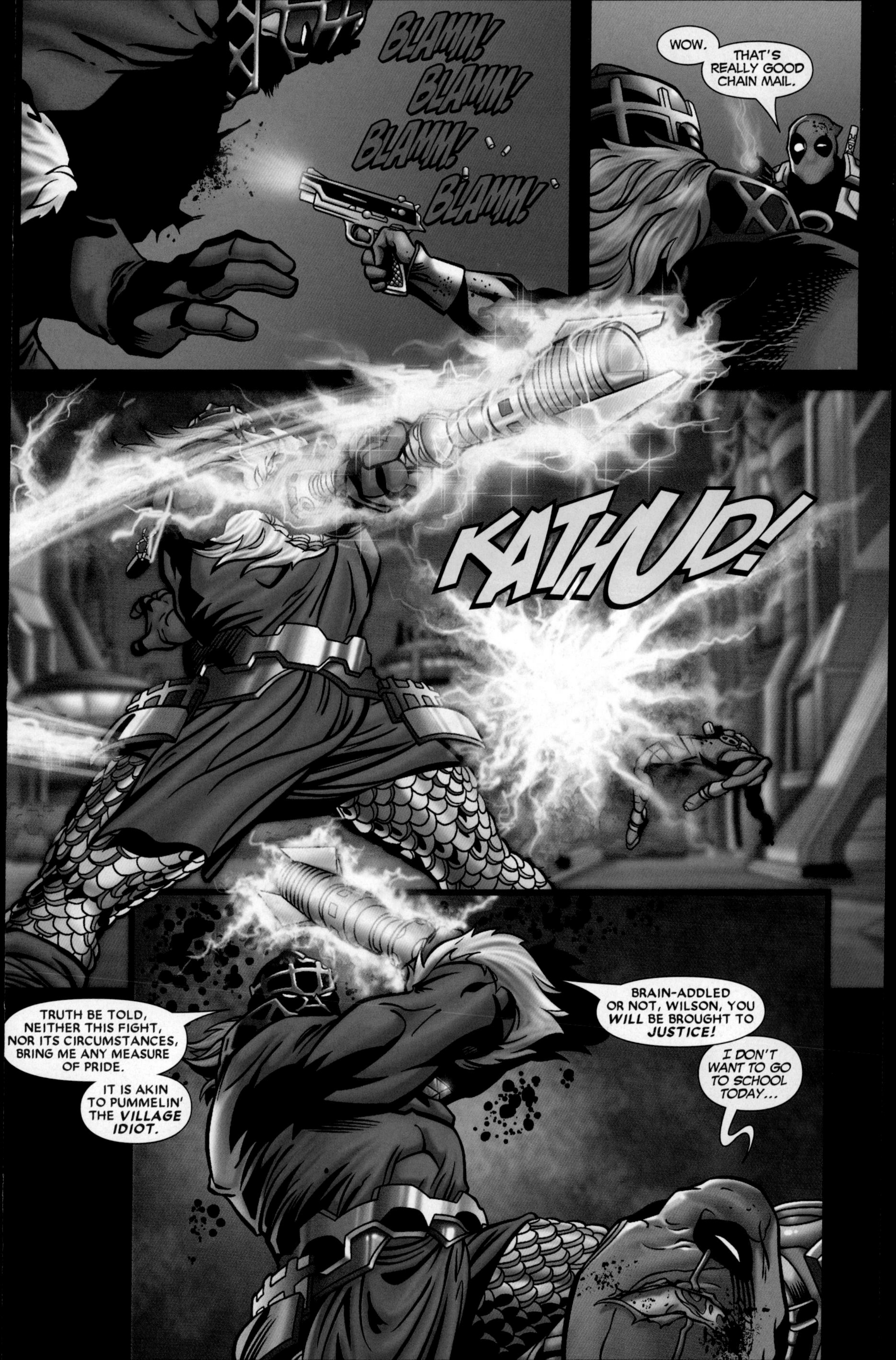
BLAMM! BLAMM! BLAMM! BLAMM!
WOW.
THAT'S REALLY GOOD CHAIN MAIL.
KATHUD!
TRUTH BE TOLD, NEITHER THIS FIGHT, NOR ITS CIRCUMSTANCES, BRING ME ANY MEASURE OF PRIDE.
IT IS AKIN TO PUMMELIN' THE VILLAGE IDIOT.
BRAIN-ADDLED OR NOT, WILSON, YOU WILL BE BROUGHT TO JUSTICE!
I DON'T WANT TO GO TO SCHOOL TODAY...

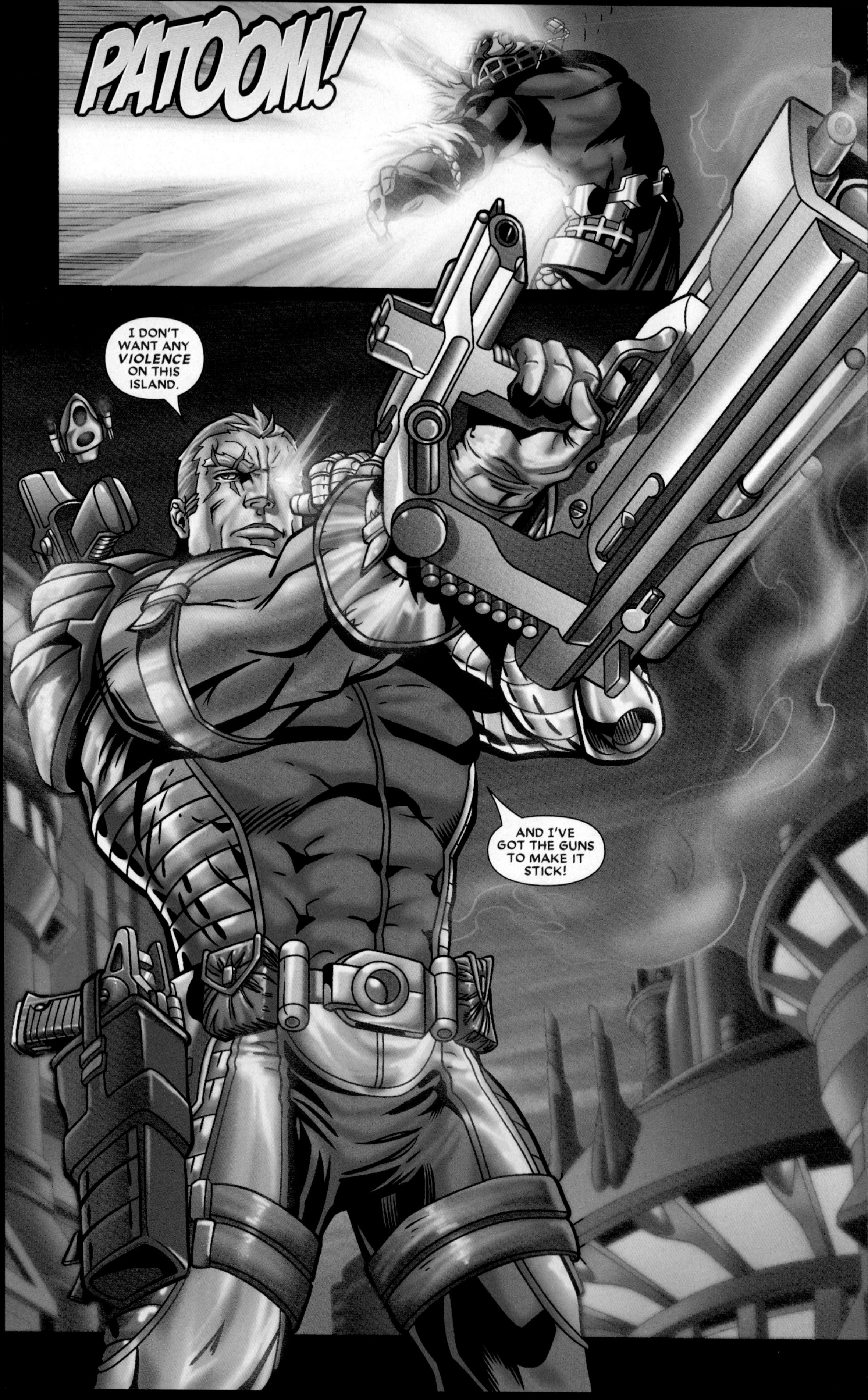
PATOOM!
I DON'T WANT ANY VIOLENCE ON THIS ISLAND.
AND I'VE GOT THE GUNS TO MAKE IT STICK!

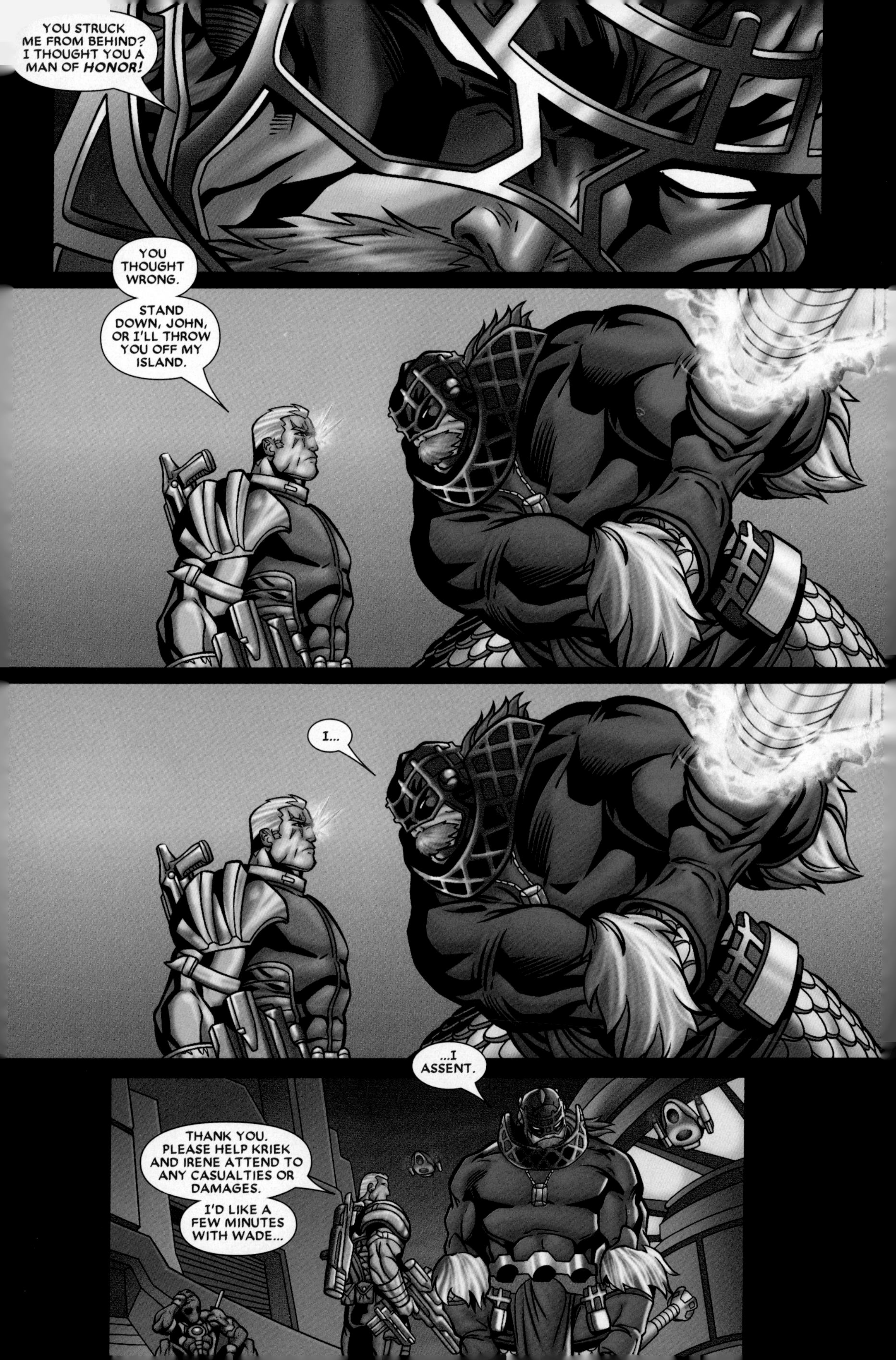
YOU STRUCK ME FROM BEHIND? I THOUGHT YOU A MAN OF *HONOR!*
YOU THOUGHT WRONG.
STAND DOWN, JOHN, OR I'LL THROW YOU OFF MY ISLAND.
I...
...I ASSENT.
THANK YOU. PLEASE HELP KRIEK AND IRENE ATTEND TO ANY CASUALTIES OR DAMAGES.
I'D LIKE A FEW MINUTES WITH WADE...

...ALONE.

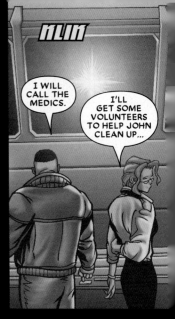

KLIN

I WILL CALL THE MEDICS.

I'LL GET SOME VOLUNTEERS TO HELP JOHN CLEAN UP...

WHAT HAPPENED?

I DON'T KNOW, NATE-- I MEAN, I DON'T REMEMBER.

WE DON'T EVEN KNOW FOR SURE THAT I KILLED HIM.

OKAY, YOU GOT A POINT.

DID YOU SEE BARAT OUT ON THE STREETS?

HEAR ABOUT HIM?

HAD YOU WORKED WITH HIM BEFORE?

DON'T KNOW, DON'T KNOW, DON'T KNOW.

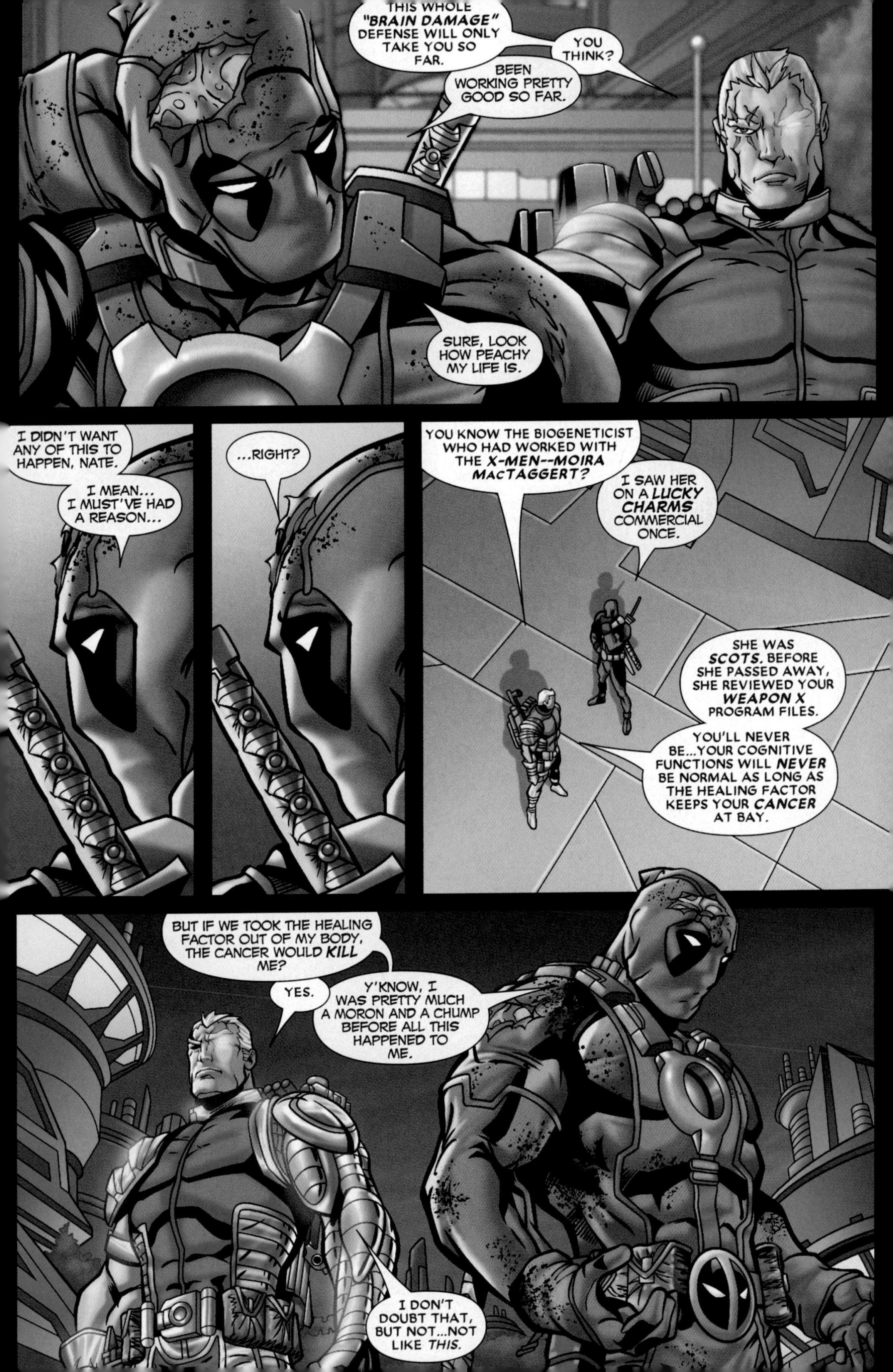
THIS WHOLE "BRAIN DAMAGE" DEFENSE WILL ONLY TAKE YOU SO FAR.
YOU THINK?
BEEN WORKING PRETTY GOOD SO FAR.
SURE, LOOK HOW PEACHY MY LIFE IS.
I DIDN'T WANT ANY OF THIS TO HAPPEN, NATE.
I MEAN... I MUST'VE HAD A REASON...
...RIGHT?
YOU KNOW THE BIOGENETICIST WHO HAD WORKED WITH THE X-MEN--MOIRA MacTAGGERT?
I SAW HER ON A LUCKY CHARMS COMMERCIAL ONCE.
SHE WAS SCOTS. BEFORE SHE PASSED AWAY, SHE REVIEWED YOUR WEAPON X PROGRAM FILES.
YOU'LL NEVER BE...YOUR COGNITIVE FUNCTIONS WILL NEVER BE NORMAL AS LONG AS THE HEALING FACTOR KEEPS YOUR CANCER AT BAY.
BUT IF WE TOOK THE HEALING FACTOR OUT OF MY BODY, THE CANCER WOULD KILL ME?
YES.
Y'KNOW, I WAS PRETTY MUCH A MORON AND A CHUMP BEFORE ALL THIS HAPPENED TO ME.
I DON'T DOUBT THAT, BUT NOT...NOT LIKE THIS.

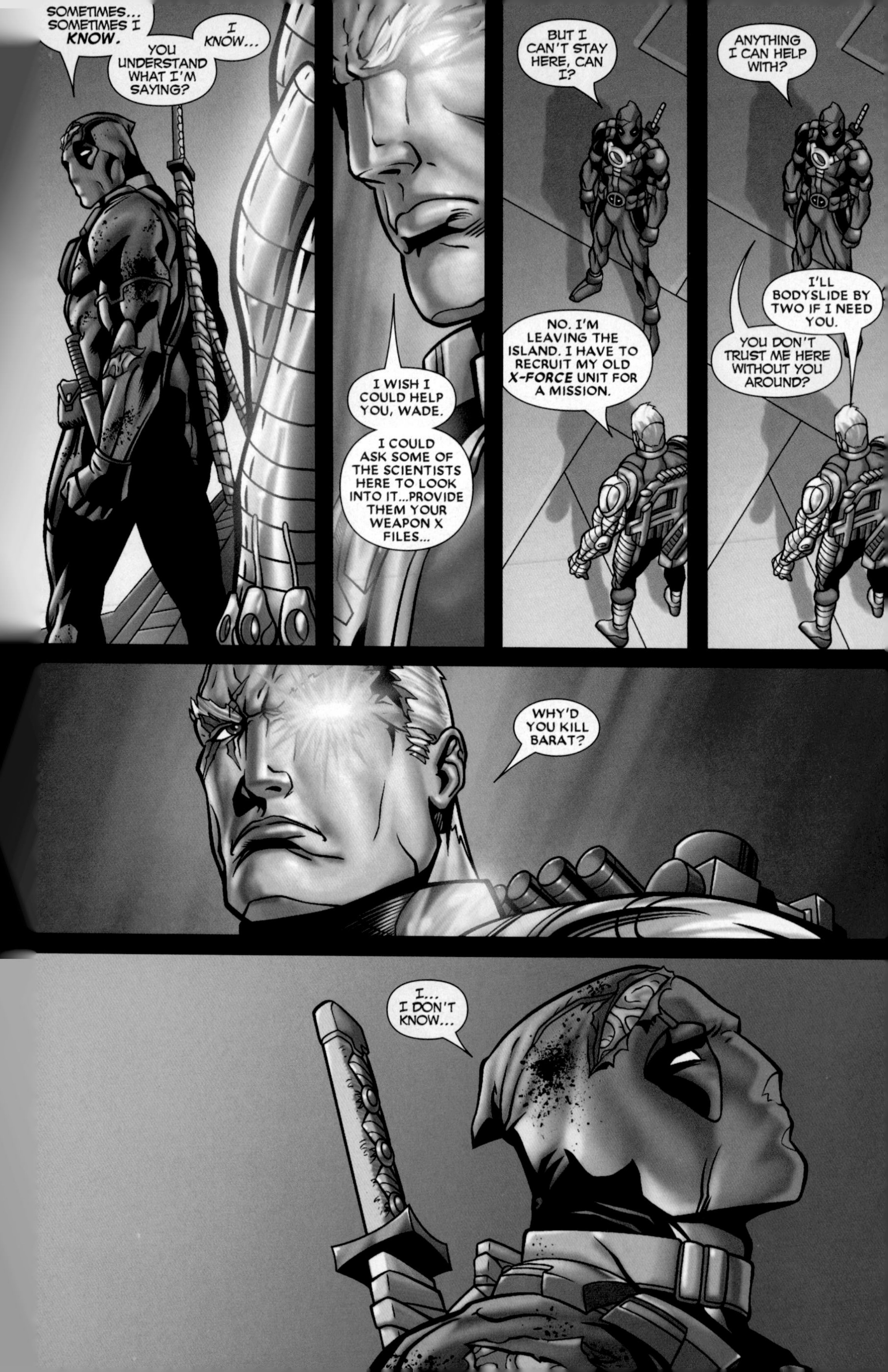
SOMETIMES... SOMETIMES I KNOW.
YOU UNDERSTAND WHAT I'M SAYING?
I KNOW...
I WISH I COULD HELP YOU, WADE.
I COULD ASK SOME OF THE SCIENTISTS HERE TO LOOK INTO IT...PROVIDE THEM YOUR WEAPON X FILES...
BUT I CAN'T STAY HERE, CAN I?
NO. I'M LEAVING THE ISLAND. I HAVE TO RECRUIT MY OLD X-FORCE UNIT FOR A MISSION.
ANYTHING I CAN HELP WITH?
YOU DON'T TRUST ME HERE WITHOUT YOU AROUND?
I'LL BODYSLIDE BY TWO IF I NEED YOU.
WHY'D YOU KILL BARAT?
I... I DON'T KNOW...

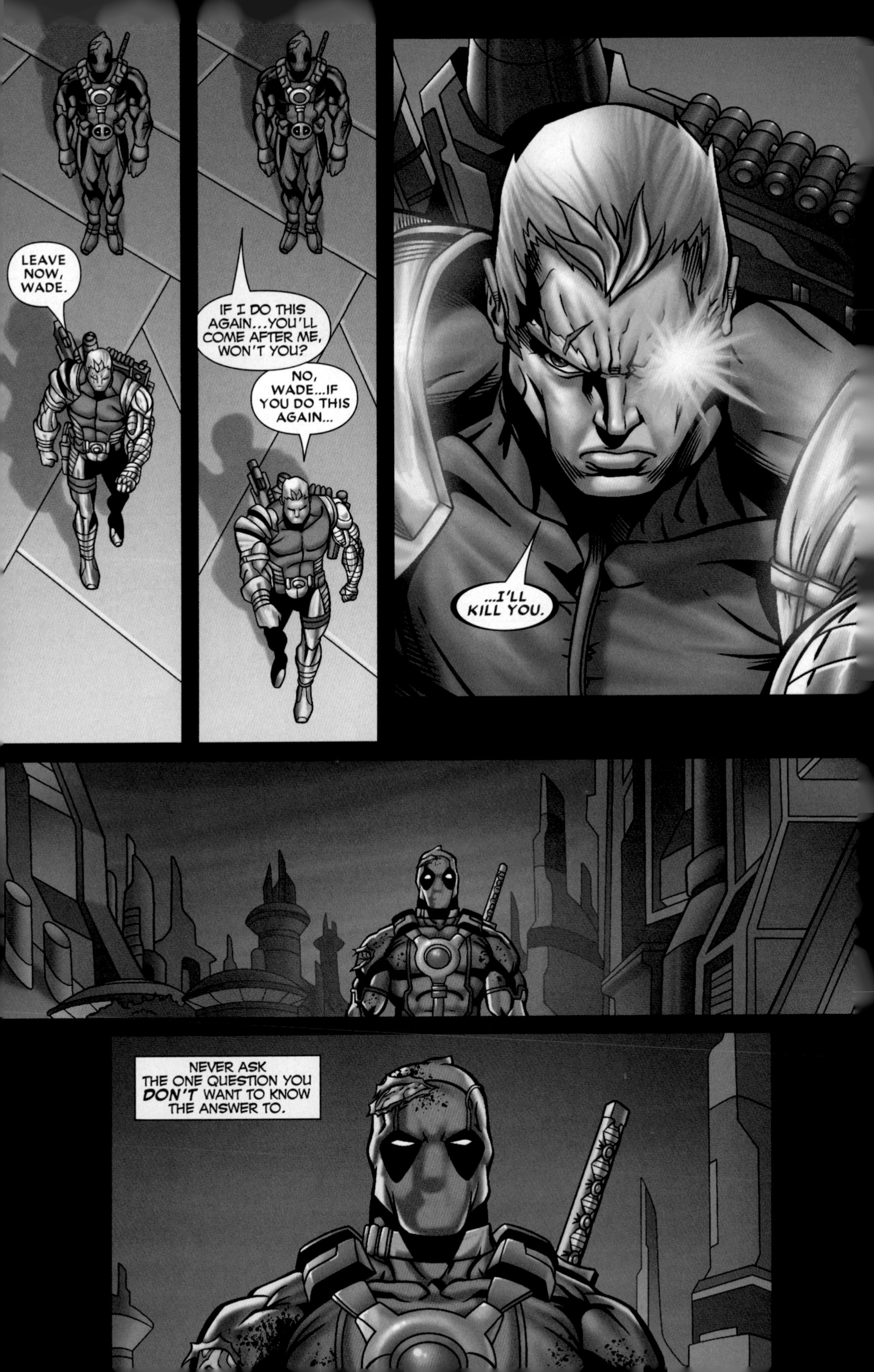
LEAVE NOW, WADE.
IF I DO THIS AGAIN...YOU'LL COME AFTER ME, WON'T YOU?
NO, WADE...IF YOU DO THIS AGAIN...
...I'LL KILL YOU.
NEVER ASK THE ONE QUESTION YOU DON'T WANT TO KNOW THE ANSWER TO.

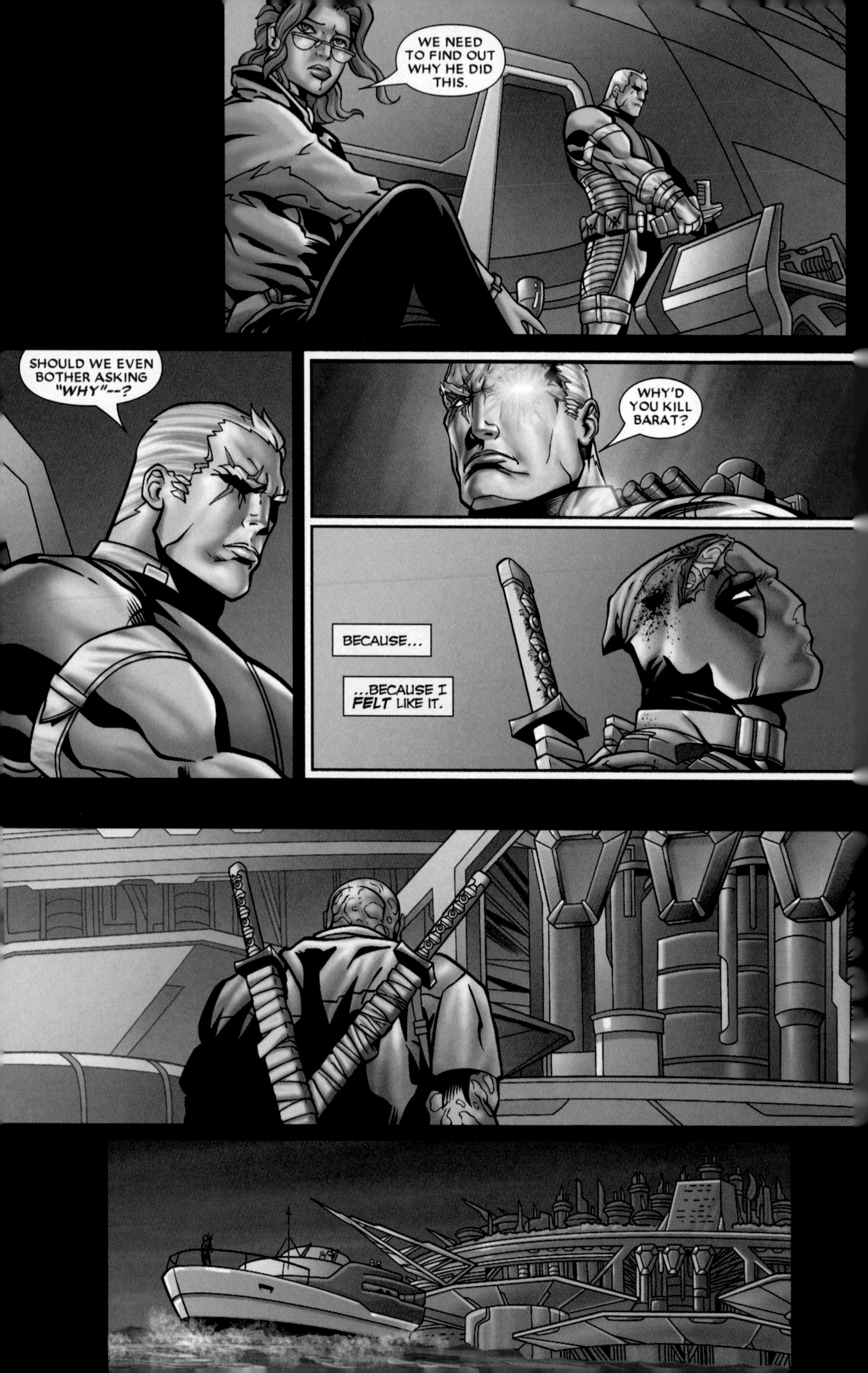
WE NEED TO FIND OUT WHY HE DID THIS.
SHOULD WE EVEN BOTHER ASKING "WHY"--?
WHY'D YOU KILL BARAT?
BECAUSE...
...BECAUSE I FELT LIKE IT.

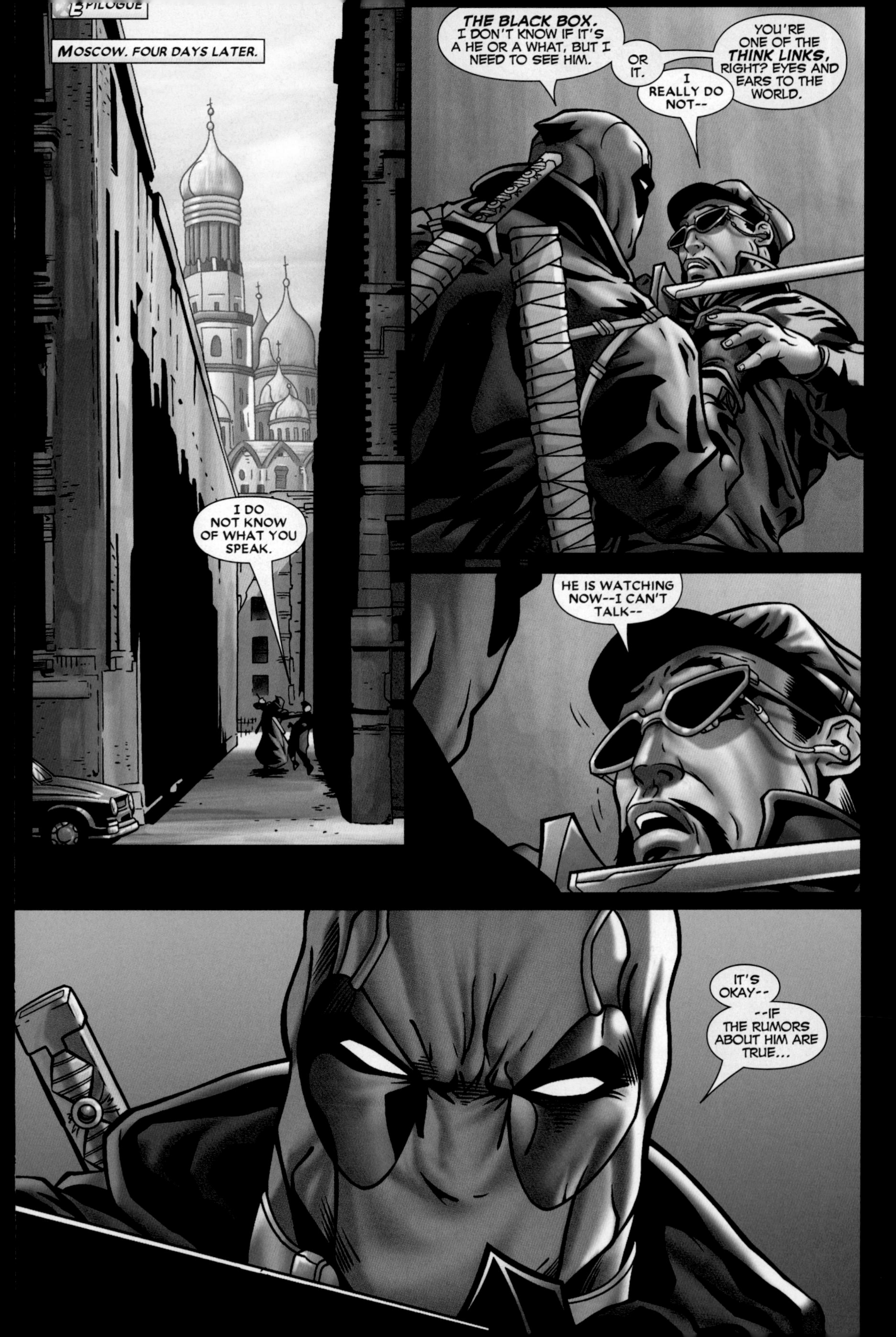
EPILOGUE
MOSCOW. FOUR DAYS LATER.
I DO NOT KNOW OF WHAT YOU SPEAK.
THE BLACK BOX. I DON'T KNOW IF IT'S A HE OR A WHAT, BUT I NEED TO SEE HIM.
OR IT.
YOU'RE ONE OF THE THINK LINKS, RIGHT? EYES AND EARS TO THE WORLD.
I REALLY DO NOT--
HE IS WATCHING NOW--I CAN'T TALK--
IT'S OKAY--
--IF THE RUMORS ABOUT HIM ARE TRUE...

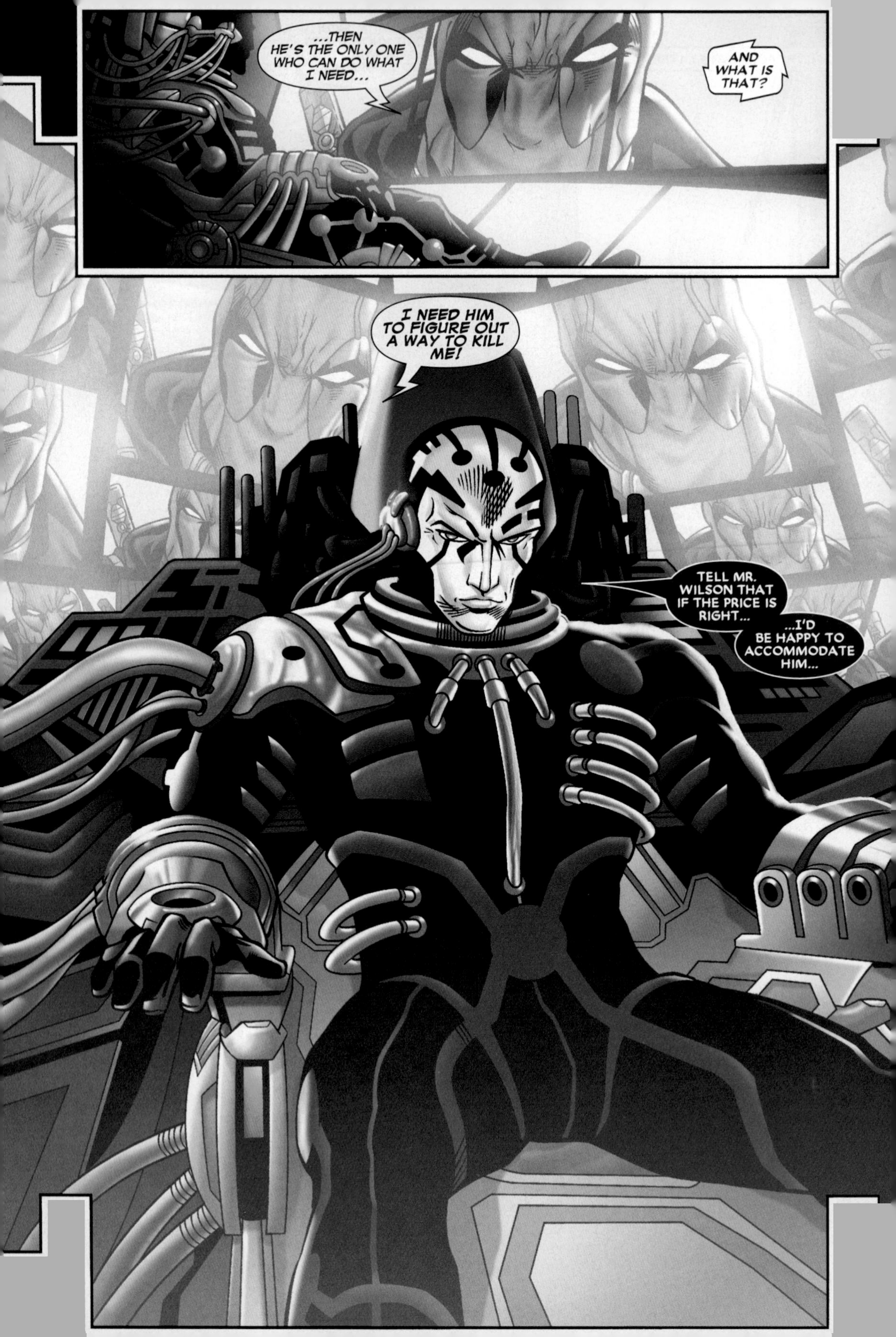
...THEN HE'S THE ONLY ONE WHO CAN DO WHAT I NEED...
AND WHAT IS THAT?
I NEED HIM TO FIGURE OUT A WAY TO KILL ME!
TELL MR. WILSON THAT IF THE PRICE IS RIGHT...
...I'D BE HAPPY TO ACCOMMODATE HIM...

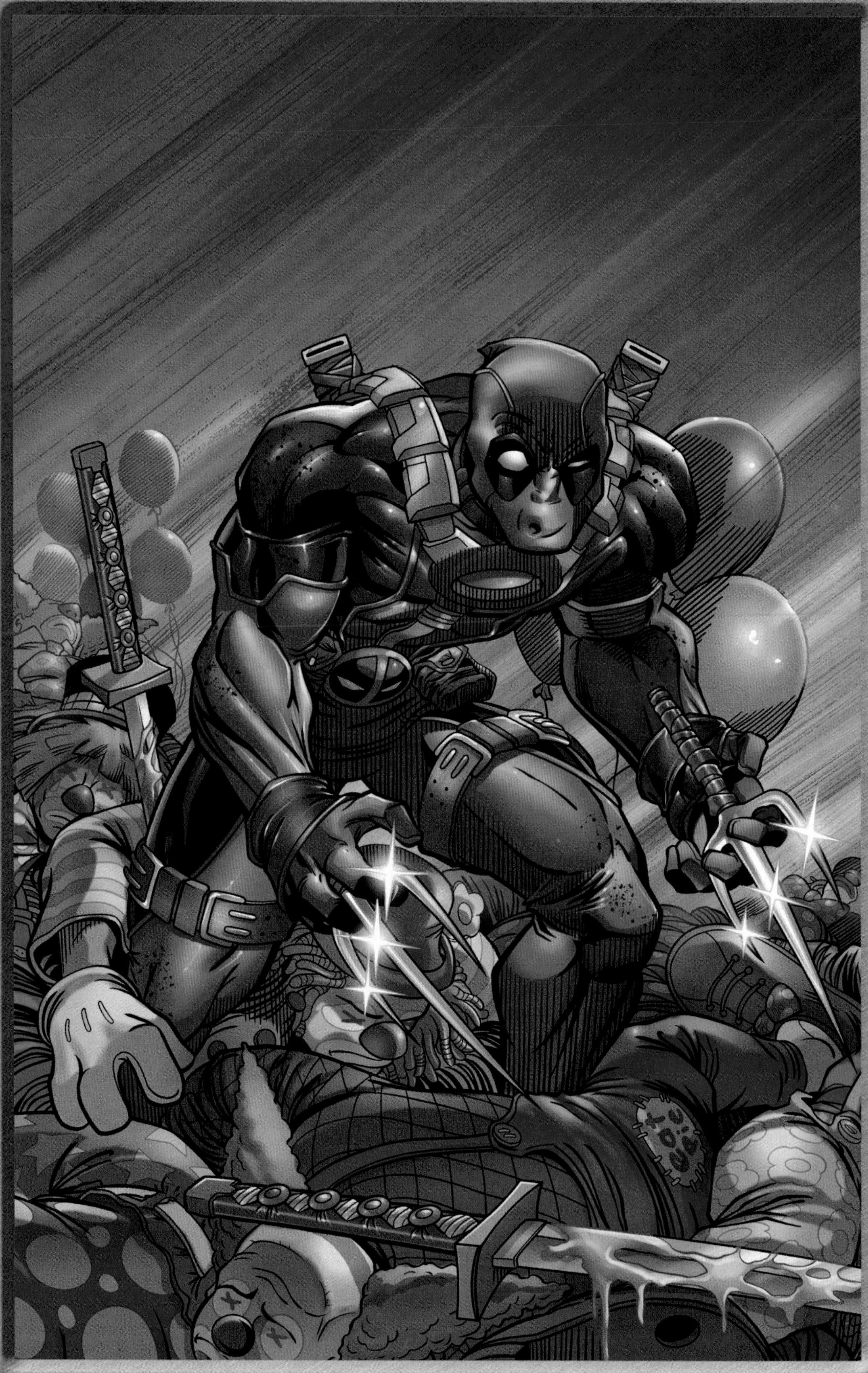

#15

ENEMA OF THE STATE

PART ONE: KILLER CLOWNS

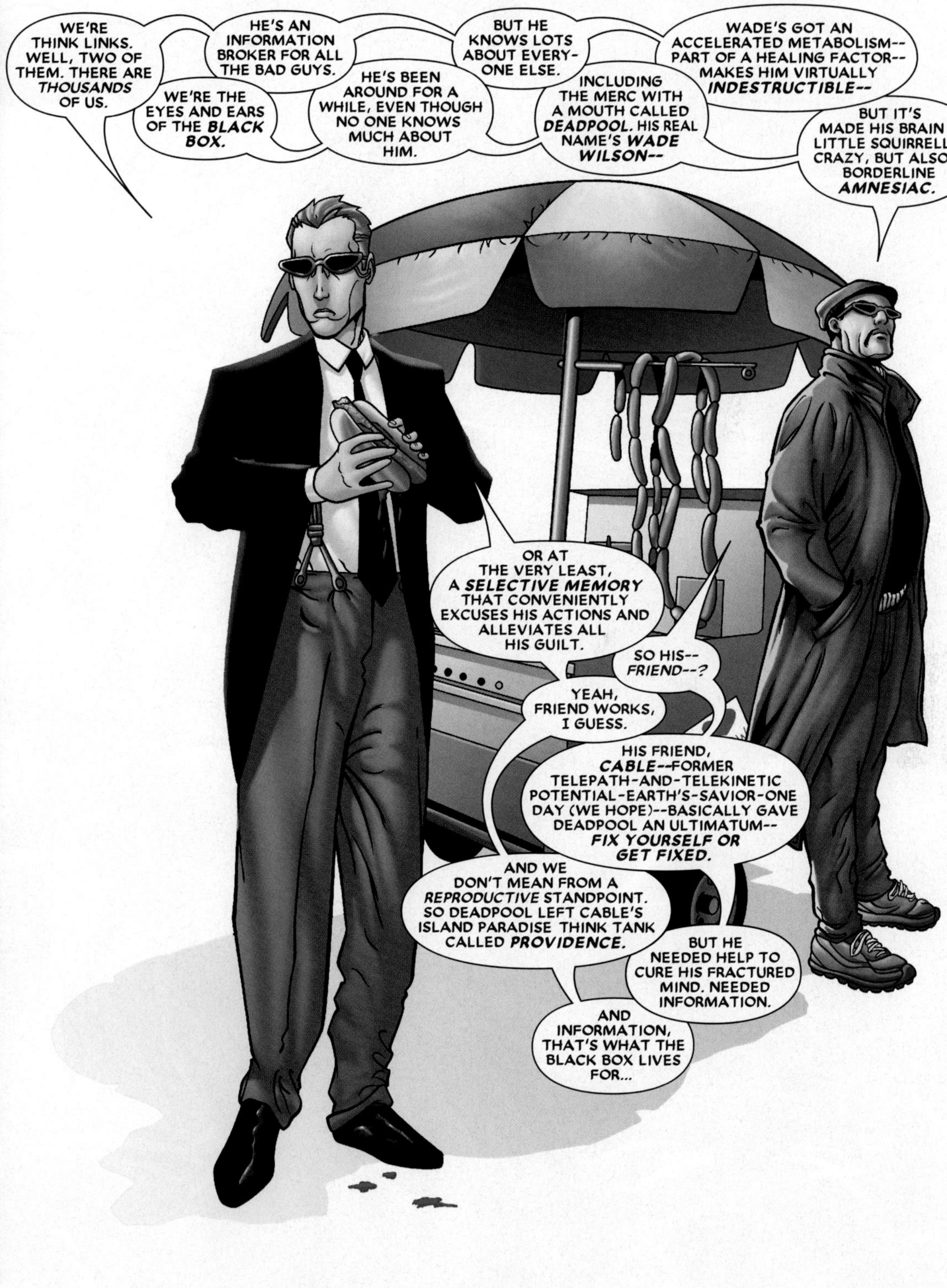
WE'RE THINK LINKS. WELL, TWO OF THEM. THERE ARE *THOUSANDS* OF US.
WE'RE THE EYES AND EARS OF THE ***BLACK BOX.***
HE'S AN INFORMATION BROKER FOR ALL THE BAD GUYS.
HE'S BEEN AROUND FOR A WHILE, EVEN THOUGH NO ONE KNOWS MUCH ABOUT HIM.
BUT HE KNOWS LOTS ABOUT EVERY-ONE ELSE.
INCLUDING THE MERC WITH A MOUTH CALLED ***DEADPOOL.*** HIS REAL NAME'S ***WADE WILSON--***
WADE'S GOT AN ACCELERATED METABOLISM--PART OF A HEALING FACTOR--MAKES HIM VIRTUALLY ***INDESTRUCTIBLE--***
BUT IT'S MADE HIS BRAIN A LITTLE SQUIRRELLY. CRAZY, BUT ALSO A BORDERLINE ***AMNESIAC.***
OR AT THE VERY LEAST, A ***SELECTIVE MEMORY*** THAT CONVENIENTLY EXCUSES HIS ACTIONS AND ALLEVIATES ALL HIS GUILT.
SO HIS-- *FRIEND--?*
YEAH, FRIEND WORKS, I GUESS.
HIS FRIEND, ***CABLE--***FORMER TELEPATH-AND-TELEKINETIC POTENTIAL-EARTH'S-SAVIOR-ONE DAY (WE HOPE)--BASICALLY GAVE DEADPOOL AN ULTIMATUM-- ***FIX YOURSELF OR GET FIXED.***
AND WE DON'T MEAN FROM A *REPRODUCTIVE* STANDPOINT. SO DEADPOOL LEFT CABLE'S ISLAND PARADISE THINK TANK CALLED ***PROVIDENCE.***
BUT HE NEEDED HELP TO CURE HIS FRACTURED MIND. NEEDED INFORMATION.
AND INFORMATION, THAT'S WHAT THE BLACK BOX LIVES FOR...

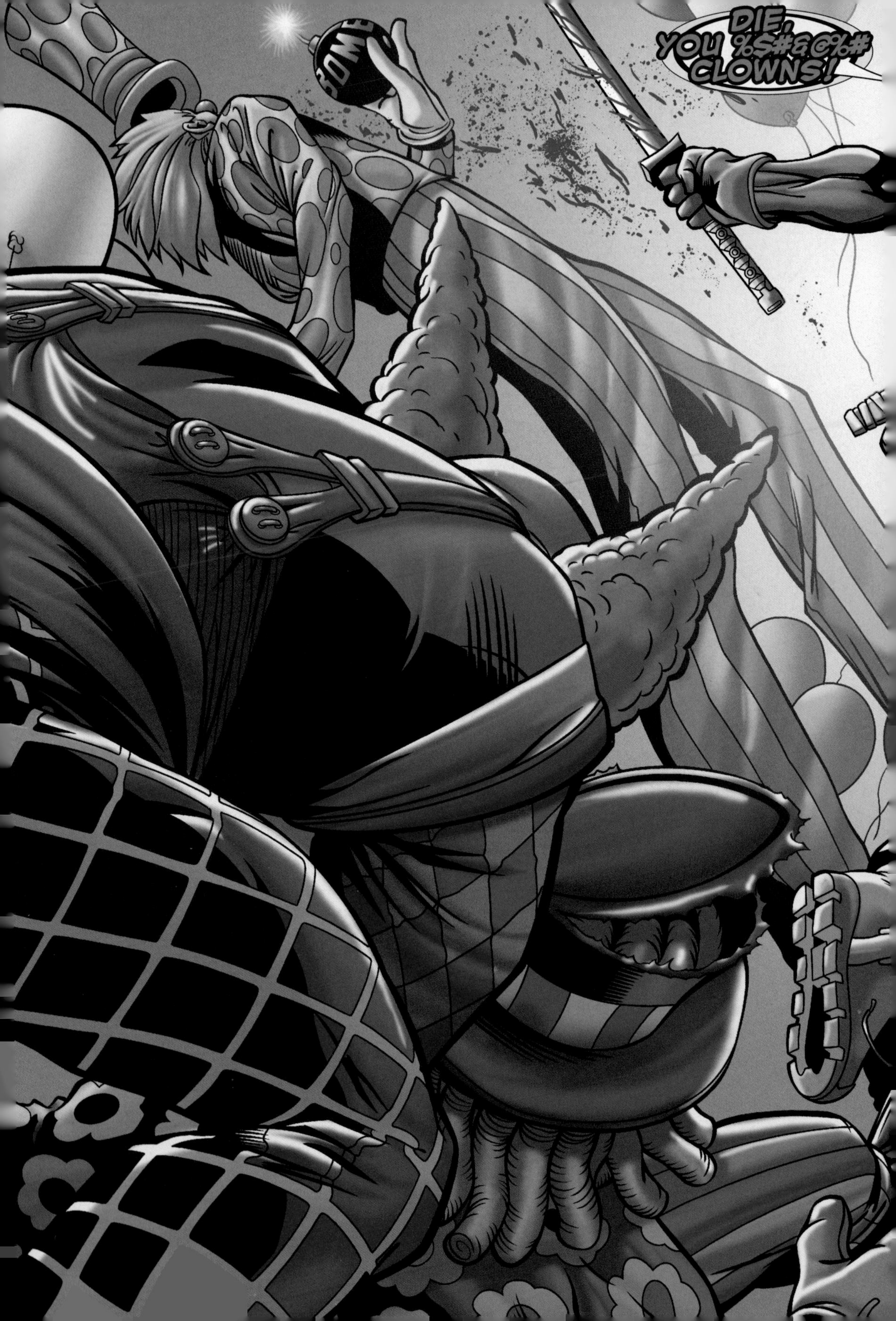
DIE, YOU %$#&@%# CLOWNS!

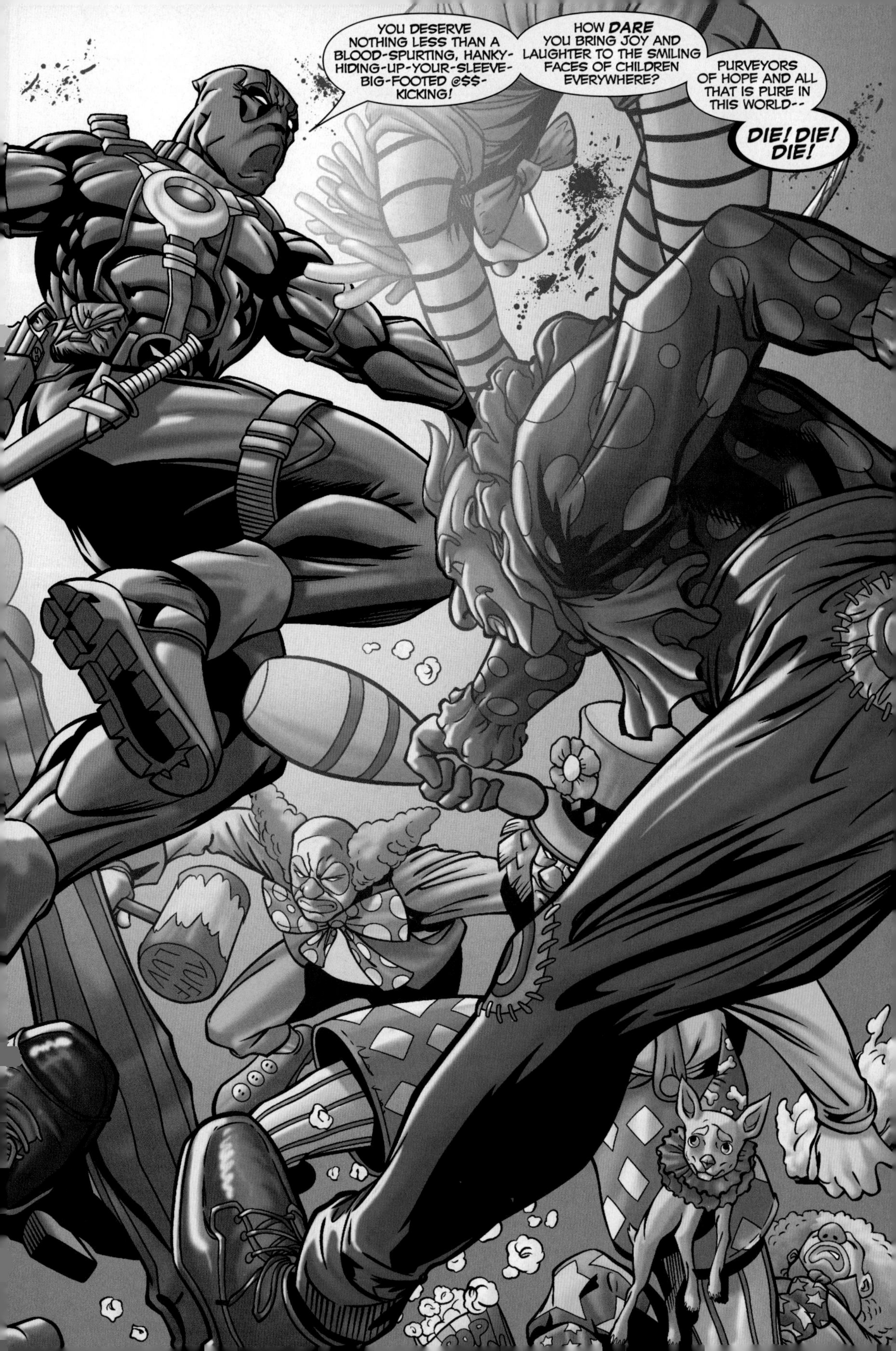
YOU DESERVE NOTHING LESS THAN A BLOOD-SPURTING, HANKY-HIDING-UP-YOUR-SLEEVE-BIG-FOOTED @$$-KICKING!
HOW **DARE** YOU BRING JOY AND LAUGHTER TO THE SMILING FACES OF CHILDREN EVERYWHERE?
PURVEYORS OF HOPE AND ALL THAT IS PURE IN THIS WORLD--
DIE! DIE! DIE!

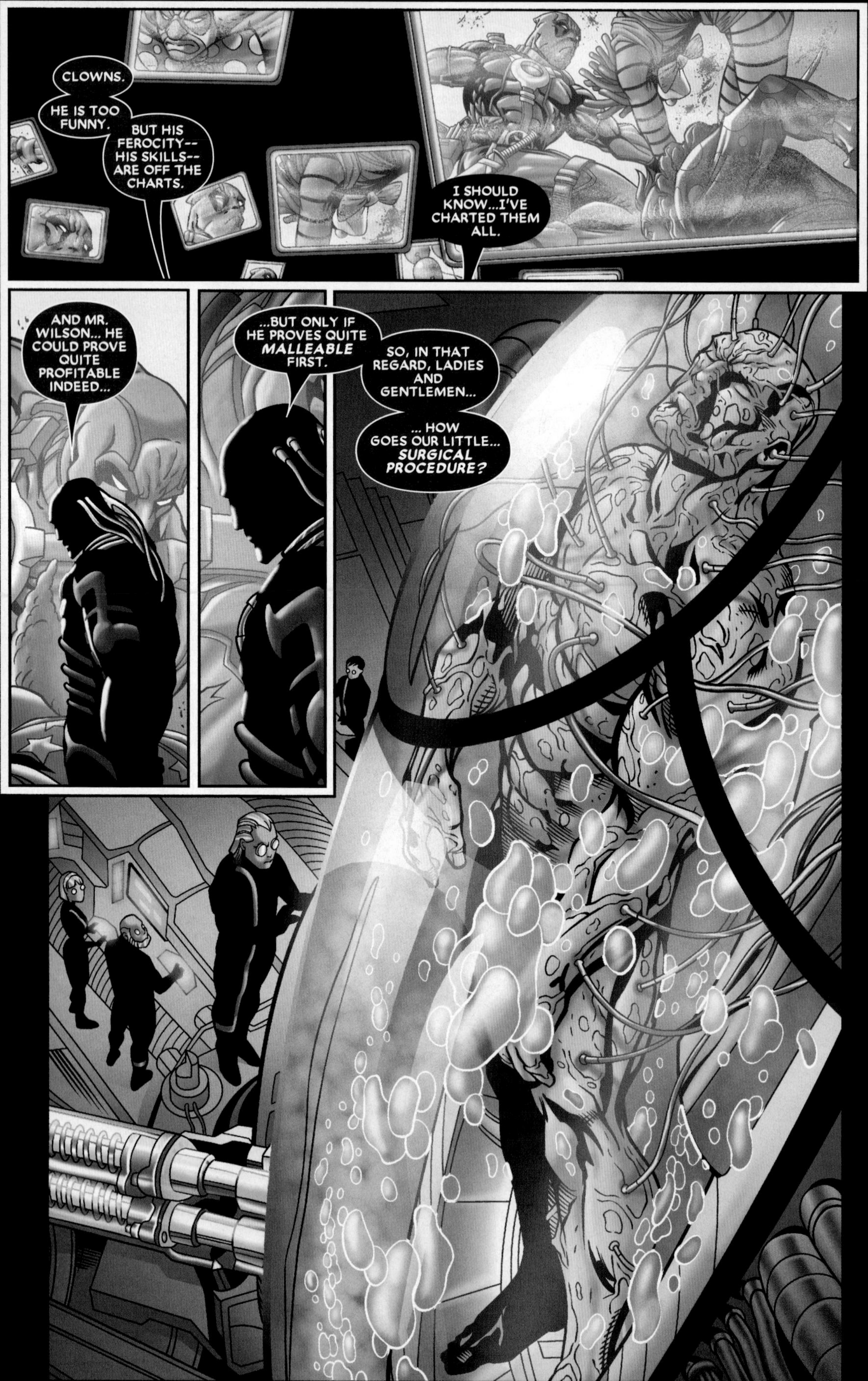
CLOWNS.
HE IS TOO FUNNY.
BUT HIS FEROCITY-- HIS SKILLS-- ARE OFF THE CHARTS.
I SHOULD KNOW...I'VE CHARTED THEM ALL.
AND MR. WILSON... HE COULD PROVE QUITE PROFITABLE INDEED...
...BUT ONLY IF HE PROVES QUITE MALLEABLE FIRST.
SO, IN THAT REGARD, LADIES AND GENTLEMEN...
... HOW GOES OUR LITTLE... SURGICAL PROCEDURE?

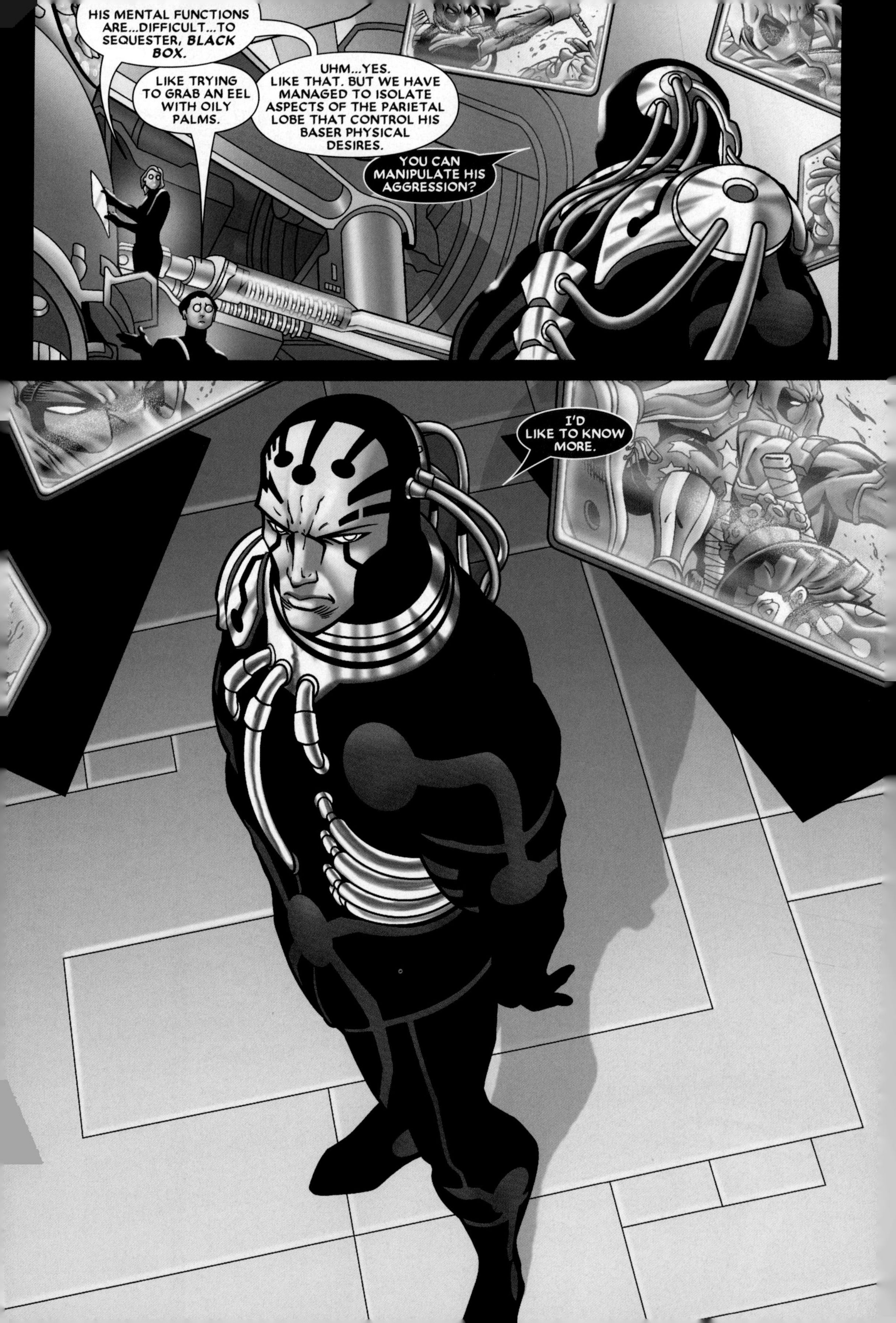
HIS MENTAL FUNCTIONS ARE...DIFFICULT...TO SEQUESTER, *BLACK BOX.*
LIKE TRYING TO GRAB AN EEL WITH OILY PALMS.
UHM...YES. LIKE THAT. BUT WE HAVE MANAGED TO ISOLATE ASPECTS OF THE PARIETAL LOBE THAT CONTROL HIS BASER PHYSICAL DESIRES.
YOU CAN MANIPULATE HIS AGGRESSION?
I'D LIKE TO KNOW MORE.

DAYS LATER...

NO, MR. WILSON, LET US TRY THIS AGAIN. WHO IS THE GREATEST THREAT TO THE PUBLIC SAFETY?

CLOWNS!

OKAY...AGAIN...CAN WE PLEASE MOVE BEYOND THIS FIXATION WITH CLOWNS?

I'LL GRANT YOU THAT CLOWNS ARE A THREAT. THERE'S YOUR BONE. BUT WHO IS AN EVEN GREATER THREAT?

SIMON COWELL!

WORSE.

GALACTUS!

KARL ROVE!

LESS THAN THAT.

SOMEWHERE BETWEEN GALACTUS AND KARL, WHO, BY THE WAY, IS A VALUED CUSTOMER.

SUPERHUMANS! SUPERHUMANS ARE THE GREATEST THREAT TO MODERN CIVILIZATION.

YOU ARE READY TO BECOME A GREAT HERO, MR. WILSON-- YOU ARE READY TO FULFILL YOUR ASSIGNMENT:

GO AND ELIMINATE THE GREATEST THREAT TO MANKIND!

BODYSLIDE BY ONE!

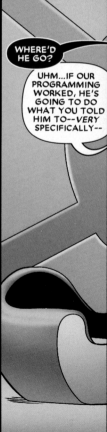

WHERE'D HE GO?

UHM...IF OUR PROGRAMMING WORKED, HE'S GOING TO DO WHAT YOU TOLD HIM TO-- VERY SPECIFICALLY--

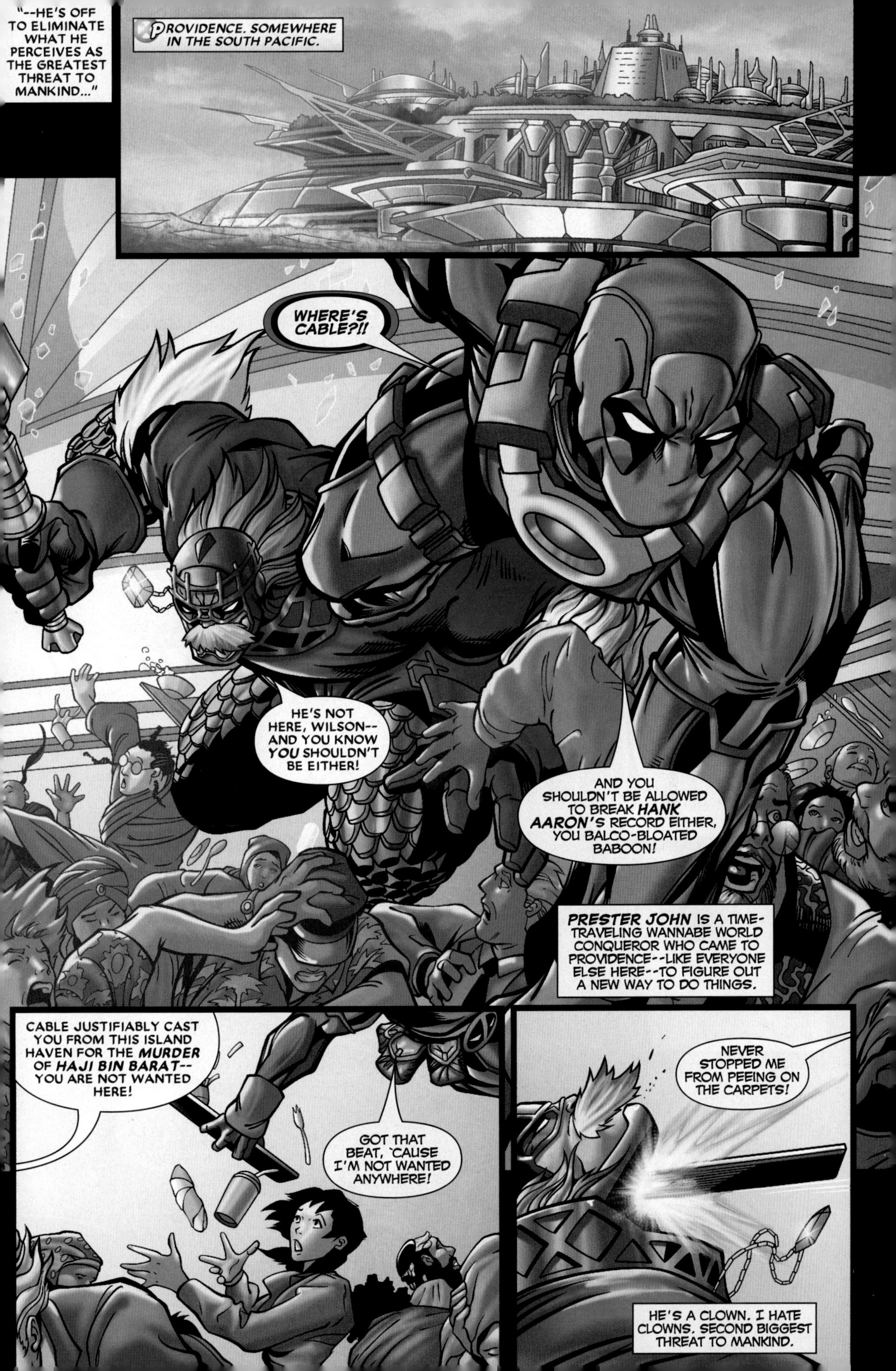
"--HE'S OFF TO ELIMINATE WHAT HE PERCEIVES AS THE GREATEST THREAT TO MANKIND..."
PROVIDENCE. SOMEWHERE IN THE SOUTH PACIFIC.
WHERE'S CABLE?!!
HE'S NOT HERE, WILSON-- AND YOU KNOW YOU SHOULDN'T BE EITHER!
AND YOU SHOULDN'T BE ALLOWED TO BREAK HANK AARON'S RECORD EITHER, YOU BALCO-BLOATED BABOON!
PRESTER JOHN IS A TIME-TRAVELING WANNABE WORLD CONQUEROR WHO CAME TO PROVIDENCE--LIKE EVERYONE ELSE HERE--TO FIGURE OUT A NEW WAY TO DO THINGS.
CABLE JUSTIFIABLY CAST YOU FROM THIS ISLAND HAVEN FOR THE MURDER OF HAJI BIN BARAT-- YOU ARE NOT WANTED HERE!
GOT THAT BEAT, 'CAUSE I'M NOT WANTED ANYWHERE!
NEVER STOPPED ME FROM PEEING ON THE CARPETS!
HE'S A CLOWN. I HATE CLOWNS. SECOND BIGGEST THREAT TO MANKIND.

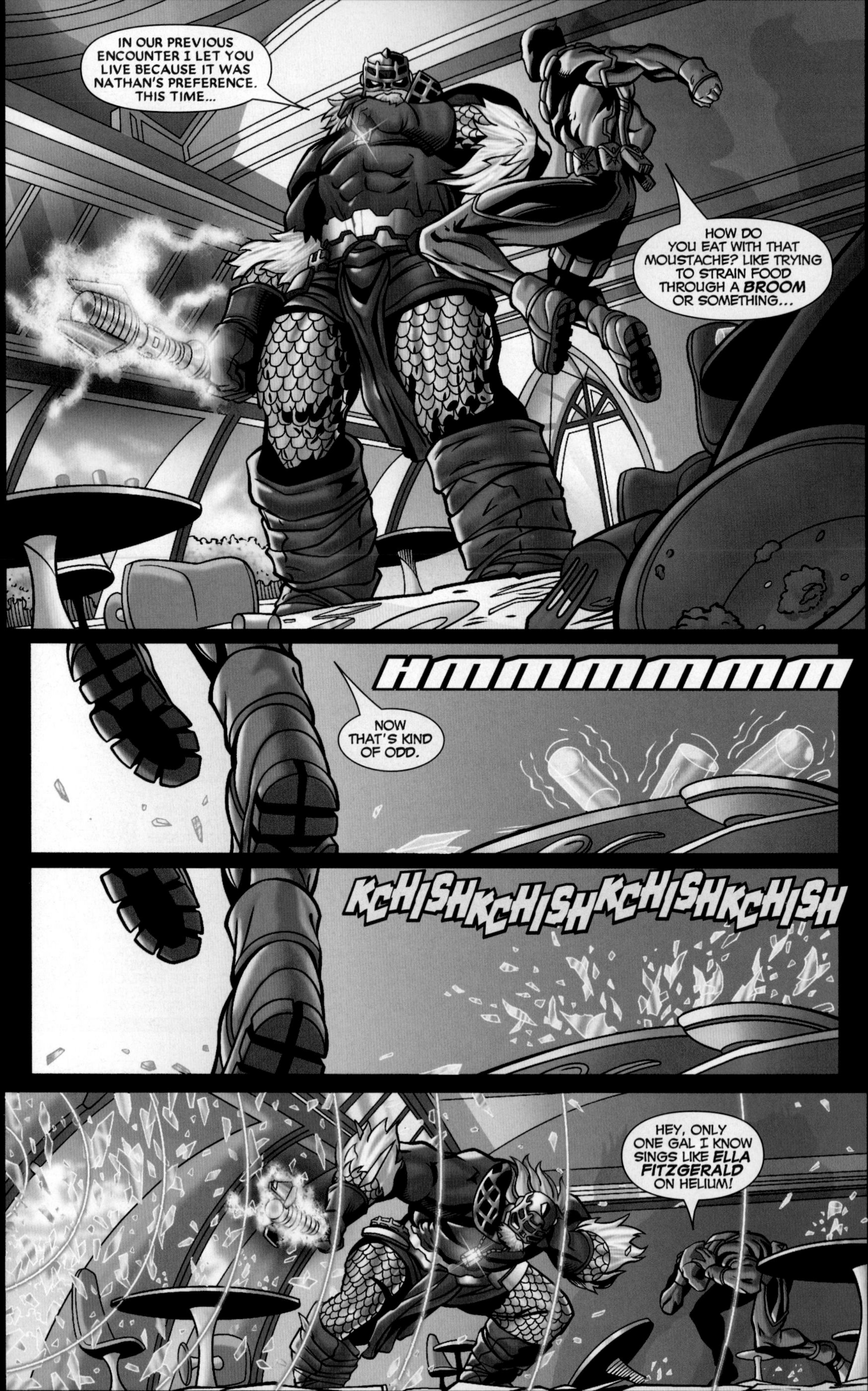
IN OUR PREVIOUS ENCOUNTER I LET YOU LIVE BECAUSE IT WAS NATHAN'S PREFERENCE. THIS TIME...
HOW DO YOU EAT WITH THAT MOUSTACHE? LIKE TRYING TO STRAIN FOOD THROUGH A BROOM OR SOMETHING...
HMMMMMMM
NOW THAT'S KIND OF ODD.
KCHISHKCHISHKCHISHKCHISH
HEY, ONLY ONE GAL I KNOW SINGS LIKE ELLA FITZGERALD ON HELIUM!

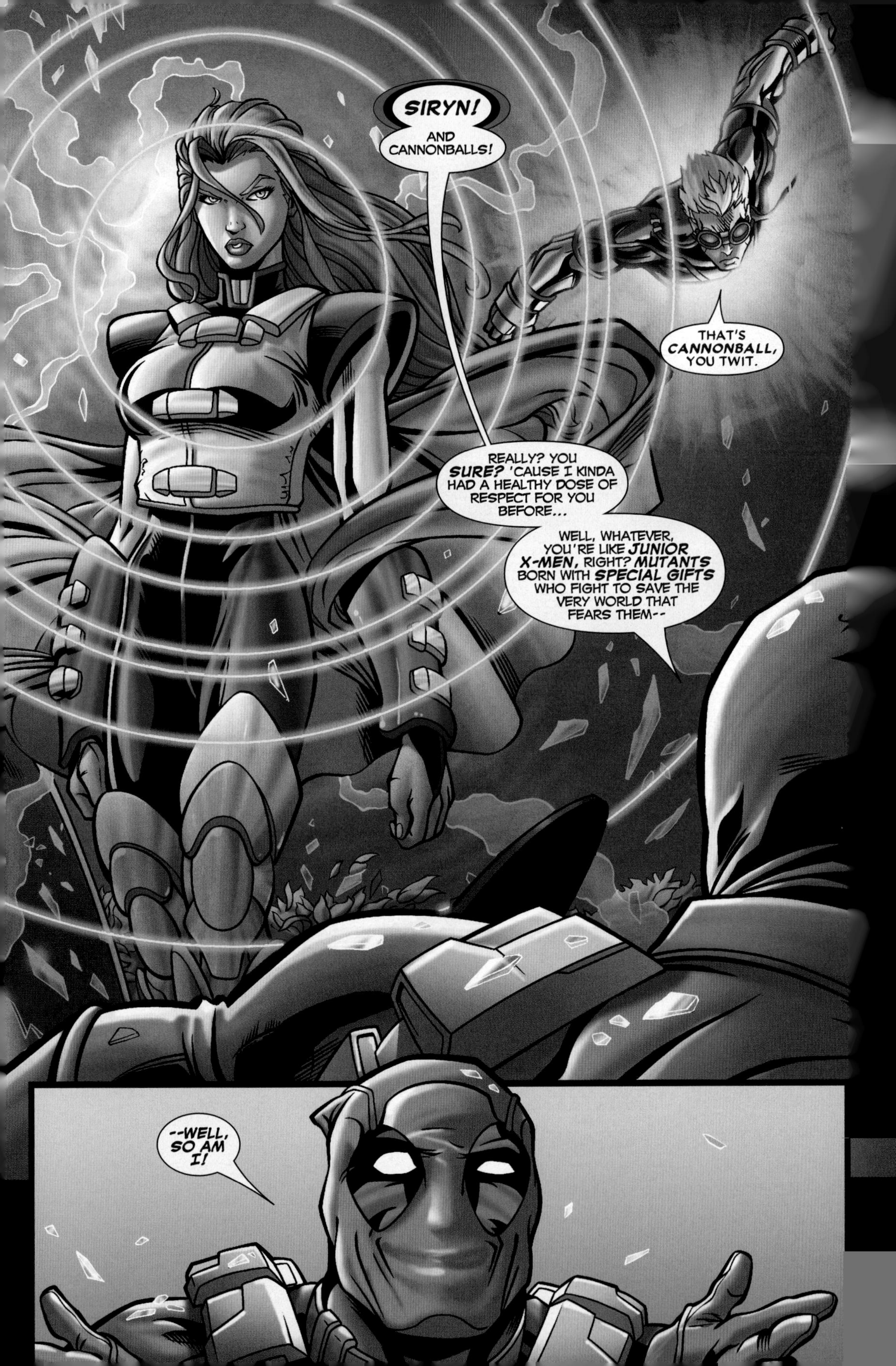
SIRYN!
AND CANNONBALLS!
THAT'S CANNONBALL, YOU TWIT.
REALLY? YOU SURE? 'CAUSE I KINDA HAD A HEALTHY DOSE OF RESPECT FOR YOU BEFORE...
WELL, WHATEVER, YOU'RE LIKE JUNIOR X-MEN, RIGHT? MUTANTS BORN WITH SPECIAL GIFTS WHO FIGHT TO SAVE THE VERY WORLD THAT FEARS THEM--
--WELL, SO AM I!

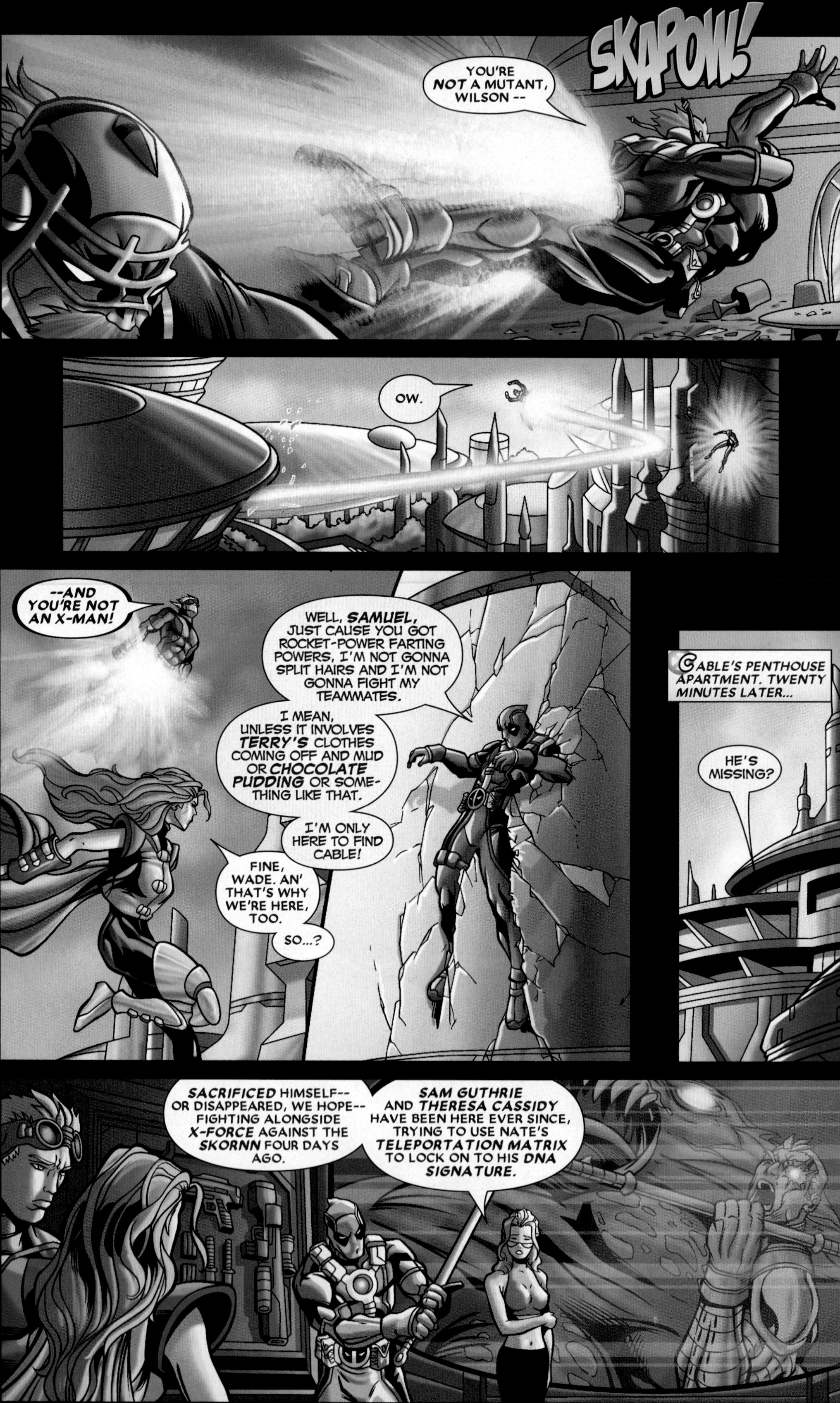
SKAPOW!
YOU'RE NOT A MUTANT, WILSON --
OW.
--AND YOU'RE NOT AN X-MAN!
WELL, SAMUEL, JUST CAUSE YOU GOT ROCKET-POWER FARTING POWERS, I'M NOT GONNA SPLIT HAIRS AND I'M NOT GONNA FIGHT MY TEAMMATES.
I MEAN, UNLESS IT INVOLVES TERRY'S CLOTHES COMING OFF AND MUD OR CHOCOLATE PUDDING OR SOMETHING LIKE THAT.
I'M ONLY HERE TO FIND CABLE!
FINE, WADE. AN' THAT'S WHY WE'RE HERE, TOO.
SO...?
CABLE'S PENTHOUSE APARTMENT. TWENTY MINUTES LATER...
HE'S MISSING?
SACRIFICED HIMSELF-- OR DISAPPEARED, WE HOPE-- FIGHTING ALONGSIDE X-FORCE AGAINST THE SKORNN FOUR DAYS AGO.
SAM GUTHRIE AND THERESA CASSIDY HAVE BEEN HERE EVER SINCE, TRYING TO USE NATE'S TELEPORTATION MATRIX TO LOCK ON TO HIS DNA SIGNATURE.

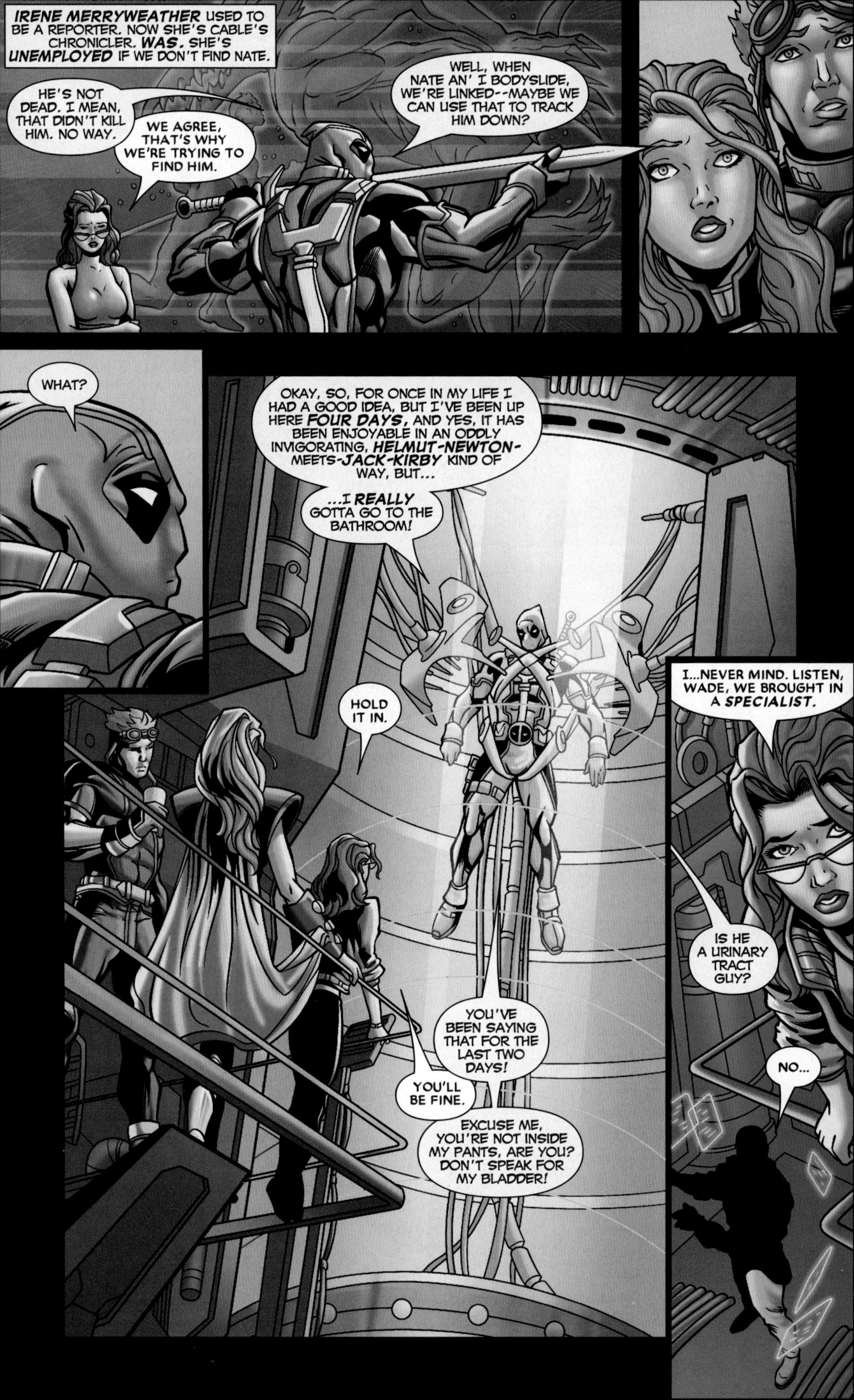
IRENE MERRYWEATHER USED TO BE A REPORTER. NOW SHE'S CABLE'S CHRONICLER. WAS. SHE'S UNEMPLOYED IF WE DON'T FIND NATE.
HE'S NOT DEAD. I MEAN, THAT DIDN'T KILL HIM. NO WAY.
WE AGREE, THAT'S WHY WE'RE TRYING TO FIND HIM.
WELL, WHEN NATE AN' I BODYSLIDE, WE'RE LINKED--MAYBE WE CAN USE THAT TO TRACK HIM DOWN?
WHAT?
OKAY, SO, FOR ONCE IN MY LIFE I HAD A GOOD IDEA, BUT I'VE BEEN UP HERE FOUR DAYS, AND YES, IT HAS BEEN ENJOYABLE IN AN ODDLY INVIGORATING, HELMUT-NEWTON-MEETS-JACK-KIRBY KIND OF WAY, BUT...
...I REALLY GOTTA GO TO THE BATHROOM!
HOLD IT IN.
YOU'VE BEEN SAYING THAT FOR THE LAST TWO DAYS!
YOU'LL BE FINE.
EXCUSE ME, YOU'RE NOT INSIDE MY PANTS, ARE YOU? DON'T SPEAK FOR MY BLADDER!
I...NEVER MIND. LISTEN, WADE, WE BROUGHT IN A SPECIALIST.
IS HE A URINARY TRACT GUY?
NO...

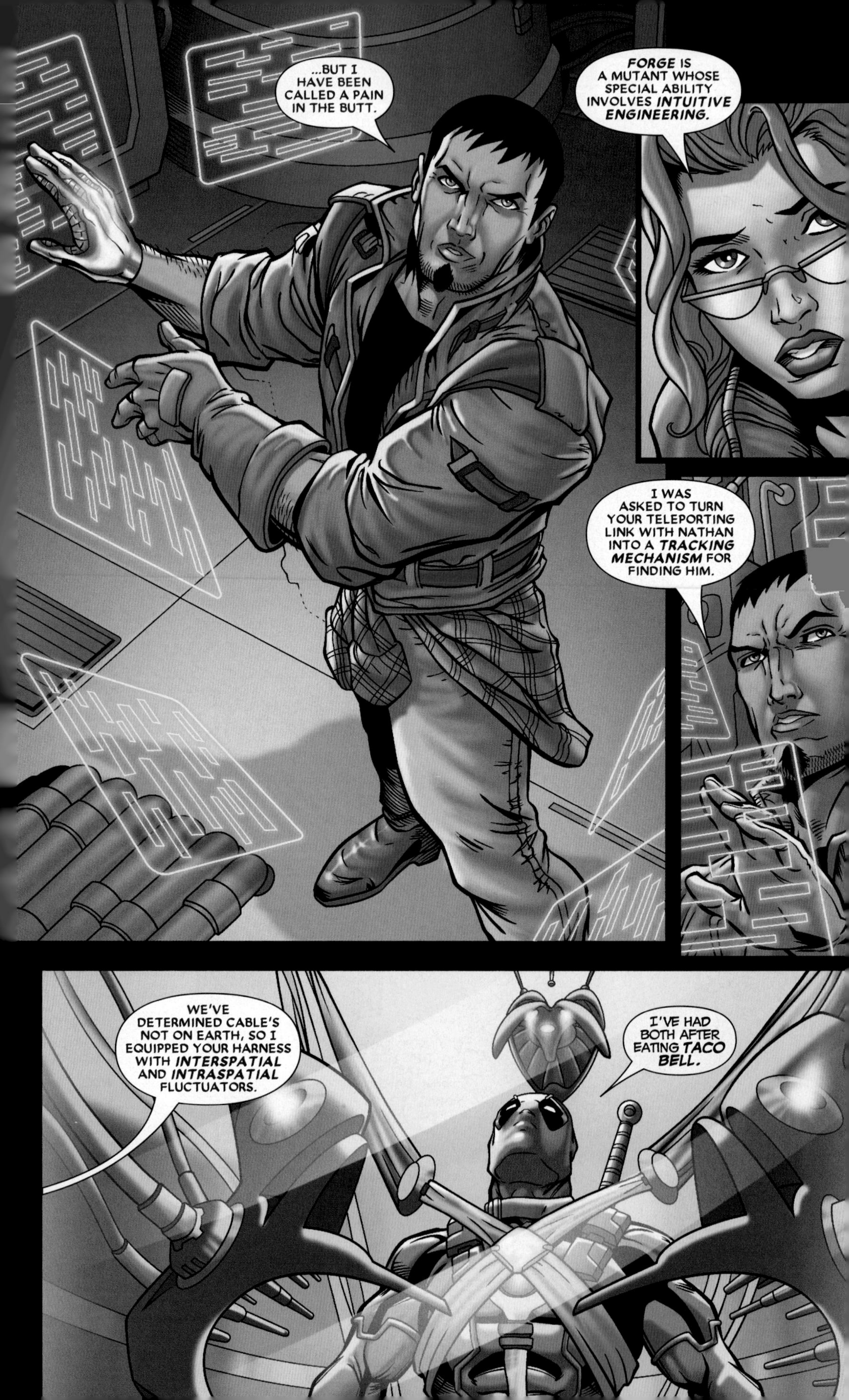
...BUT I HAVE BEEN CALLED A PAIN IN THE BUTT.
FORGE IS A MUTANT WHOSE SPECIAL ABILITY INVOLVES INTUITIVE ENGINEERING.
I WAS ASKED TO TURN YOUR TELEPORTING LINK WITH NATHAN INTO A TRACKING MECHANISM FOR FINDING HIM.
WE'VE DETERMINED CABLE'S NOT ON EARTH, SO I EQUIPPED YOUR HARNESS WITH INTERSPATIAL AND INTRASPATIAL FLUCTUATORS.
I'VE HAD BOTH AFTER EATING TACO BELL.

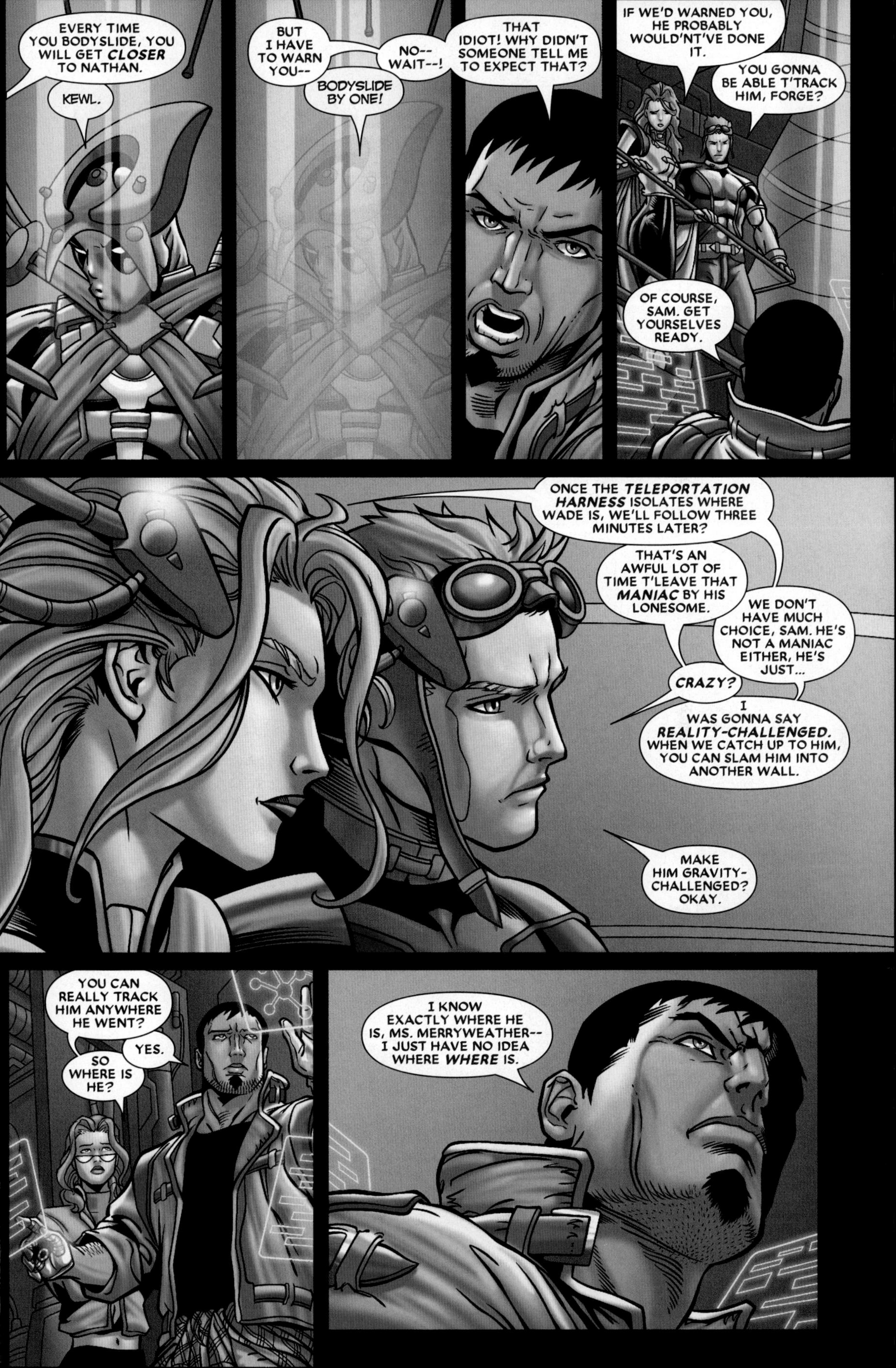
EVERY TIME YOU BODYSLIDE, YOU WILL GET CLOSER TO NATHAN.
KEWL.
BUT I HAVE TO WARN YOU--
BODYSLIDE BY ONE!
NO-- WAIT--!
THAT IDIOT! WHY DIDN'T SOMEONE TELL ME TO EXPECT THAT?
IF WE'D WARNED YOU, HE PROBABLY WOULD'NT'VE DONE IT.
YOU GONNA BE ABLE T'TRACK HIM, FORGE?
OF COURSE, SAM. GET YOURSELVES READY.
ONCE THE TELEPORTATION HARNESS ISOLATES WHERE WADE IS, WE'LL FOLLOW THREE MINUTES LATER?
THAT'S AN AWFUL LOT OF TIME T'LEAVE THAT MANIAC BY HIS LONESOME.
WE DON'T HAVE MUCH CHOICE, SAM. HE'S NOT A MANIAC EITHER, HE'S JUST...
CRAZY?
I WAS GONNA SAY REALITY-CHALLENGED. WHEN WE CATCH UP TO HIM, YOU CAN SLAM HIM INTO ANOTHER WALL.
MAKE HIM GRAVITY-CHALLENGED? OKAY.
YOU CAN REALLY TRACK HIM ANYWHERE HE WENT?
YES.
SO WHERE IS HE?
I KNOW EXACTLY WHERE HE IS, MS. MERRYWEATHER-- I JUST HAVE NO IDEA WHERE WHERE IS.

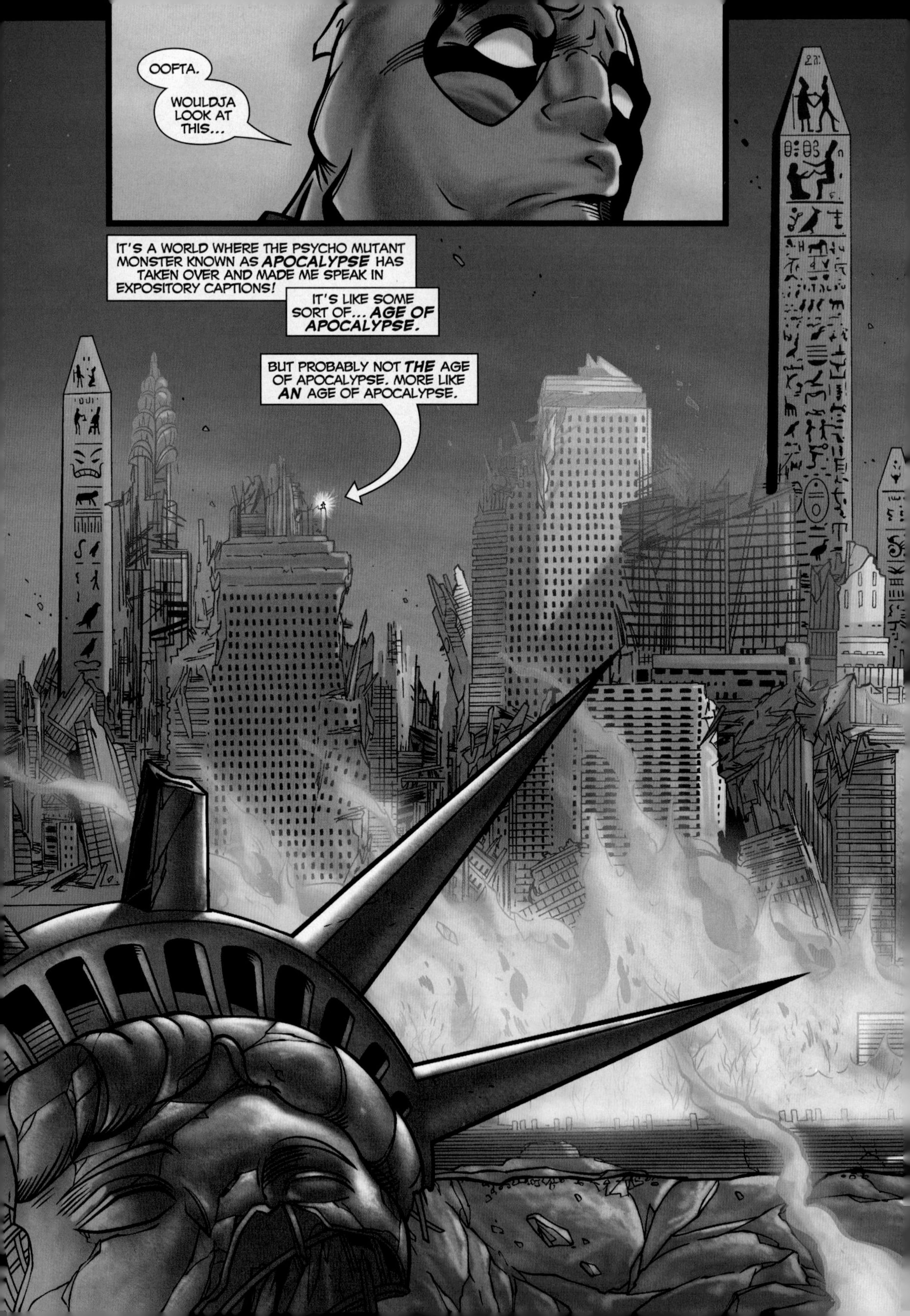
OOFTA.
WOULDJA LOOK AT THIS...
IT'S A WORLD WHERE THE PSYCHO MUTANT MONSTER KNOWN AS APOCALYPSE HAS TAKEN OVER AND MADE ME SPEAK IN EXPOSITORY CAPTIONS!
IT'S LIKE SOME SORT OF... AGE OF APOCALYPSE.
BUT PROBABLY NOT THE AGE OF APOCALYPSE. MORE LIKE AN AGE OF APOCALYPSE.

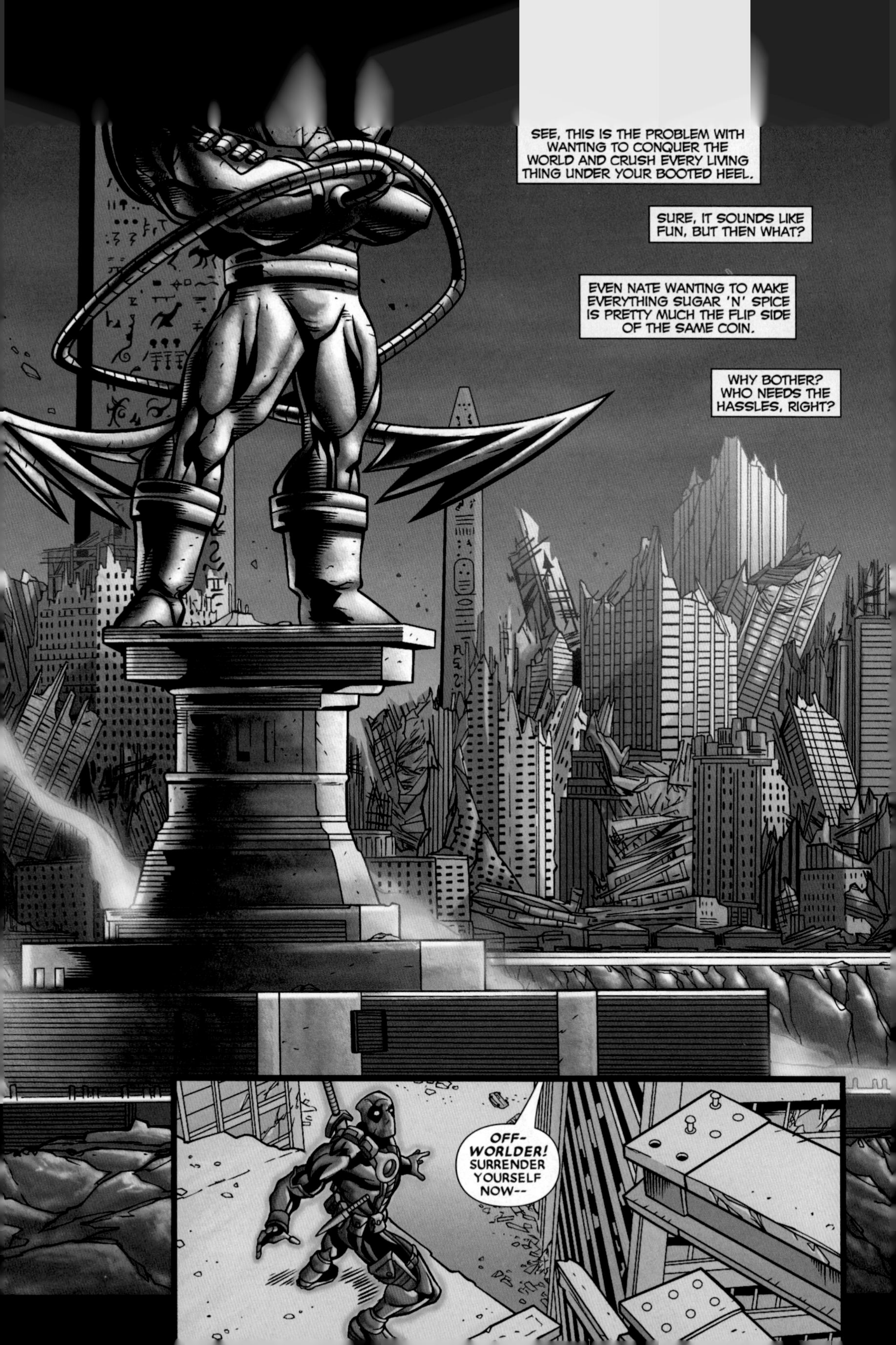
SEE, THIS IS THE PROBLEM WITH WANTING TO CONQUER THE WORLD AND CRUSH EVERY LIVING THING UNDER YOUR BOOTED HEEL.
SURE, IT SOUNDS LIKE FUN, BUT THEN WHAT?
EVEN NATE WANTING TO MAKE EVERYTHING SUGAR 'N' SPICE IS PRETTY MUCH THE FLIP SIDE OF THE SAME COIN.
WHY BOTHER? WHO NEEDS THE HASSLES, RIGHT?
OFF-WORLDER! SURRENDER YOURSELF NOW--

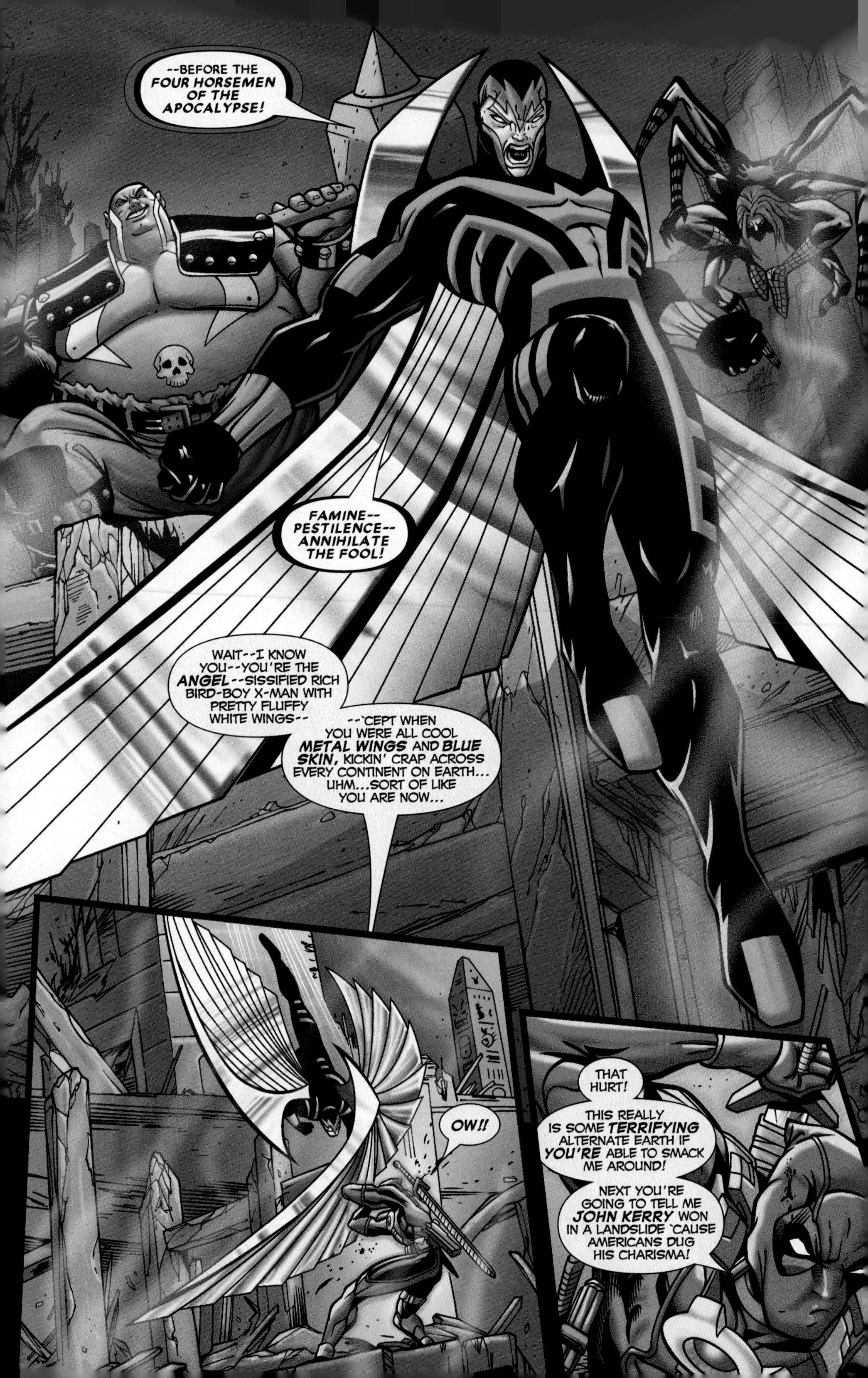
--BEFORE THE FOUR HORSEMEN OF THE APOCALYPSE!
FAMINE--PESTILENCE--ANNIHILATE THE FOOL!
WAIT--I KNOW YOU--YOU'RE THE ANGEL--SISSIFIED RICH BIRD-BOY X-MAN WITH PRETTY FLUFFY WHITE WINGS--
--`CEPT WHEN YOU WERE ALL COOL METAL WINGS AND BLUE SKIN, KICKIN' CRAP ACROSS EVERY CONTINENT ON EARTH... UHM...SORT OF LIKE YOU ARE NOW...
OW!!
THAT HURT!
THIS REALLY IS SOME TERRIFYING ALTERNATE EARTH IF YOU'RE ABLE TO SMACK ME AROUND!
NEXT YOU'RE GOING TO TELL ME JOHN KERRY WON IN A LANDSLIDE 'CAUSE AMERICANS DUG HIS CHARISMA!

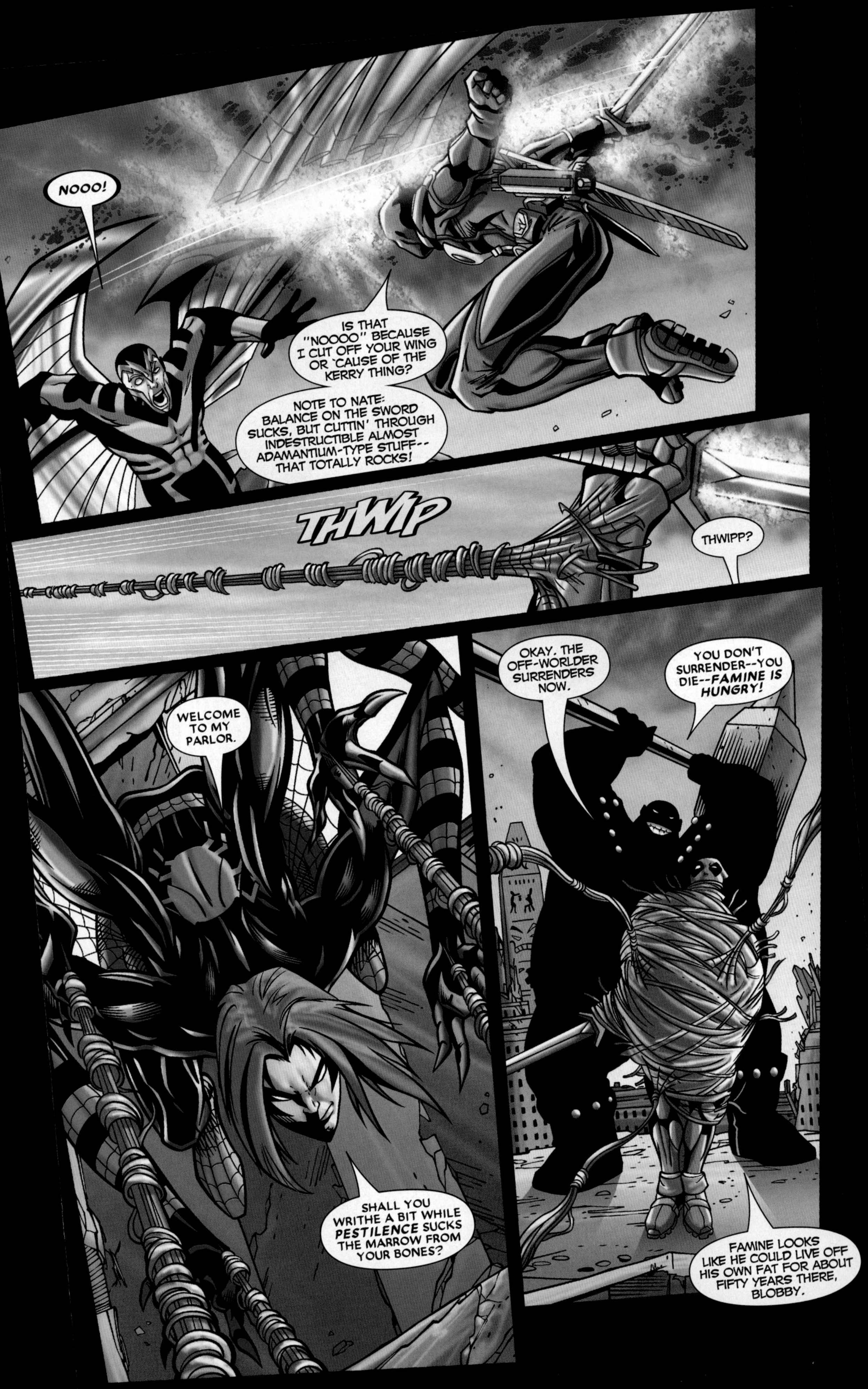
NOOO!
IS THAT "NOOOO" BECAUSE I CUT OFF YOUR WING OR 'CAUSE OF THE KERRY THING?
NOTE TO NATE: BALANCE ON THE SWORD SUCKS, BUT CUTTIN' THROUGH INDESTRUCTIBLE ALMOST ADAMANTIUM-TYPE STUFF-- THAT TOTALLY ROCKS!
THWIP
THWIPP?
WELCOME TO MY PARLOR.
SHALL YOU WRITHE A BIT WHILE PESTILENCE SUCKS THE MARROW FROM YOUR BONES?
OKAY. THE OFF-WORLDER SURRENDERS NOW.
YOU DON'T SURRENDER--YOU DIE--FAMINE IS HUNGRY!
FAMINE LOOKS LIKE HE COULD LIVE OFF HIS OWN FAT FOR ABOUT FIFTY YEARS THERE, BLOBBY.

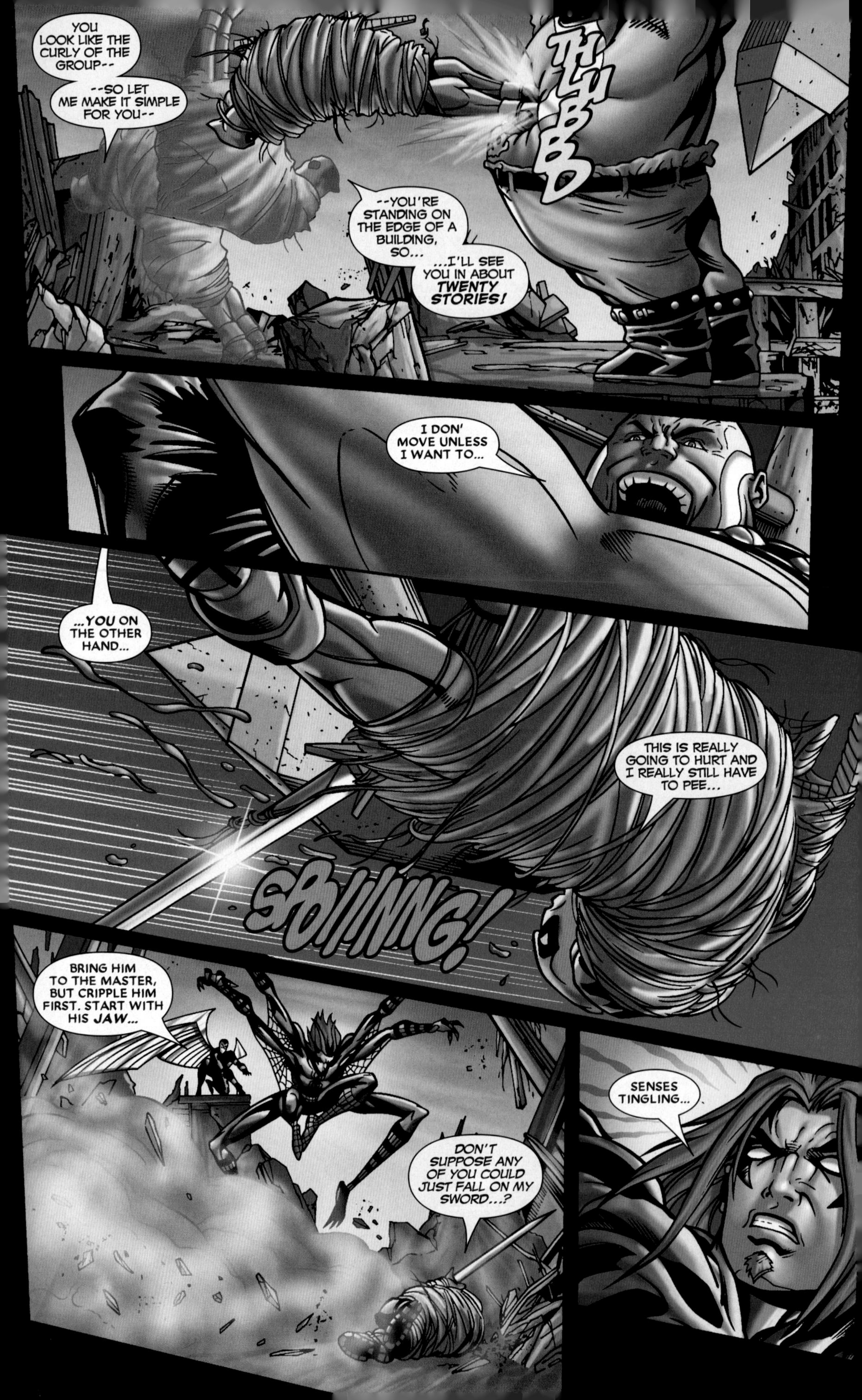
YOU LOOK LIKE THE CURLY OF THE GROUP--
--SO LET ME MAKE IT SIMPLE FOR YOU--
THUBB
--YOU'RE STANDING ON THE EDGE OF A BUILDING, SO...
...I'LL SEE YOU IN ABOUT TWENTY STORIES!
I DON' MOVE UNLESS I WANT TO...
...YOU ON THE OTHER HAND...
THIS IS REALLY GOING TO HURT AND I REALLY STILL HAVE TO PEE...
SPOIIINNG!
BRING HIM TO THE MASTER, BUT CRIPPLE HIM FIRST. START WITH HIS JAW...
DON'T SUPPOSE ANY OF YOU COULD JUST FALL ON MY SWORD...?
SENSES TINGLING...

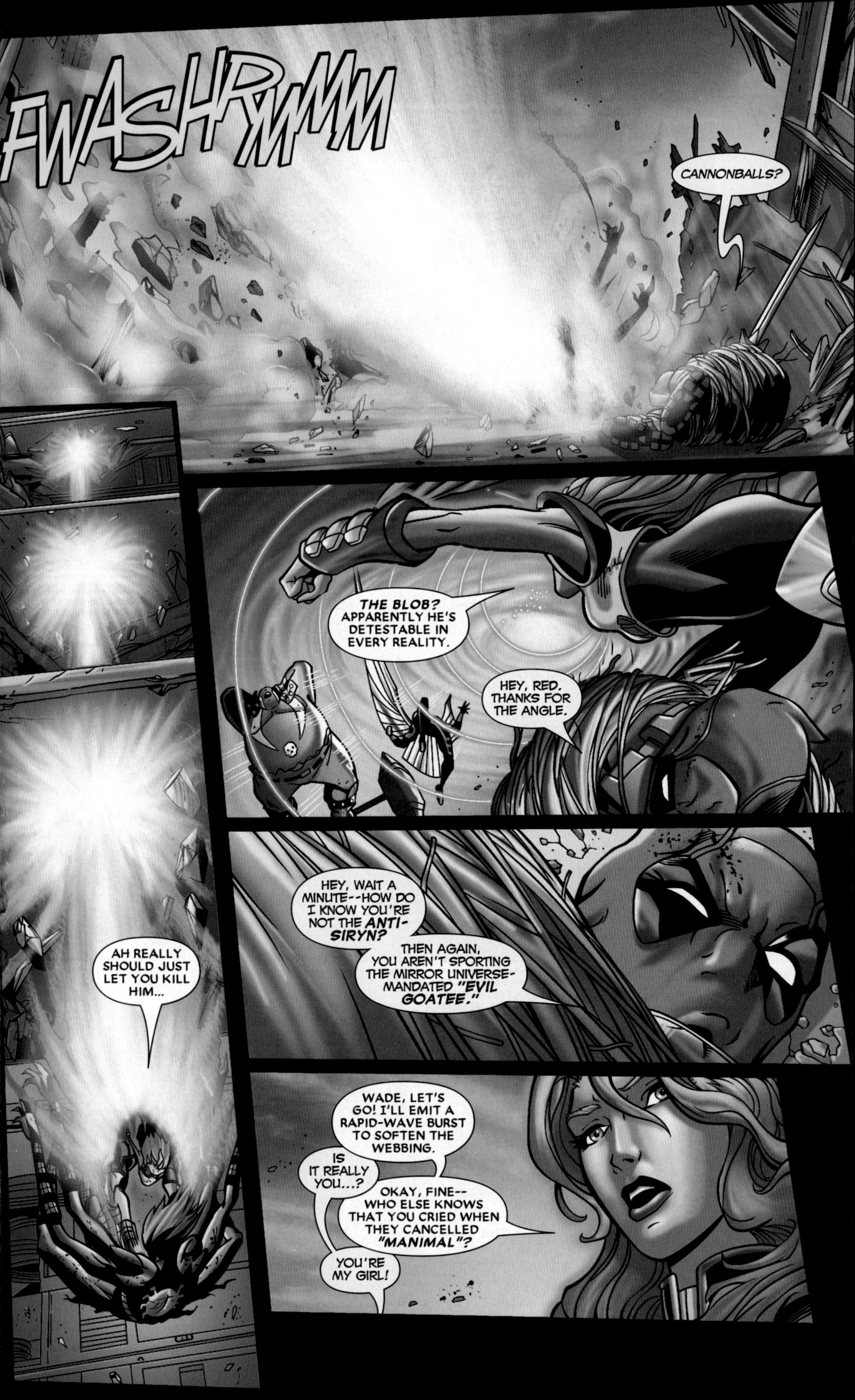
FWASHRMMMM
CANNONBALLS?
AH REALLY SHOULD JUST LET YOU KILL HIM...
THE BLOB? APPARENTLY HE'S DETESTABLE IN EVERY REALITY.
HEY, RED. THANKS FOR THE ANGLE.
HEY, WAIT A MINUTE--HOW DO I KNOW YOU'RE NOT THE ANTI-SIRYN?
THEN AGAIN, YOU AREN'T SPORTING THE MIRROR UNIVERSE-MANDATED "EVIL GOATEE."
WADE, LET'S GO! I'LL EMIT A RAPID-WAVE BURST TO SOFTEN THE WEBBING.
IS IT REALLY YOU...?
OKAY, FINE--WHO ELSE KNOWS THAT YOU CRIED WHEN THEY CANCELLED "MANIMAL"?
YOU'RE MY GIRL!

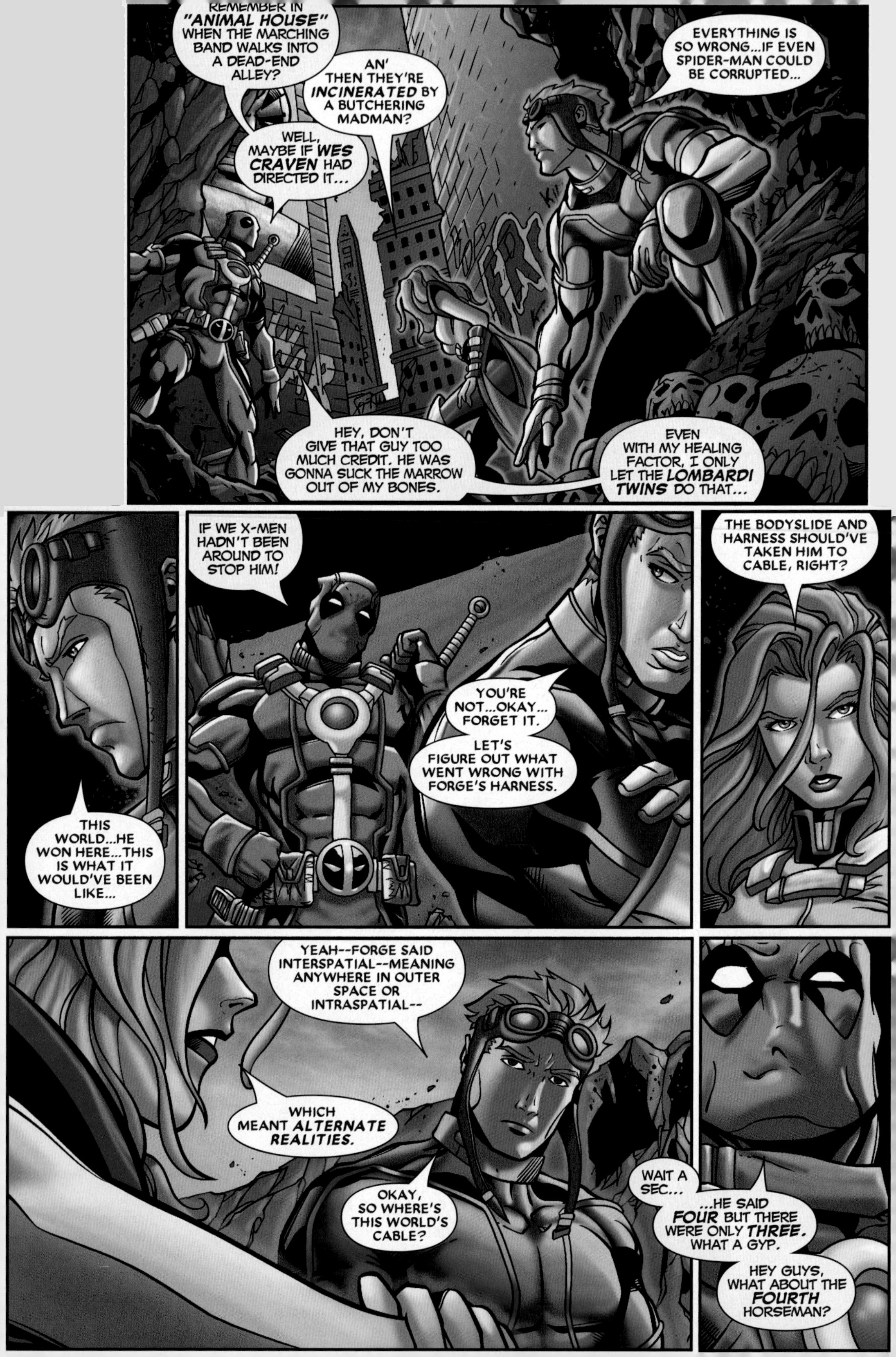

REMEMBER IN "ANIMAL HOUSE" WHEN THE MARCHING BAND WALKS INTO A DEAD-END ALLEY?
AN' THEN THEY'RE INCINERATED BY A BUTCHERING MADMAN?
WELL, MAYBE IF WES CRAVEN HAD DIRECTED IT...
EVERYTHING IS SO WRONG...IF EVEN SPIDER-MAN COULD BE CORRUPTED...
HEY, DON'T GIVE THAT GUY TOO MUCH CREDIT. HE WAS GONNA SUCK THE MARROW OUT OF MY BONES.
EVEN WITH MY HEALING FACTOR, I ONLY LET THE LOMBARDI TWINS DO THAT...
THIS WORLD...HE WON HERE...THIS IS WHAT IT WOULD'VE BEEN LIKE...
IF WE X-MEN HADN'T BEEN AROUND TO STOP HIM!
YOU'RE NOT...OKAY... FORGET IT.
LET'S FIGURE OUT WHAT WENT WRONG WITH FORGE'S HARNESS.
THE BODYSLIDE AND HARNESS SHOULD'VE TAKEN HIM TO CABLE, RIGHT?
YEAH--FORGE SAID INTERSPATIAL--MEANING ANYWHERE IN OUTER SPACE OR INTRASPATIAL--
WHICH MEANT ALTERNATE REALITIES.
OKAY, SO WHERE'S THIS WORLD'S CABLE?
WAIT A SEC...
...HE SAID FOUR BUT THERE WERE ONLY THREE. WHAT A GYP.
HEY GUYS, WHAT ABOUT THE FOURTH HORSEMAN?

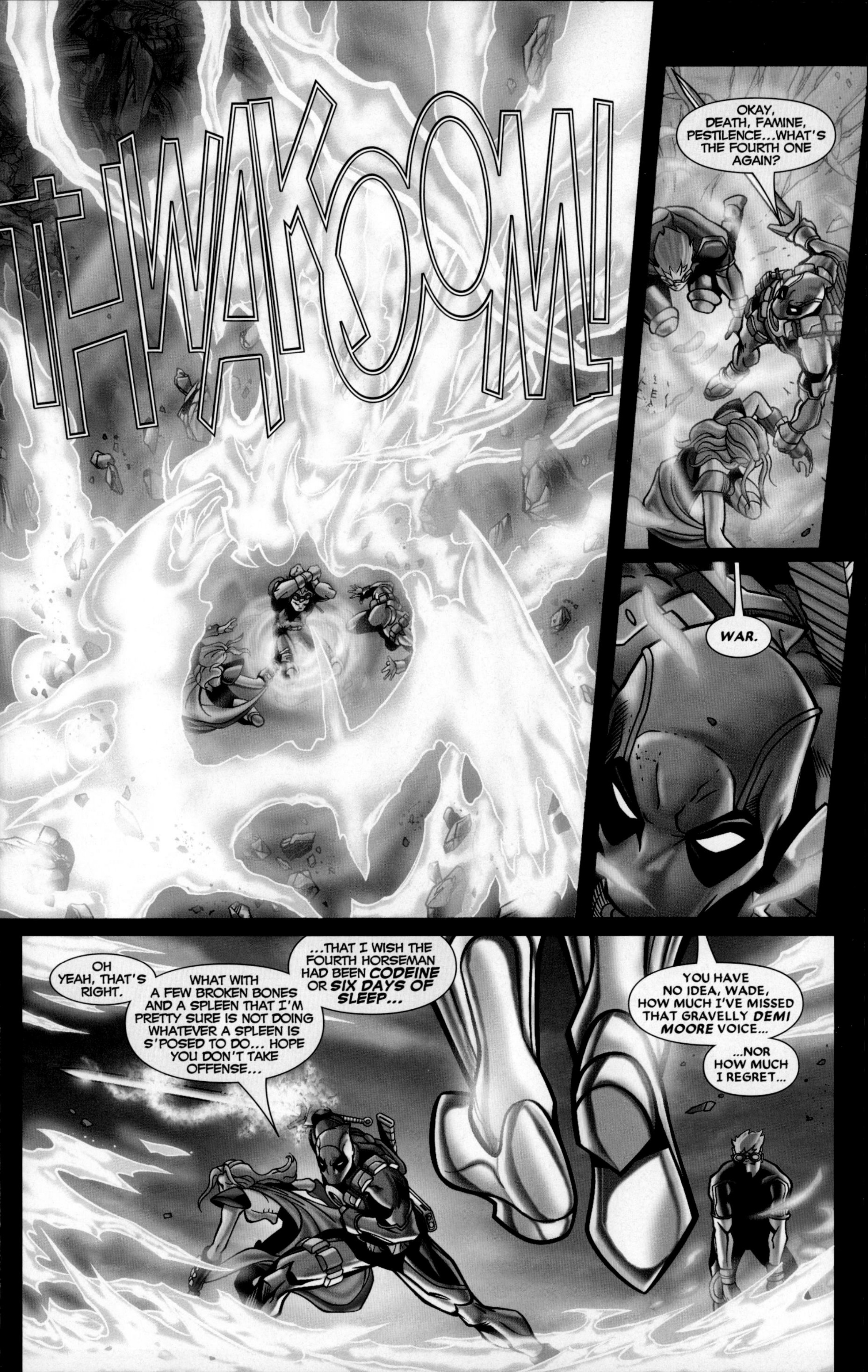
THWAKOOM!
OKAY, DEATH, FAMINE, PESTILENCE...WHAT'S THE FOURTH ONE AGAIN?
WAR.
OH YEAH, THAT'S RIGHT.
WHAT WITH A FEW BROKEN BONES AND A SPLEEN THAT I'M PRETTY SURE IS NOT DOING WHATEVER A SPLEEN IS S'POSED TO DO... HOPE YOU DON'T TAKE OFFENSE...
...THAT I WISH THE FOURTH HORSEMAN HAD BEEN CODEINE OR SIX DAYS OF SLEEP...
YOU HAVE NO IDEA, WADE, HOW MUCH I'VE MISSED THAT GRAVELLY DEMI MOORE VOICE...
...NOR HOW MUCH I REGRET...

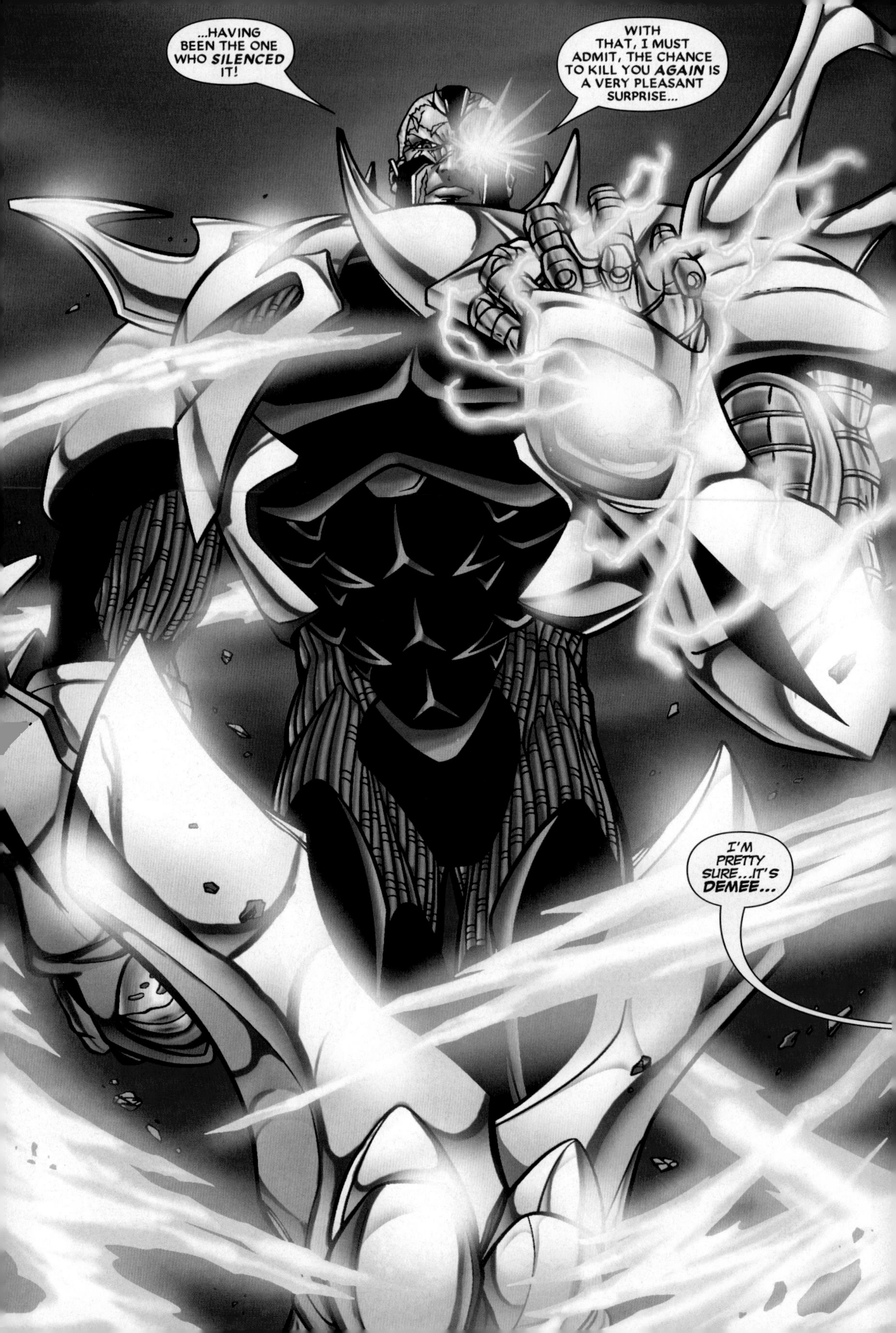
...HAVING BEEN THE ONE WHO SILENCED IT!
WITH THAT, I MUST ADMIT, THE CHANCE TO KILL YOU AGAIN IS A VERY PLEASANT SURPRISE...
I'M PRETTY SURE...IT'S DEMEE...

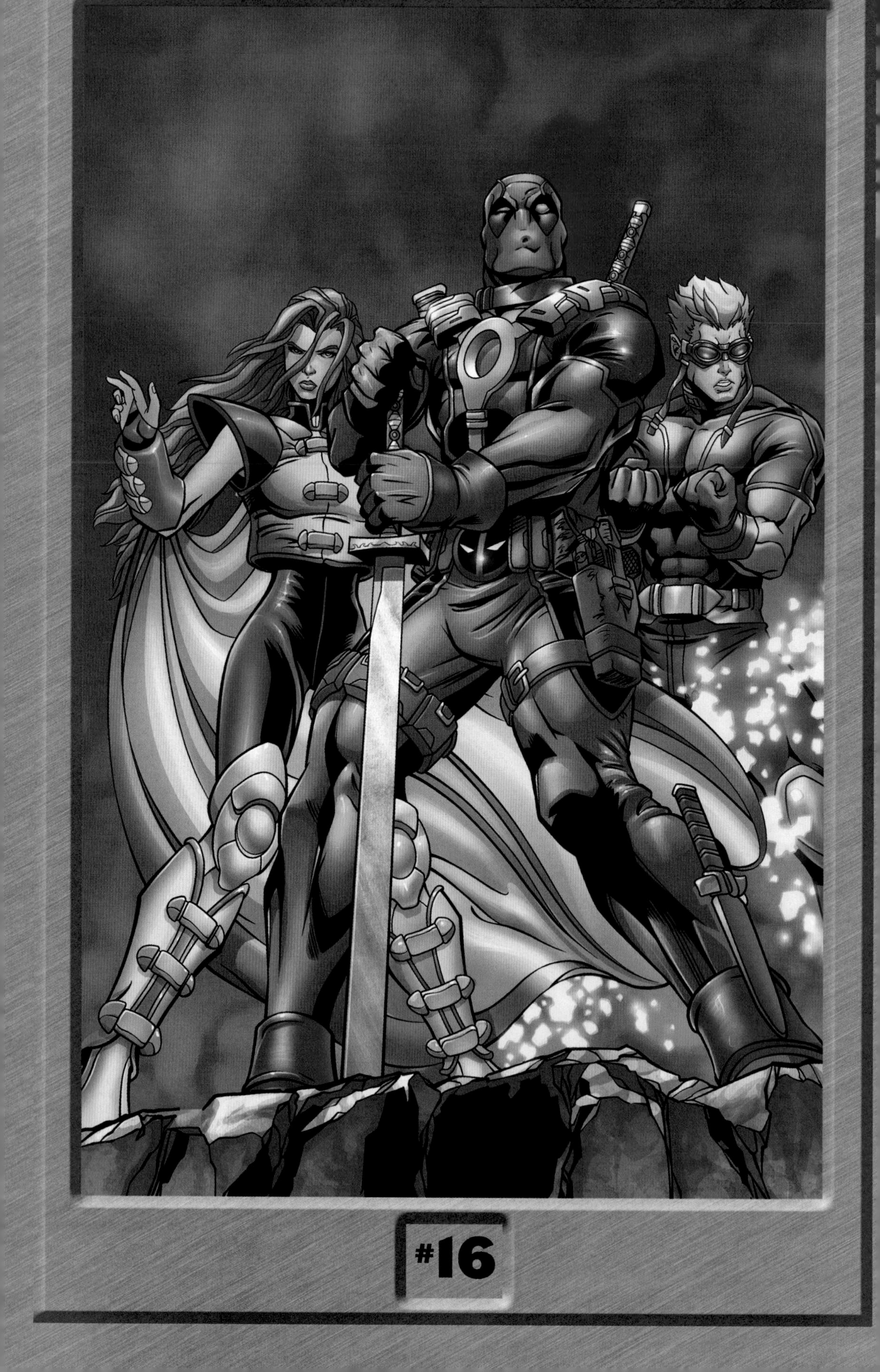

#16

ENEMA OF THE STATE

PART TWO: WHAT IF...?

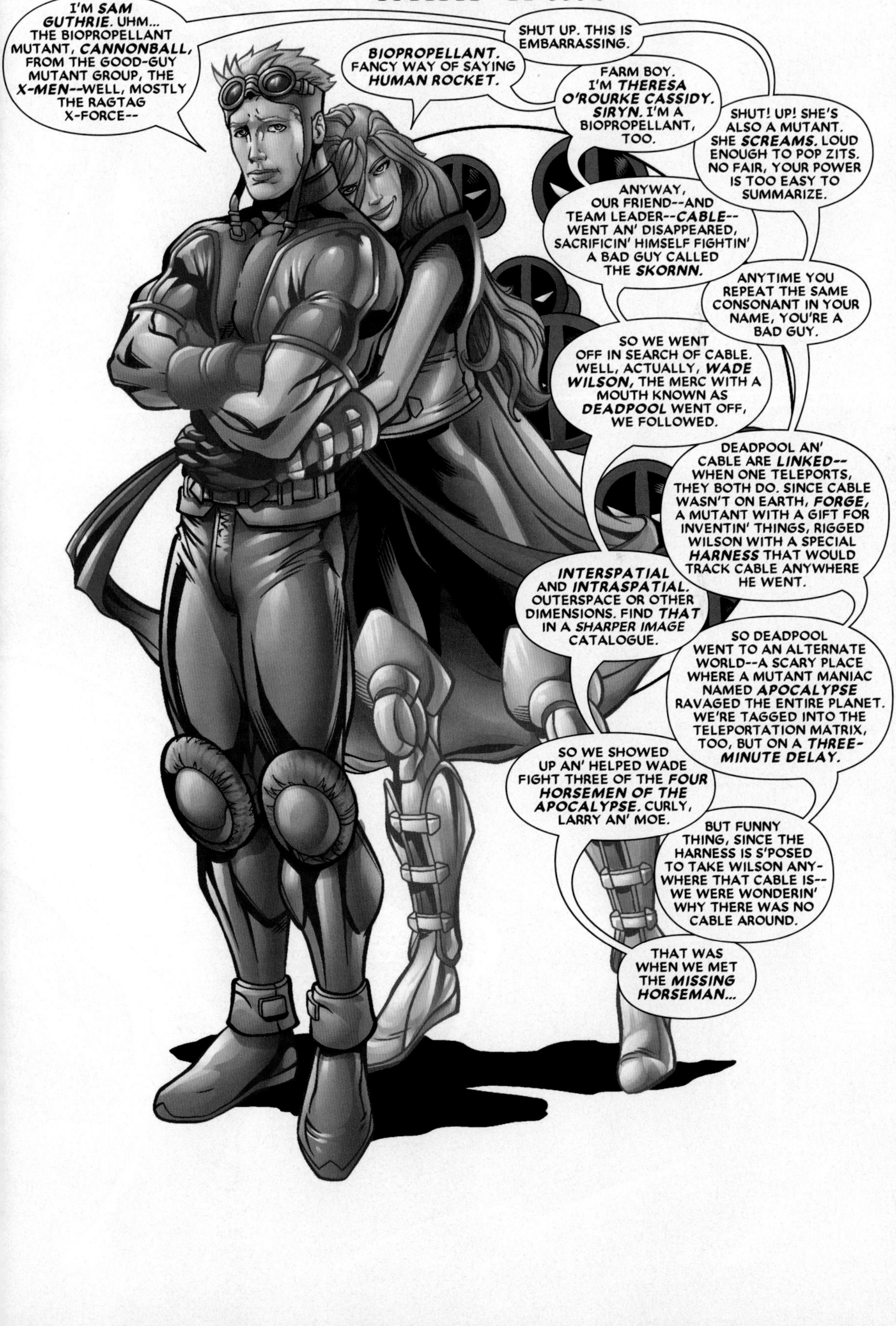

I'M *SAM GUTHRIE*. UHM... THE BIOPROPELLANT MUTANT, *CANNONBALL*, FROM THE GOOD-GUY MUTANT GROUP, THE *X-MEN*--WELL, MOSTLY THE RAGTAG X-FORCE--
SHUT UP. THIS IS EMBARRASSING.
BIOPROPELLANT. FANCY WAY OF SAYING *HUMAN ROCKET.*
FARM BOY. I'M *THERESA O'ROURKE CASSIDY. SIRYN.* I'M A BIOPROPELLANT, TOO.
SHUT! UP! SHE'S ALSO A MUTANT. SHE *SCREAMS.* LOUD ENOUGH TO POP ZITS. NO FAIR, YOUR POWER IS TOO EASY TO SUMMARIZE.
ANYWAY, OUR FRIEND--AND TEAM LEADER--*CABLE*--WENT AN' DISAPPEARED, SACRIFICIN' HIMSELF FIGHTIN' A BAD GUY CALLED THE *SKORNN.*
ANYTIME YOU REPEAT THE SAME CONSONANT IN YOUR NAME, YOU'RE A BAD GUY.
SO WE WENT OFF IN SEARCH OF CABLE. WELL, ACTUALLY, *WADE WILSON,* THE MERC WITH A MOUTH KNOWN AS *DEADPOOL* WENT OFF, WE FOLLOWED.
DEADPOOL AN' CABLE ARE *LINKED*--WHEN ONE TELEPORTS, THEY BOTH DO. SINCE CABLE WASN'T ON EARTH, *FORGE,* A MUTANT WITH A GIFT FOR INVENTIN' THINGS, RIGGED WILSON WITH A SPECIAL *HARNESS* THAT WOULD TRACK CABLE ANYWHERE HE WENT.
INTERSPATIAL AND *INTRASPATIAL.* OUTERSPACE OR OTHER DIMENSIONS. FIND *THAT* IN A *SHARPER IMAGE* CATALOGUE.
SO DEADPOOL WENT TO AN ALTERNATE WORLD--A SCARY PLACE WHERE A MUTANT MANIAC NAMED *APOCALYPSE* RAVAGED THE ENTIRE PLANET. WE'RE TAGGED INTO THE TELEPORTATION MATRIX, TOO, BUT ON A *THREE-MINUTE DELAY.*
SO WE SHOWED UP AN' HELPED WADE FIGHT THREE OF THE *FOUR HORSEMEN OF THE APOCALYPSE.* CURLY, LARRY AN' MOE.
BUT FUNNY THING, SINCE THE HARNESS IS S'POSED TO TAKE WILSON ANYWHERE THAT CABLE IS--WE WERE WONDERIN' WHY THERE WAS NO CABLE AROUND.
THAT WAS WHEN WE MET THE *MISSING HORSEMAN...*

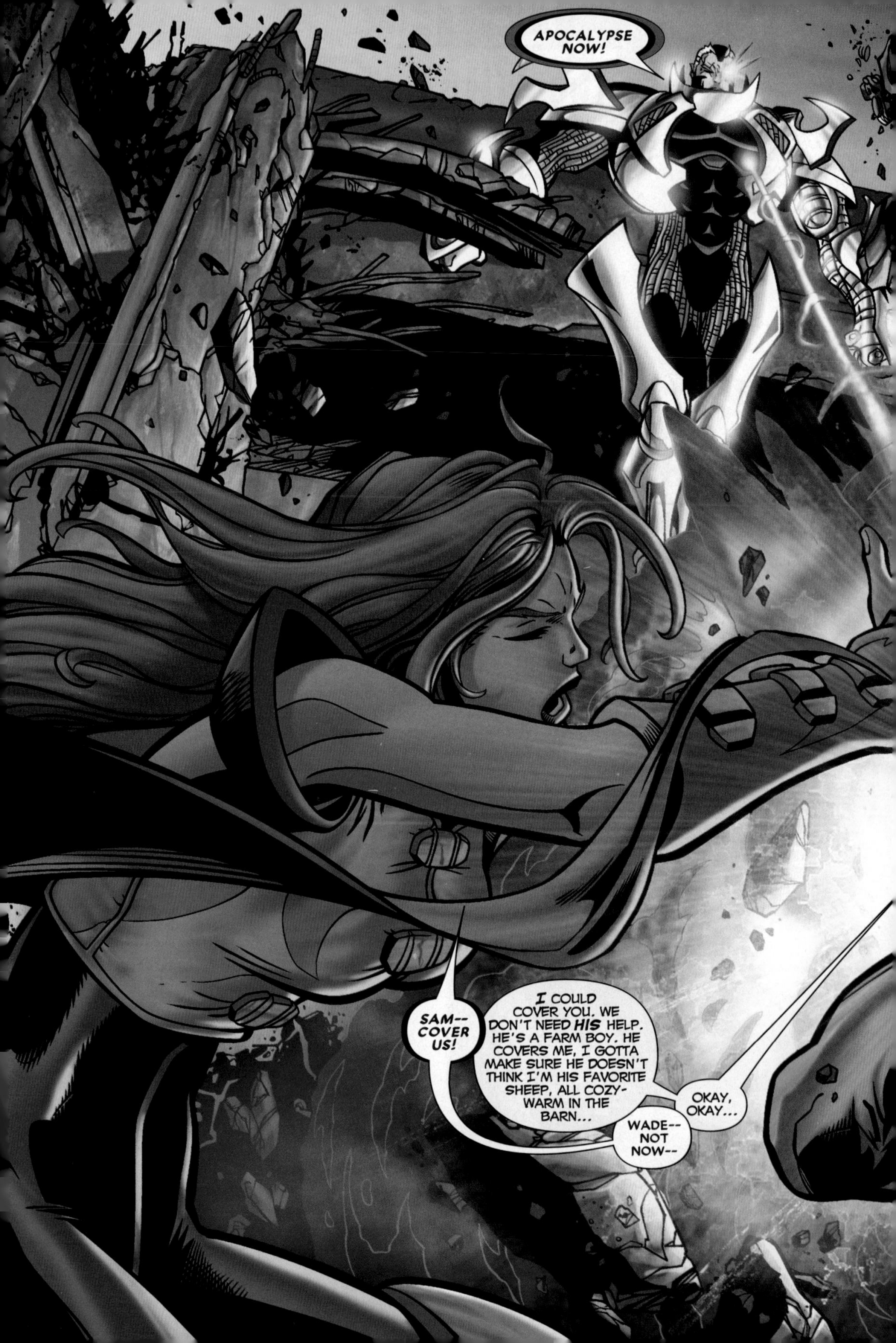
APOCALYPSE NOW!
SAM-- COVER US!
I COULD COVER YOU. WE DON'T NEED HIS HELP. HE'S A FARM BOY. HE COVERS ME, I GOTTA MAKE SURE HE DOESN'T THINK I'M HIS FAVORITE SHEEP, ALL COZY-WARM IN THE BARN...
WADE-- NOT NOW--
OKAY, OKAY...

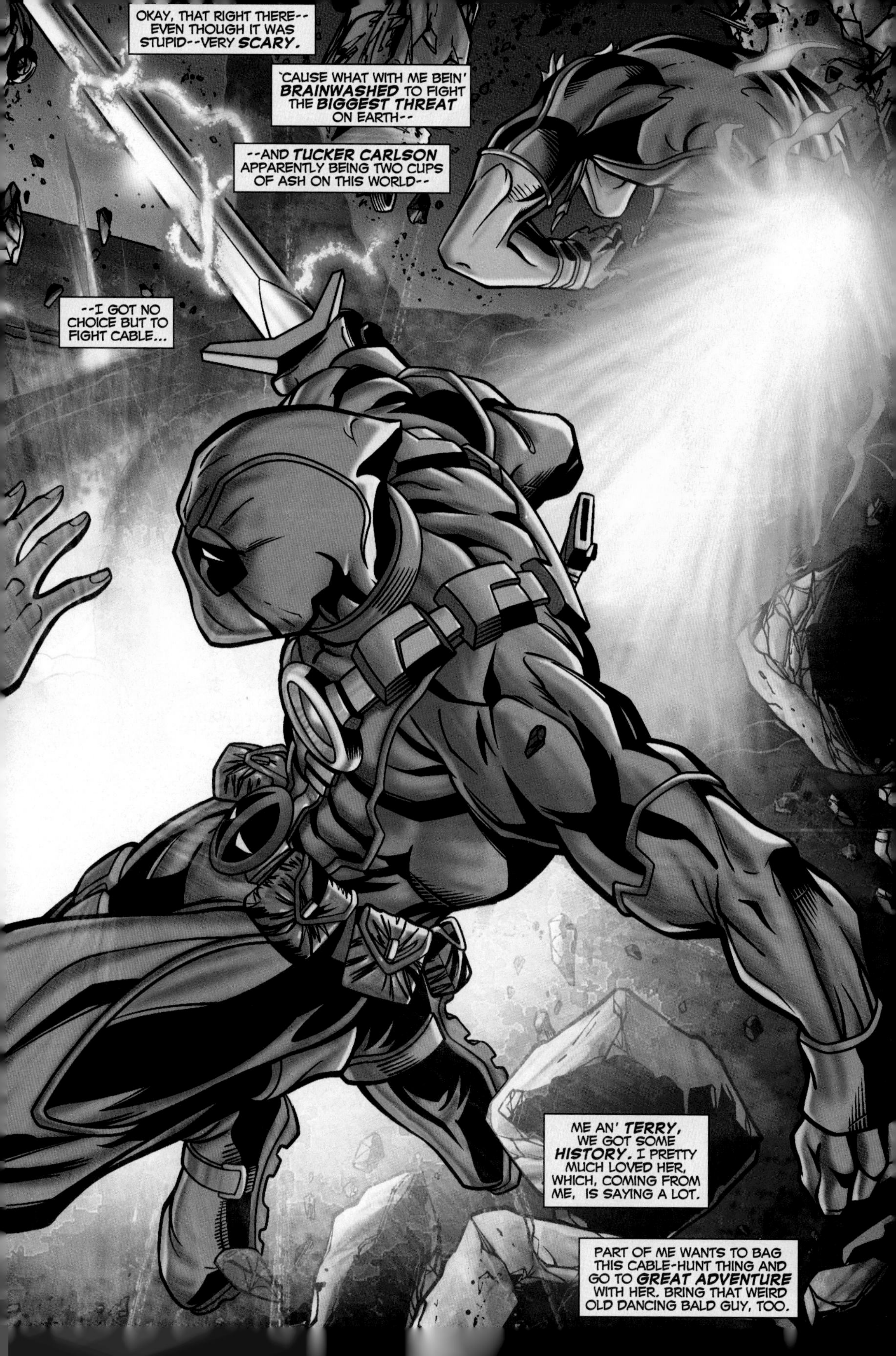
OKAY, THAT RIGHT THERE-- EVEN THOUGH IT WAS STUPID--VERY SCARY.
`CAUSE WHAT WITH ME BEIN' BRAINWASHED TO FIGHT THE BIGGEST THREAT ON EARTH--
--AND TUCKER CARLSON APPARENTLY BEING TWO CUPS OF ASH ON THIS WORLD--
--I GOT NO CHOICE BUT TO FIGHT CABLE...
ME AN' TERRY, WE GOT SOME HISTORY. I PRETTY MUCH LOVED HER, WHICH, COMING FROM ME, IS SAYING A LOT.
PART OF ME WANTS TO BAG THIS CABLE-HUNT THING AND GO TO GREAT ADVENTURE WITH HER. BRING THAT WEIRD OLD DANCING BALD GUY, TOO.

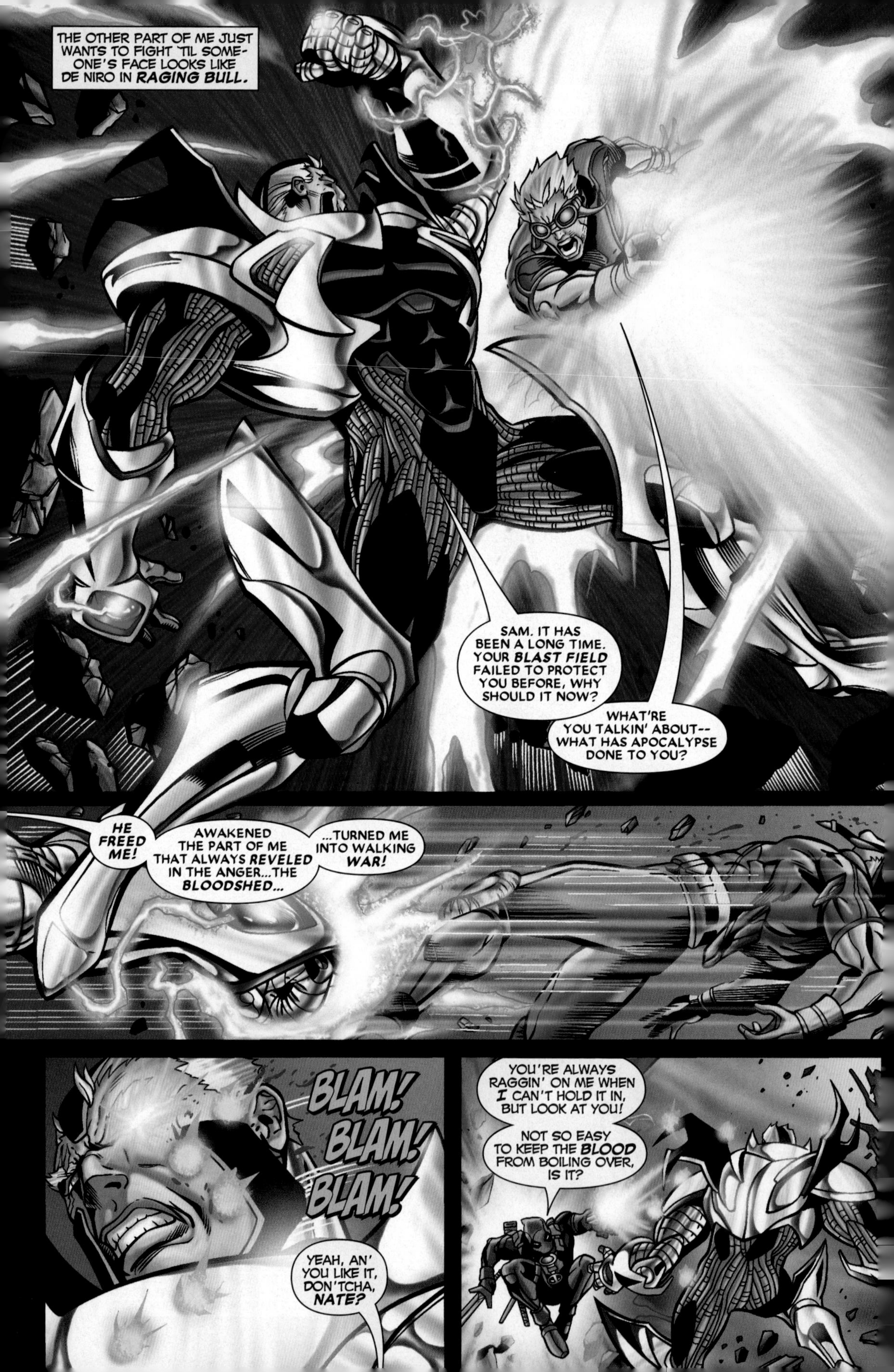
THE OTHER PART OF ME JUST WANTS TO FIGHT 'TIL SOME-ONE'S FACE LOOKS LIKE DE NIRO IN RAGING BULL.
SAM. IT HAS BEEN A LONG TIME. YOUR BLAST FIELD FAILED TO PROTECT YOU BEFORE, WHY SHOULD IT NOW?
WHAT'RE YOU TALKIN' ABOUT-- WHAT HAS APOCALYPSE DONE TO YOU?
HE FREED ME!
AWAKENED THE PART OF ME THAT ALWAYS REVELED IN THE ANGER...THE BLOODSHED...
...TURNED ME INTO WALKING WAR!
BLAM! BLAM! BLAM!
YEAH, AN' YOU LIKE IT, DON'TCHA, NATE?
YOU'RE ALWAYS RAGGIN' ON ME WHEN I CAN'T HOLD IT IN, BUT LOOK AT YOU!
NOT SO EASY TO KEEP THE BLOOD FROM BOILING OVER, IS IT?

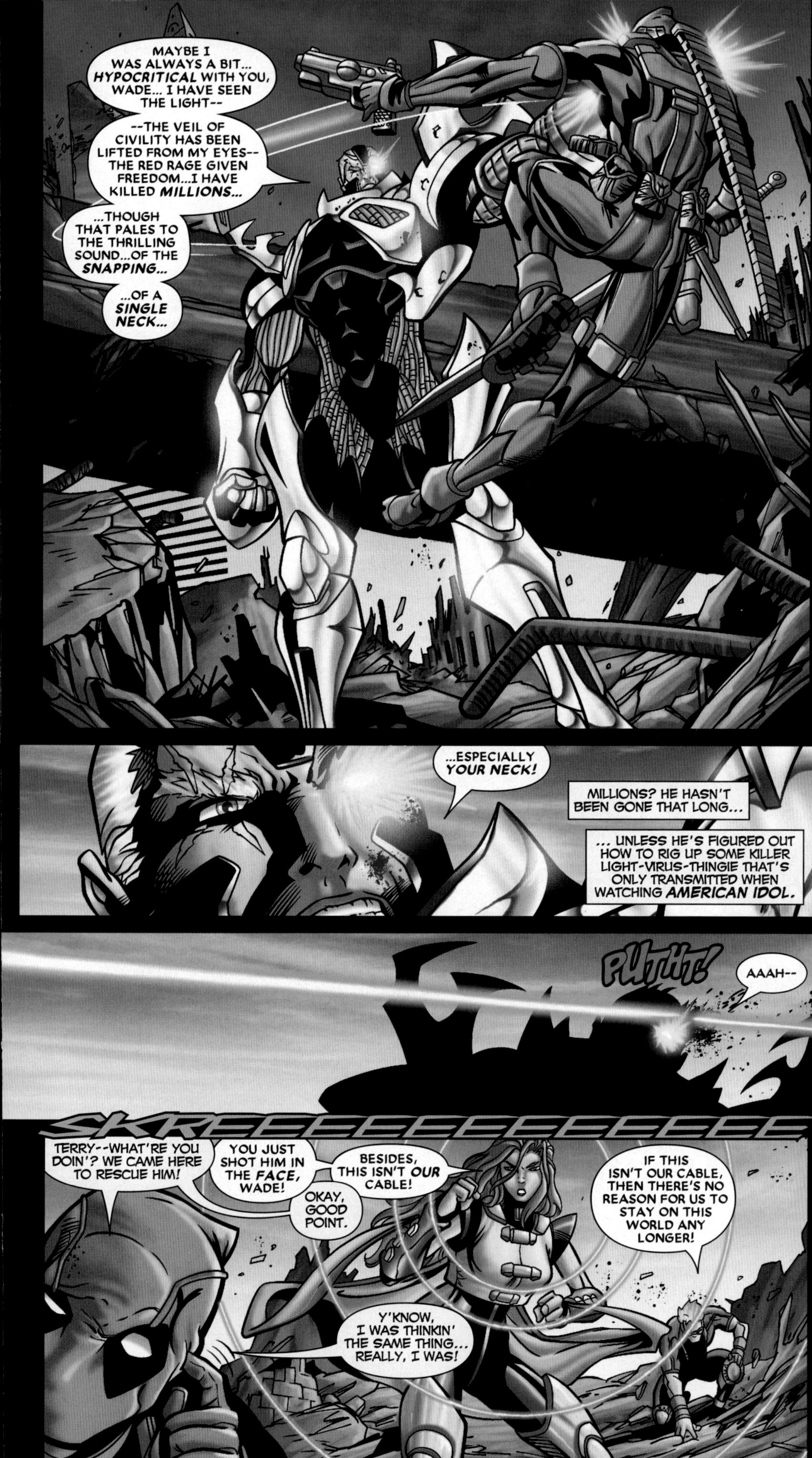
MAYBE I WAS ALWAYS A BIT... *HYPOCRITICAL* WITH YOU, WADE... I HAVE SEEN THE LIGHT--
--THE VEIL OF CIVILITY HAS BEEN LIFTED FROM MY EYES-- THE RED RAGE GIVEN FREEDOM...I HAVE KILLED *MILLIONS*...
...THOUGH THAT PALES TO THE THRILLING SOUND...OF THE *SNAPPING*...
...OF A *SINGLE NECK*...
...ESPECIALLY *YOUR NECK!*
MILLIONS? HE HASN'T BEEN GONE THAT LONG...
... UNLESS HE'S FIGURED OUT HOW TO RIG UP SOME KILLER LIGHT-VIRUS-THINGIE THAT'S ONLY TRANSMITTED WHEN WATCHING *AMERICAN IDOL.*
PUTHT!
AAAH--
SKREEEEEEEEEEEEEE
TERRY--WHAT'RE YOU DOIN'? WE CAME HERE TO RESCUE HIM!
YOU JUST SHOT HIM IN THE *FACE*, WADE!
BESIDES, THIS ISN'T *OUR* CABLE!
OKAY, GOOD POINT.
IF THIS ISN'T OUR CABLE, THEN THERE'S NO REASON FOR US TO STAY ON THIS WORLD ANY LONGER!
Y'KNOW, I WAS THINKIN' THE SAME THING... REALLY, I WAS!

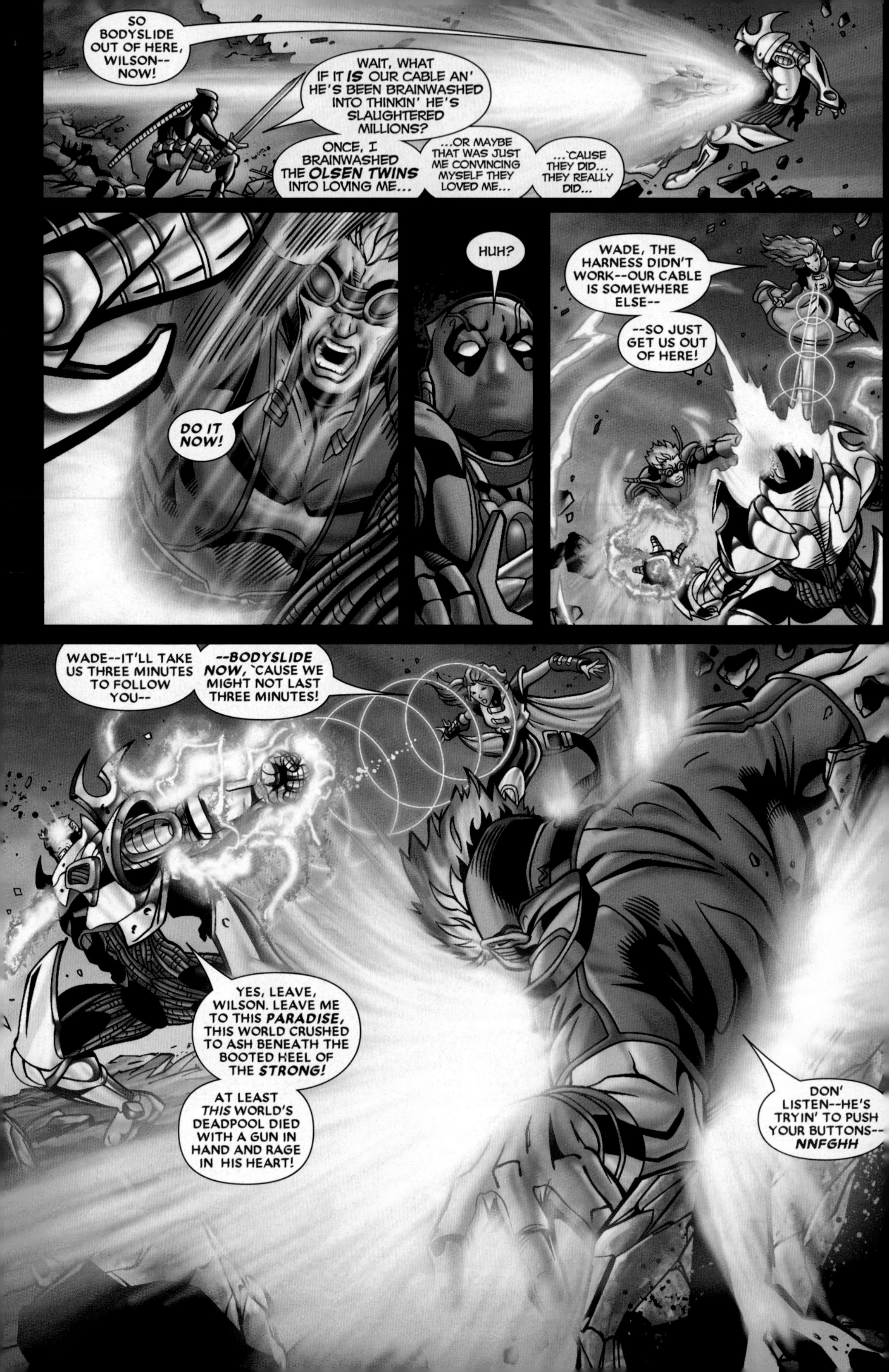
SO BODYSLIDE OUT OF HERE, WILSON--NOW!
WAIT, WHAT IF IT IS OUR CABLE AN' HE'S BEEN BRAINWASHED INTO THINKIN' HE'S SLAUGHTERED MILLIONS?
ONCE, I BRAINWASHED THE OLSEN TWINS INTO LOVING ME...
...OR MAYBE THAT WAS JUST ME CONVINCING MYSELF THEY LOVED ME...
...`CAUSE THEY DID... THEY REALLY DID...
DO IT NOW!
HUH?
WADE, THE HARNESS DIDN'T WORK--OUR CABLE IS SOMEWHERE ELSE--
--SO JUST GET US OUT OF HERE!
WADE--IT'LL TAKE US THREE MINUTES TO FOLLOW YOU--
--BODYSLIDE NOW, `CAUSE WE MIGHT NOT LAST THREE MINUTES!
YES, LEAVE, WILSON. LEAVE ME TO THIS PARADISE, THIS WORLD CRUSHED TO ASH BENEATH THE BOOTED HEEL OF THE STRONG!
AT LEAST THIS WORLD'S DEADPOOL DIED WITH A GUN IN HAND AND RAGE IN HIS HEART!
DON' LISTEN--HE'S TRYIN' TO PUSH YOUR BUTTONS--NNFGHH

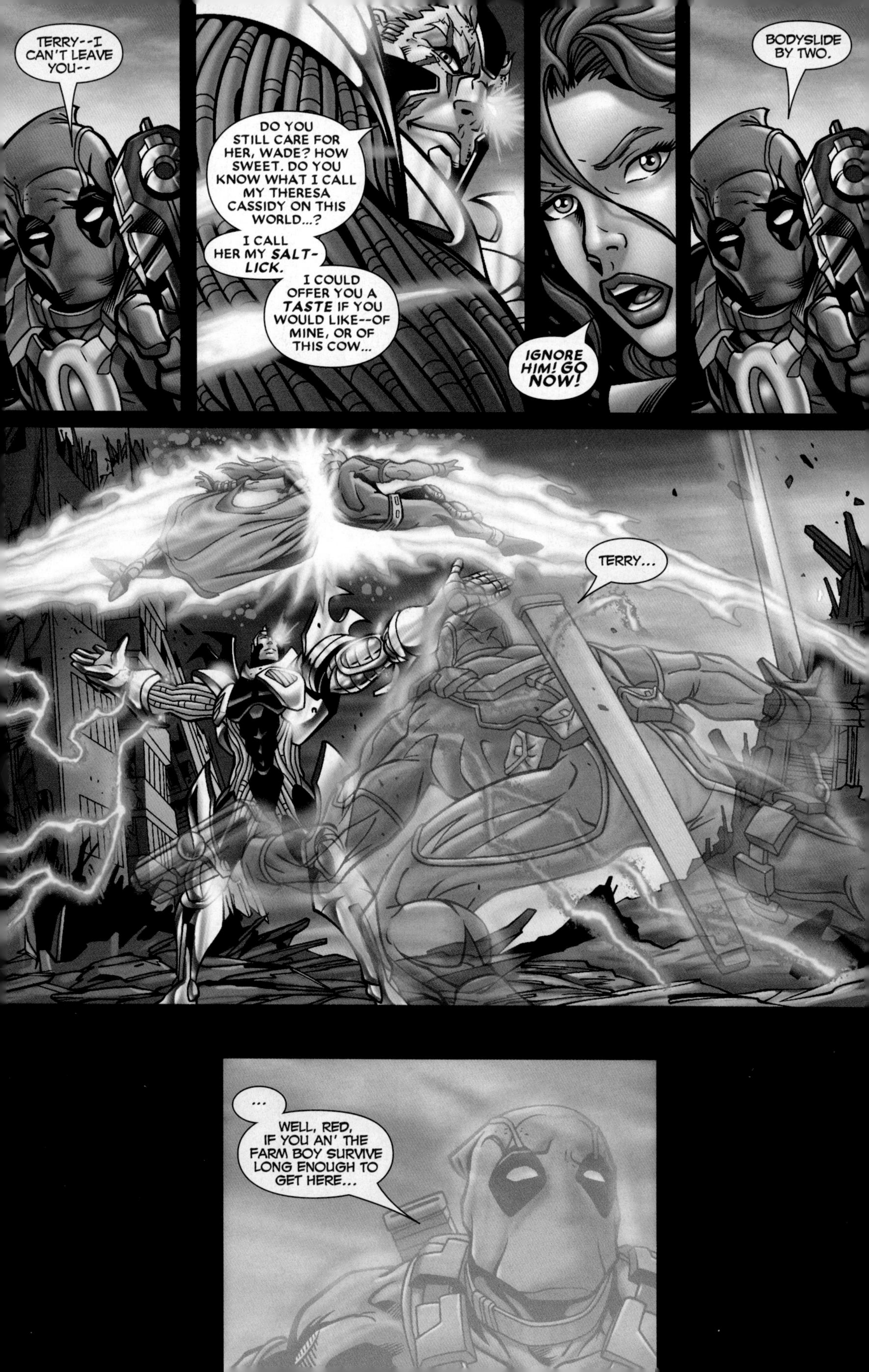
TERRY--I CAN'T LEAVE YOU--
DO YOU STILL CARE FOR HER, WADE? HOW SWEET. DO YOU KNOW WHAT I CALL MY THERESA CASSIDY ON THIS WORLD...?
I CALL HER MY SALT-LICK.
I COULD OFFER YOU A TASTE IF YOU WOULD LIKE--OF MINE, OR OF THIS COW...
IGNORE HIM! GO NOW!
BODYSLIDE BY TWO.
TERRY...
...
WELL, RED, IF YOU AN' THE FARM BOY SURVIVE LONG ENOUGH TO GET HERE...

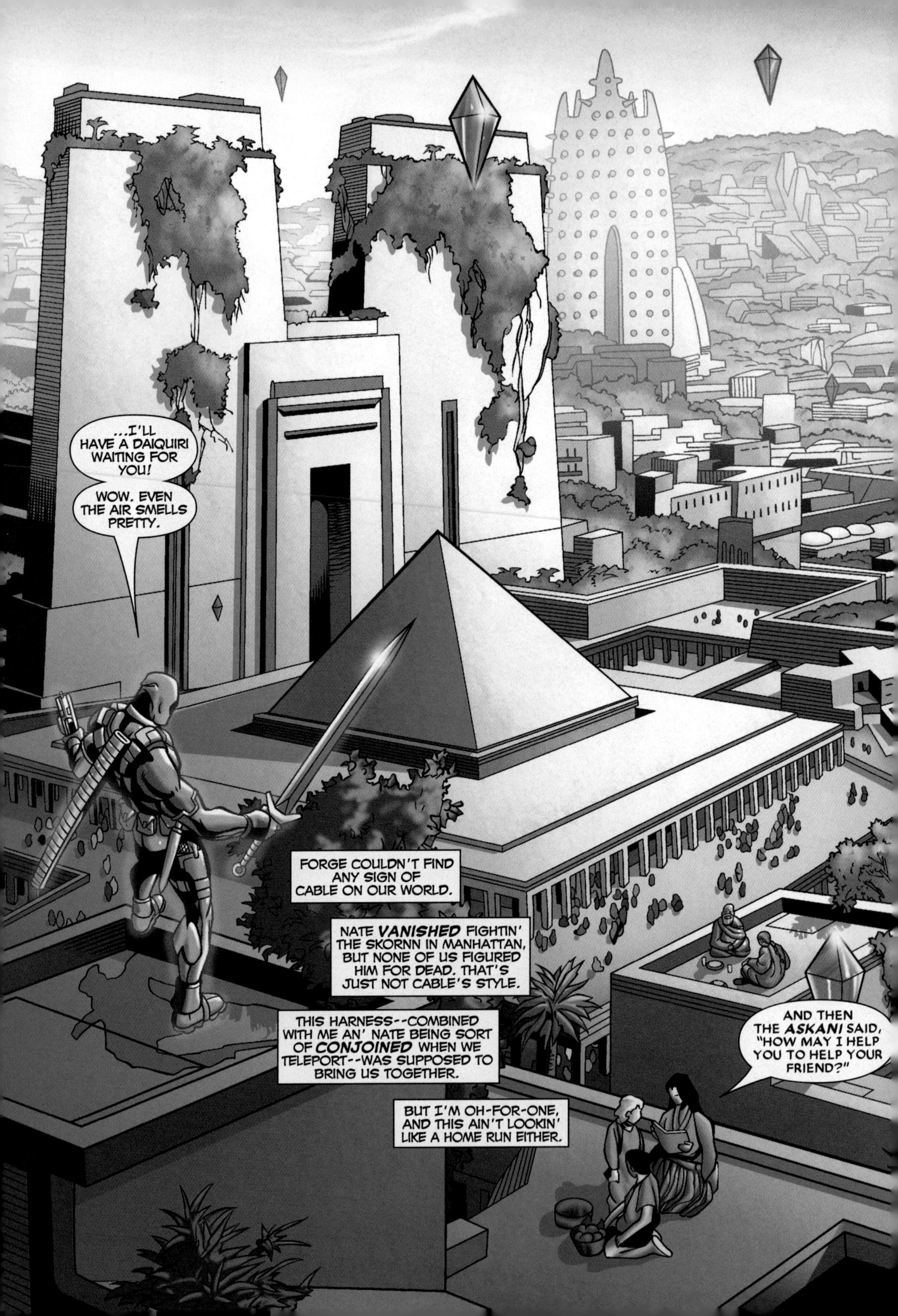

...I'LL HAVE A DAIQUIRI WAITING FOR YOU!
WOW. EVEN THE AIR SMELLS PRETTY.
FORGE COULDN'T FIND ANY SIGN OF CABLE ON OUR WORLD.
NATE VANISHED FIGHTIN' THE SKORNN IN MANHATTAN, BUT NONE OF US FIGURED HIM FOR DEAD. THAT'S JUST NOT CABLE'S STYLE.
THIS HARNESS--COMBINED WITH ME AN' NATE BEING SORT OF CONJOINED WHEN WE TELEPORT--WAS SUPPOSED TO BRING US TOGETHER.
BUT I'M OH-FOR-ONE, AND THIS AIN'T LOOKIN' LIKE A HOME RUN EITHER.
AND THEN THE ASKANI SAID, "HOW MAY I HELP YOU TO HELP YOUR FRIEND?"

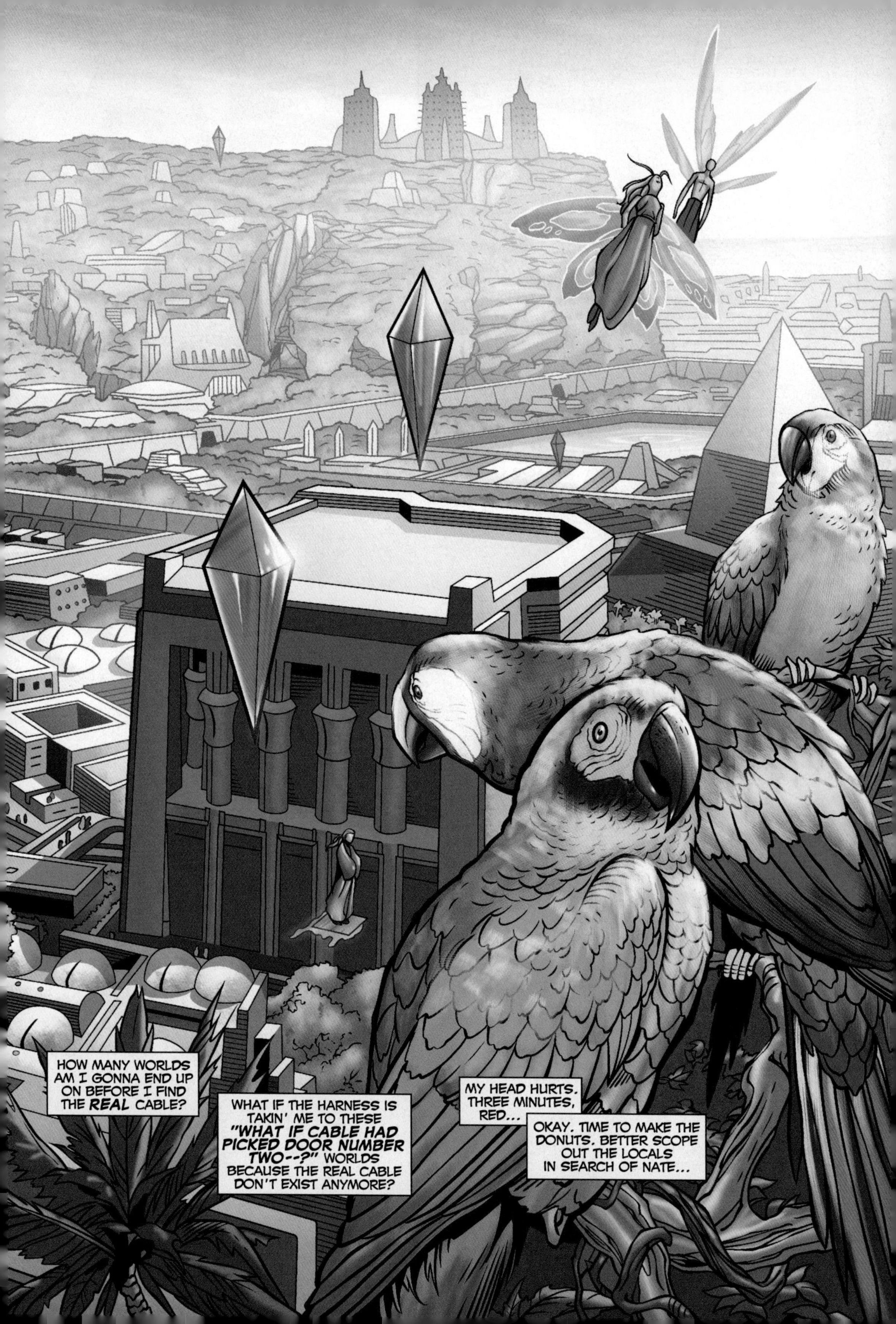
HOW MANY WORLDS AM I GONNA END UP ON BEFORE I FIND THE *REAL* CABLE?
WHAT IF THE HARNESS IS TAKIN' ME TO THESE ***"WHAT IF CABLE HAD PICKED DOOR NUMBER TWO--?"*** WORLDS BECAUSE THE REAL CABLE DON'T EXIST ANYMORE?
MY HEAD HURTS. THREE MINUTES, RED...
OKAY. TIME TO MAKE THE DONUTS. BETTER SCOPE OUT THE LOCALS IN SEARCH OF NATE...

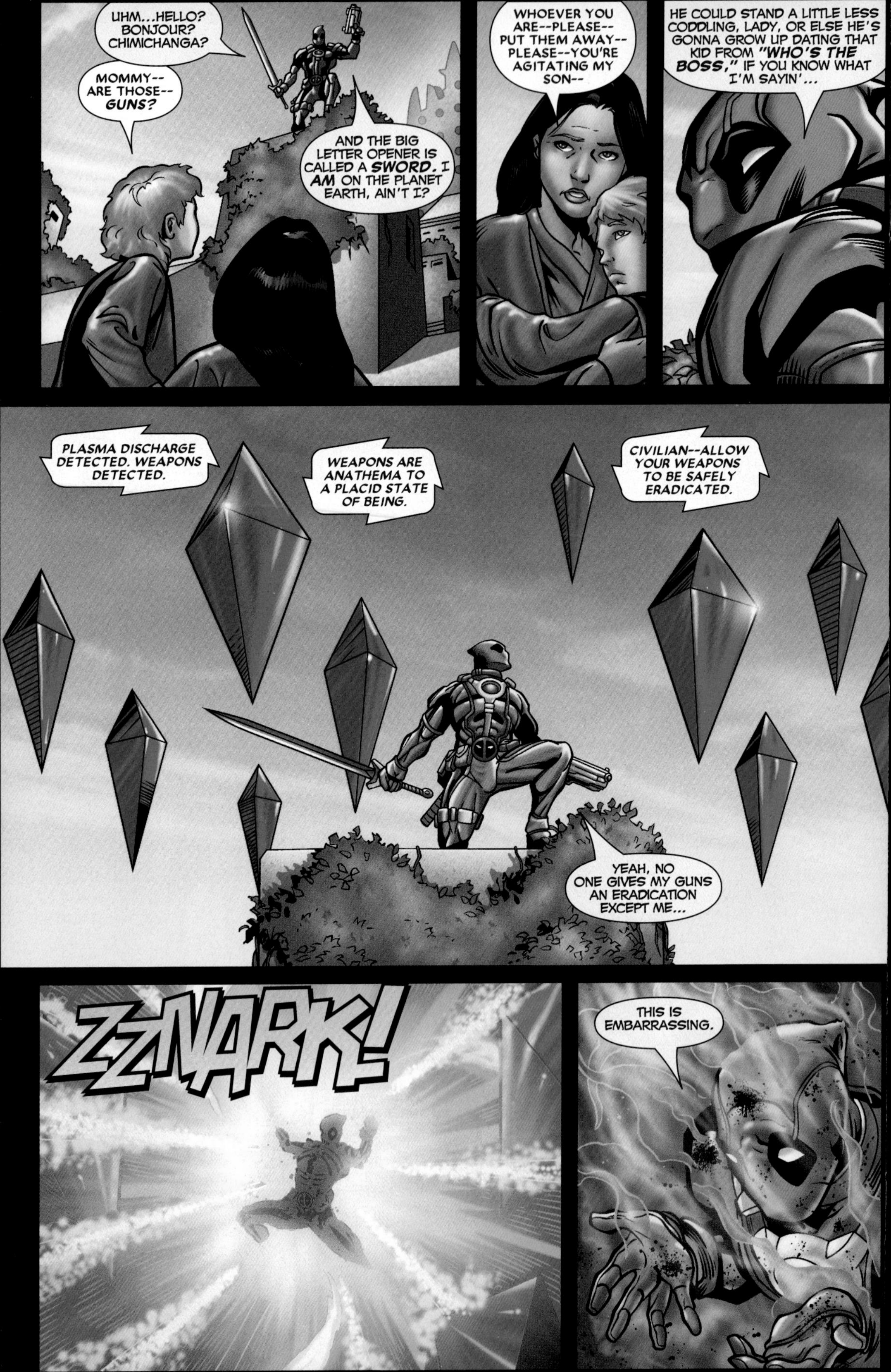
UHM...HELLO? BONJOUR? CHIMICHANGA?
MOMMY-- ARE THOSE-- GUNS?
AND THE BIG LETTER OPENER IS CALLED A SWORD. I AM ON THE PLANET EARTH, AIN'T I?
WHOEVER YOU ARE--PLEASE-- PUT THEM AWAY-- PLEASE--YOU'RE AGITATING MY SON--
HE COULD STAND A LITTLE LESS CODDLING, LADY, OR ELSE HE'S GONNA GROW UP DATING THAT KID FROM "WHO'S THE BOSS," IF YOU KNOW WHAT I'M SAYIN'...
PLASMA DISCHARGE DETECTED. WEAPONS DETECTED.
WEAPONS ARE ANATHEMA TO A PLACID STATE OF BEING.
CIVILIAN--ALLOW YOUR WEAPONS TO BE SAFELY ERADICATED.
YEAH, NO ONE GIVES MY GUNS AN ERADICATION EXCEPT ME...
ZZNARK!
THIS IS EMBARRASSING.

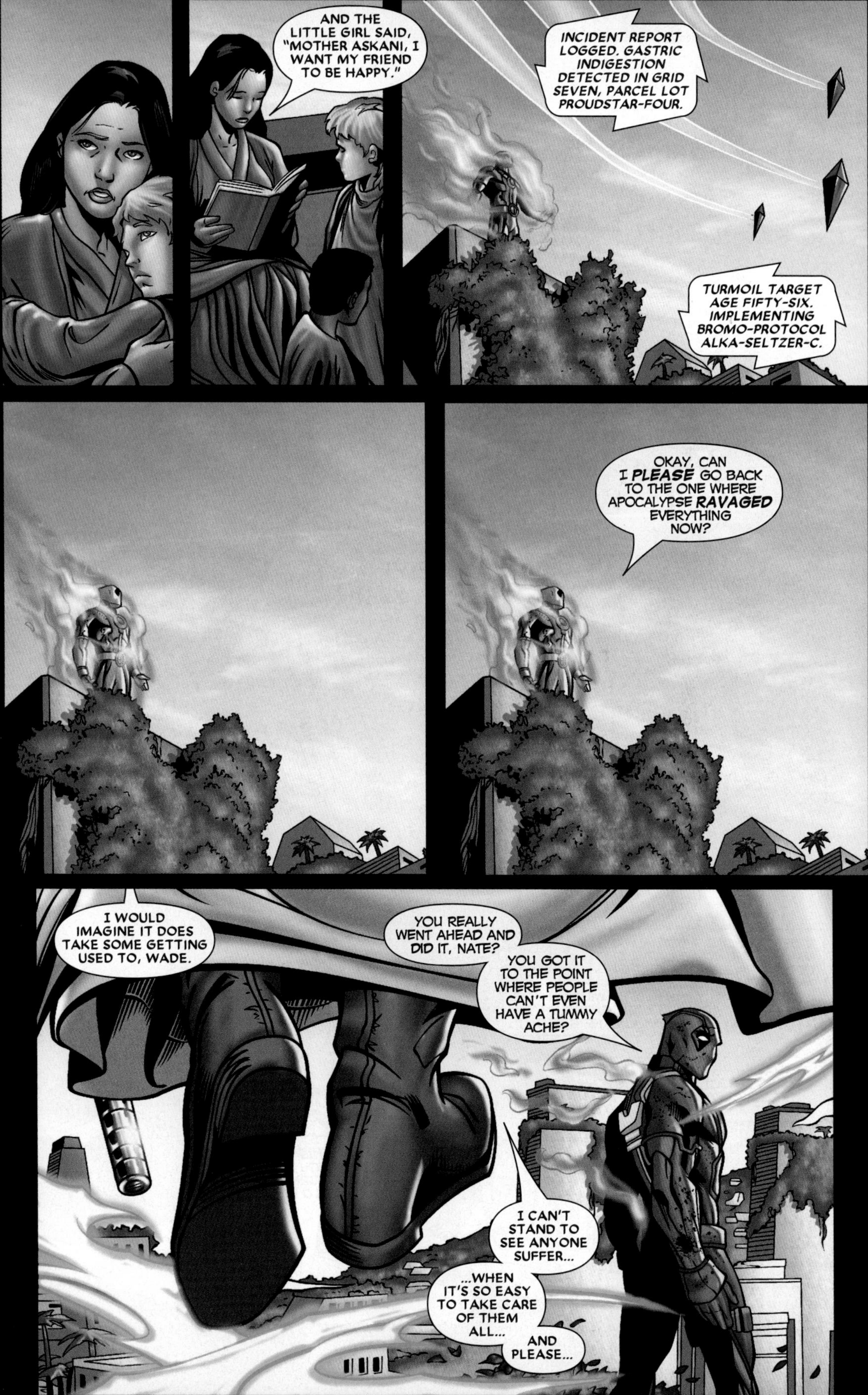
AND THE LITTLE GIRL SAID, "MOTHER ASKANI, I WANT MY FRIEND TO BE HAPPY."
INCIDENT REPORT LOGGED. GASTRIC INDIGESTION DETECTED IN GRID SEVEN, PARCEL LOT PROUDSTAR-FOUR.
TURMOIL TARGET AGE FIFTY-SIX. IMPLEMENTING BROMO-PROTOCOL ALKA-SELTZER-C.
OKAY, CAN I PLEASE GO BACK TO THE ONE WHERE APOCALYPSE RAVAGED EVERYTHING NOW?
I WOULD IMAGINE IT DOES TAKE SOME GETTING USED TO, WADE.
YOU REALLY WENT AHEAD AND DID IT, NATE?
YOU GOT IT TO THE POINT WHERE PEOPLE CAN'T EVEN HAVE A TUMMY ACHE?
I CAN'T STAND TO SEE ANYONE SUFFER...
...WHEN IT'S SO EASY TO TAKE CARE OF THEM ALL...
AND PLEASE...

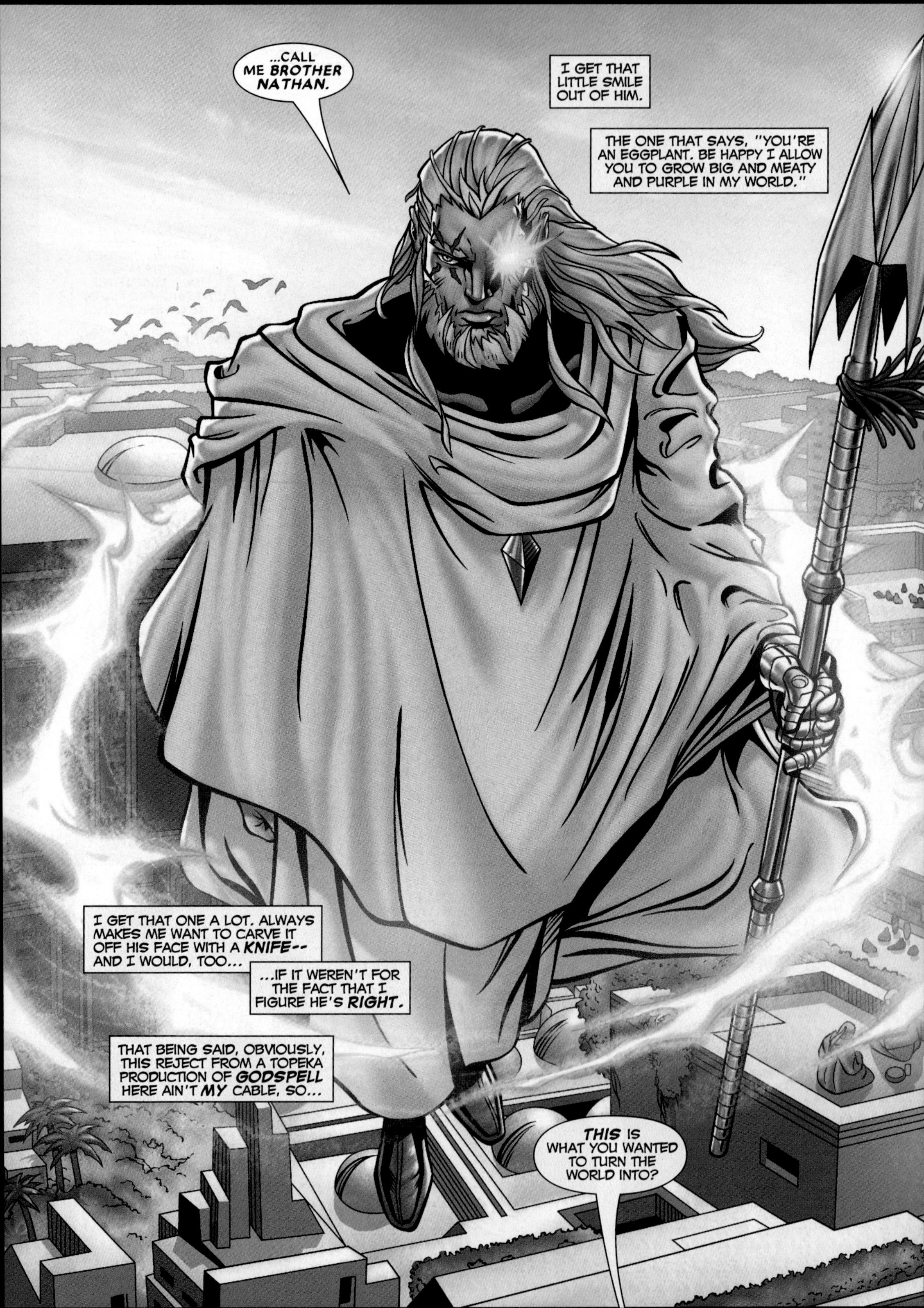
...CALL ME BROTHER NATHAN.
I GET THAT LITTLE SMILE OUT OF HIM.
THE ONE THAT SAYS, "YOU'RE AN EGGPLANT. BE HAPPY I ALLOW YOU TO GROW BIG AND MEATY AND PURPLE IN MY WORLD."
I GET THAT ONE A LOT. ALWAYS MAKES ME WANT TO CARVE IT OFF HIS FACE WITH A KNIFE-- AND I WOULD, TOO...
...IF IT WEREN'T FOR THE FACT THAT I FIGURE HE'S RIGHT.
THAT BEING SAID, OBVIOUSLY, THIS REJECT FROM A TOPEKA PRODUCTION OF GODSPELL HERE AIN'T MY CABLE, SO...
THIS IS WHAT YOU WANTED TO TURN THE WORLD INTO?

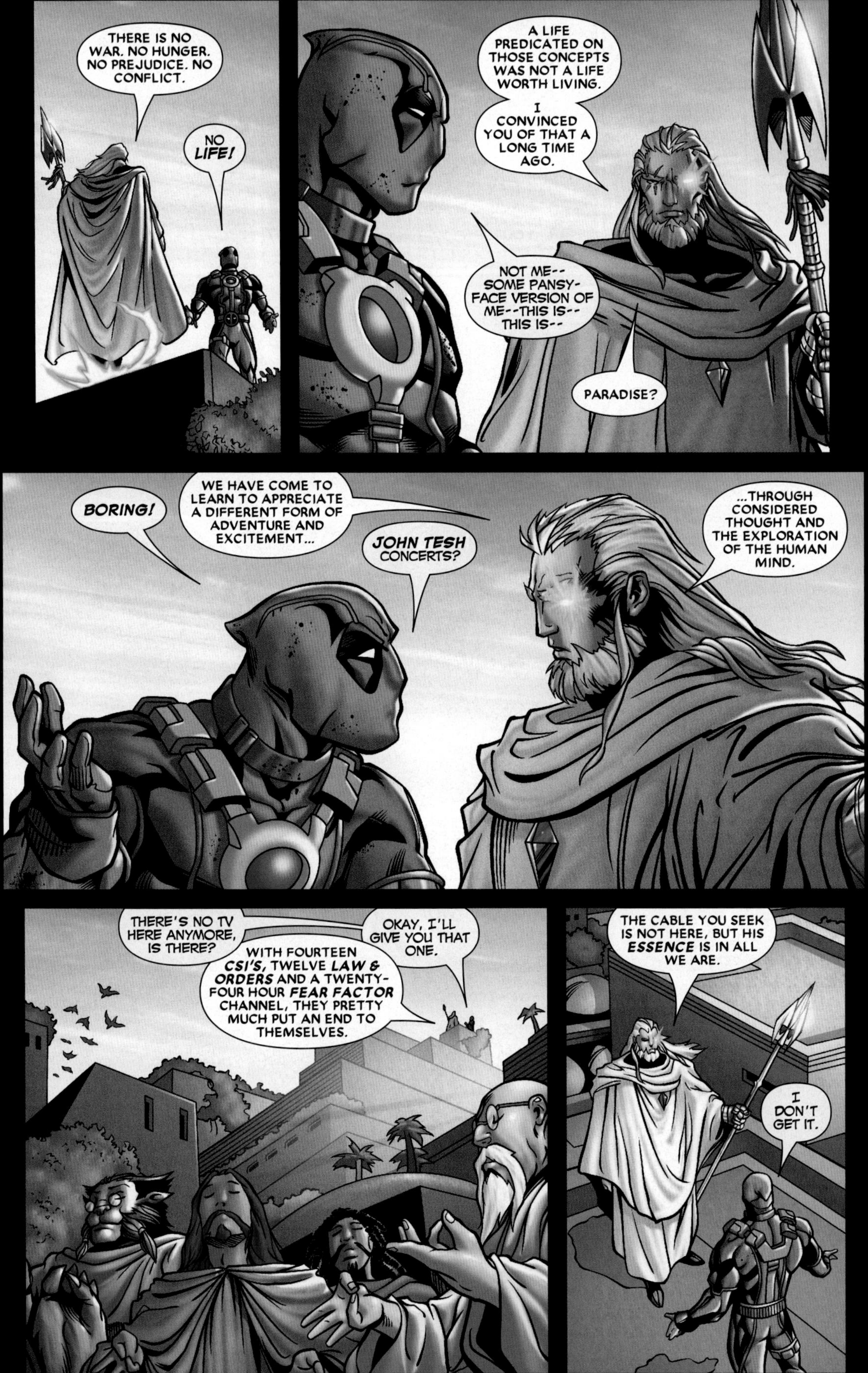
THERE IS NO WAR. NO HUNGER. NO PREJUDICE. NO CONFLICT.
NO LIFE!
A LIFE PREDICATED ON THOSE CONCEPTS WAS NOT A LIFE WORTH LIVING.
I CONVINCED YOU OF THAT A LONG TIME AGO.
NOT ME-- SOME PANSY-FACE VERSION OF ME--THIS IS-- THIS IS--
PARADISE?
BORING!
WE HAVE COME TO LEARN TO APPRECIATE A DIFFERENT FORM OF ADVENTURE AND EXCITEMENT...
JOHN TESH CONCERTS?
...THROUGH CONSIDERED THOUGHT AND THE EXPLORATION OF THE HUMAN MIND.
THERE'S NO TV HERE ANYMORE, IS THERE?
OKAY, I'LL GIVE YOU THAT ONE.
WITH FOURTEEN CSI'S, TWELVE LAW & ORDERS AND A TWENTY-FOUR HOUR FEAR FACTOR CHANNEL, THEY PRETTY MUCH PUT AN END TO THEMSELVES.
THE CABLE YOU SEEK IS NOT HERE, BUT HIS ESSENCE IS IN ALL WE ARE.
I DON'T GET IT.

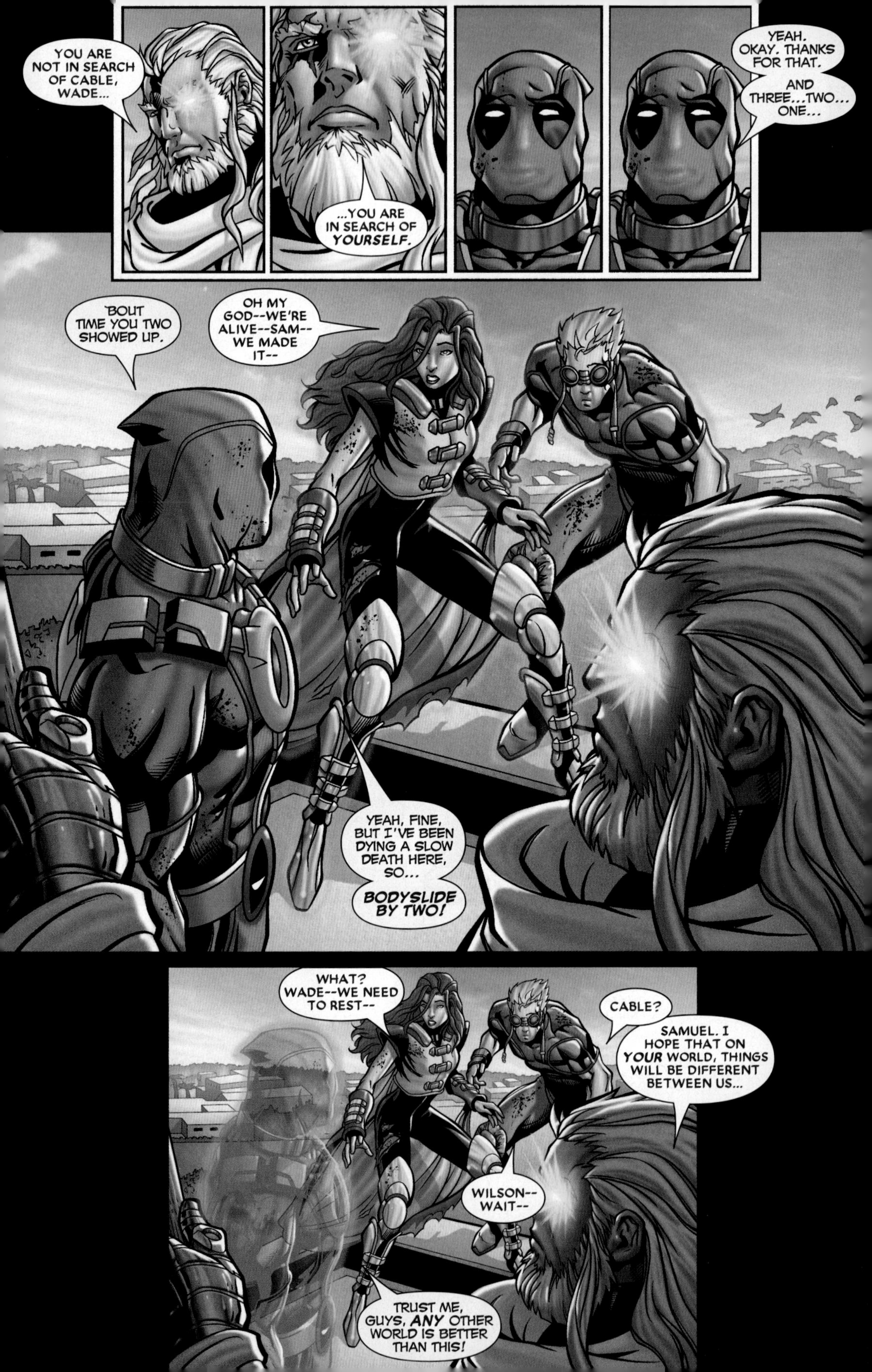
YOU ARE NOT IN SEARCH OF CABLE, WADE...
...YOU ARE IN SEARCH OF *YOURSELF*.
YEAH. OKAY. THANKS FOR THAT.
AND THREE...TWO... ONE...
'BOUT TIME YOU TWO SHOWED UP.
OH MY GOD--WE'RE ALIVE--SAM--WE MADE IT--
YEAH, FINE, BUT I'VE BEEN DYING A SLOW DEATH HERE, SO...
BODYSLIDE BY TWO!
WHAT? WADE--WE NEED TO REST--
CABLE?
SAMUEL. I HOPE THAT ON *YOUR* WORLD, THINGS WILL BE DIFFERENT BETWEEN US...
WILSON--WAIT--
TRUST ME, GUYS, *ANY* OTHER WORLD IS BETTER THAN THIS!

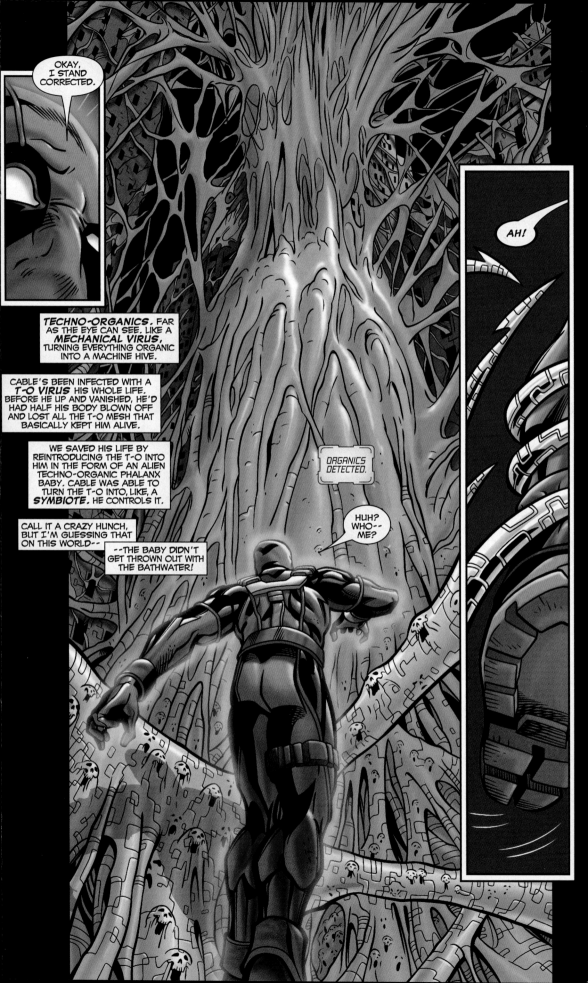

OKAY, I STAND CORRECTED.

TECHNO-ORGANICS. FAR AS THE EYE CAN SEE. LIKE A *MECHANICAL VIRUS*, TURNING EVERYTHING ORGANIC INTO A MACHINE HIVE.

CABLE'S BEEN INFECTED WITH A *T-O VIRUS* HIS WHOLE LIFE. BEFORE HE UP AND VANISHED, HE'D HAD HALF HIS BODY BLOWN OFF AND LOST ALL THE T-O MESH THAT BASICALLY KEPT HIM ALIVE.

WE SAVED HIS LIFE BY REINTRODUCING THE T-O INTO HIM IN THE FORM OF AN ALIEN TECHNO-ORGANIC PHALANX BABY. CABLE WAS ABLE TO TURN THE T-O INTO, LIKE, A *SYMBIOTE.* HE CONTROLS IT.

CALL IT A CRAZY HUNCH, BUT I'M GUESSING THAT ON THIS WORLD--

--THE BABY DIDN'T GET THROWN OUT WITH THE BATHWATER!

ORGANICS DETECTED.

HUH? WHO-- ME?

AH!

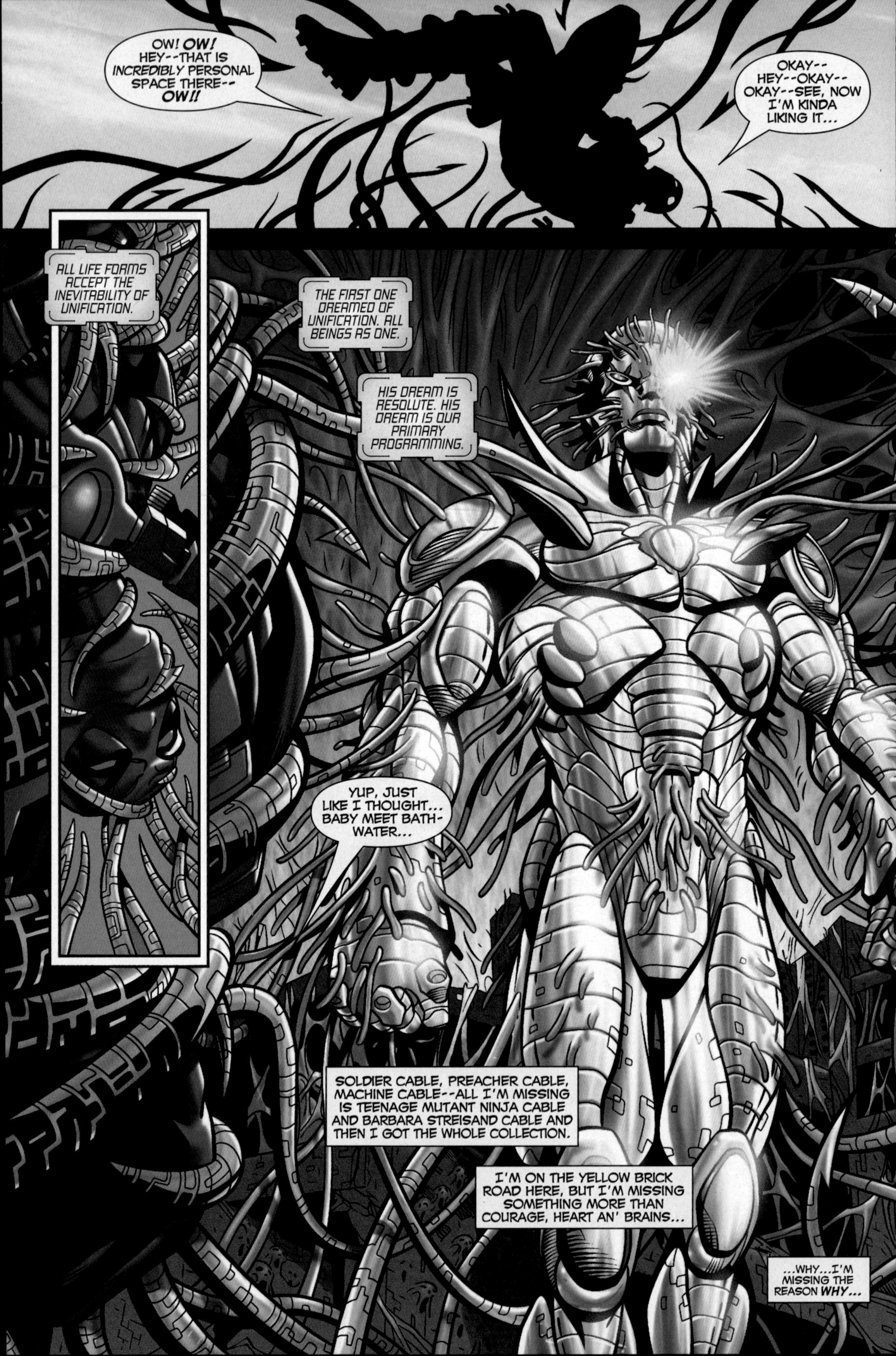
OW! OW! HEY--THAT IS INCREDIBLY PERSONAL SPACE THERE--OW!!
OKAY--HEY--OKAY--OKAY--SEE, NOW I'M KINDA LIKING IT...
ALL LIFE FORMS ACCEPT THE INEVITABILITY OF UNIFICATION.
THE FIRST ONE DREAMED OF UNIFICATION. ALL BEINGS AS ONE.
HIS DREAM IS RESOLUTE. HIS DREAM IS OUR PRIMARY PROGRAMMING.
YUP, JUST LIKE I THOUGHT... BABY MEET BATH-WATER...
SOLDIER CABLE, PREACHER CABLE, MACHINE CABLE--ALL I'M MISSING IS TEENAGE MUTANT NINJA CABLE AND BARBARA STREISAND CABLE AND THEN I GOT THE WHOLE COLLECTION.
I'M ON THE YELLOW BRICK ROAD HERE, BUT I'M MISSING SOMETHING MORE THAN COURAGE, HEART AN' BRAINS...
...WHY...I'M MISSING THE REASON WHY...

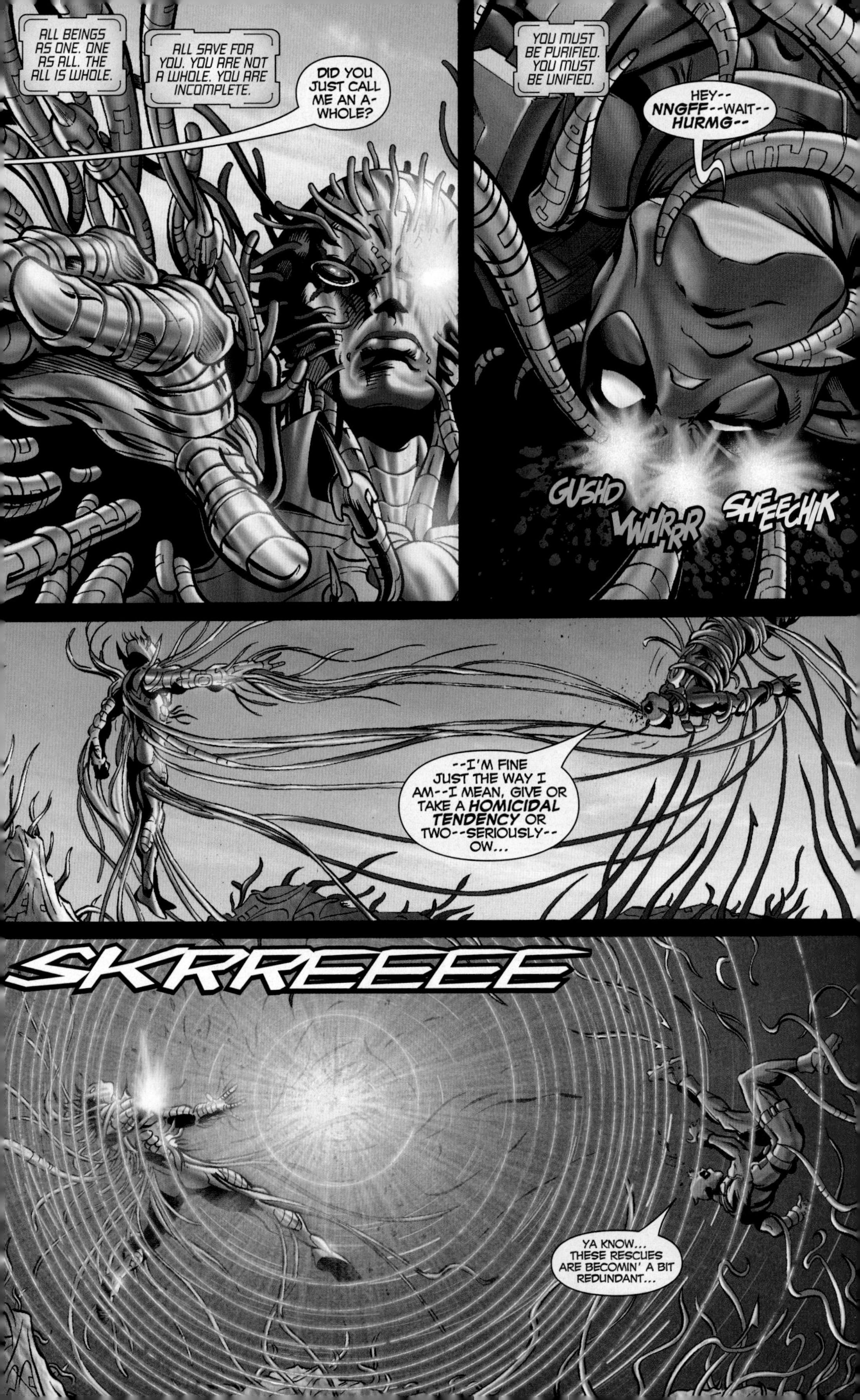

ALL BEINGS AS ONE. ONE AS ALL. THE ALL IS WHOLE.
ALL SAVE FOR YOU. YOU ARE NOT A WHOLE. YOU ARE INCOMPLETE.
DID YOU JUST CALL ME AN A-WHOLE?
YOU MUST BE PURIFIED. YOU MUST BE UNIFIED.
HEY-- NNGFF--WAIT-- HURMG--
GUSHD
VWHRRR
SHEEECHIK
--I'M FINE JUST THE WAY I AM--I MEAN, GIVE OR TAKE A HOMICIDAL TENDENCY OR TWO--SERIOUSLY--OW...
SKRREEEEE
YA KNOW... THESE RESCUES ARE BECOMIN' A BIT REDUNDANT...

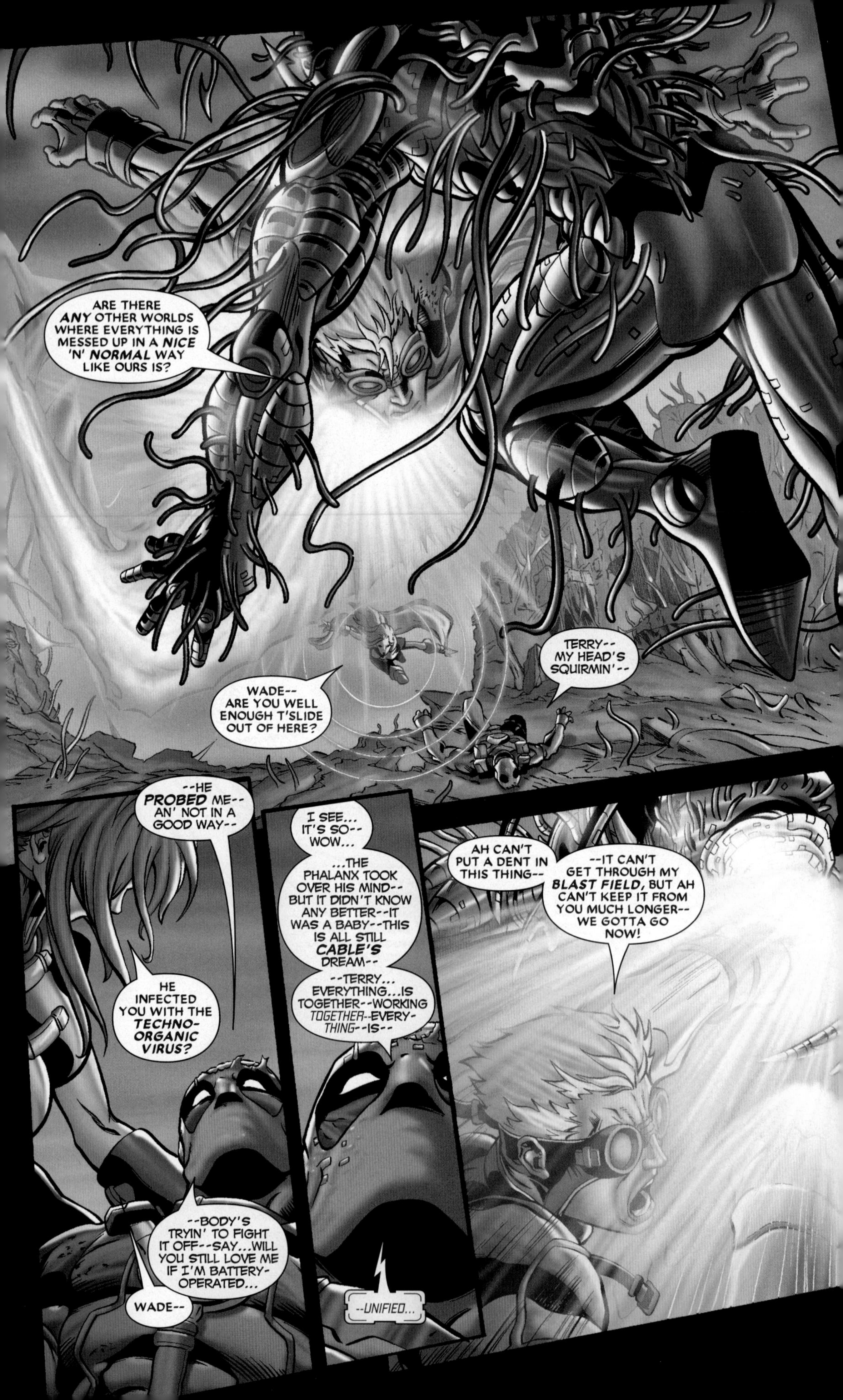
ARE THERE ANY OTHER WORLDS WHERE EVERYTHING IS MESSED UP IN A NICE 'N' NORMAL WAY LIKE OURS IS?
WADE-- ARE YOU WELL ENOUGH T'SLIDE OUT OF HERE?
TERRY-- MY HEAD'S SQUIRMIN'--
--HE PROBED ME-- AN' NOT IN A GOOD WAY--
HE INFECTED YOU WITH THE TECHNO-ORGANIC VIRUS?
--BODY'S TRYIN' TO FIGHT IT OFF--SAY...WILL YOU STILL LOVE ME IF I'M BATTERY-OPERATED...
WADE--
I SEE... IT'S SO--WOW...
...THE PHALANX TOOK OVER HIS MIND--BUT IT DIDN'T KNOW ANY BETTER--IT WAS A BABY--THIS IS ALL STILL CABLE'S DREAM--
--TERRY... EVERYTHING...IS TOGETHER--WORKING TOGETHER--EVERY-THING--IS--
--UNIFIED...
AH CAN'T PUT A DENT IN THIS THING--
--IT CAN'T GET THROUGH MY BLAST FIELD, BUT AH CAN'T KEEP IT FROM YOU MUCH LONGER--WE GOTTA GO NOW!

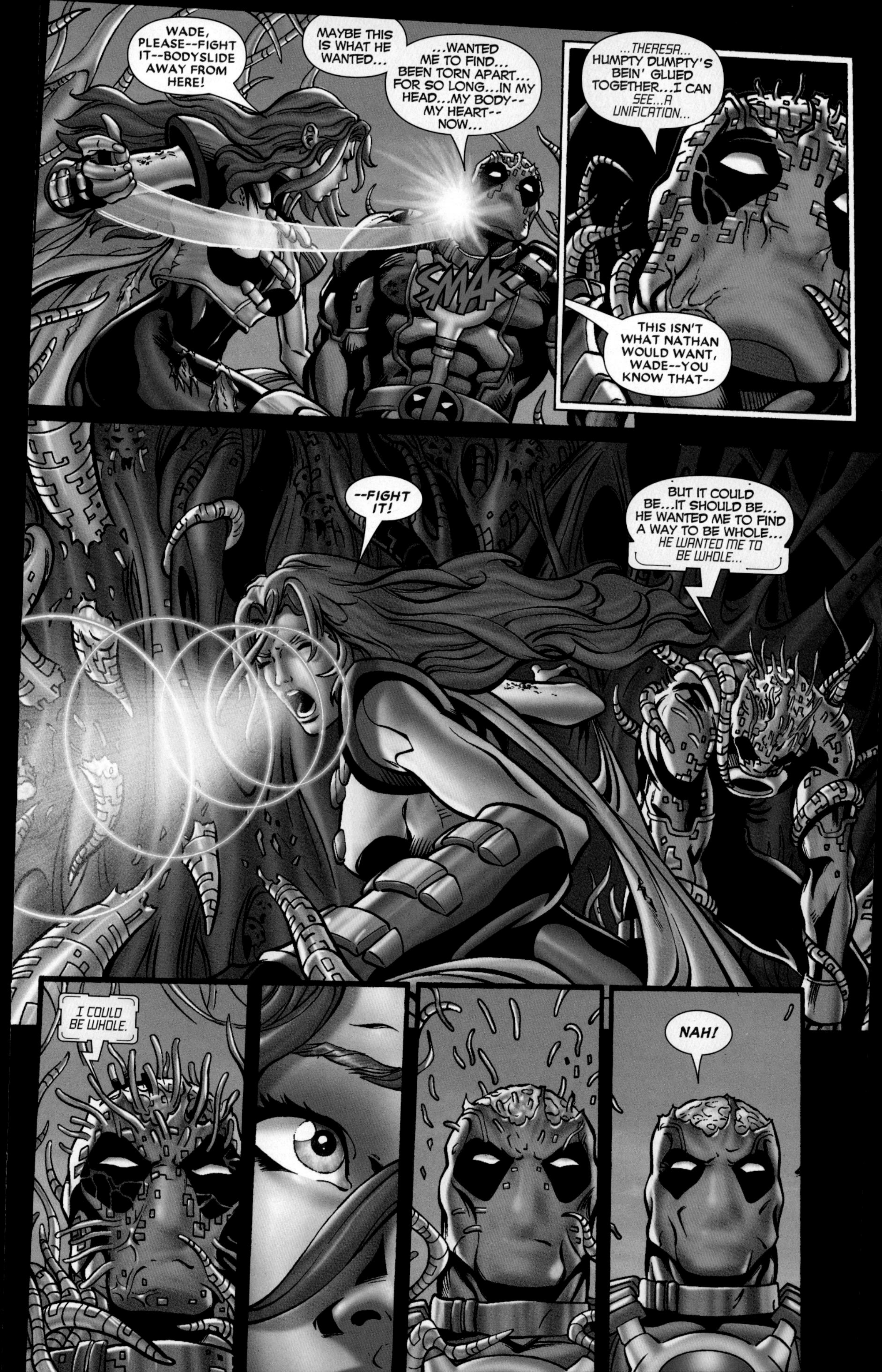
WADE, PLEASE--FIGHT IT--BODYSLIDE AWAY FROM HERE!
MAYBE THIS IS WHAT HE WANTED...
...WANTED ME TO FIND... BEEN TORN APART... FOR SO LONG...IN MY HEAD...MY BODY-- MY HEART-- NOW...
SMAK
...THERESA... HUMPTY DUMPTY'S BEIN' GLUED TOGETHER...I CAN SEE...A UNIFICATION...
THIS ISN'T WHAT NATHAN WOULD WANT, WADE--YOU KNOW THAT--
--FIGHT IT!
BUT IT COULD BE...IT SHOULD BE... HE WANTED ME TO FIND A WAY TO BE WHOLE...
HE WANTED ME TO BE WHOLE...
I COULD BE WHOLE.
NAH!

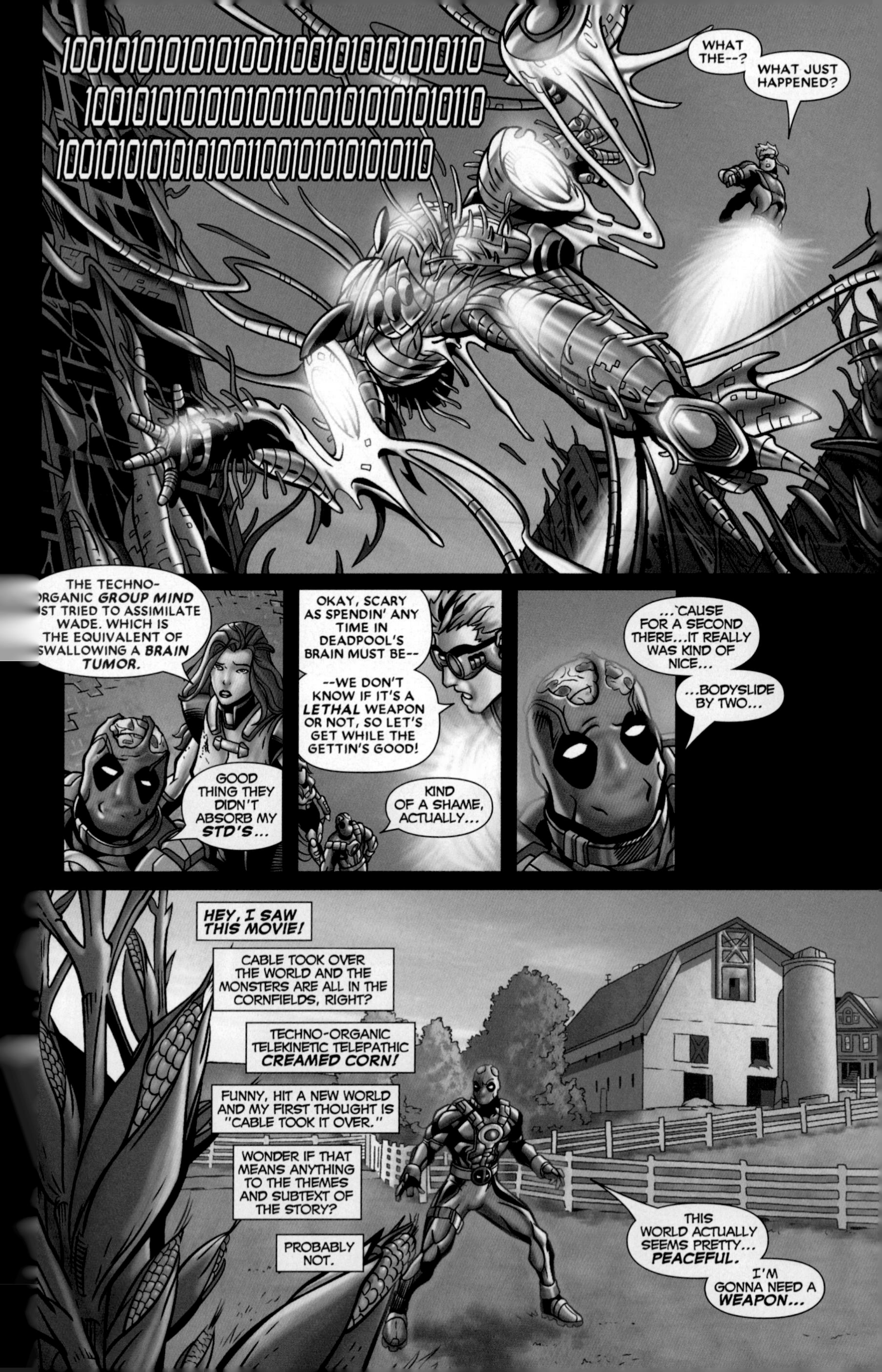
100101010101010100110010101010101110
100101010101010100110010101010101110
100101010101010100110010101010101110
WHAT THE--?
WHAT JUST HAPPENED?
THE TECHNO-ORGANIC GROUP MIND JUST TRIED TO ASSIMILATE WADE. WHICH IS THE EQUIVALENT OF SWALLOWING A BRAIN TUMOR.
GOOD THING THEY DIDN'T ABSORB MY STD'S...
OKAY, SCARY AS SPENDIN' ANY TIME IN DEADPOOL'S BRAIN MUST BE--
--WE DON'T KNOW IF IT'S A LETHAL WEAPON OR NOT, SO LET'S GET WHILE THE GETTIN'S GOOD!
KIND OF A SHAME, ACTUALLY...
...`CAUSE FOR A SECOND THERE...IT REALLY WAS KIND OF NICE...
...BODYSLIDE BY TWO...
HEY, I SAW THIS MOVIE!
CABLE TOOK OVER THE WORLD AND THE MONSTERS ARE ALL IN THE CORNFIELDS, RIGHT?
TECHNO-ORGANIC TELEKINETIC TELEPATHIC CREAMED CORN!
FUNNY, HIT A NEW WORLD AND MY FIRST THOUGHT IS "CABLE TOOK IT OVER."
WONDER IF THAT MEANS ANYTHING TO THE THEMES AND SUBTEXT OF THE STORY?
PROBABLY NOT.
THIS WORLD ACTUALLY SEEMS PRETTY... PEACEFUL.
I'M GONNA NEED A WEAPON...

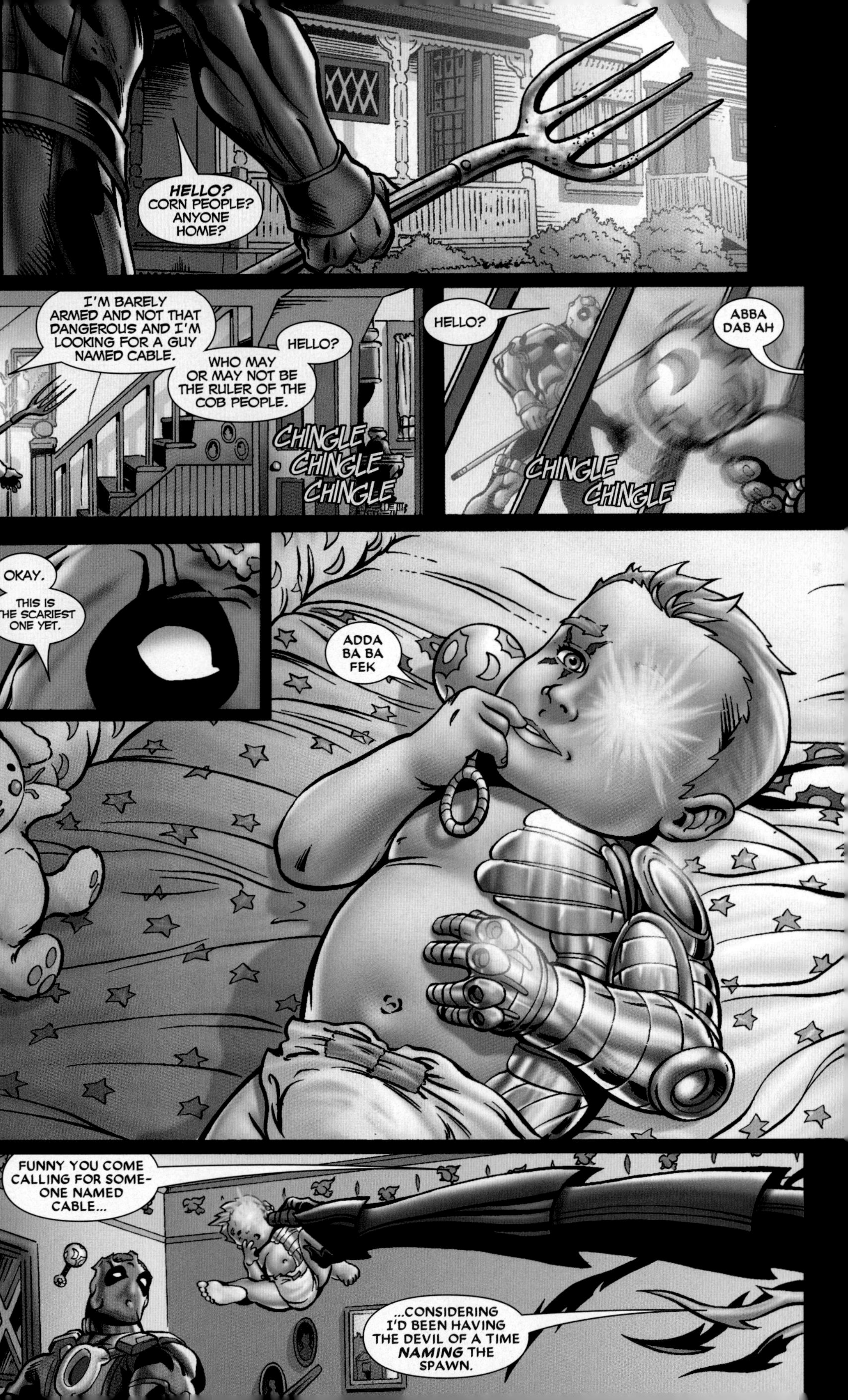
HELLO? CORN PEOPLE? ANYONE HOME?
I'M BARELY ARMED AND NOT THAT DANGEROUS AND I'M LOOKING FOR A GUY NAMED CABLE.
HELLO?
WHO MAY OR MAY NOT BE THE RULER OF THE COB PEOPLE.
CHINGLE CHINGLE CHINGLE
HELLO?
ABBA DAB AH
CHINGLE CHINGLE
OKAY.
THIS IS THE SCARIEST ONE YET.
ADDA BA BA FEK
FUNNY YOU COME CALLING FOR SOME-ONE NAMED CABLE...
...CONSIDERING I'D BEEN HAVING THE DEVIL OF A TIME NAMING THE SPAWN.

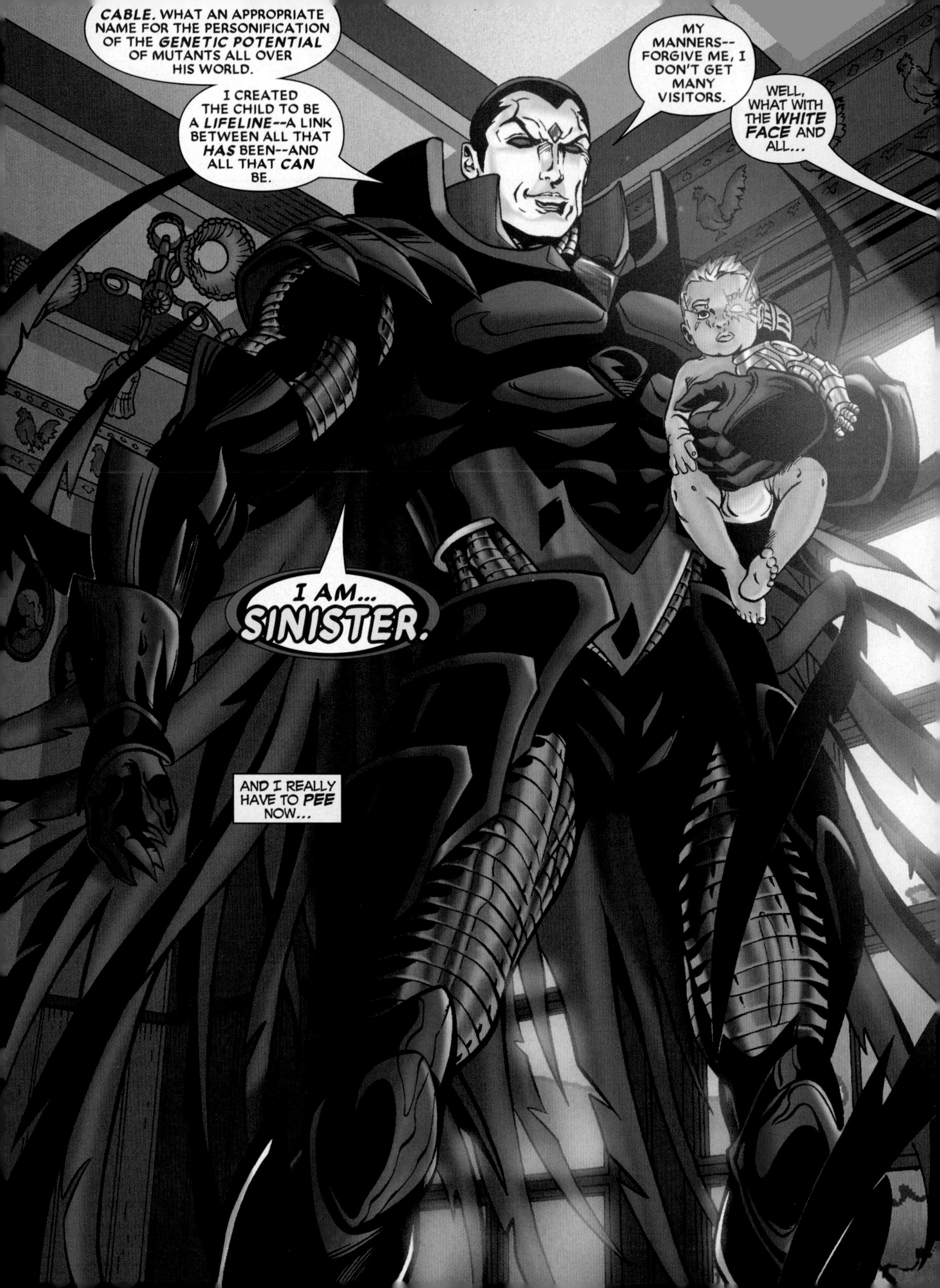
CABLE. WHAT AN APPROPRIATE NAME FOR THE PERSONIFICATION OF THE GENETIC POTENTIAL OF MUTANTS ALL OVER HIS WORLD.
I CREATED THE CHILD TO BE A LIFELINE--A LINK BETWEEN ALL THAT HAS BEEN--AND ALL THAT CAN BE.
MY MANNERS--FORGIVE ME, I DON'T GET MANY VISITORS.
WELL, WHAT WITH THE WHITE FACE AND ALL...
I AM... SINISTER.
AND I REALLY HAVE TO PEE NOW...

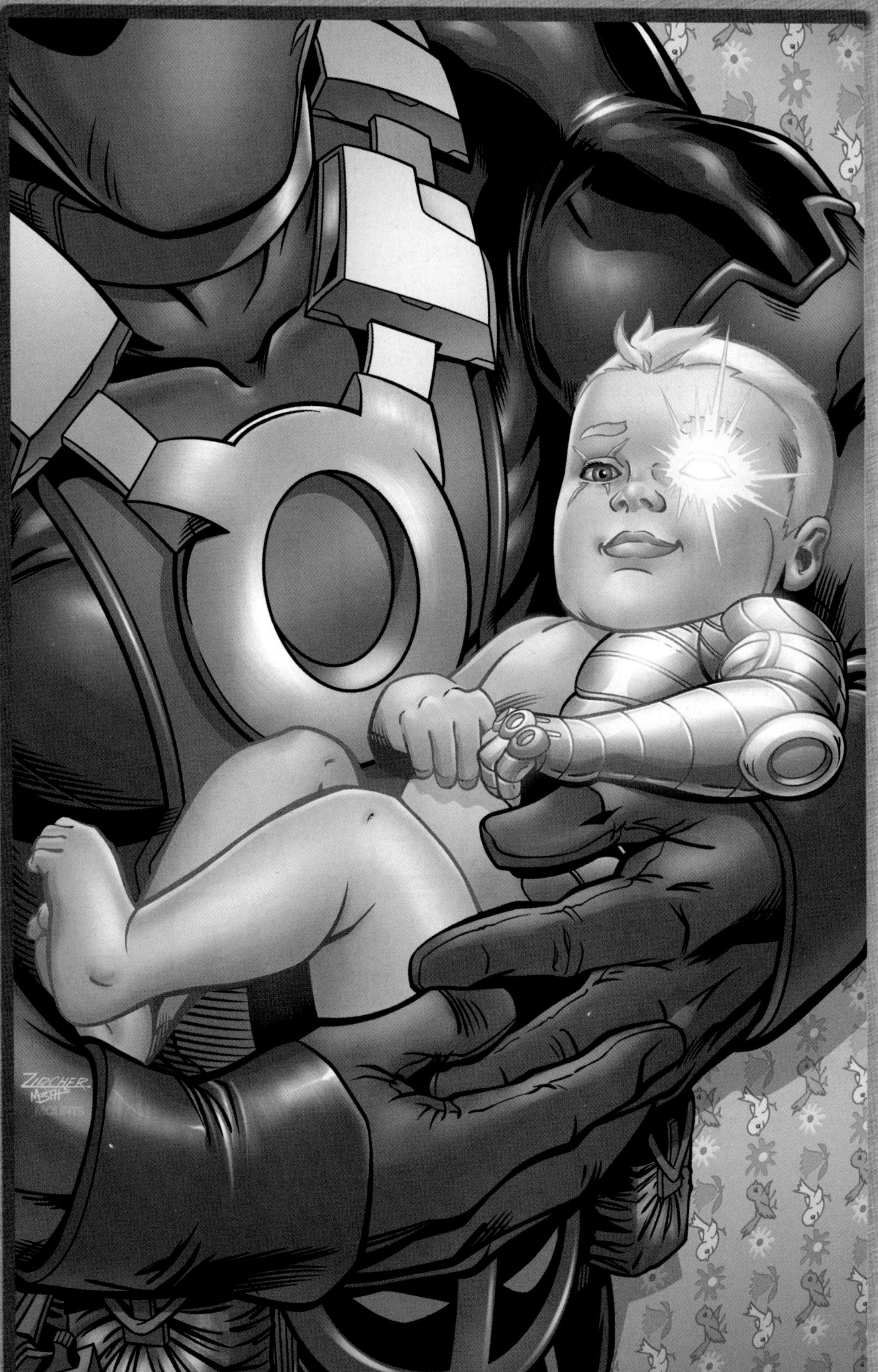

#17

The New Avengers and the Astonishing X-Men met to discuss the fate of
Wanda Maximoff, the Scarlet Witch—the daughter of the powerful mutant
terrorist Magneto. After losing control of her reality-altering powers and
suffering a total nervous breakdown, Wanda unleashed chaos upon the
Avengers, killing and injuring many of their number. Magneto intervened and
took his daughter to the devastated island-nation of Genosha, where Charles
Xavier—Professor X, the founder of the X-Men—was to help her recover.
Xavier failed, and now it is up to Wanda's friends and teammates to decide
whether she will live or die. But Magneto, Wanda, and her brother Pietro
disappear...

Then the world burns to white. Reality as we knew it is gone...

...to be replaced by a society in which humans are the oppressed minority
and mutants run the culture, ruling over all existing countries, religions, and
politics. A kingdom united under the House of M.

HOUSE OF M

CABLE & DEADPOOL

ENEMA OF THE STATE
PART THREE: "HOUSE OF MMMM"

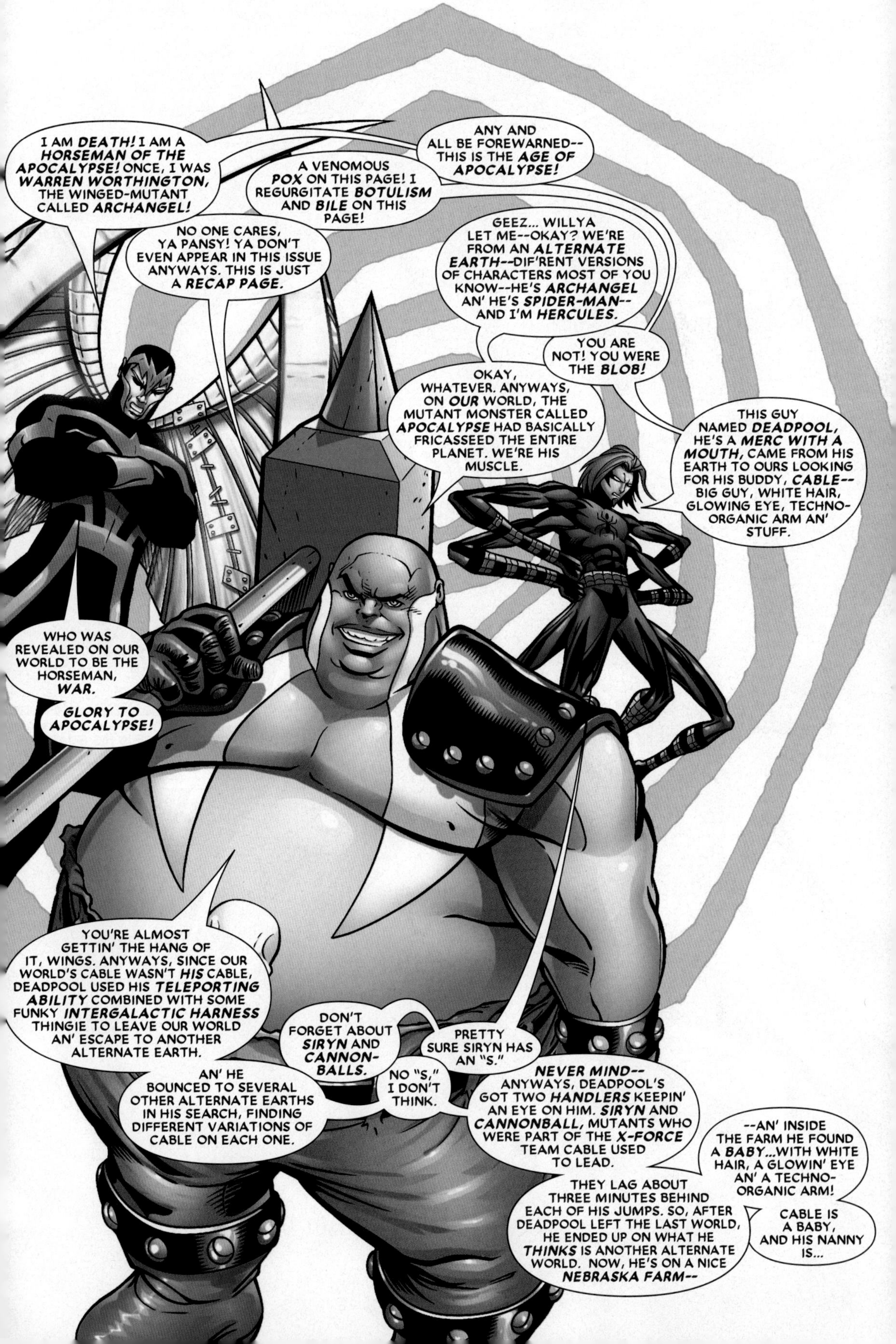
I AM DEATH! I AM A HORSEMAN OF THE APOCALYPSE! ONCE, I WAS WARREN WORTHINGTON, THE WINGED-MUTANT CALLED ARCHANGEL!
ANY AND ALL BE FOREWARNED-- THIS IS THE AGE OF APOCALYPSE!
A VENOMOUS POX ON THIS PAGE! I REGURGITATE BOTULISM AND BILE ON THIS PAGE!
NO ONE CARES, YA PANSY! YA DON'T EVEN APPEAR IN THIS ISSUE ANYWAYS. THIS IS JUST A RECAP PAGE.
GEEZ... WILLYA LET ME--OKAY? WE'RE FROM AN ALTERNATE EARTH--DIF'RENT VERSIONS OF CHARACTERS MOST OF YOU KNOW--HE'S ARCHANGEL AN' HE'S SPIDER-MAN-- AND I'M HERCULES.
YOU ARE NOT! YOU WERE THE BLOB!
OKAY, WHATEVER. ANYWAYS, ON OUR WORLD, THE MUTANT MONSTER CALLED APOCALYPSE HAD BASICALLY FRICASSEED THE ENTIRE PLANET. WE'RE HIS MUSCLE.
THIS GUY NAMED DEADPOOL, HE'S A MERC WITH A MOUTH, CAME FROM HIS EARTH TO OURS LOOKING FOR HIS BUDDY, CABLE-- BIG GUY, WHITE HAIR, GLOWING EYE, TECHNO-ORGANIC ARM AN' STUFF.
WHO WAS REVEALED ON OUR WORLD TO BE THE HORSEMAN, WAR.
GLORY TO APOCALYPSE!
YOU'RE ALMOST GETTIN' THE HANG OF IT, WINGS. ANYWAYS, SINCE OUR WORLD'S CABLE WASN'T HIS CABLE, DEADPOOL USED HIS TELEPORTING ABILITY COMBINED WITH SOME FUNKY INTERGALACTIC HARNESS THINGIE TO LEAVE OUR WORLD AN' ESCAPE TO ANOTHER ALTERNATE EARTH.
AN' HE BOUNCED TO SEVERAL OTHER ALTERNATE EARTHS IN HIS SEARCH, FINDING DIFFERENT VARIATIONS OF CABLE ON EACH ONE.
DON'T FORGET ABOUT SIRYN AND CANNON-BALLS.
PRETTY SURE SIRYN HAS AN "S."
NO "S," I DON'T THINK.
NEVER MIND-- ANYWAYS, DEADPOOL'S GOT TWO HANDLERS KEEPIN' AN EYE ON HIM. SIRYN AND CANNONBALL, MUTANTS WHO WERE PART OF THE X-FORCE TEAM CABLE USED TO LEAD.
THEY LAG ABOUT THREE MINUTES BEHIND EACH OF HIS JUMPS. SO, AFTER DEADPOOL LEFT THE LAST WORLD, HE ENDED UP ON WHAT HE THINKS IS ANOTHER ALTERNATE WORLD. NOW, HE'S ON A NICE NEBRASKA FARM--
--AN' INSIDE THE FARM HE FOUND A BABY...WITH WHITE HAIR, A GLOWIN' EYE AN' A TECHNO-ORGANIC ARM!
CABLE IS A BABY, AND HIS NANNY IS...

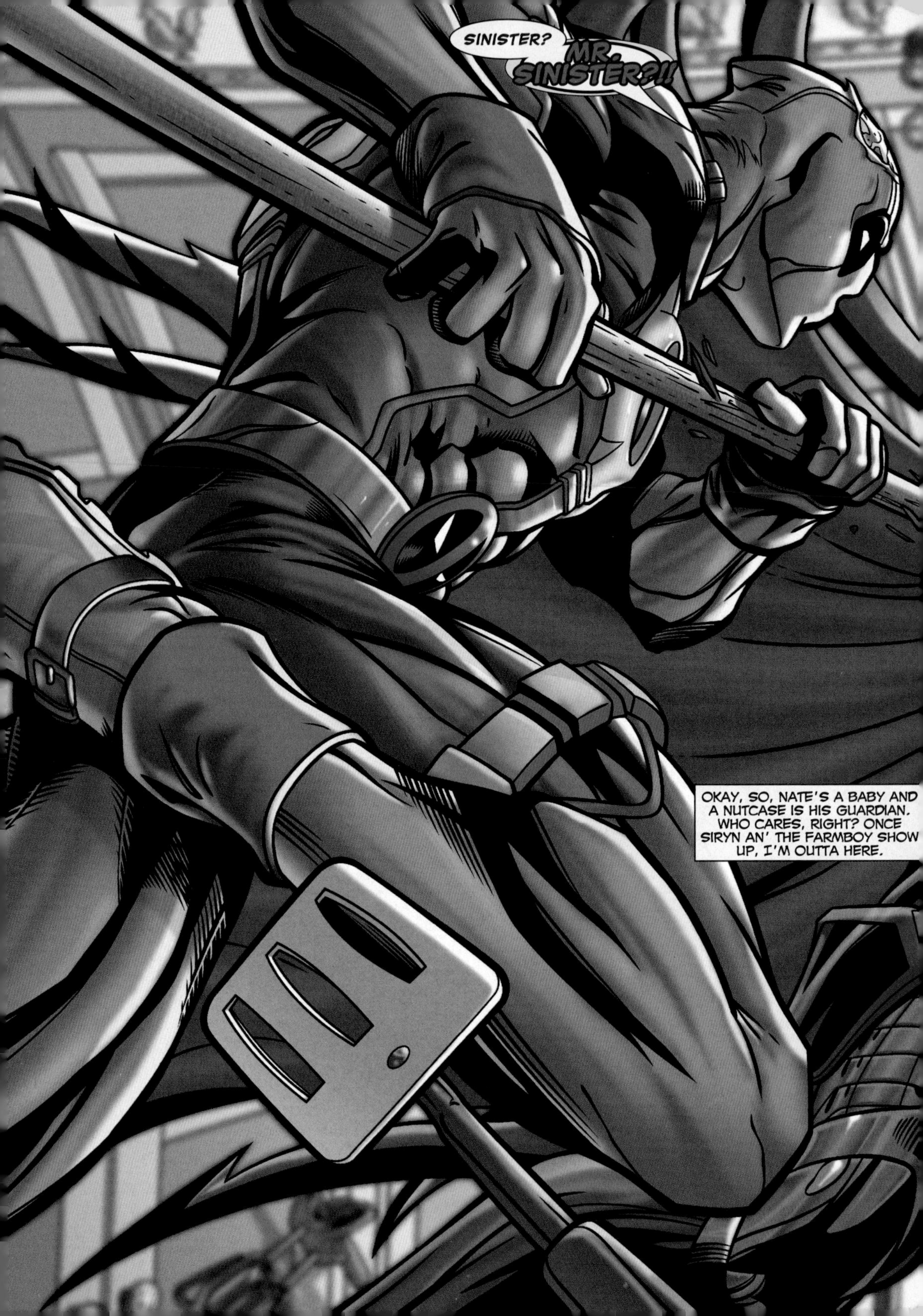
SINISTER?
MR. SINISTER?!!
OKAY, SO, NATE'S A BABY AND A NUTCASE IS HIS GUARDIAN. WHO CARES, RIGHT? ONCE SIRYN AN' THE FARMBOY SHOW UP, I'M OUTTA HERE.

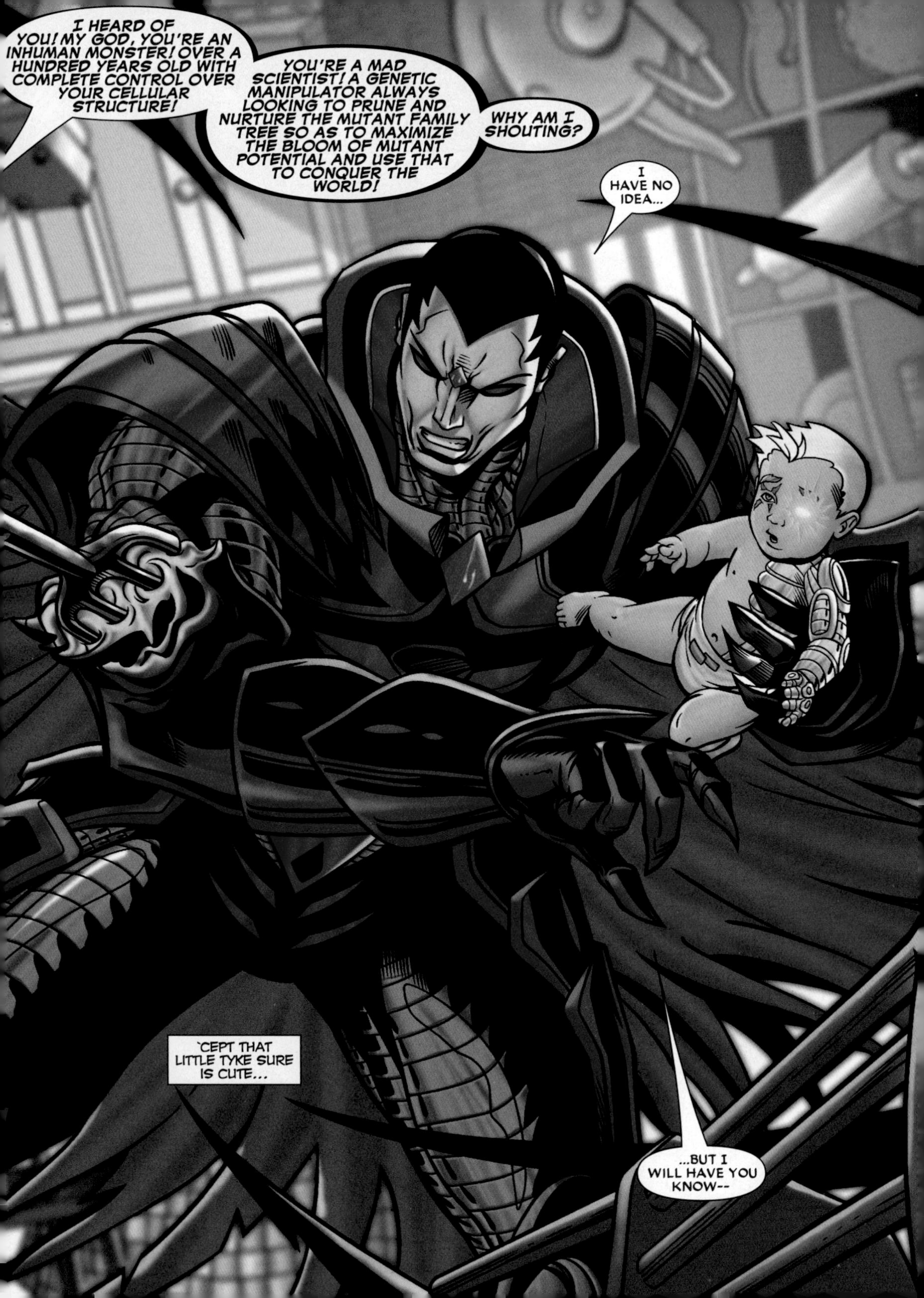
I HEARD OF YOU! MY GOD, YOU'RE AN INHUMAN MONSTER! OVER A HUNDRED YEARS OLD WITH COMPLETE CONTROL OVER YOUR CELLULAR STRUCTURE!
YOU'RE A MAD SCIENTIST! A GENETIC MANIPULATOR ALWAYS LOOKING TO PRUNE AND NURTURE THE MUTANT FAMILY TREE SO AS TO MAXIMIZE THE BLOOM OF MUTANT POTENTIAL AND USE THAT TO CONQUER THE WORLD!
WHY AM I SHOUTING?
I HAVE NO IDEA...
`CEPT THAT LITTLE TYKE SURE IS CUTE...
...BUT I WILL HAVE YOU KNOW--

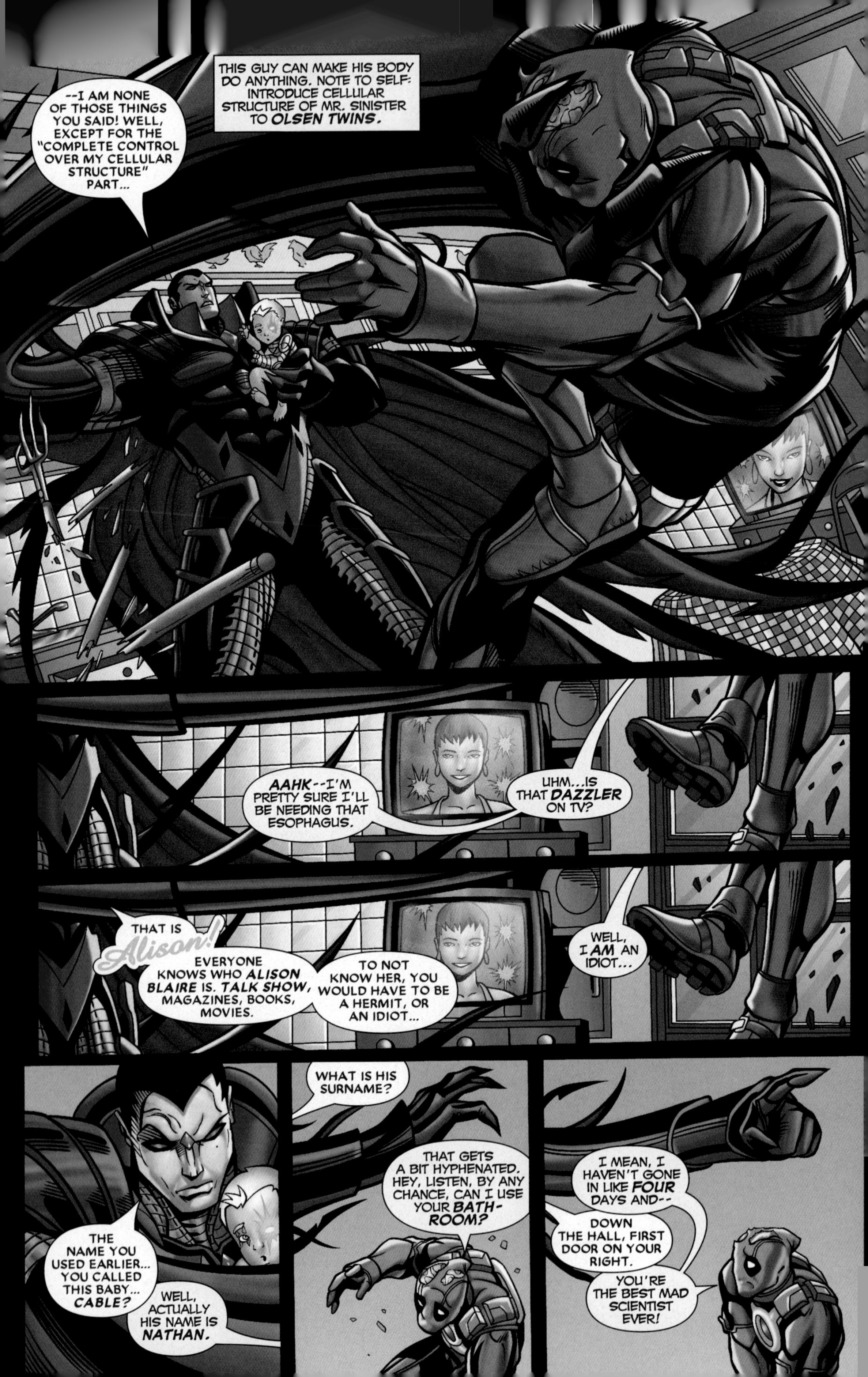
--I AM NONE OF THOSE THINGS YOU SAID! WELL, EXCEPT FOR THE "COMPLETE CONTROL OVER MY CELLULAR STRUCTURE" PART...
THIS GUY CAN MAKE HIS BODY DO ANYTHING. NOTE TO SELF: INTRODUCE CELLULAR STRUCTURE OF MR. SINISTER TO OLSEN TWINS.
AAHK--I'M PRETTY SURE I'LL BE NEEDING THAT ESOPHAGUS.
UHM...IS THAT DAZZLER ON TV?
THAT IS Alison!
EVERYONE KNOWS WHO ALISON BLAIRE IS. TALK SHOW, MAGAZINES, BOOKS, MOVIES.
TO NOT KNOW HER, YOU WOULD HAVE TO BE A HERMIT, OR AN IDIOT...
WELL, I AM AN IDIOT...
THE NAME YOU USED EARLIER... YOU CALLED THIS BABY... CABLE?
WELL, ACTUALLY HIS NAME IS NATHAN.
WHAT IS HIS SURNAME?
THAT GETS A BIT HYPHENATED. HEY, LISTEN, BY ANY CHANCE, CAN I USE YOUR BATH-ROOM?
I MEAN, I HAVEN'T GONE IN LIKE FOUR DAYS AND--
DOWN THE HALL, FIRST DOOR ON YOUR RIGHT.
YOU'RE THE BEST MAD SCIENTIST EVER!

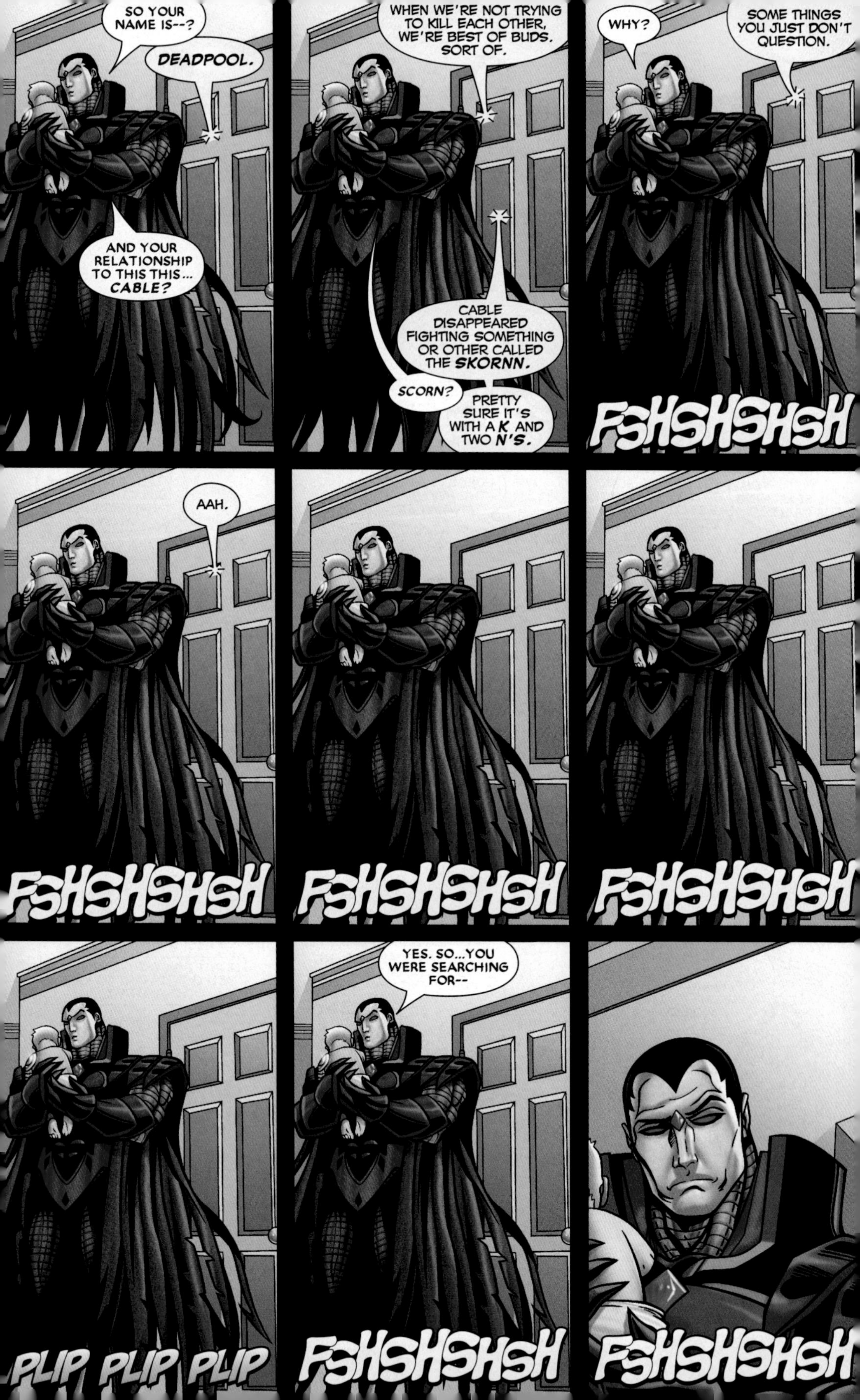
SO YOUR NAME IS--?
DEADPOOL.
AND YOUR RELATIONSHIP TO THIS THIS... CABLE?
WHEN WE'RE NOT TRYING TO KILL EACH OTHER, WE'RE BEST OF BUDS. SORT OF.
CABLE DISAPPEARED FIGHTING SOMETHING OR OTHER CALLED THE SKORNN.
SCORN?
PRETTY SURE IT'S WITH A K AND TWO N'S.
WHY?
SOME THINGS YOU JUST DON'T QUESTION.
FSHSHSHSH
AAH.
FSHSHSHSH
FSHSHSHSH
FSHSHSHSH
PLIP PLIP PLIP
YES. SO...YOU WERE SEARCHING FOR--
FSHSHSHSH
FSHSHSHSH

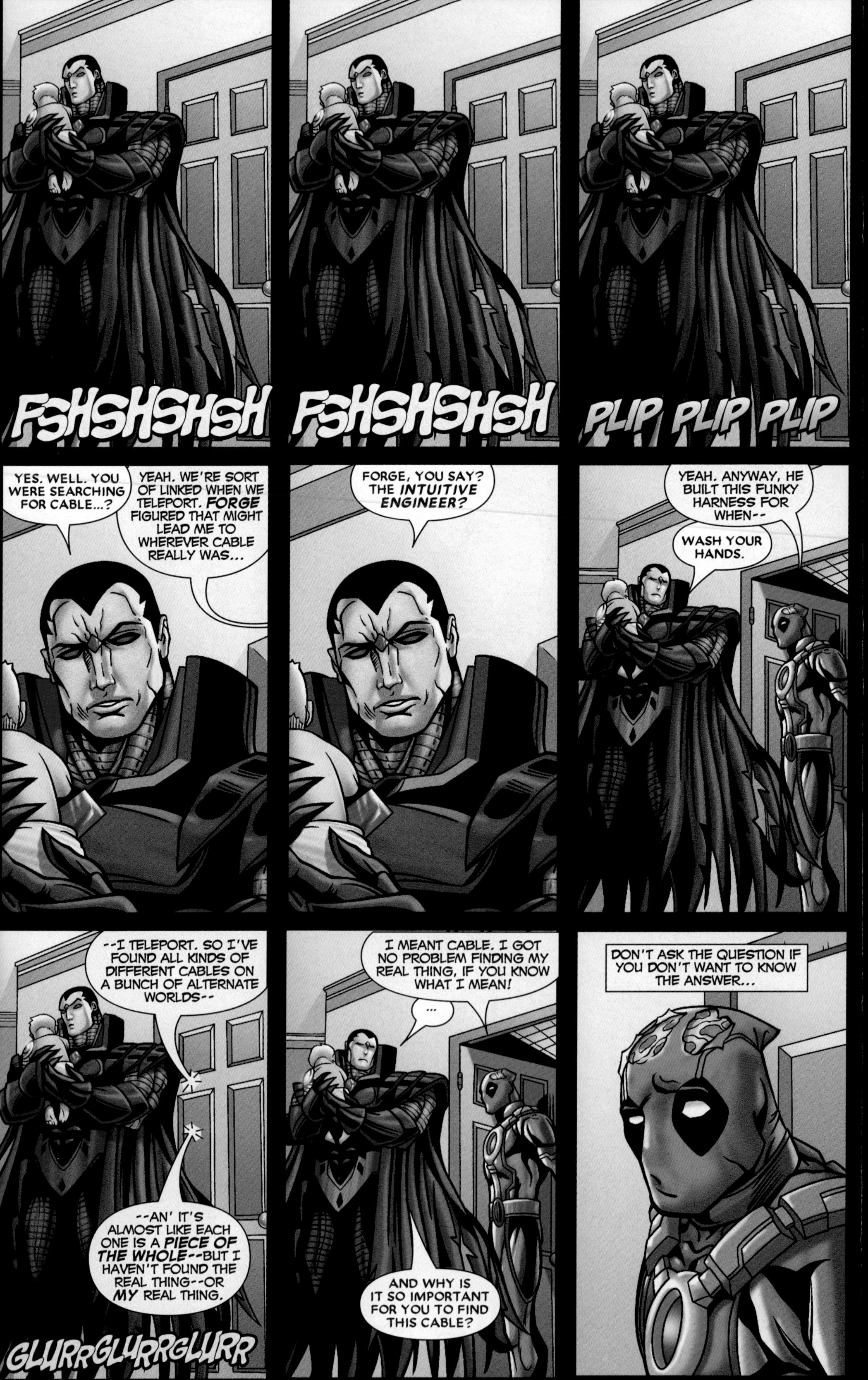
FSHSHSHSH
FSHSHSHSH
PLIP PLIP PLIP
YES. WELL. YOU WERE SEARCHING FOR CABLE...?
YEAH. WE'RE SORT OF LINKED WHEN WE TELEPORT. FORGE FIGURED THAT MIGHT LEAD ME TO WHEREVER CABLE REALLY WAS...
FORGE, YOU SAY? THE INTUITIVE ENGINEER?
YEAH. ANYWAY, HE BUILT THIS FUNKY HARNESS FOR WHEN--
WASH YOUR HANDS.
--I TELEPORT. SO I'VE FOUND ALL KINDS OF DIFFERENT CABLES ON A BUNCH OF ALTERNATE WORLDS--
--AN' IT'S ALMOST LIKE EACH ONE IS A PIECE OF THE WHOLE--BUT I HAVEN'T FOUND THE REAL THING--OR MY REAL THING.
GLURRGLURRGLURR
AND WHY IS IT SO IMPORTANT FOR YOU TO FIND THIS CABLE?
I MEANT CABLE. I GOT NO PROBLEM FINDING MY REAL THING, IF YOU KNOW WHAT I MEAN!
...
DON'T ASK THE QUESTION IF YOU DON'T WANT TO KNOW THE ANSWER...

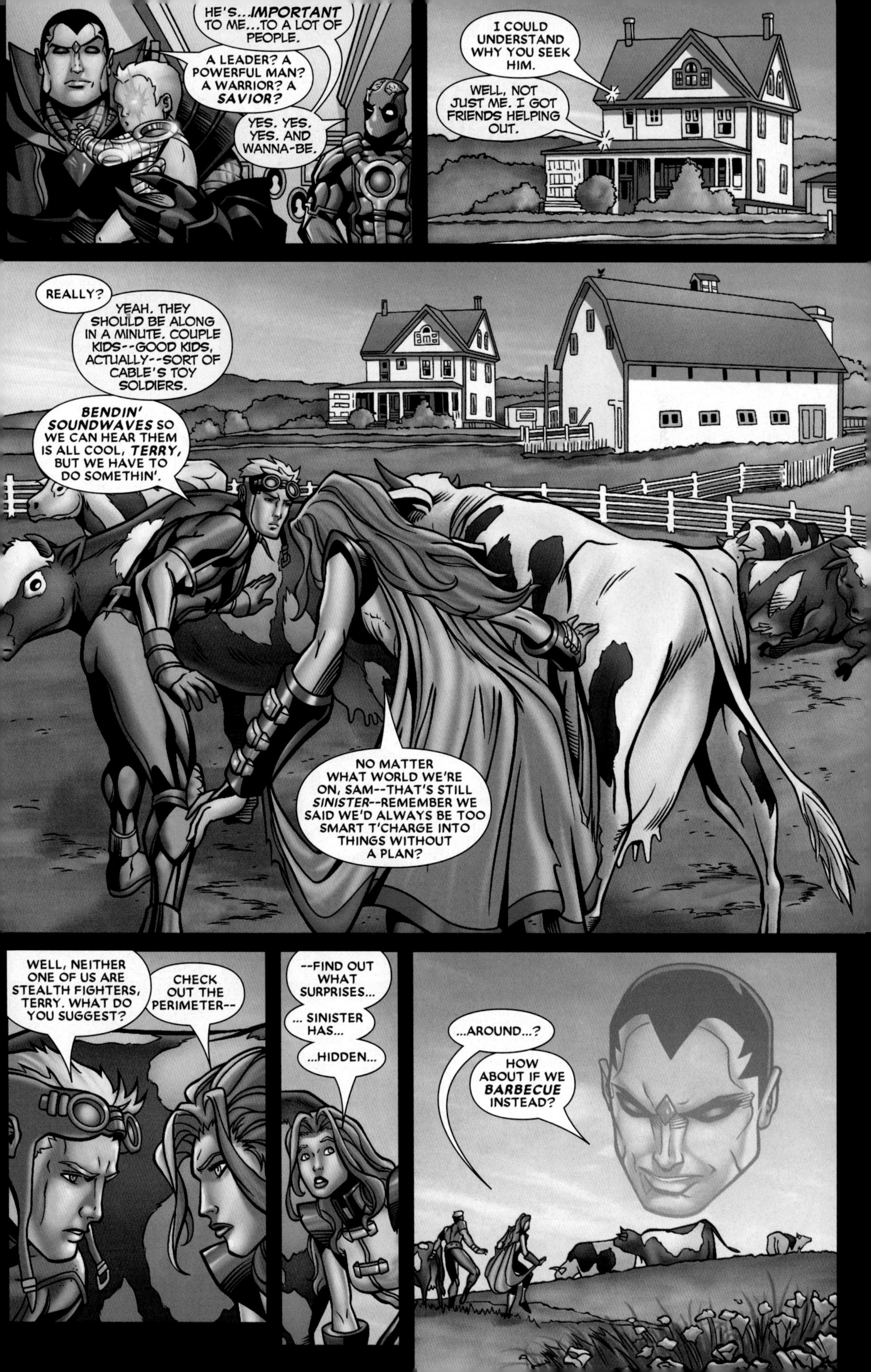
HE'S...IMPORTANT TO ME...TO A LOT OF PEOPLE.
A LEADER? A POWERFUL MAN? A WARRIOR? A SAVIOR?
YES. YES. YES. AND WANNA-BE.
I COULD UNDERSTAND WHY YOU SEEK HIM.
WELL, NOT JUST ME. I GOT FRIENDS HELPING OUT.
REALLY?
YEAH. THEY SHOULD BE ALONG IN A MINUTE. COUPLE KIDS--GOOD KIDS, ACTUALLY--SORT OF CABLE'S TOY SOLDIERS.
BENDIN' SOUNDWAVES SO WE CAN HEAR THEM IS ALL COOL, TERRY, BUT WE HAVE TO DO SOMETHIN'.
NO MATTER WHAT WORLD WE'RE ON, SAM--THAT'S STILL SINISTER--REMEMBER WE SAID WE'D ALWAYS BE TOO SMART T'CHARGE INTO THINGS WITHOUT A PLAN?
WELL, NEITHER ONE OF US ARE STEALTH FIGHTERS, TERRY. WHAT DO YOU SUGGEST?
CHECK OUT THE PERIMETER--
--FIND OUT WHAT SURPRISES...
... SINISTER HAS...
...HIDDEN...
...AROUND...?
HOW ABOUT IF WE BARBECUE INSTEAD?

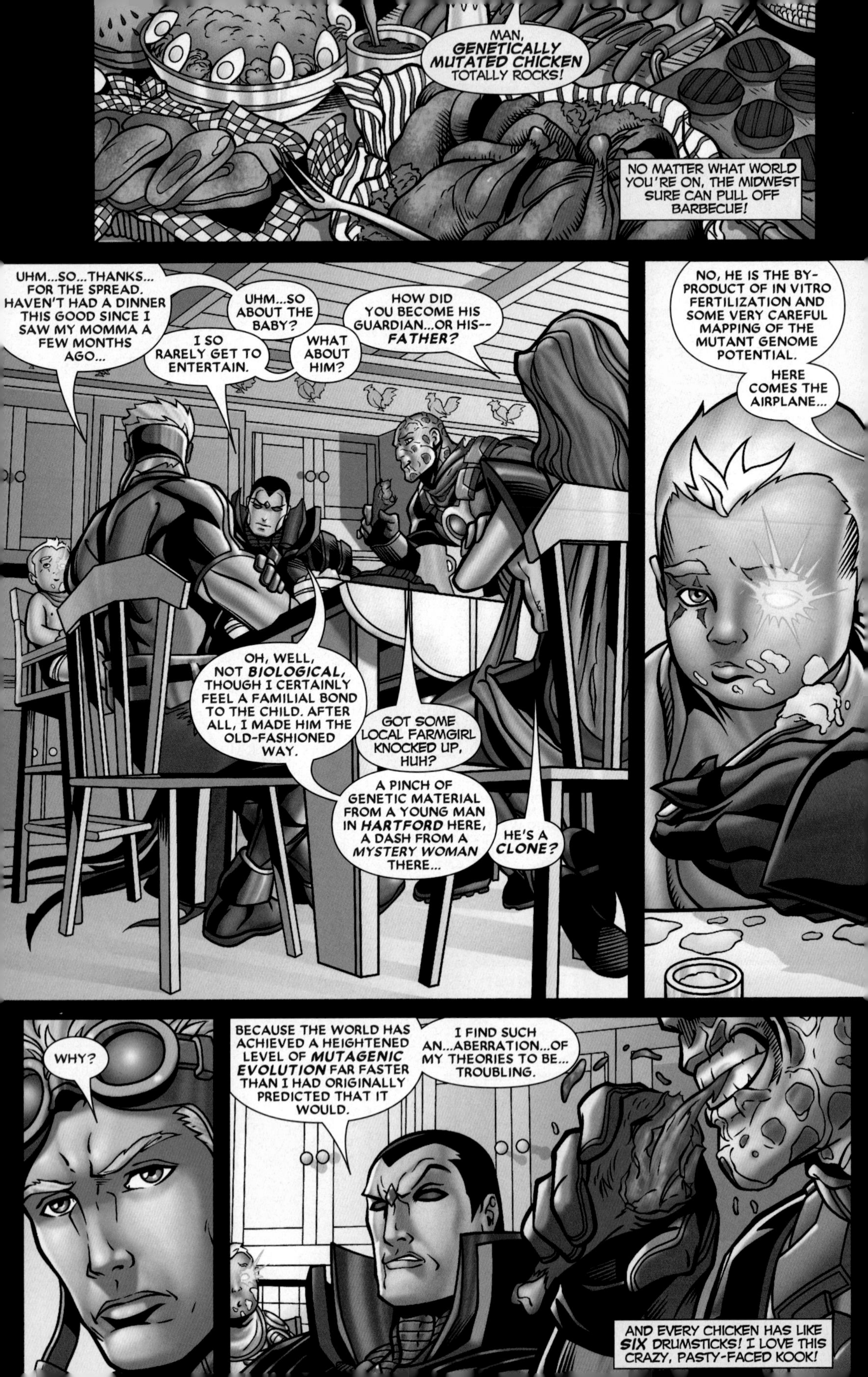
MAN, GENETICALLY MUTATED CHICKEN TOTALLY ROCKS!
NO MATTER WHAT WORLD YOU'RE ON, THE MIDWEST SURE CAN PULL OFF BARBECUE!
UHM...SO...THANKS... FOR THE SPREAD. HAVEN'T HAD A DINNER THIS GOOD SINCE I SAW MY MOMMA A FEW MONTHS AGO...
I SO RARELY GET TO ENTERTAIN.
UHM...SO ABOUT THE BABY?
WHAT ABOUT HIM?
HOW DID YOU BECOME HIS GUARDIAN...OR HIS-- FATHER?
OH, WELL, NOT BIOLOGICAL, THOUGH I CERTAINLY FEEL A FAMILIAL BOND TO THE CHILD. AFTER ALL, I MADE HIM THE OLD-FASHIONED WAY.
GOT SOME LOCAL FARMGIRL KNOCKED UP, HUH?
A PINCH OF GENETIC MATERIAL FROM A YOUNG MAN IN HARTFORD HERE, A DASH FROM A MYSTERY WOMAN THERE...
HE'S A CLONE?
NO, HE IS THE BY-PRODUCT OF IN VITRO FERTILIZATION AND SOME VERY CAREFUL MAPPING OF THE MUTANT GENOME POTENTIAL.
HERE COMES THE AIRPLANE...
WHY?
BECAUSE THE WORLD HAS ACHIEVED A HEIGHTENED LEVEL OF MUTAGENIC EVOLUTION FAR FASTER THAN I HAD ORIGINALLY PREDICTED THAT IT WOULD.
I FIND SUCH AN...ABERRATION...OF MY THEORIES TO BE... TROUBLING.
AND EVERY CHICKEN HAS LIKE SIX DRUMSTICKS! I LOVE THIS CRAZY, PASTY-FACED KOOK!

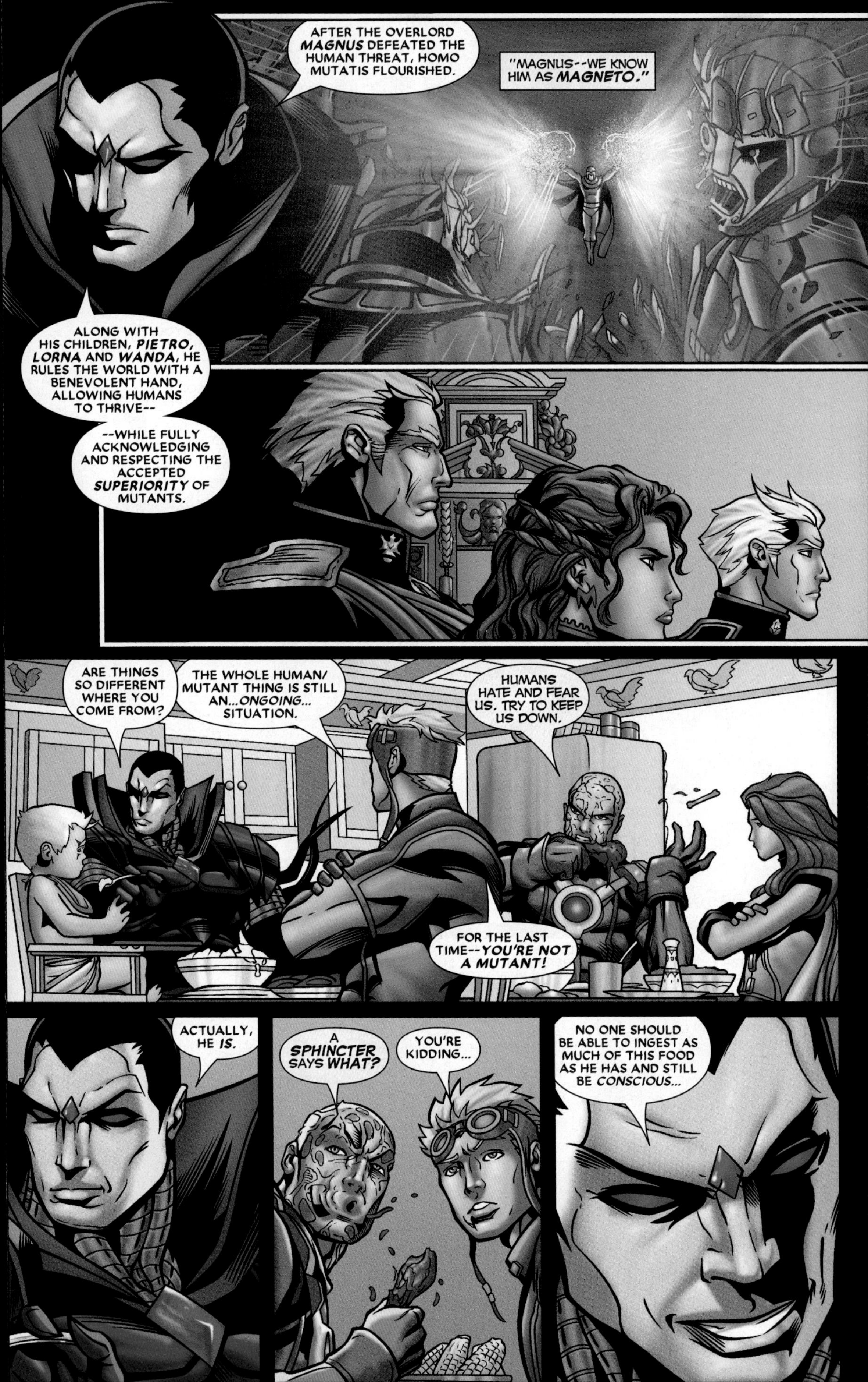
AFTER THE OVERLORD *MAGNUS* DEFEATED THE HUMAN THREAT, HOMO MUTATIS FLOURISHED.
"MAGNUS--WE KNOW HIM AS *MAGNETO*."
ALONG WITH HIS CHILDREN, *PIETRO, LORNA* AND *WANDA*, HE RULES THE WORLD WITH A BENEVOLENT HAND, ALLOWING HUMANS TO THRIVE--
--WHILE FULLY ACKNOWLEDGING AND RESPECTING THE ACCEPTED *SUPERIORITY* OF MUTANTS.
ARE THINGS SO DIFFERENT WHERE YOU COME FROM?
THE WHOLE HUMAN/ MUTANT THING IS STILL AN...*ONGOING*... SITUATION.
HUMANS HATE AND FEAR US. TRY TO KEEP US DOWN.
FOR THE LAST TIME--*YOU'RE NOT A MUTANT!*
ACTUALLY, HE *IS*.
A *SPHINCTER* SAYS *WHAT?*
YOU'RE KIDDING...
NO ONE SHOULD BE ABLE TO INGEST AS MUCH OF THIS FOOD AS HE HAS AND STILL BE *CONSCIOUS*...

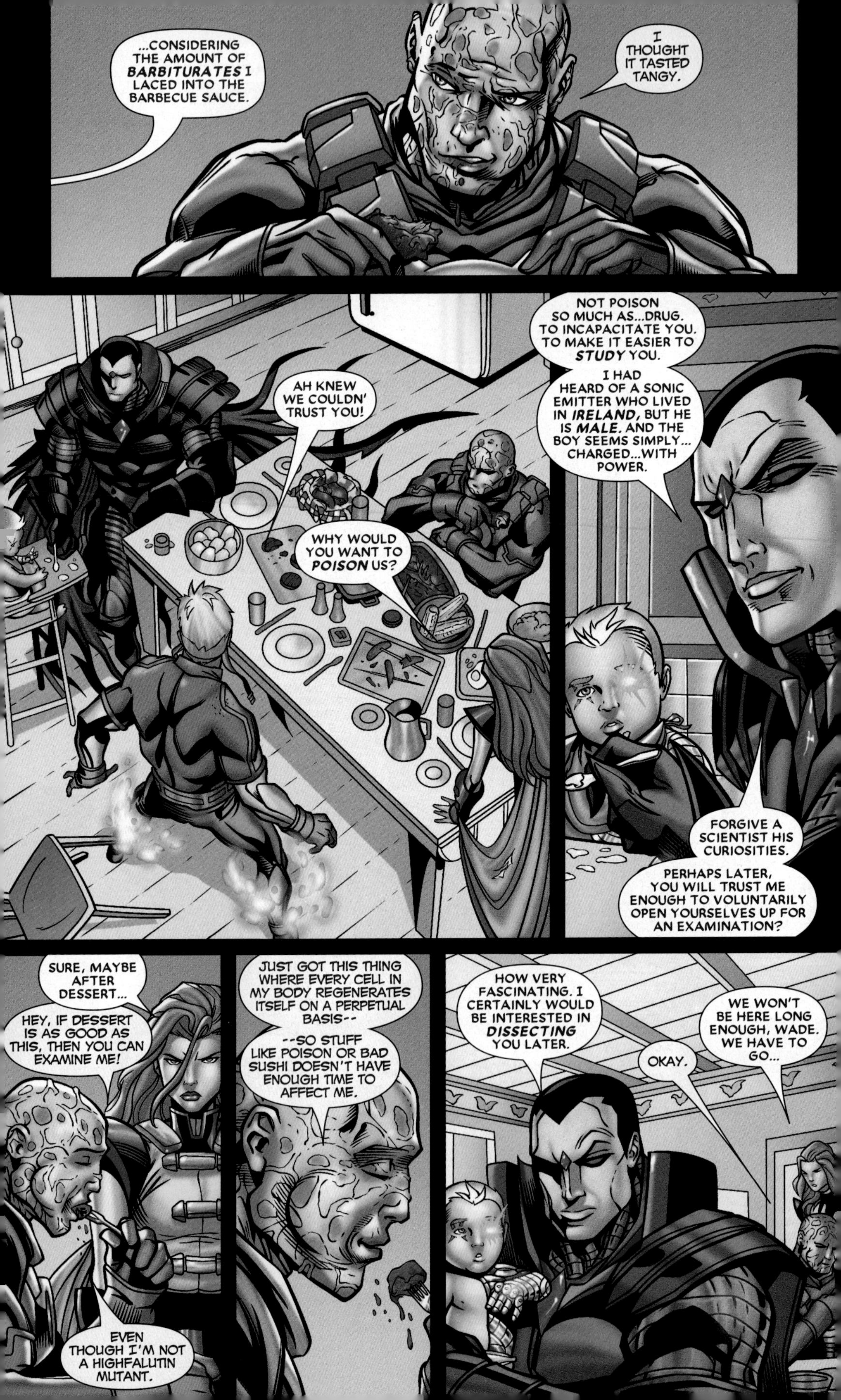

...CONSIDERING THE AMOUNT OF BARBITURATES I LACED INTO THE BARBECUE SAUCE.
I THOUGHT IT TASTED TANGY.
AH KNEW WE COULDN' TRUST YOU!
WHY WOULD YOU WANT TO POISON US?
NOT POISON SO MUCH AS...DRUG. TO INCAPACITATE YOU. TO MAKE IT EASIER TO STUDY YOU.
I HAD HEARD OF A SONIC EMITTER WHO LIVED IN IRELAND, BUT HE IS MALE. AND THE BOY SEEMS SIMPLY... CHARGED...WITH POWER.
FORGIVE A SCIENTIST HIS CURIOSITIES.
PERHAPS LATER, YOU WILL TRUST ME ENOUGH TO VOLUNTARILY OPEN YOURSELVES UP FOR AN EXAMINATION?
SURE, MAYBE AFTER DESSERT...
HEY, IF DESSERT IS AS GOOD AS THIS, THEN YOU CAN EXAMINE ME!
EVEN THOUGH I'M NOT A HIGHFALUTIN MUTANT.
JUST GOT THIS THING WHERE EVERY CELL IN MY BODY REGENERATES ITSELF ON A PERPETUAL BASIS--
--SO STUFF LIKE POISON OR BAD SUSHI DOESN'T HAVE ENOUGH TIME TO AFFECT ME.
HOW VERY FASCINATING. I CERTAINLY WOULD BE INTERESTED IN DISSECTING YOU LATER.
OKAY.
WE WON'T BE HERE LONG ENOUGH, WADE. WE HAVE TO GO...

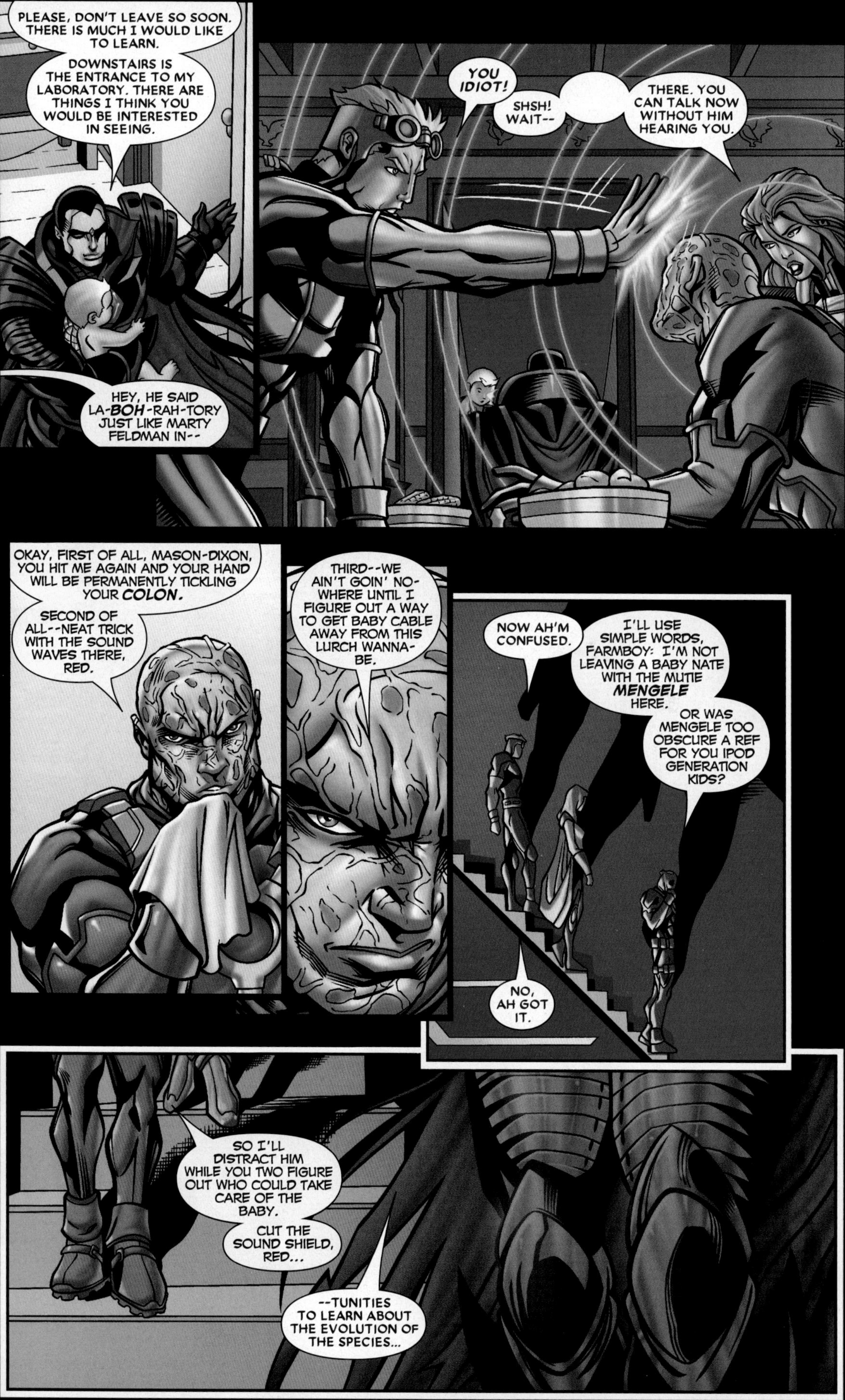
PLEASE, DON'T LEAVE SO SOON. THERE IS MUCH I WOULD LIKE TO LEARN.
DOWNSTAIRS IS THE ENTRANCE TO MY LABORATORY. THERE ARE THINGS I THINK YOU WOULD BE INTERESTED IN SEEING.
HEY, HE SAID LA-BOH-RAH-TORY JUST LIKE MARTY FELDMAN IN--
YOU IDIOT!
SHSH! WAIT--
THERE. YOU CAN TALK NOW WITHOUT HIM HEARING YOU.
OKAY, FIRST OF ALL, MASON-DIXON, YOU HIT ME AGAIN AND YOUR HAND WILL BE PERMANENTLY TICKLING YOUR COLON.
SECOND OF ALL--NEAT TRICK WITH THE SOUND WAVES THERE, RED.
THIRD--WE AIN'T GOIN' NO-WHERE UNTIL I FIGURE OUT A WAY TO GET BABY CABLE AWAY FROM THIS LURCH WANNA-BE.
NOW AH'M CONFUSED.
I'LL USE SIMPLE WORDS, FARMBOY: I'M NOT LEAVING A BABY NATE WITH THE MUTIE MENGELE HERE.
OR WAS MENGELE TOO OBSCURE A REF FOR YOU IPOD GENERATION KIDS?
NO, AH GOT IT.
SO I'LL DISTRACT HIM WHILE YOU TWO FIGURE OUT WHO COULD TAKE CARE OF THE BABY.
CUT THE SOUND SHIELD, RED...
--TUNITIES TO LEARN ABOUT THE EVOLUTION OF THE SPECIES...

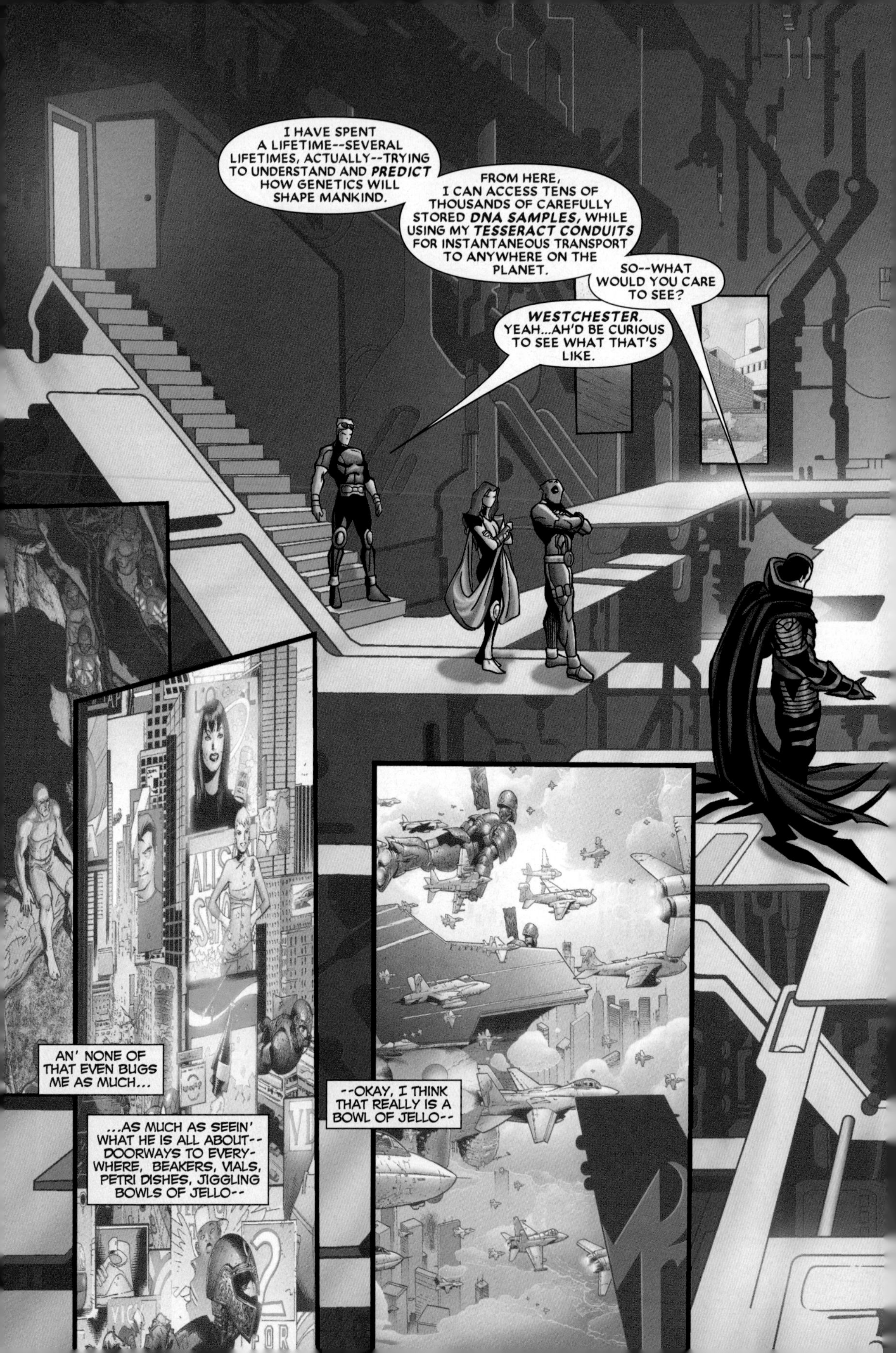

I HAVE SPENT A LIFETIME--SEVERAL LIFETIMES, ACTUALLY--TRYING TO UNDERSTAND AND PREDICT HOW GENETICS WILL SHAPE MANKIND.
FROM HERE, I CAN ACCESS TENS OF THOUSANDS OF CAREFULLY STORED DNA SAMPLES, WHILE USING MY TESSERACT CONDUITS FOR INSTANTANEOUS TRANSPORT TO ANYWHERE ON THE PLANET.
SO--WHAT WOULD YOU CARE TO SEE?
WESTCHESTER. YEAH...AH'D BE CURIOUS TO SEE WHAT THAT'S LIKE.
AN' NONE OF THAT EVEN BUGS ME AS MUCH...
...AS MUCH AS SEEIN' WHAT HE IS ALL ABOUT--DOORWAYS TO EVERY-WHERE, BEAKERS, VIALS, PETRI DISHES, JIGGLING BOWLS OF JELLO--
--OKAY, I THINK THAT REALLY IS A BOWL OF JELLO--

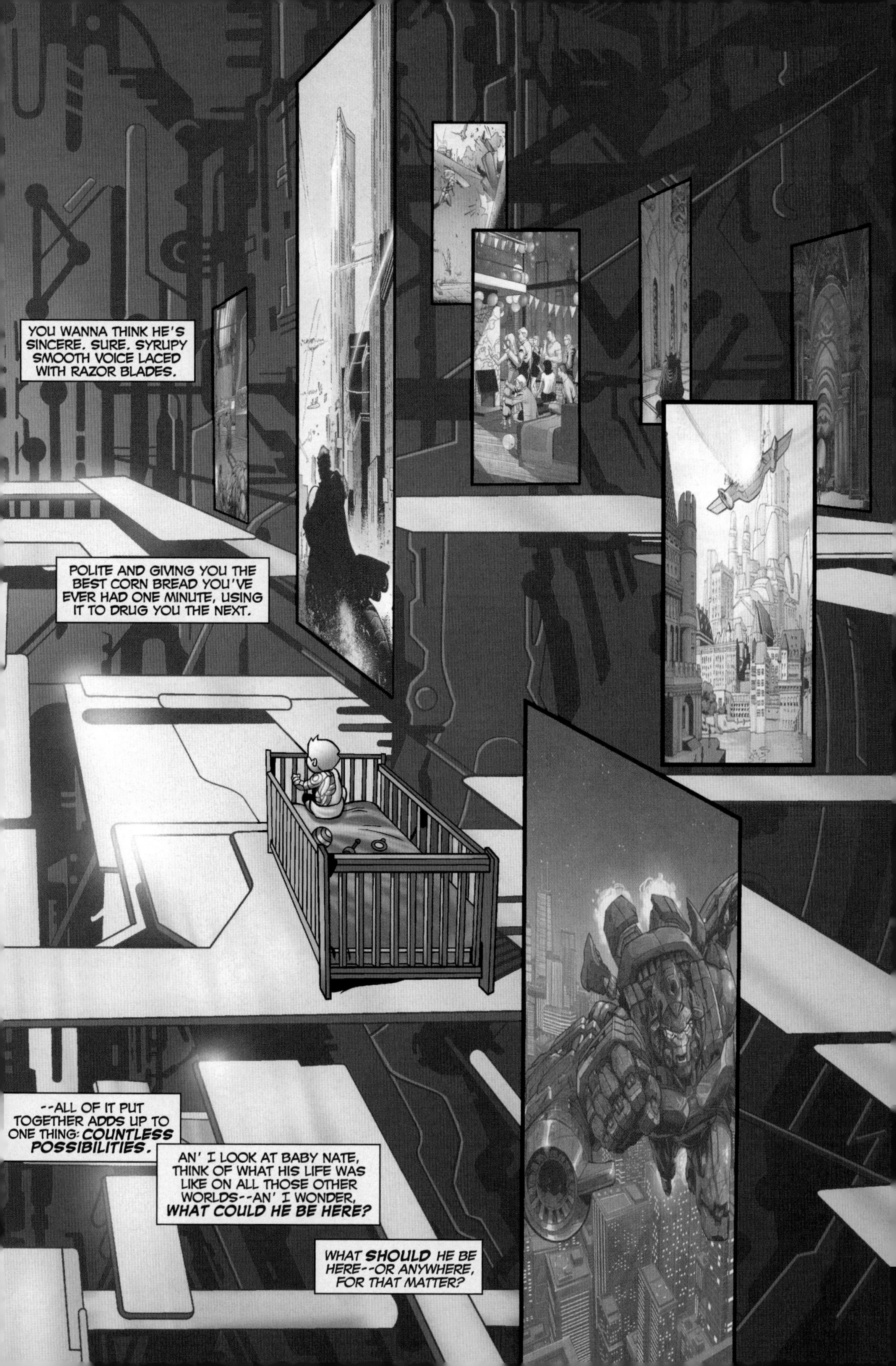

YOU WANNA THINK HE'S SINCERE. SURE. SYRUPY SMOOTH VOICE LACED WITH RAZOR BLADES.
POLITE AND GIVING YOU THE BEST CORN BREAD YOU'VE EVER HAD ONE MINUTE, USING IT TO DRUG YOU THE NEXT.
--ALL OF IT PUT TOGETHER ADDS UP TO ONE THING: *COUNTLESS POSSIBILITIES.*
AN' I LOOK AT BABY NATE, THINK OF WHAT HIS LIFE WAS LIKE ON ALL THOSE OTHER WORLDS--AN' I WONDER, *WHAT COULD HE BE HERE?*
*WHAT **SHOULD** HE BE HERE--OR ANYWHERE, FOR THAT MATTER?*

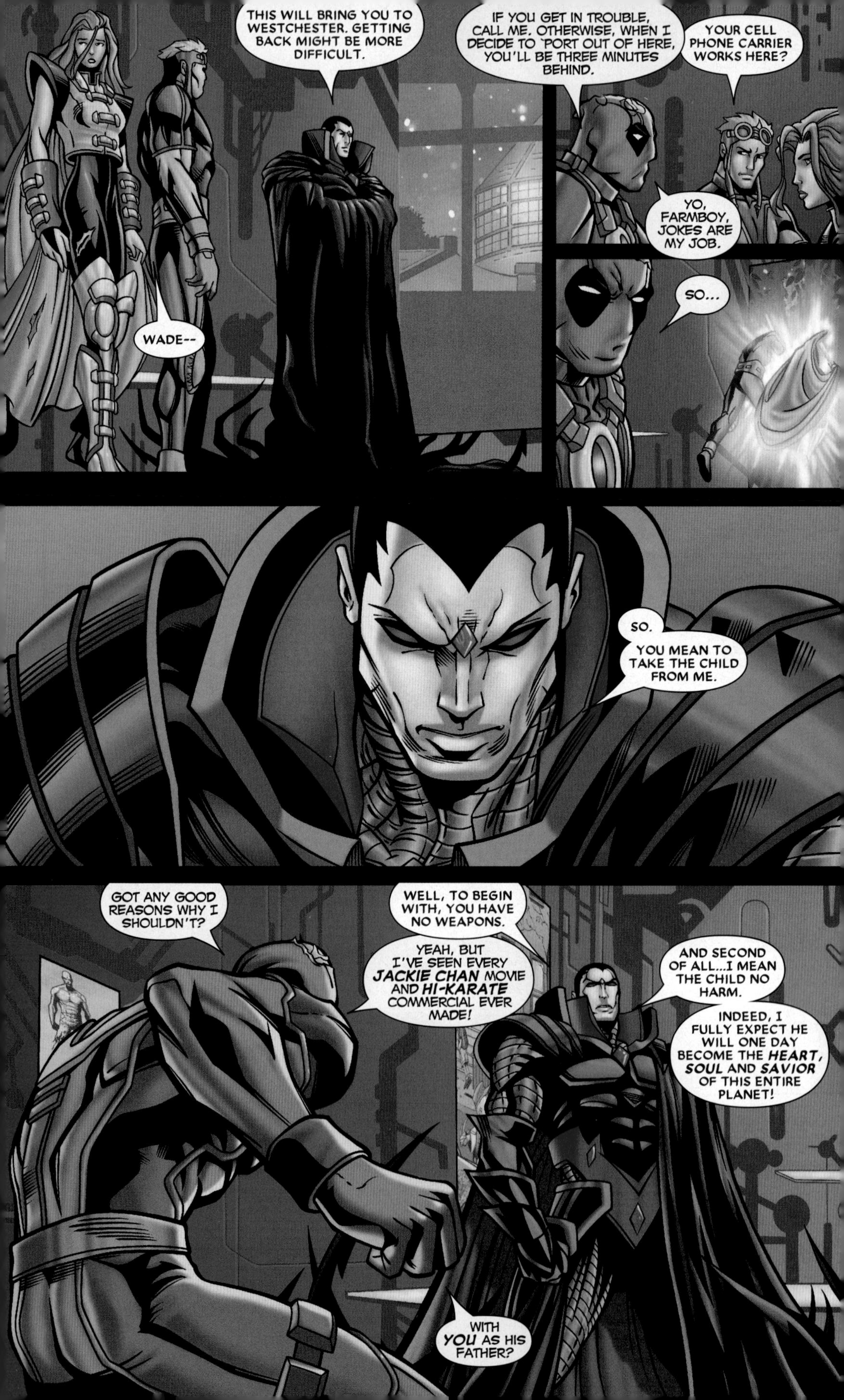
THIS WILL BRING YOU TO WESTCHESTER. GETTING BACK MIGHT BE MORE DIFFICULT.
WADE--
IF YOU GET IN TROUBLE, CALL ME. OTHERWISE, WHEN I DECIDE TO 'PORT OUT OF HERE, YOU'LL BE THREE MINUTES BEHIND.
YOUR CELL PHONE CARRIER WORKS HERE?
YO, FARMBOY, JOKES ARE MY JOB.
SO...
SO.
YOU MEAN TO TAKE THE CHILD FROM ME.
GOT ANY GOOD REASONS WHY I SHOULDN'T?
WELL, TO BEGIN WITH, YOU HAVE NO WEAPONS.
YEAH, BUT I'VE SEEN EVERY JACKIE CHAN MOVIE AND HI-KARATE COMMERCIAL EVER MADE!
AND SECOND OF ALL...I MEAN THE CHILD NO HARM.
INDEED, I FULLY EXPECT HE WILL ONE DAY BECOME THE HEART, SOUL AND SAVIOR OF THIS ENTIRE PLANET!
WITH YOU AS HIS FATHER?

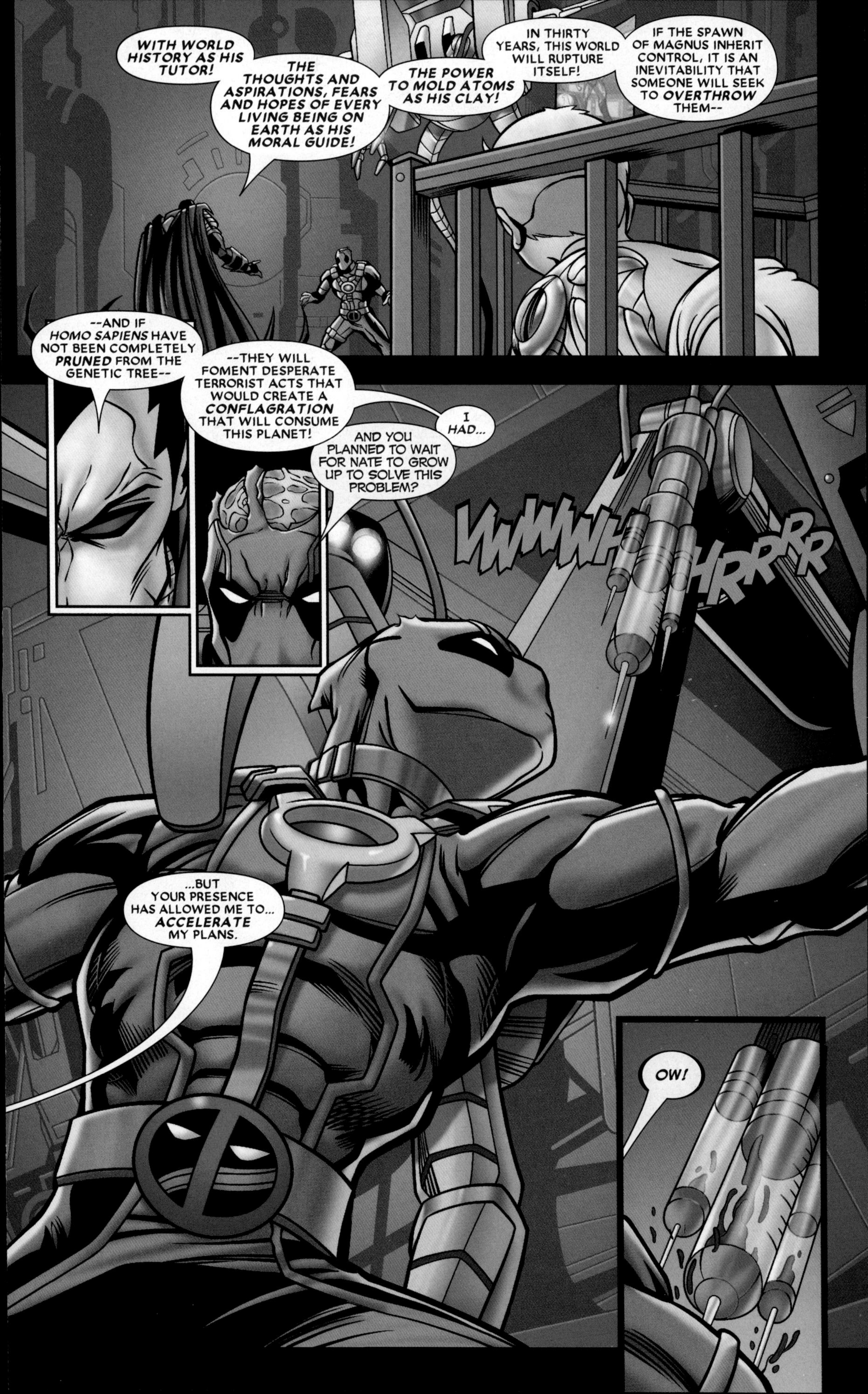
WITH WORLD HISTORY AS HIS TUTOR!
THE THOUGHTS AND ASPIRATIONS, FEARS AND HOPES OF EVERY LIVING BEING ON EARTH AS HIS MORAL GUIDE!
THE POWER TO MOLD ATOMS AS HIS CLAY!
IN THIRTY YEARS, THIS WORLD WILL RUPTURE ITSELF!
IF THE SPAWN OF MAGNUS INHERIT CONTROL, IT IS AN INEVITABILITY THAT SOMEONE WILL SEEK TO OVERTHROW THEM--
--AND IF HOMO SAPIENS HAVE NOT BEEN COMPLETELY PRUNED FROM THE GENETIC TREE--
--THEY WILL FOMENT DESPERATE TERRORIST ACTS THAT WOULD CREATE A CONFLAGRATION THAT WILL CONSUME THIS PLANET!
AND YOU PLANNED TO WAIT FOR NATE TO GROW UP TO SOLVE THIS PROBLEM?
I HAD...
VWWWHRRRR
...BUT YOUR PRESENCE HAS ALLOWED ME TO... ACCELERATE MY PLANS.
OW!

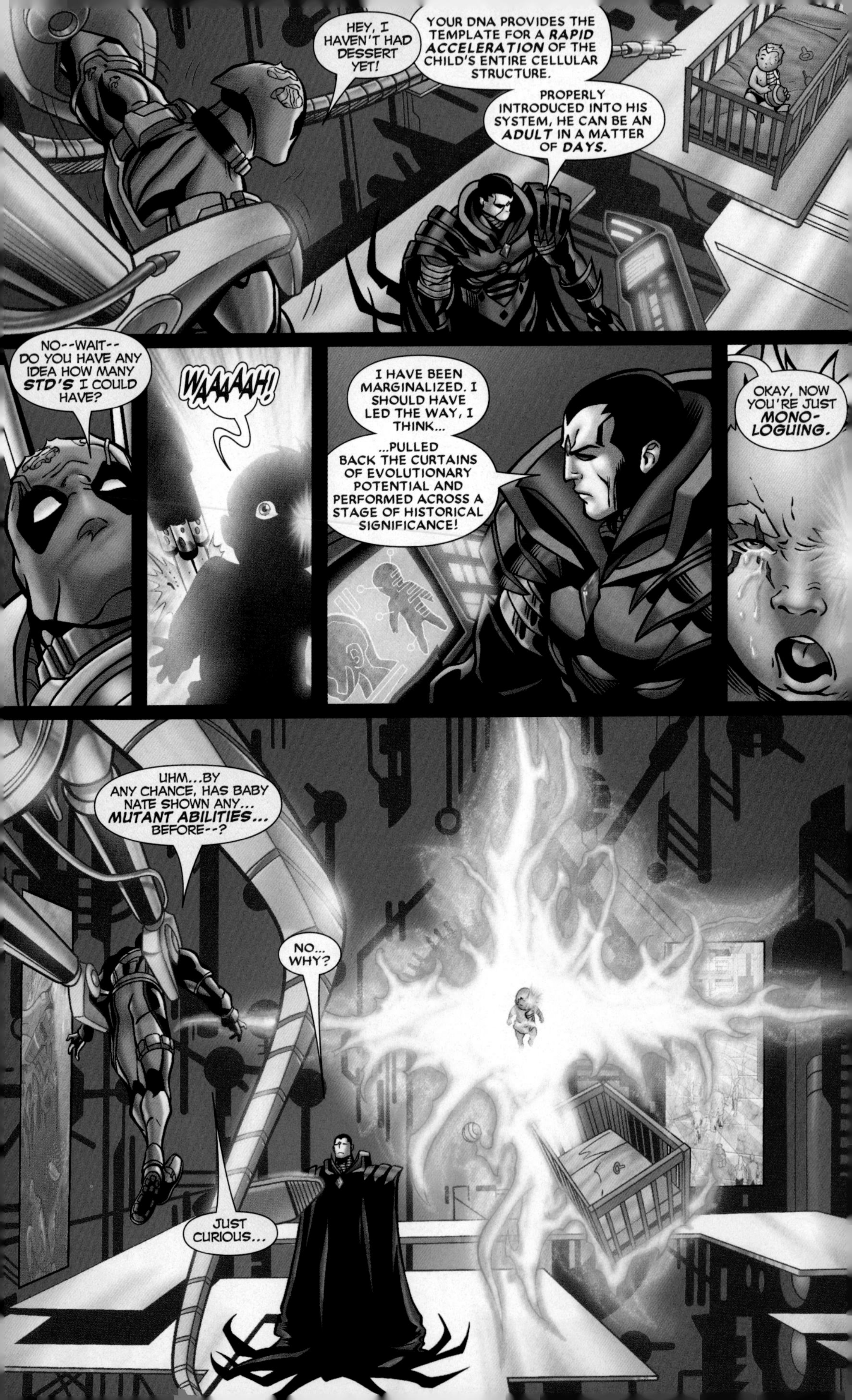
HEY, I HAVEN'T HAD DESSERT YET!
YOUR DNA PROVIDES THE TEMPLATE FOR A RAPID ACCELERATION OF THE CHILD'S ENTIRE CELLULAR STRUCTURE.
PROPERLY INTRODUCED INTO HIS SYSTEM, HE CAN BE AN ADULT IN A MATTER OF DAYS.
NO--WAIT-- DO YOU HAVE ANY IDEA HOW MANY STD'S I COULD HAVE?
WAAAAAH!
I HAVE BEEN MARGINALIZED. I SHOULD HAVE LED THE WAY, I THINK...
...PULLED BACK THE CURTAINS OF EVOLUTIONARY POTENTIAL AND PERFORMED ACROSS A STAGE OF HISTORICAL SIGNIFICANCE!
OKAY, NOW YOU'RE JUST MONO-LOGUING.
UHM...BY ANY CHANCE, HAS BABY NATE SHOWN ANY... MUTANT ABILITIES... BEFORE--?
NO... WHY?
JUST CURIOUS...

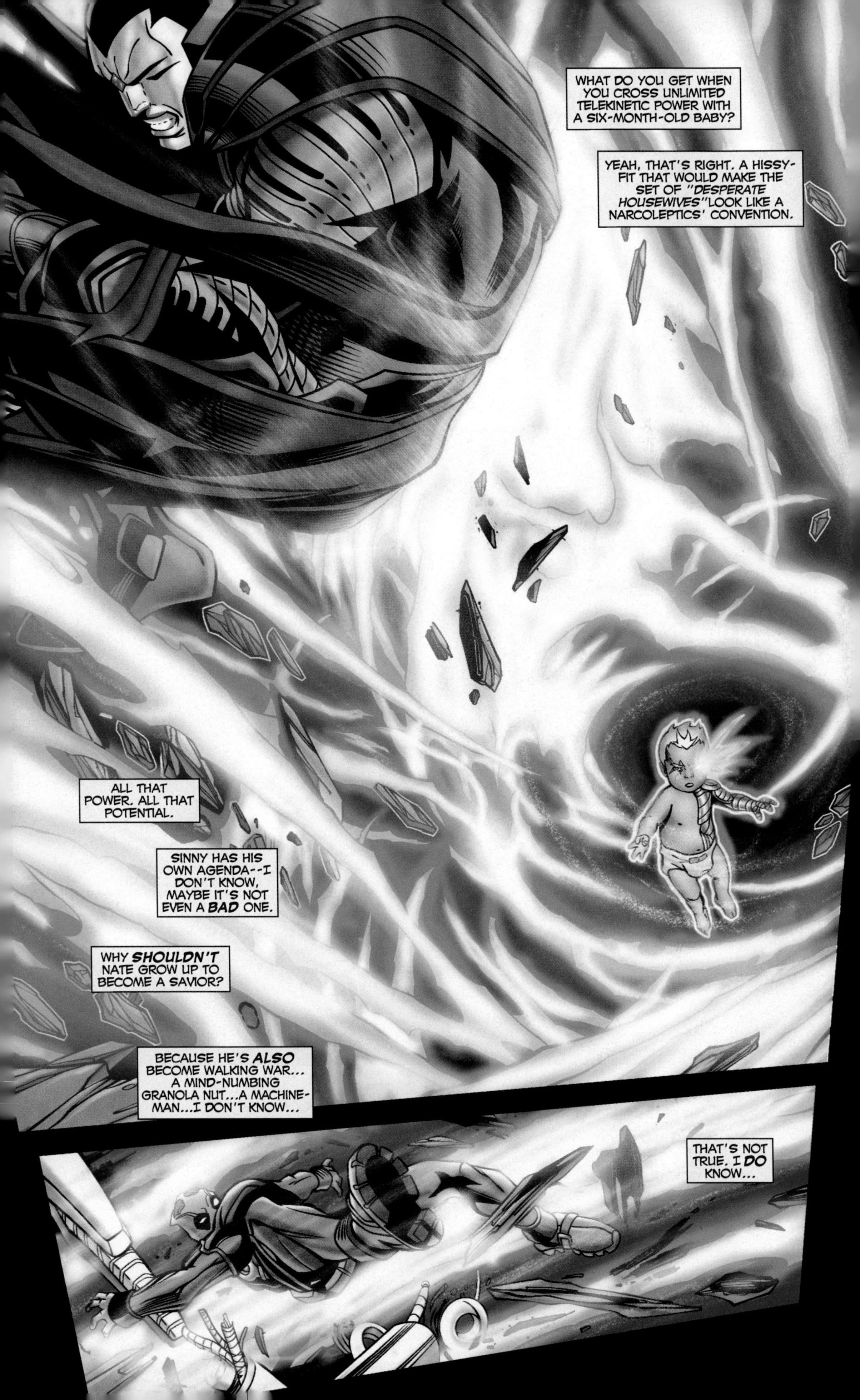
WHAT DO YOU GET WHEN YOU CROSS UNLIMITED TELEKINETIC POWER WITH A SIX-MONTH-OLD BABY?
YEAH, THAT'S RIGHT. A HISSY-FIT THAT WOULD MAKE THE SET OF "DESPERATE HOUSEWIVES" LOOK LIKE A NARCOLEPTICS' CONVENTION.
ALL THAT POWER. ALL THAT POTENTIAL.
SINNY HAS HIS OWN AGENDA--I DON'T KNOW, MAYBE IT'S NOT EVEN A BAD ONE.
WHY SHOULDN'T NATE GROW UP TO BECOME A SAVIOR?
BECAUSE HE'S ALSO BECOME WALKING WAR... A MIND-NUMBING GRANOLA NUT...A MACHINE-MAN...I DON'T KNOW...
THAT'S NOT TRUE. I DO KNOW...

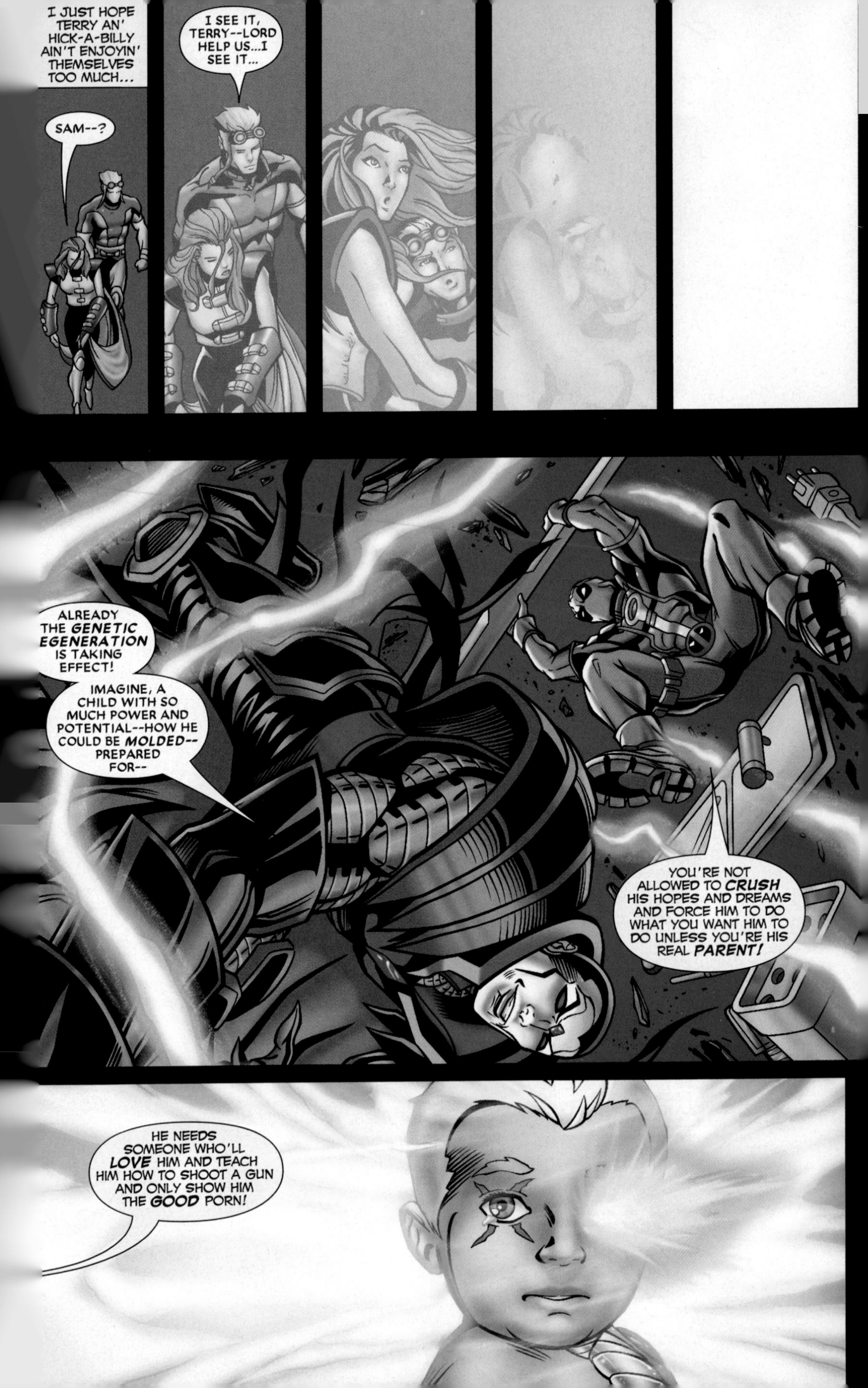
I JUST HOPE TERRY AN' HICK-A-BILLY AIN'T ENJOYIN' THEMSELVES TOO MUCH...
SAM--?
I SEE IT, TERRY--LORD HELP US...I SEE IT...
ALREADY THE GENETIC EGENERATION IS TAKING EFFECT!
IMAGINE, A CHILD WITH SO MUCH POWER AND POTENTIAL--HOW HE COULD BE MOLDED--PREPARED FOR--
YOU'RE NOT ALLOWED TO CRUSH HIS HOPES AND DREAMS AND FORCE HIM TO DO WHAT YOU WANT HIM TO DO UNLESS YOU'RE HIS REAL PARENT!
HE NEEDS SOMEONE WHO'LL LOVE HIM AND TEACH HIM HOW TO SHOOT A GUN AND ONLY SHOW HIM THE GOOD PORN!

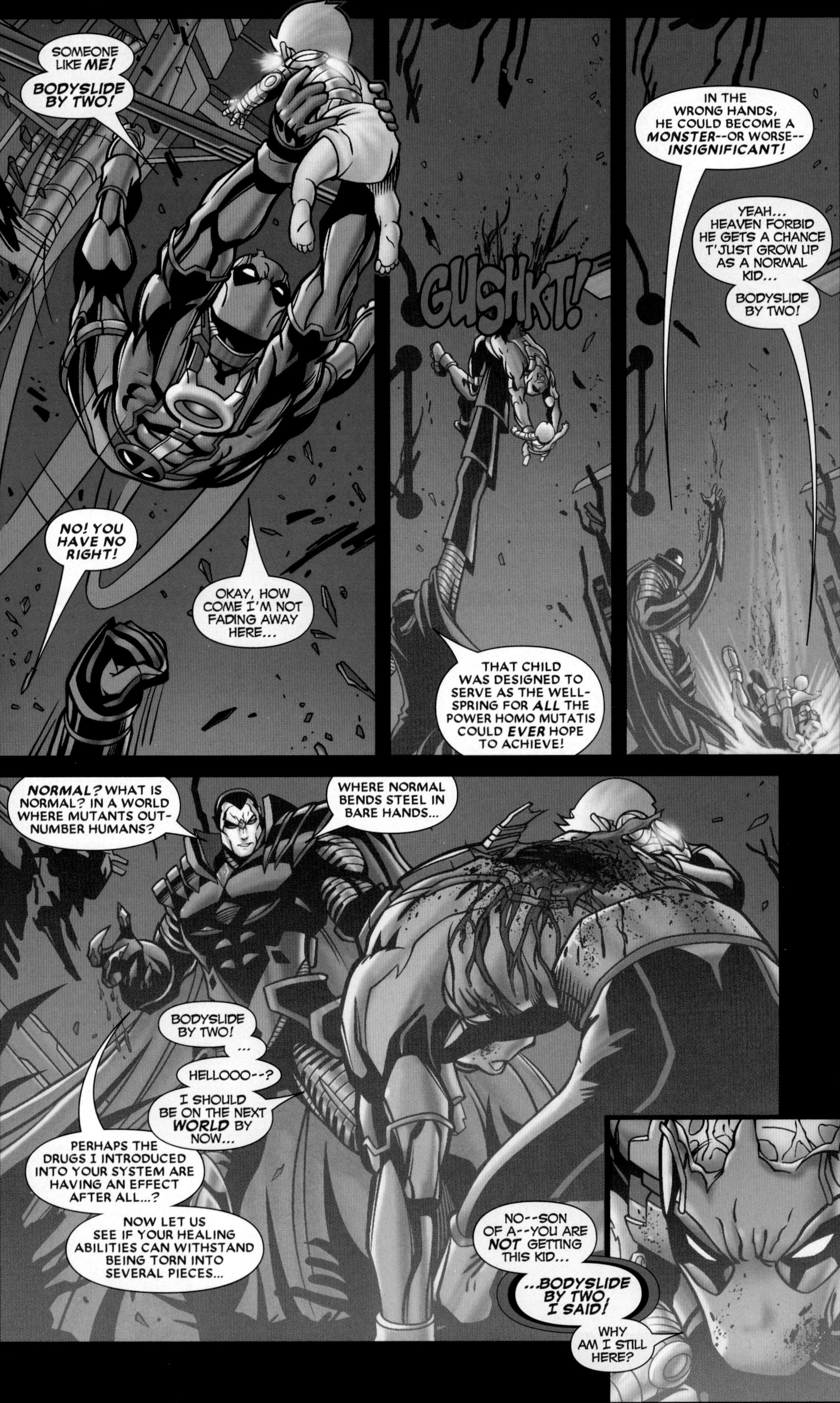
SOMEONE LIKE ME!
BODYSLIDE BY TWO!
NO! YOU HAVE NO RIGHT!
OKAY, HOW COME I'M NOT FADING AWAY HERE...
GUSHKT!
THAT CHILD WAS DESIGNED TO SERVE AS THE WELL-SPRING FOR ALL THE POWER HOMO MUTATIS COULD EVER HOPE TO ACHIEVE!
IN THE WRONG HANDS, HE COULD BECOME A MONSTER--OR WORSE-- INSIGNIFICANT!
YEAH... HEAVEN FORBID HE GETS A CHANCE T'JUST GROW UP AS A NORMAL KID...
BODYSLIDE BY TWO!
NORMAL? WHAT IS NORMAL? IN A WORLD WHERE MUTANTS OUT-NUMBER HUMANS?
WHERE NORMAL BENDS STEEL IN BARE HANDS...
BODYSLIDE BY TWO!
...
HELLOOO--?
I SHOULD BE ON THE NEXT WORLD BY NOW...
PERHAPS THE DRUGS I INTRODUCED INTO YOUR SYSTEM ARE HAVING AN EFFECT AFTER ALL...?
NOW LET US SEE IF YOUR HEALING ABILITIES CAN WITHSTAND BEING TORN INTO SEVERAL PIECES...
NO--SON OF A--YOU ARE NOT GETTING THIS KID...
...BODYSLIDE BY TWO, I SAID!
WHY AM I STILL HERE?

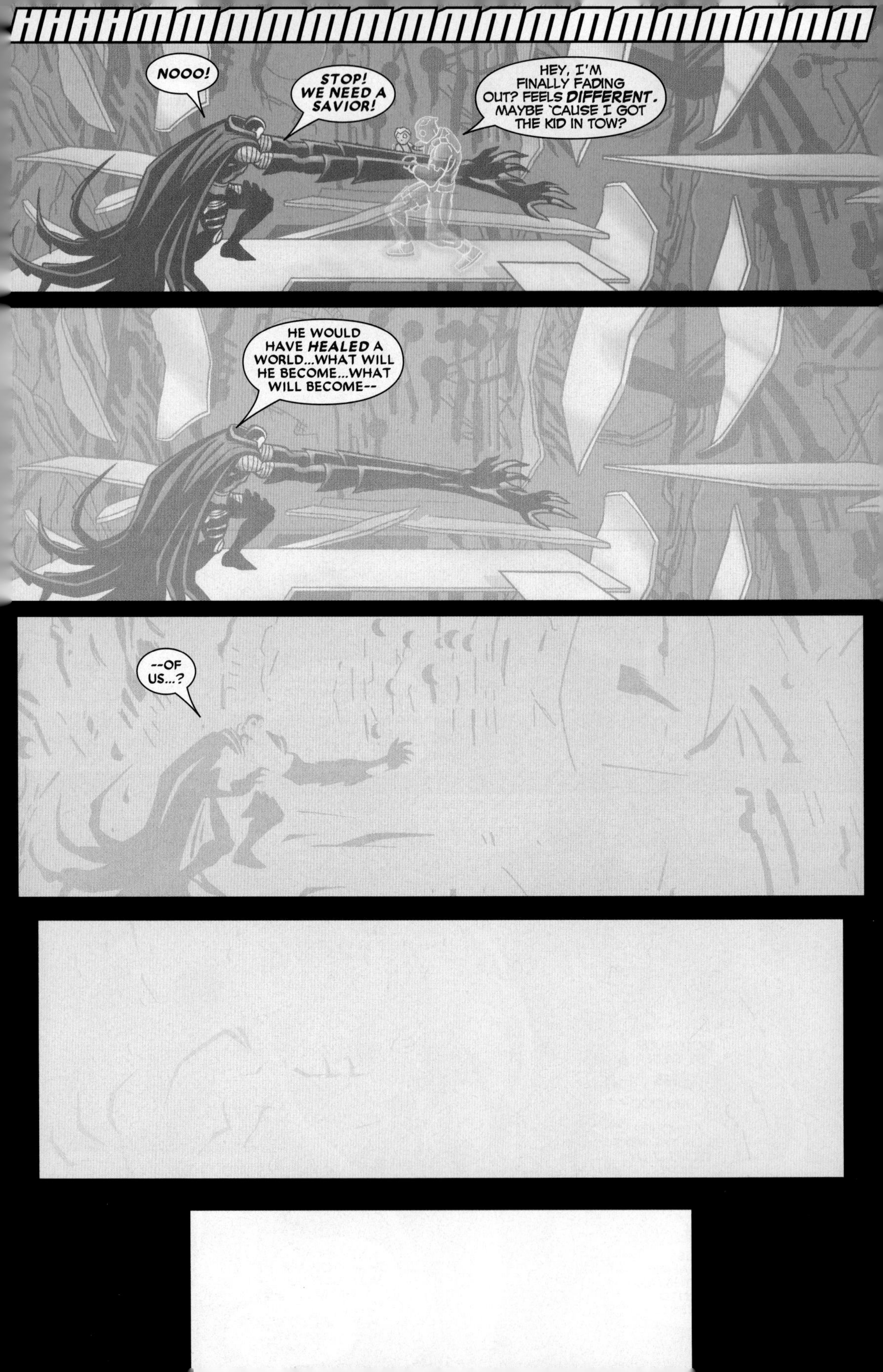

HHHHMMMMMMMMMMMMMMMMMMM
NOOO!
STOP! WE NEED A SAVIOR!
HEY, I'M FINALLY FADING OUT? FEELS DIFFERENT. MAYBE `CAUSE I GOT THE KID IN TOW?
HE WOULD HAVE HEALED A WORLD...WHAT WILL HE BECOME...WHAT WILL BECOME--
--OF US...?

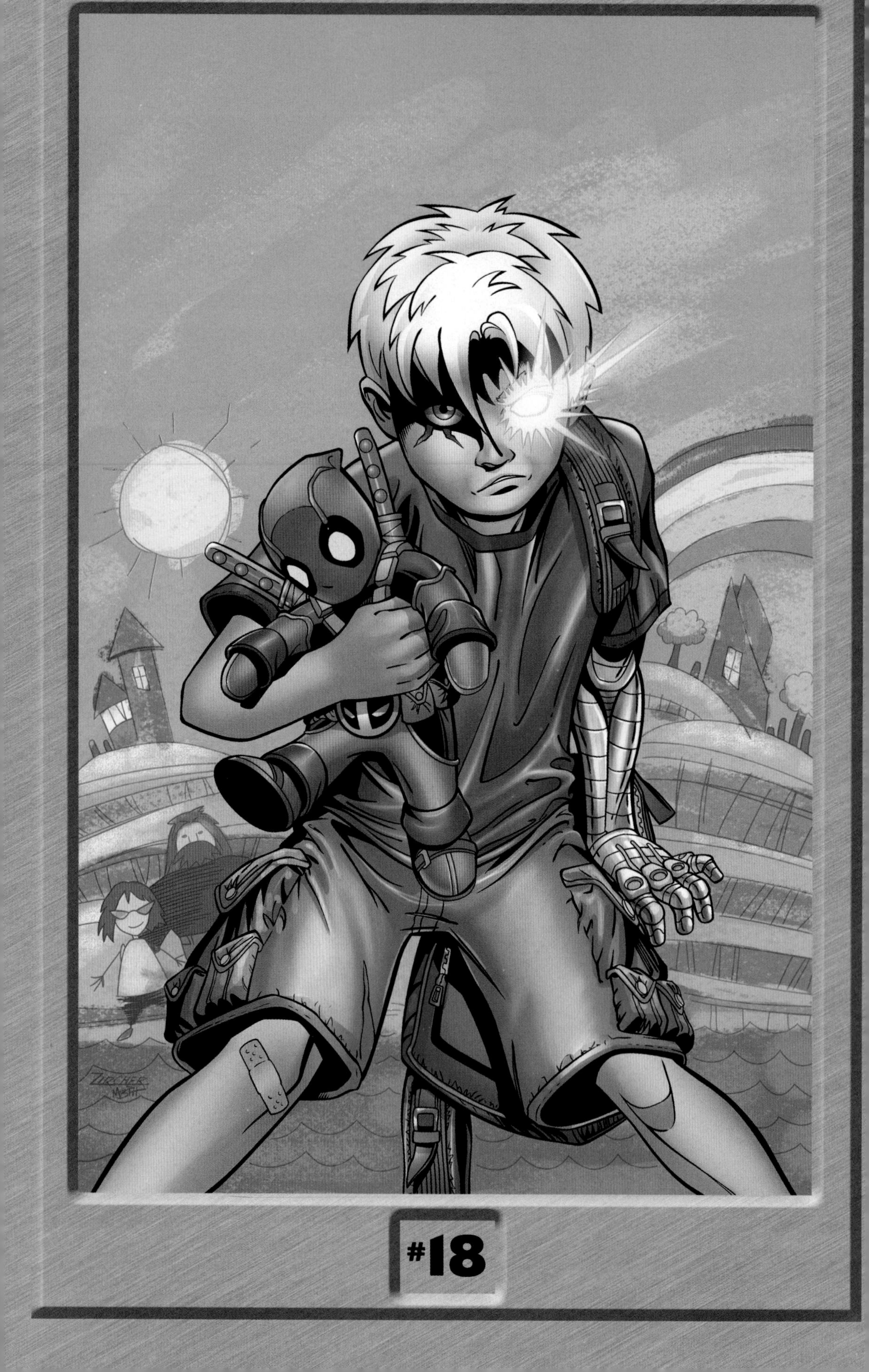
ZIRCHER

#18

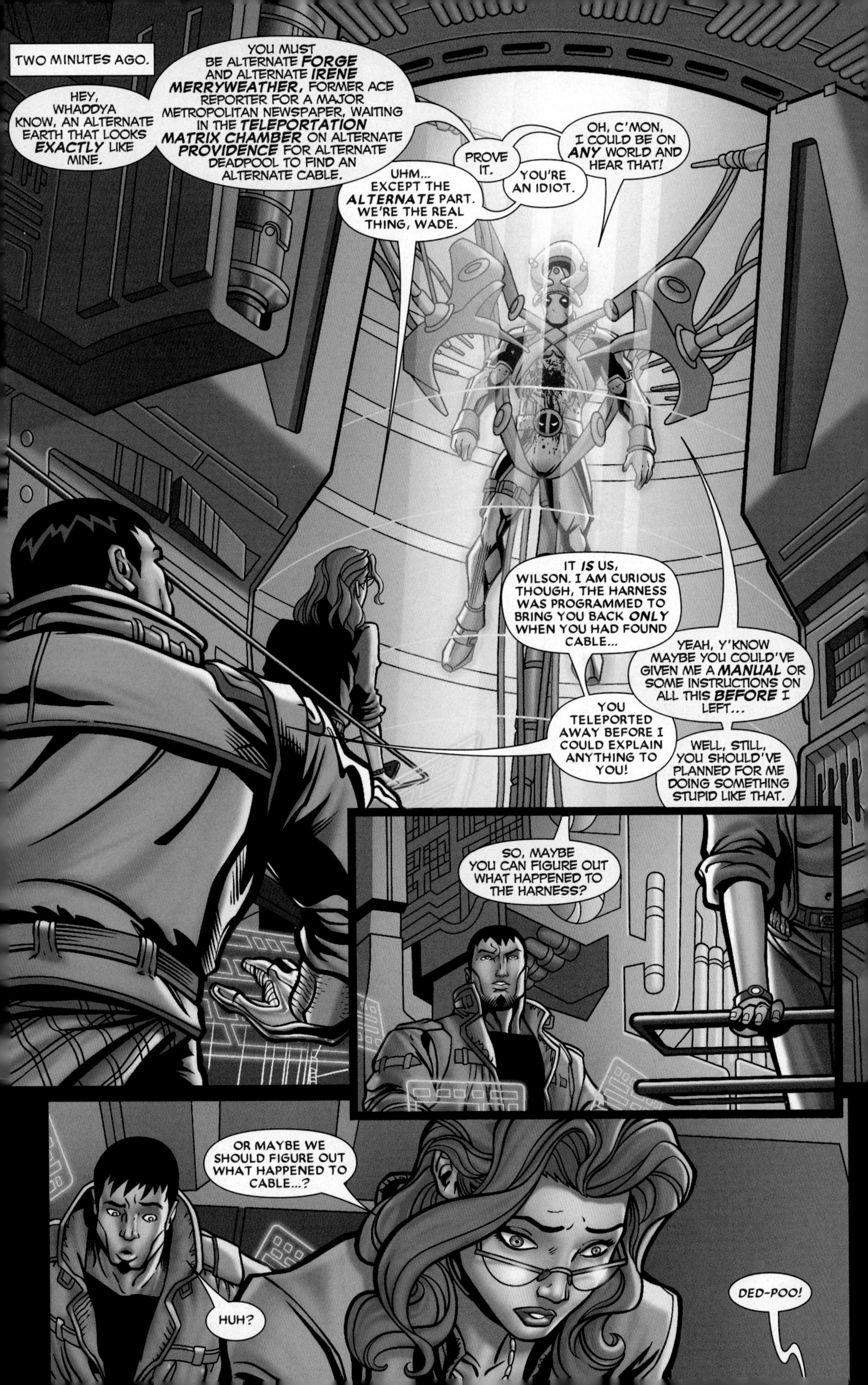
TWO MINUTES AGO.
HEY, WHADDYA KNOW, AN ALTERNATE EARTH THAT LOOKS EXACTLY LIKE MINE.
YOU MUST BE ALTERNATE FORGE AND ALTERNATE IRENE MERRYWEATHER, FORMER ACE REPORTER FOR A MAJOR METROPOLITAN NEWSPAPER, WAITING IN THE TELEPORTATION MATRIX CHAMBER ON ALTERNATE PROVIDENCE FOR ALTERNATE DEADPOOL TO FIND AN ALTERNATE CABLE.
UHM... EXCEPT THE ALTERNATE PART. WE'RE THE REAL THING, WADE.
PROVE IT.
YOU'RE AN IDIOT.
OH, C'MON, I COULD BE ON ANY WORLD AND HEAR THAT!
IT IS US, WILSON. I AM CURIOUS THOUGH, THE HARNESS WAS PROGRAMMED TO BRING YOU BACK ONLY WHEN YOU HAD FOUND CABLE...
YEAH, Y'KNOW MAYBE YOU COULD'VE GIVEN ME A MANUAL OR SOME INSTRUCTIONS ON ALL THIS BEFORE I LEFT...
YOU TELEPORTED AWAY BEFORE I COULD EXPLAIN ANYTHING TO YOU!
WELL, STILL, YOU SHOULD'VE PLANNED FOR ME DOING SOMETHING STUPID LIKE THAT.
SO, MAYBE YOU CAN FIGURE OUT WHAT HAPPENED TO THE HARNESS?
OR MAYBE WE SHOULD FIGURE OUT WHAT HAPPENED TO CABLE...?
HUH?
DED-POO!

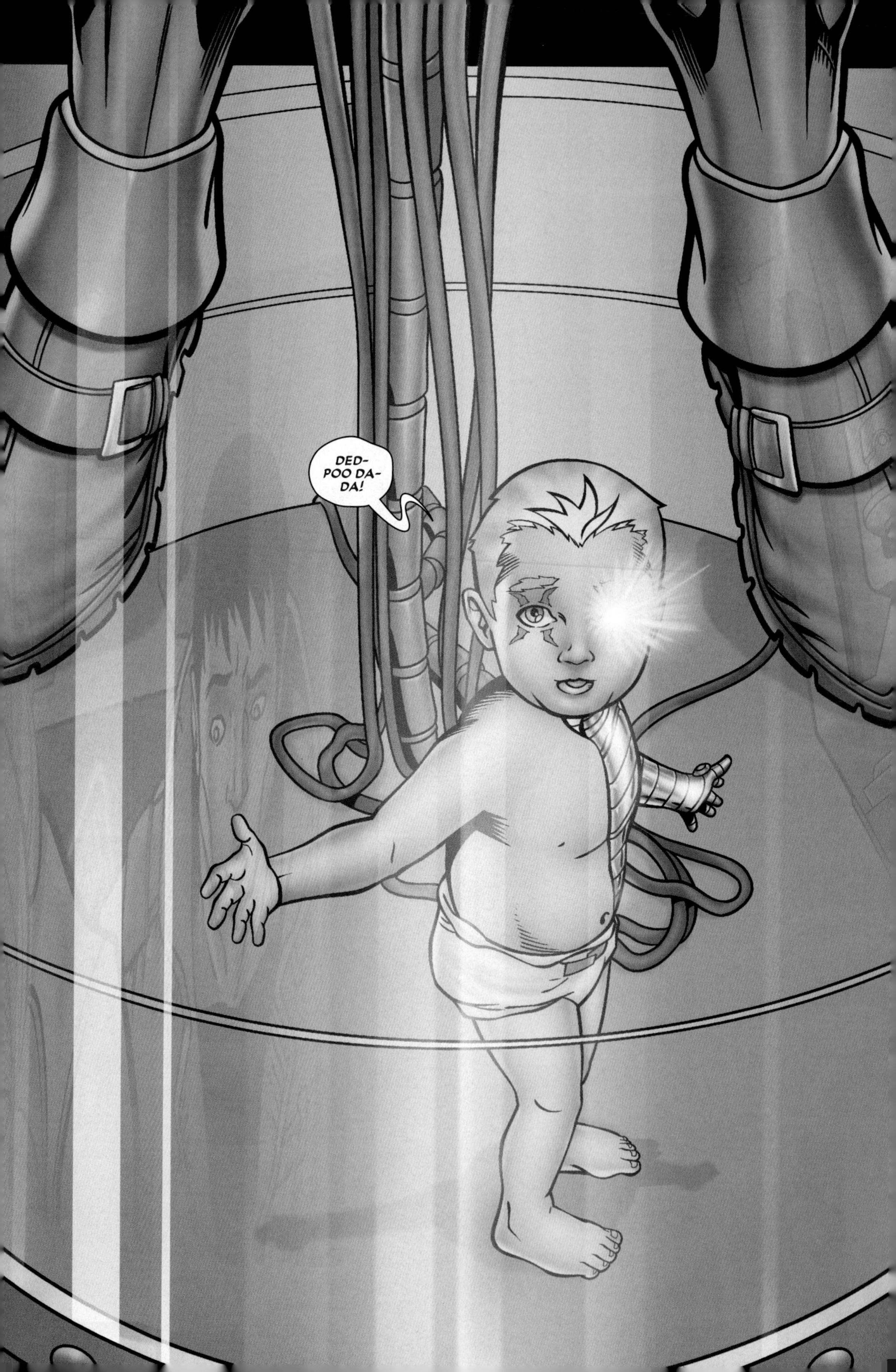
DED-POO DA-DA!

ENEMA OF THE STATE
PART FOUR: "BRINGING UP BABY"

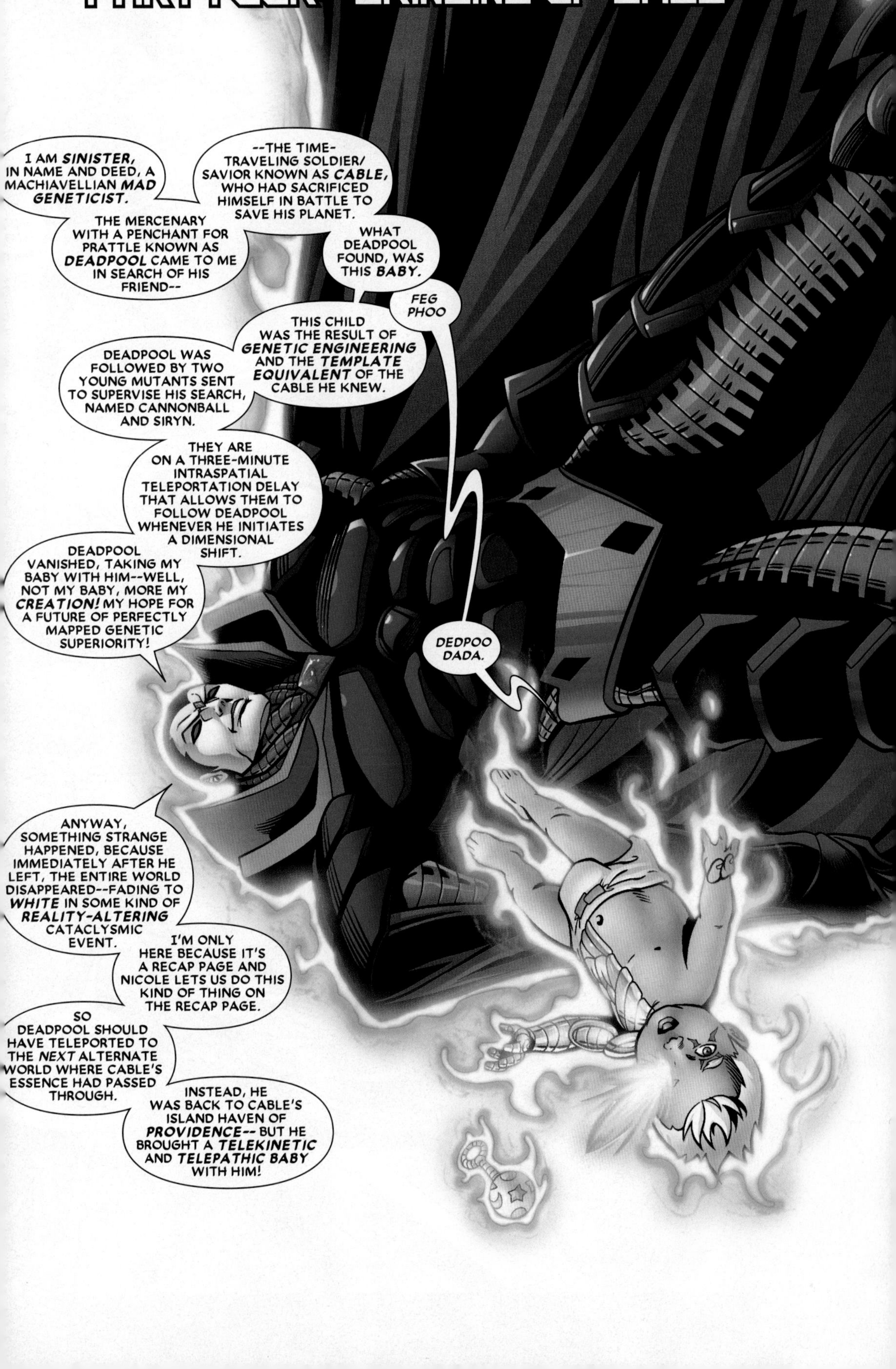
I AM SINISTER, IN NAME AND DEED, A MACHIAVELLIAN MAD GENETICIST.
THE MERCENARY WITH A PENCHANT FOR PRATTLE KNOWN AS DEADPOOL CAME TO ME IN SEARCH OF HIS FRIEND--
--THE TIME-TRAVELING SOLDIER/ SAVIOR KNOWN AS CABLE, WHO HAD SACRIFICED HIMSELF IN BATTLE TO SAVE HIS PLANET.
WHAT DEADPOOL FOUND, WAS THIS BABY.
FEG PHOO
THIS CHILD WAS THE RESULT OF GENETIC ENGINEERING AND THE TEMPLATE EQUIVALENT OF THE CABLE HE KNEW.
DEADPOOL WAS FOLLOWED BY TWO YOUNG MUTANTS SENT TO SUPERVISE HIS SEARCH, NAMED CANNONBALL AND SIRYN.
THEY ARE ON A THREE-MINUTE INTRASPATIAL TELEPORTATION DELAY THAT ALLOWS THEM TO FOLLOW DEADPOOL WHENEVER HE INITIATES A DIMENSIONAL SHIFT.
DEADPOOL VANISHED, TAKING MY BABY WITH HIM--WELL, NOT MY BABY, MORE MY CREATION! MY HOPE FOR A FUTURE OF PERFECTLY MAPPED GENETIC SUPERIORITY!
DEDPOO DADA.
ANYWAY, SOMETHING STRANGE HAPPENED, BECAUSE IMMEDIATELY AFTER HE LEFT, THE ENTIRE WORLD DISAPPEARED--FADING TO WHITE IN SOME KIND OF REALITY-ALTERING CATACLYSMIC EVENT.
I'M ONLY HERE BECAUSE IT'S A RECAP PAGE AND NICOLE LETS US DO THIS KIND OF THING ON THE RECAP PAGE.
SO DEADPOOL SHOULD HAVE TELEPORTED TO THE NEXT ALTERNATE WORLD WHERE CABLE'S ESSENCE HAD PASSED THROUGH.
INSTEAD, HE WAS BACK TO CABLE'S ISLAND HAVEN OF PROVIDENCE-- BUT HE BROUGHT A TELEKINETIC AND TELEPATHIC BABY WITH HIM!

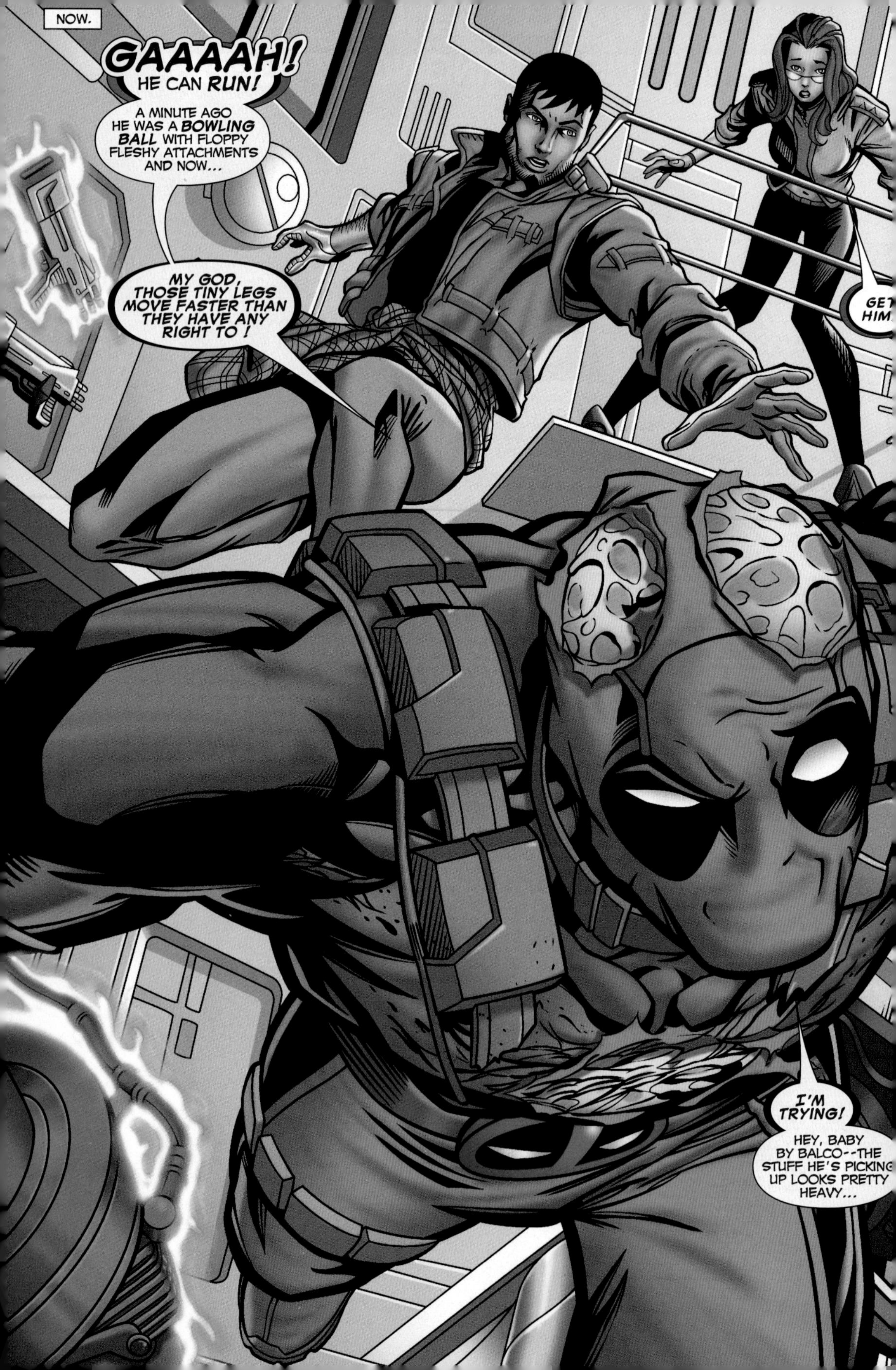
NOW.
GAAAAH! HE CAN RUN!
A MINUTE AGO HE WAS A BOWLING BALL WITH FLOPPY FLESHY ATTACHMENTS AND NOW...
MY GOD, THOSE TINY LEGS MOVE FASTER THAN THEY HAVE ANY RIGHT TO!
GET HIM
I'M TRYING!
HEY, BABY BY BALCO--THE STUFF HE'S PICKING UP LOOKS PRETTY HEAVY...

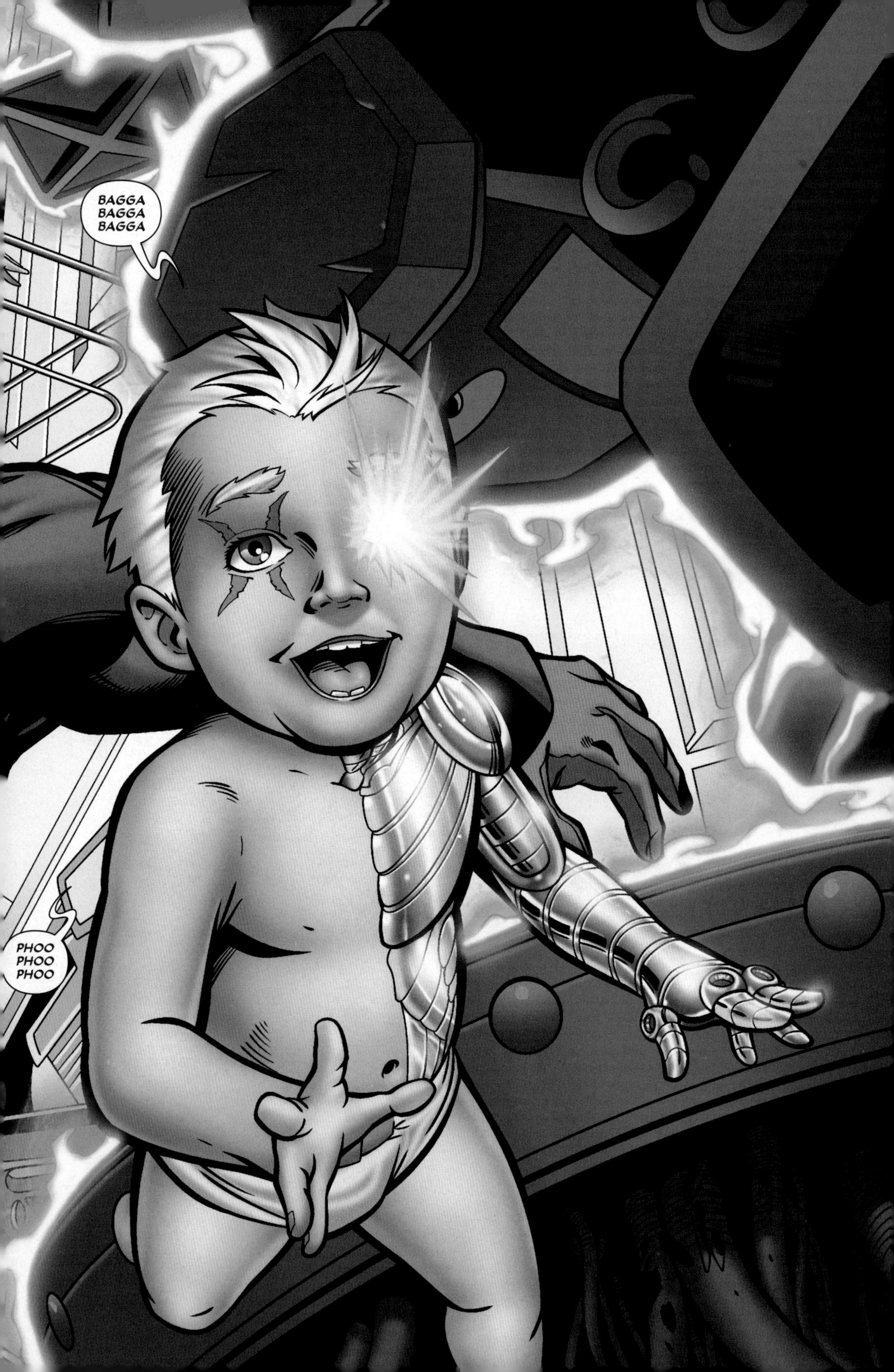
BAGGA BAGGA BAGGA
PHOO PHOO PHOO

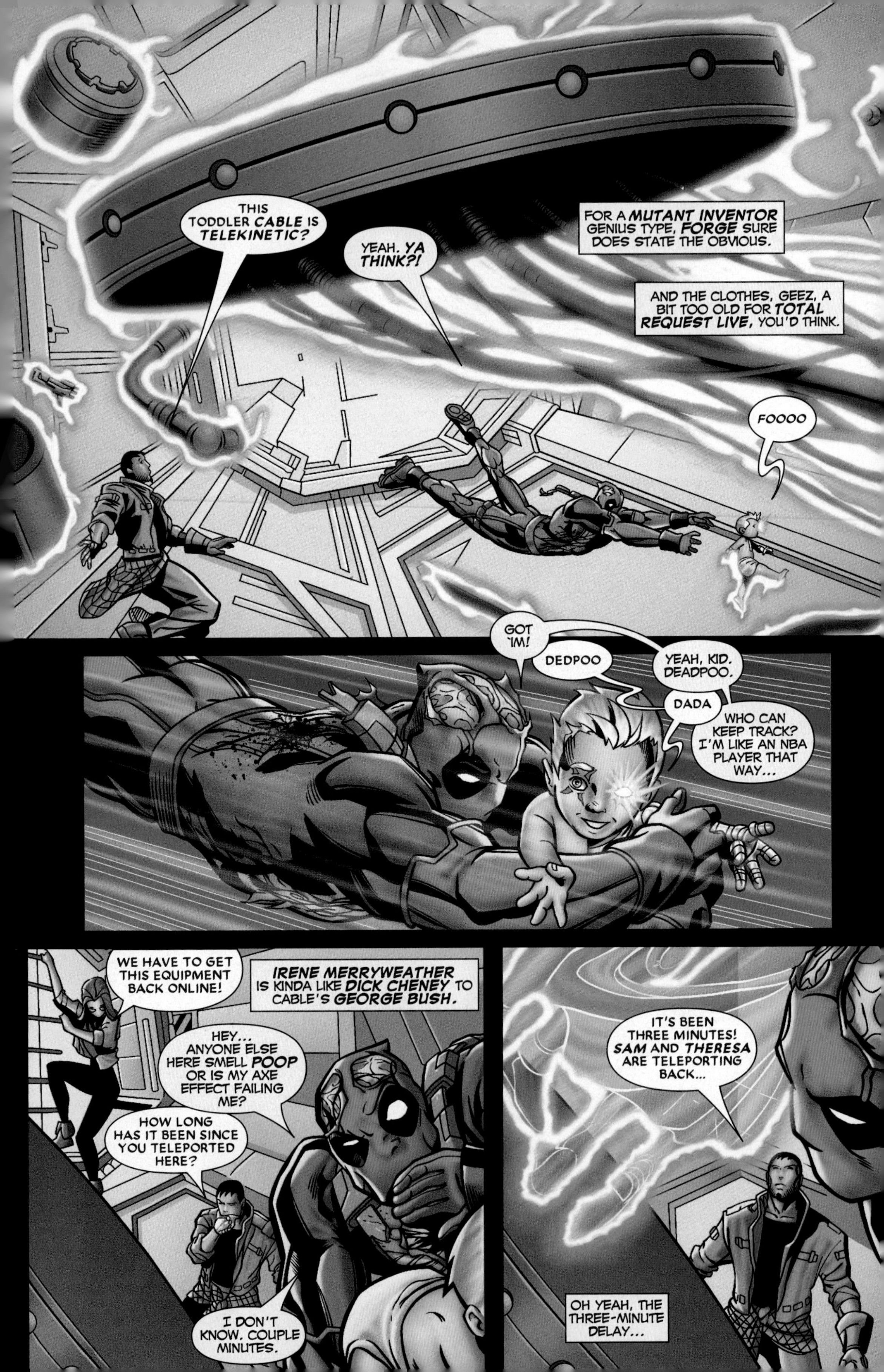
THIS TODDLER CABLE IS TELEKINETIC?
YEAH. YA THINK?!
FOR A MUTANT INVENTOR GENIUS TYPE, FORGE SURE DOES STATE THE OBVIOUS.
AND THE CLOTHES, GEEZ, A BIT TOO OLD FOR TOTAL REQUEST LIVE, YOU'D THINK.
FOOOO
GOT 'IM!
DEDPOO
YEAH, KID. DEADPOO.
DADA
WHO CAN KEEP TRACK? I'M LIKE AN NBA PLAYER THAT WAY...
WE HAVE TO GET THIS EQUIPMENT BACK ONLINE!
IRENE MERRYWEATHER IS KINDA LIKE DICK CHENEY TO CABLE'S GEORGE BUSH.
HEY... ANYONE ELSE HERE SMELL POOP OR IS MY AXE EFFECT FAILING ME?
HOW LONG HAS IT BEEN SINCE YOU TELEPORTED HERE?
I DON'T KNOW. COUPLE MINUTES.
IT'S BEEN THREE MINUTES! SAM AND THERESA ARE TELEPORTING BACK...
OH YEAH, THE THREE-MINUTE DELAY...

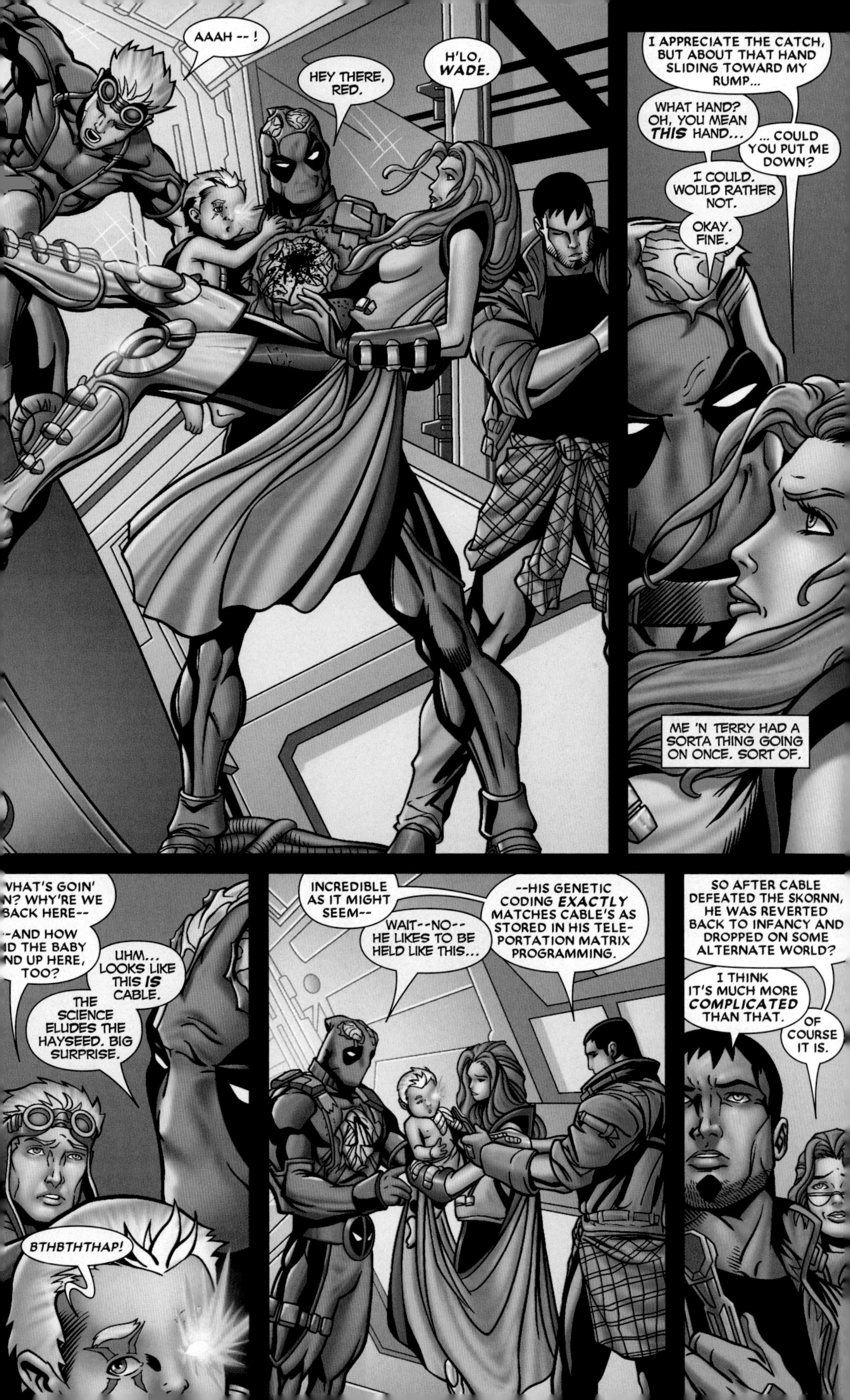
AAAH -- !
HEY THERE, RED.
H'LO, WADE.
I APPRECIATE THE CATCH, BUT ABOUT THAT HAND SLIDING TOWARD MY RUMP...
WHAT HAND? OH, YOU MEAN THIS HAND...
... COULD YOU PUT ME DOWN?
I COULD. WOULD RATHER NOT.
OKAY. FINE.
ME 'N TERRY HAD A SORTA THING GOING ON ONCE. SORT OF.
VHAT'S GOIN' N? WHY'RE WE BACK HERE--
--AND HOW ID THE BABY ND UP HERE, TOO?
UHM... LOOKS LIKE THIS IS CABLE.
THE SCIENCE ELUDES THE HAYSEED. BIG SURPRISE.
BTHBTHTHAP!
INCREDIBLE AS IT MIGHT SEEM--
WAIT--NO-- HE LIKES TO BE HELD LIKE THIS...
--HIS GENETIC CODING EXACTLY MATCHES CABLE'S AS STORED IN HIS TELE-PORTATION MATRIX PROGRAMMING.
SO AFTER CABLE DEFEATED THE SKORNN, HE WAS REVERTED BACK TO INFANCY AND DROPPED ON SOME ALTERNATE WORLD?
I THINK IT'S MUCH MORE COMPLICATED THAN THAT.
OF COURSE IT IS.

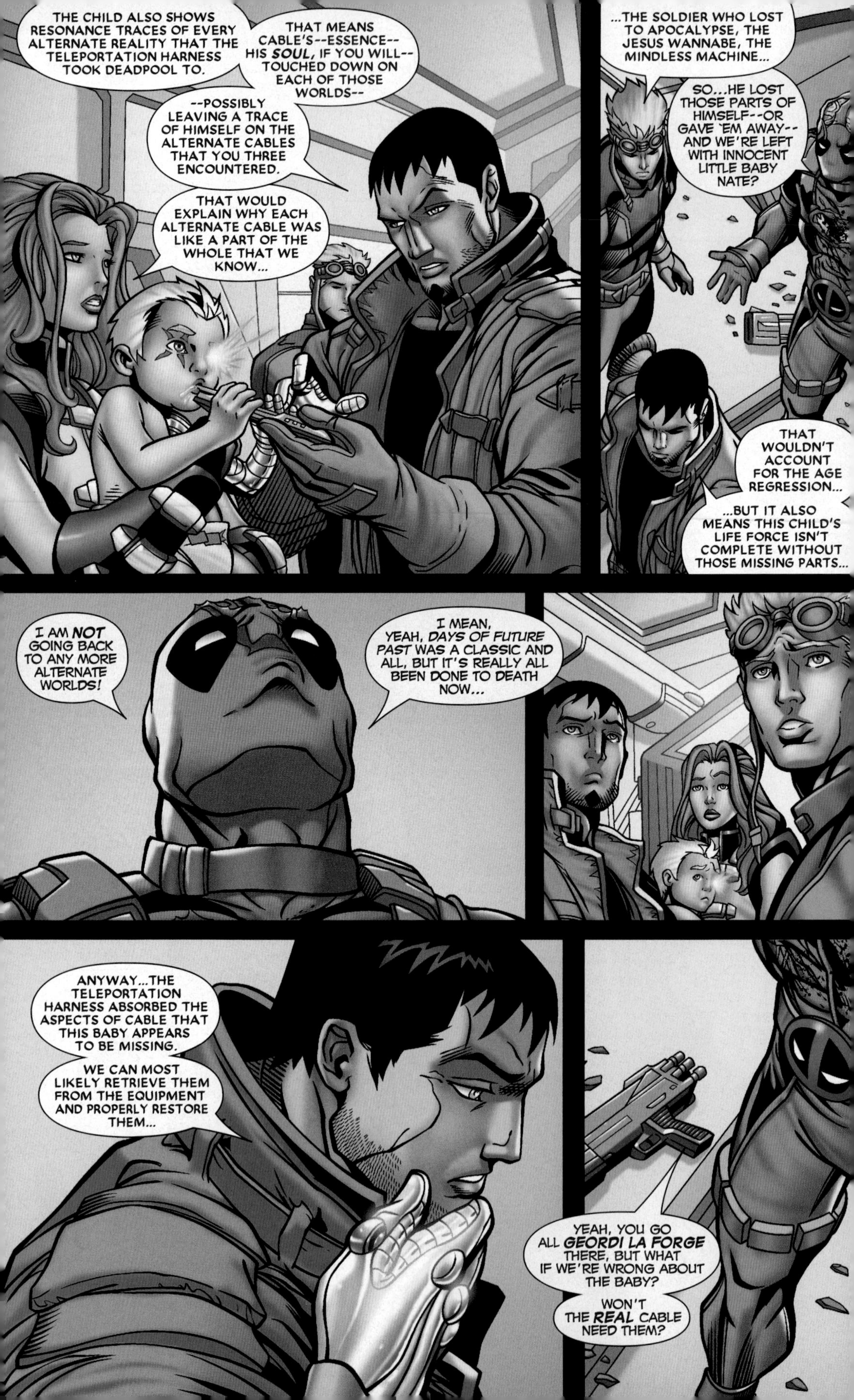
THE CHILD ALSO SHOWS RESONANCE TRACES OF EVERY ALTERNATE REALITY THAT THE TELEPORTATION HARNESS TOOK DEADPOOL TO.
THAT MEANS CABLE'S--ESSENCE--HIS SOUL, IF YOU WILL--TOUCHED DOWN ON EACH OF THOSE WORLDS--
--POSSIBLY LEAVING A TRACE OF HIMSELF ON THE ALTERNATE CABLES THAT YOU THREE ENCOUNTERED.
THAT WOULD EXPLAIN WHY EACH ALTERNATE CABLE WAS LIKE A PART OF THE WHOLE THAT WE KNOW...
...THE SOLDIER WHO LOST TO APOCALYPSE, THE JESUS WANNABE, THE MINDLESS MACHINE...
SO...HE LOST THOSE PARTS OF HIMSELF--OR GAVE 'EM AWAY--AND WE'RE LEFT WITH INNOCENT LITTLE BABY NATE?
THAT WOULDN'T ACCOUNT FOR THE AGE REGRESSION...
...BUT IT ALSO MEANS THIS CHILD'S LIFE FORCE ISN'T COMPLETE WITHOUT THOSE MISSING PARTS...
I AM NOT GOING BACK TO ANY MORE ALTERNATE WORLDS!
I MEAN, YEAH, DAYS OF FUTURE PAST WAS A CLASSIC AND ALL, BUT IT'S REALLY ALL BEEN DONE TO DEATH NOW...
ANYWAY...THE TELEPORTATION HARNESS ABSORBED THE ASPECTS OF CABLE THAT THIS BABY APPEARS TO BE MISSING.
WE CAN MOST LIKELY RETRIEVE THEM FROM THE EQUIPMENT AND PROPERLY RESTORE THEM...
YEAH, YOU GO ALL GEORDI LA FORGE THERE, BUT WHAT IF WE'RE WRONG ABOUT THE BABY?
WON'T THE REAL CABLE NEED THEM?

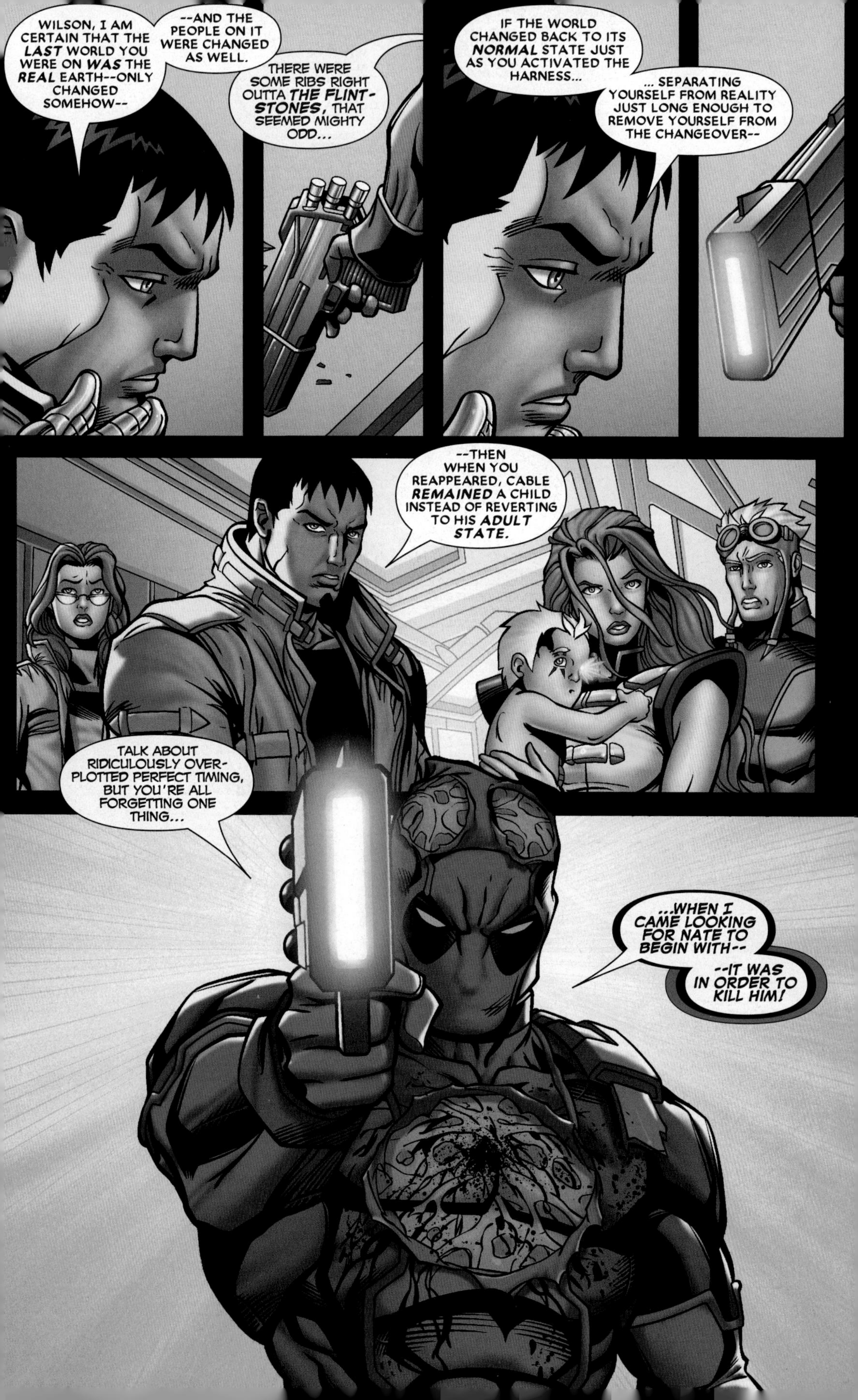
WILSON, I AM CERTAIN THAT THE LAST WORLD YOU WERE ON WAS THE REAL EARTH--ONLY CHANGED SOMEHOW--
--AND THE PEOPLE ON IT WERE CHANGED AS WELL.
THERE WERE SOME RIBS RIGHT OUTTA THE FLINT-STONES, THAT SEEMED MIGHTY ODD...
IF THE WORLD CHANGED BACK TO ITS NORMAL STATE JUST AS YOU ACTIVATED THE HARNESS...
... SEPARATING YOURSELF FROM REALITY JUST LONG ENOUGH TO REMOVE YOURSELF FROM THE CHANGEOVER--
--THEN WHEN YOU REAPPEARED, CABLE REMAINED A CHILD INSTEAD OF REVERTING TO HIS ADULT STATE.
TALK ABOUT RIDICULOUSLY OVER-PLOTTED PERFECT TIMING, BUT YOU'RE ALL FORGETTING ONE THING...
...WHEN I CAME LOOKING FOR NATE TO BEGIN WITH--
--IT WAS IN ORDER TO KILL HIM!

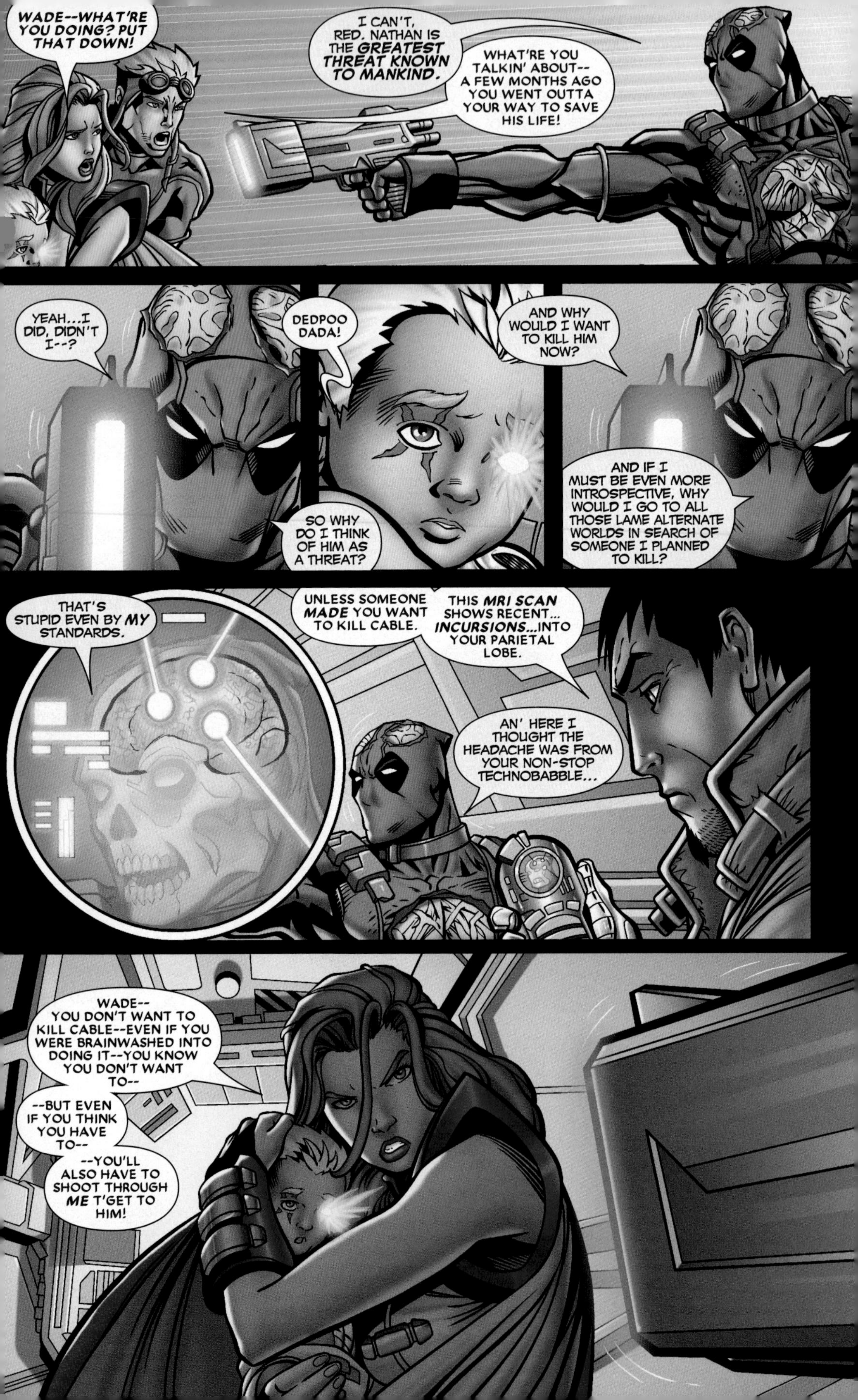
WADE--WHAT'RE YOU DOING? PUT THAT DOWN!
I CAN'T, RED. NATHAN IS THE GREATEST THREAT KNOWN TO MANKIND.
WHAT'RE YOU TALKIN' ABOUT-- A FEW MONTHS AGO YOU WENT OUTTA YOUR WAY TO SAVE HIS LIFE!
YEAH...I DID, DIDN'T I--?
SO WHY DO I THINK OF HIM AS A THREAT?
DEDPOO DADA!
AND WHY WOULD I WANT TO KILL HIM NOW?
AND IF I MUST BE EVEN MORE INTROSPECTIVE, WHY WOULD I GO TO ALL THOSE LAME ALTERNATE WORLDS IN SEARCH OF SOMEONE I PLANNED TO KILL?
THAT'S STUPID EVEN BY MY STANDARDS.
UNLESS SOMEONE MADE YOU WANT TO KILL CABLE.
THIS MRI SCAN SHOWS RECENT... INCURSIONS...INTO YOUR PARIETAL LOBE.
AN' HERE I THOUGHT THE HEADACHE WAS FROM YOUR NON-STOP TECHNOBABBLE...
WADE-- YOU DON'T WANT TO KILL CABLE--EVEN IF YOU WERE BRAINWASHED INTO DOING IT--YOU KNOW YOU DON'T WANT TO--
--BUT EVEN IF YOU THINK YOU HAVE TO--
--YOU'LL ALSO HAVE TO SHOOT THROUGH ME T'GET TO HIM!

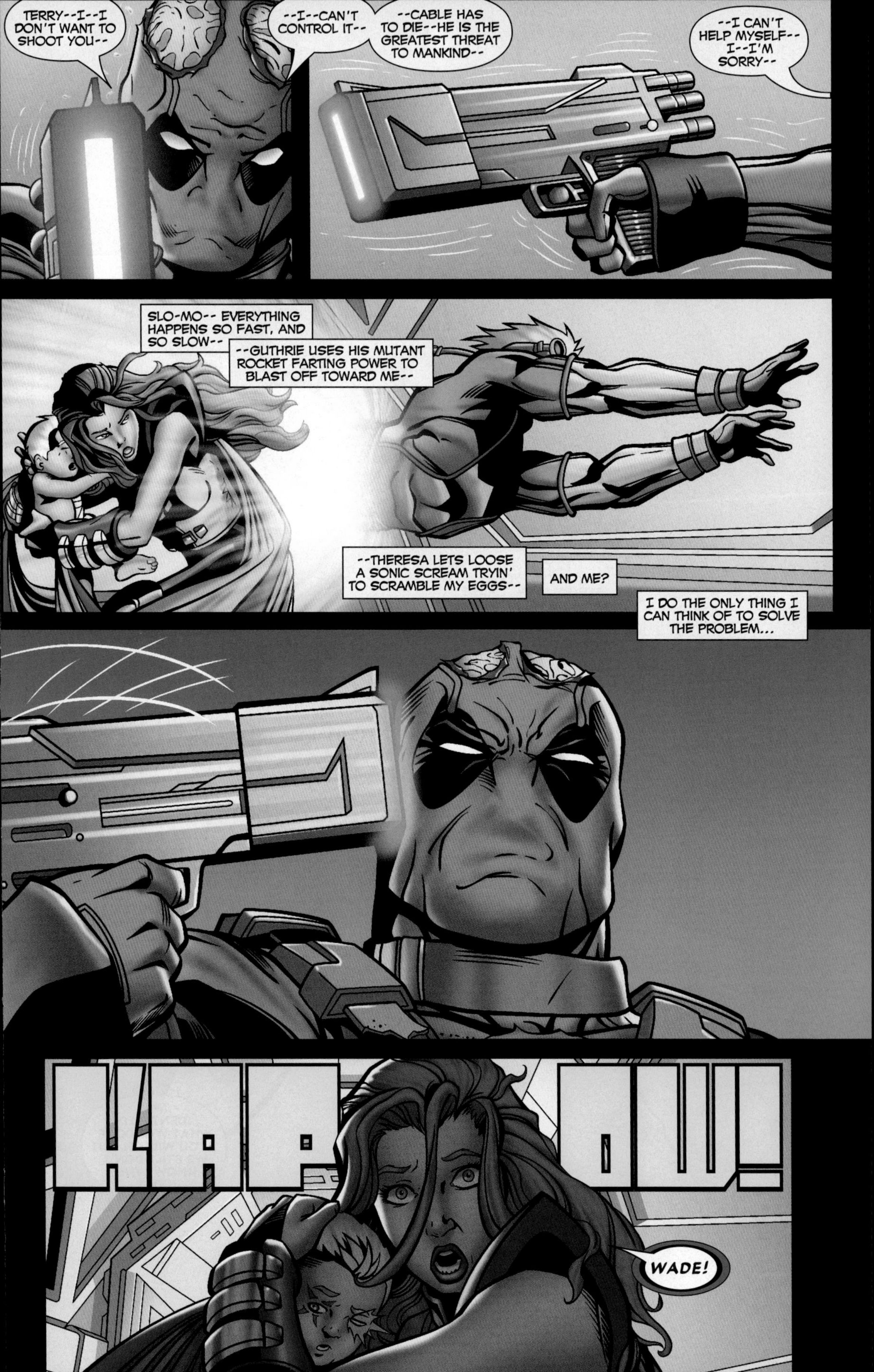
TERRY--I--I DON'T WANT TO SHOOT YOU--
--I--CAN'T CONTROL IT--
--CABLE HAS TO DIE--HE IS THE GREATEST THREAT TO MANKIND--
--I CAN'T HELP MYSELF-- I--I'M SORRY--
SLO-MO-- EVERYTHING HAPPENS SO FAST, AND SO SLOW--
--GUTHRIE USES HIS MUTANT ROCKET FARTING POWER TO BLAST OFF TOWARD ME--
--THERESA LETS LOOSE A SONIC SCREAM TRYIN' TO SCRAMBLE MY EGGS--
AND ME?
I DO THE ONLY THING I CAN THINK OF TO SOLVE THE PROBLEM...
KAP OW!
WADE!

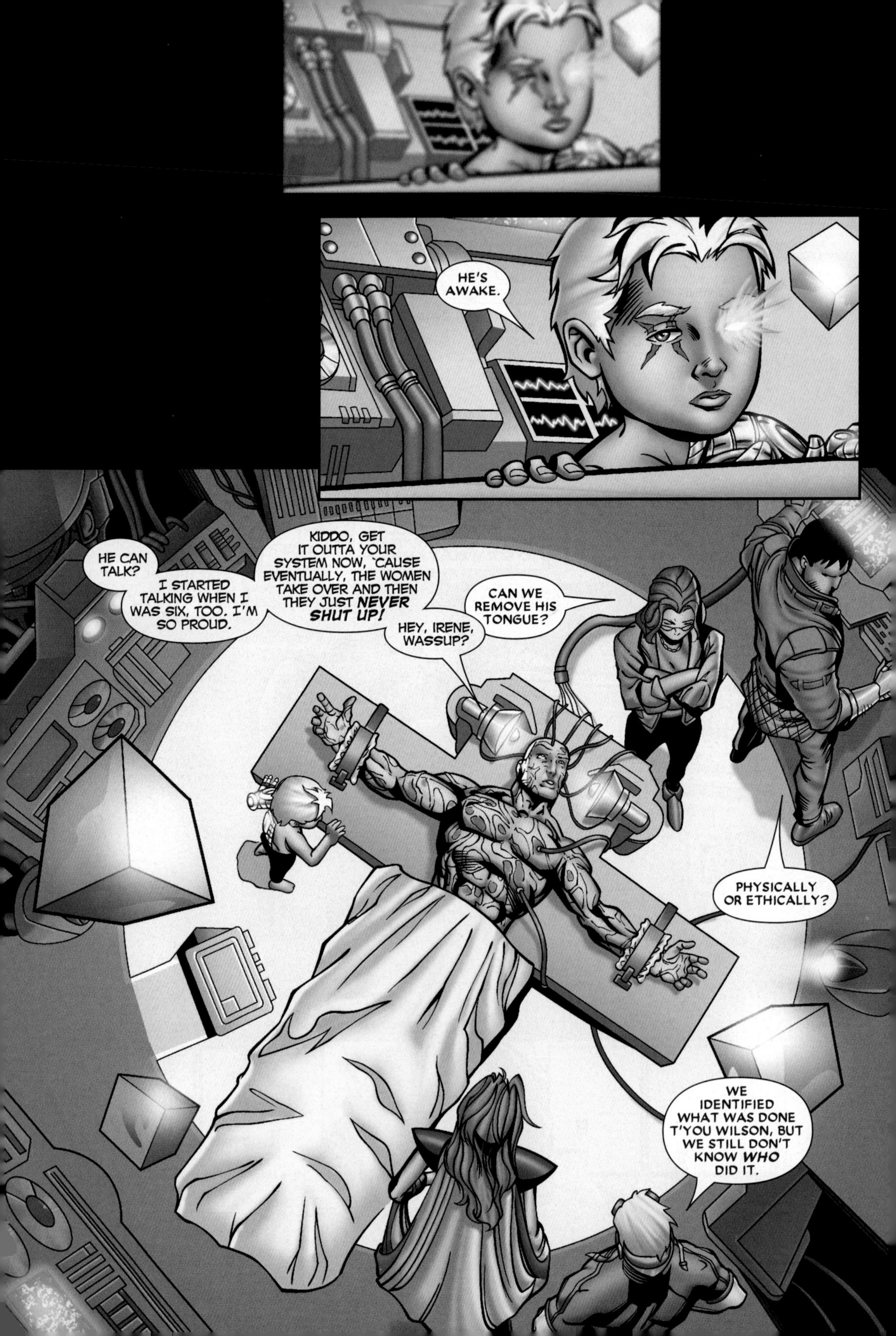
HE'S AWAKE.
HE CAN TALK?
I STARTED TALKING WHEN I WAS SIX, TOO. I'M SO PROUD.
KIDDO, GET IT OUTTA YOUR SYSTEM NOW, 'CAUSE EVENTUALLY, THE WOMEN TAKE OVER AND THEN THEY JUST ***NEVER SHUT UP!***
HEY, IRENE, WASSUP?
CAN WE REMOVE HIS TONGUE?
PHYSICALLY OR ETHICALLY?
WE IDENTIFIED WHAT WAS DONE T'YOU WILSON, BUT WE STILL DON'T KNOW ***WHO*** DID IT.

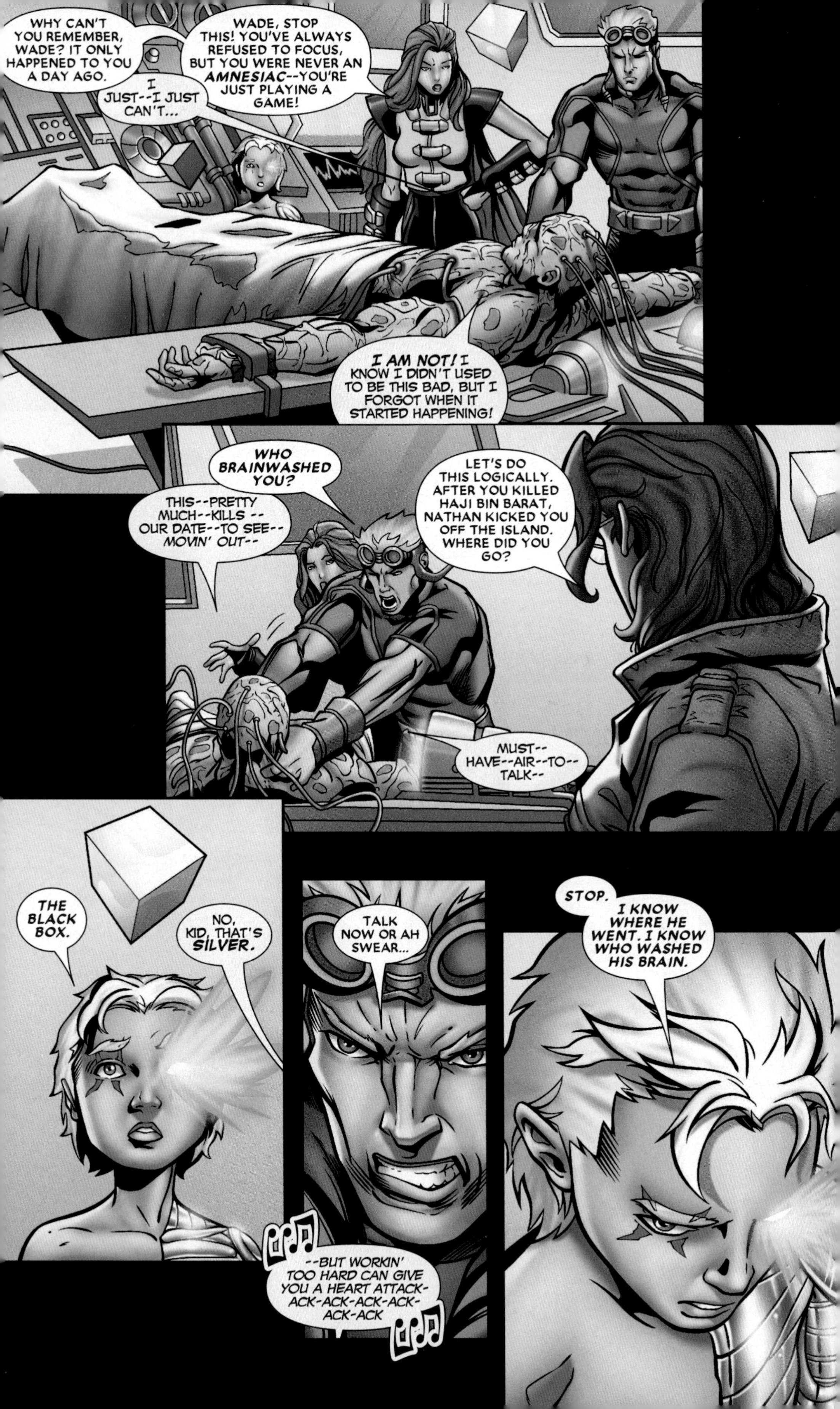

WHY CAN'T YOU REMEMBER, WADE? IT ONLY HAPPENED TO YOU A DAY AGO.
WADE, STOP THIS! YOU'VE ALWAYS REFUSED TO FOCUS, BUT YOU WERE NEVER AN AMNESIAC--YOU'RE JUST PLAYING A GAME!
I JUST--I JUST CAN'T...
I AM NOT! I KNOW I DIDN'T USED TO BE THIS BAD, BUT I FORGOT WHEN IT STARTED HAPPENING!
WHO BRAINWASHED YOU?
THIS--PRETTY MUCH--KILLS -- OUR DATE--TO SEE-- MOVIN' OUT--
LET'S DO THIS LOGICALLY. AFTER YOU KILLED HAJI BIN BARAT, NATHAN KICKED YOU OFF THE ISLAND. WHERE DID YOU GO?
MUST-- HAVE--AIR--TO-- TALK--
THE BLACK BOX.
NO, KID, THAT'S SILVER.
TALK NOW OR AH SWEAR...
--BUT WORKIN' TOO HARD CAN GIVE YOU A HEART ATTACK-ACK-ACK-ACK-ACK-ACK-ACK
STOP. I KNOW WHERE HE WENT. I KNOW WHO WASHED HIS BRAIN.

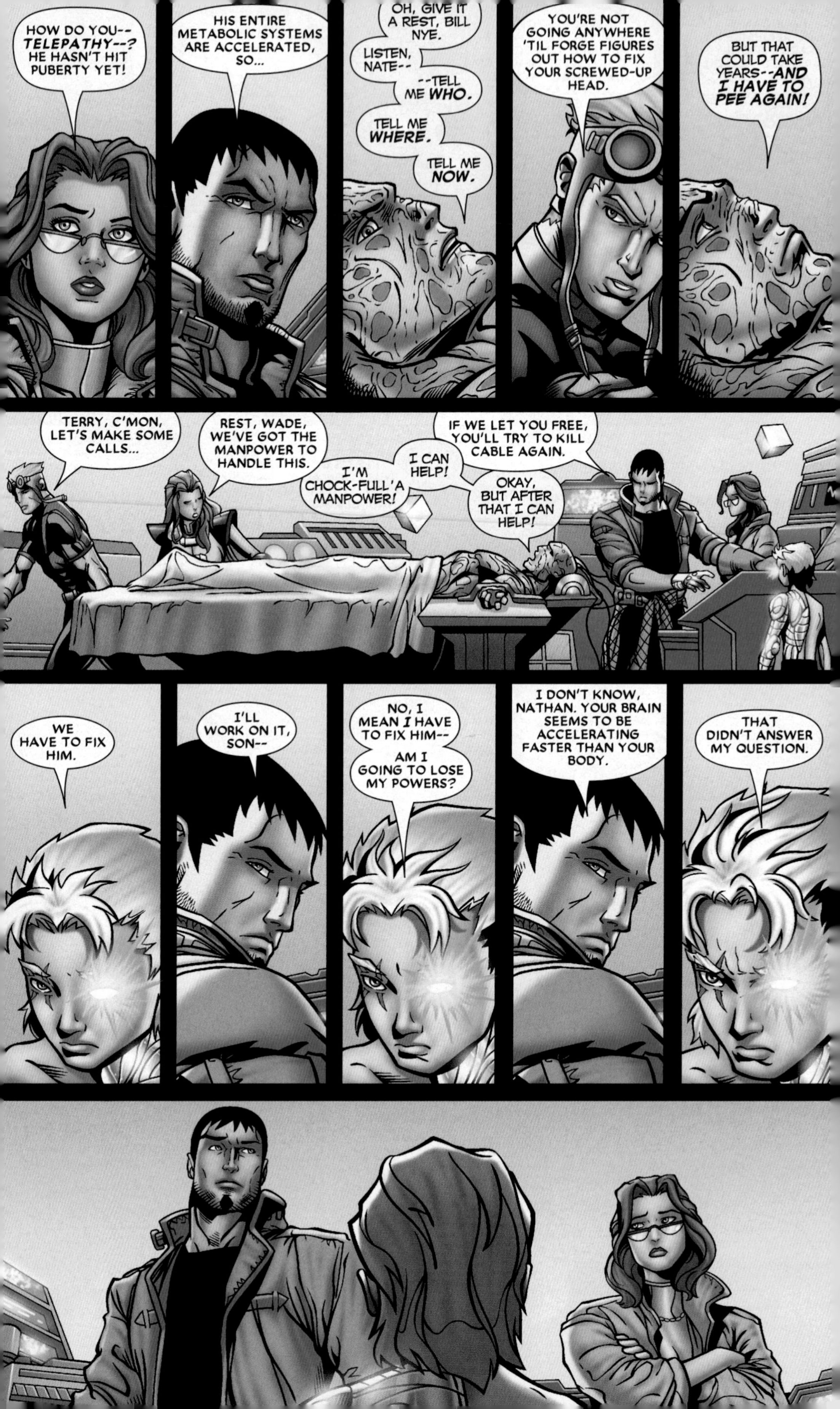
HOW DO YOU--*TELEPATHY*--? HE HASN'T HIT PUBERTY YET!
HIS ENTIRE METABOLIC SYSTEMS ARE ACCELERATED, SO...
OH, GIVE IT A REST, BILL NYE.
LISTEN, NATE--
--TELL ME **WHO.**
TELL ME **WHERE.**
TELL ME **NOW.**
YOU'RE NOT GOING ANYWHERE 'TIL FORGE FIGURES OUT HOW TO FIX YOUR SCREWED-UP HEAD.
BUT THAT COULD TAKE YEARS--***AND I HAVE TO PEE AGAIN!***
TERRY, C'MON, LET'S MAKE SOME CALLS...
REST, WADE, WE'VE GOT THE MANPOWER TO HANDLE THIS.
I'M CHOCK-FULL'A MANPOWER!
I CAN HELP!
IF WE LET YOU FREE, YOU'LL TRY TO KILL CABLE AGAIN.
OKAY, BUT AFTER THAT I CAN HELP!
WE HAVE TO FIX HIM.
I'LL WORK ON IT, SON--
NO, I MEAN *I* HAVE TO FIX HIM--
AM I GOING TO LOSE MY POWERS?
I DON'T KNOW, NATHAN. YOUR BRAIN SEEMS TO BE ACCELERATING FASTER THAN YOUR BODY.
THAT DIDN'T ANSWER MY QUESTION.

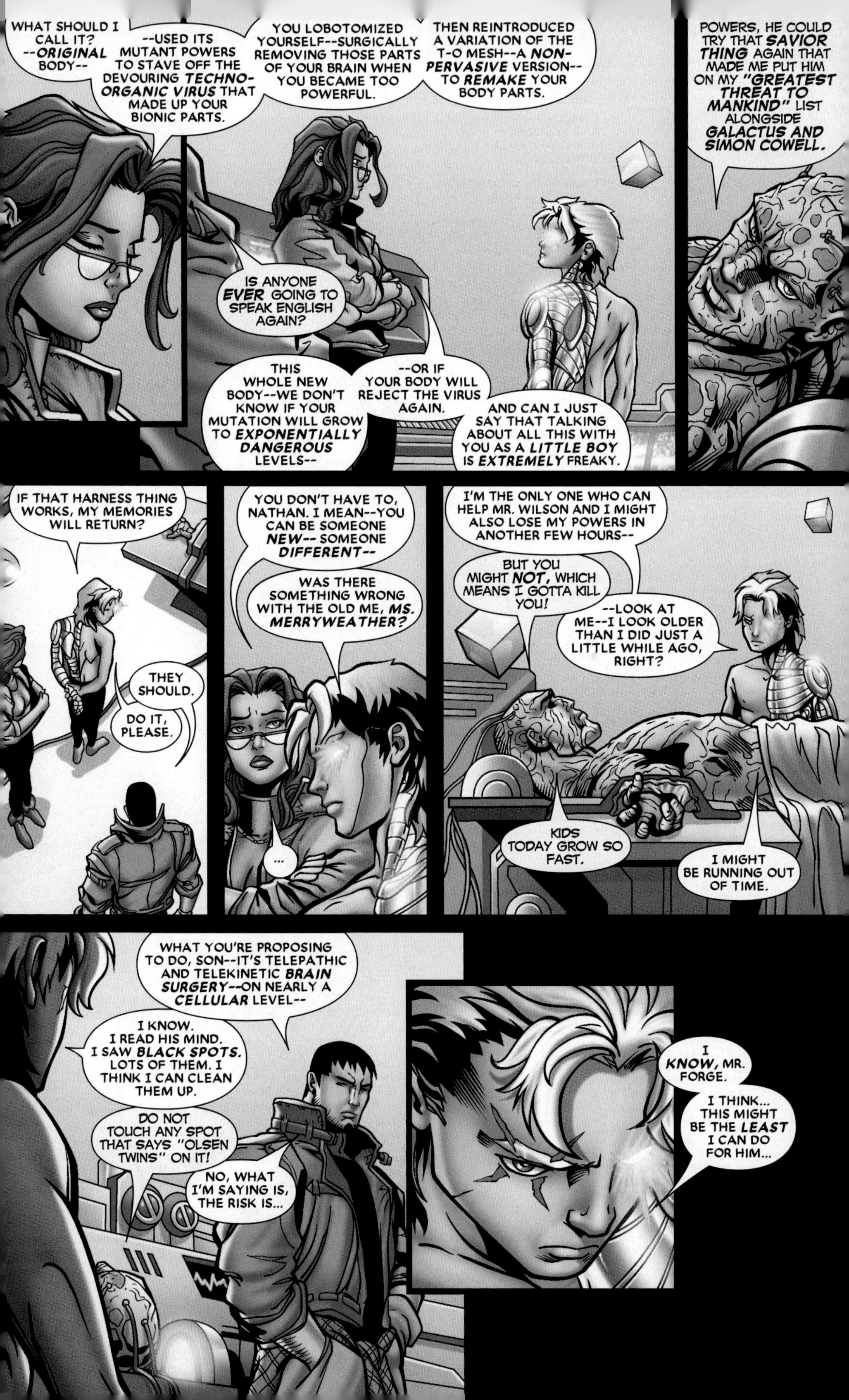
WHAT SHOULD I CALL IT? --ORIGINAL BODY--
--USED ITS MUTANT POWERS TO STAVE OFF THE DEVOURING TECHNO-ORGANIC VIRUS THAT MADE UP YOUR BIONIC PARTS.
YOU LOBOTOMIZED YOURSELF--SURGICALLY REMOVING THOSE PARTS OF YOUR BRAIN WHEN YOU BECAME TOO POWERFUL.
THEN REINTRODUCED A VARIATION OF THE T-O MESH--A NON-PERVASIVE VERSION--TO REMAKE YOUR BODY PARTS.
IS ANYONE EVER GOING TO SPEAK ENGLISH AGAIN?
THIS WHOLE NEW BODY--WE DON'T KNOW IF YOUR MUTATION WILL GROW TO EXPONENTIALLY DANGEROUS LEVELS--
--OR IF YOUR BODY WILL REJECT THE VIRUS AGAIN.
AND CAN I JUST SAY THAT TALKING ABOUT ALL THIS WITH YOU AS A LITTLE BOY IS EXTREMELY FREAKY.
POWERS, HE COULD TRY THAT SAVIOR THING AGAIN THAT MADE ME PUT HIM ON MY "GREATEST THREAT TO MANKIND" LIST ALONGSIDE GALACTUS AND SIMON COWELL.
IF THAT HARNESS THING WORKS, MY MEMORIES WILL RETURN?
THEY SHOULD.
DO IT, PLEASE.
YOU DON'T HAVE TO, NATHAN. I MEAN--YOU CAN BE SOMEONE NEW-- SOMEONE DIFFERENT--
WAS THERE SOMETHING WRONG WITH THE OLD ME, MS. MERRYWEATHER?
...
I'M THE ONLY ONE WHO CAN HELP MR. WILSON AND I MIGHT ALSO LOSE MY POWERS IN ANOTHER FEW HOURS--
BUT YOU MIGHT NOT, WHICH MEANS I GOTTA KILL YOU!
--LOOK AT ME--I LOOK OLDER THAN I DID JUST A LITTLE WHILE AGO, RIGHT?
KIDS TODAY GROW SO FAST.
I MIGHT BE RUNNING OUT OF TIME.
WHAT YOU'RE PROPOSING TO DO, SON--IT'S TELEPATHIC AND TELEKINETIC BRAIN SURGERY--ON NEARLY A CELLULAR LEVEL--
I KNOW. I READ HIS MIND. I SAW BLACK SPOTS. LOTS OF THEM. I THINK I CAN CLEAN THEM UP.
DO NOT TOUCH ANY SPOT THAT SAYS "OLSEN TWINS" ON IT!
NO, WHAT I'M SAYING IS, THE RISK IS...
I KNOW, MR. FORGE.
I THINK... THIS MIGHT BE THE LEAST I CAN DO FOR HIM...

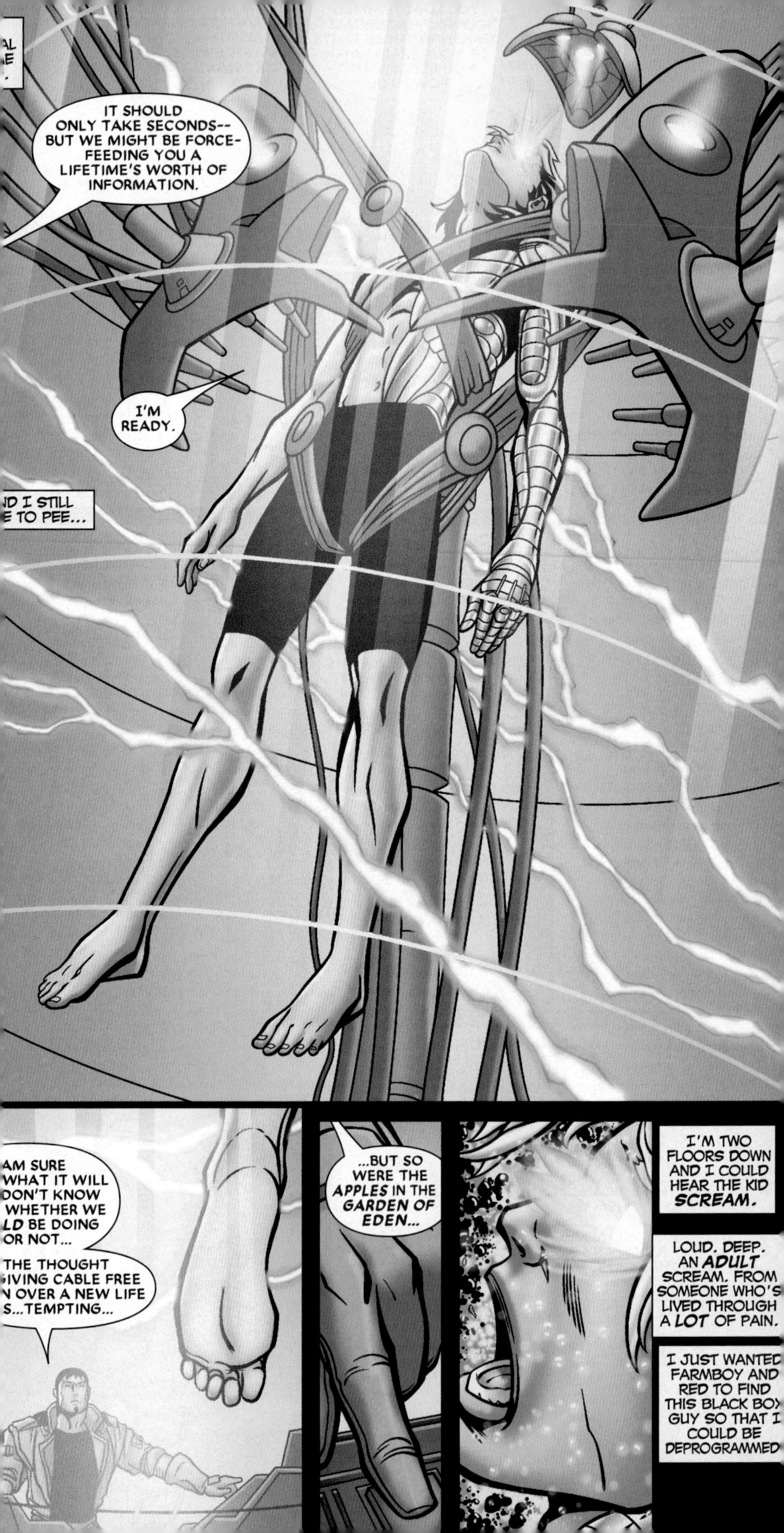
IT SHOULD ONLY TAKE SECONDS-- BUT WE MIGHT BE FORCE-FEEDING YOU A LIFETIME'S WORTH OF INFORMATION.
I'M READY.
ND I STILL E TO PEE...
AM SURE WHAT IT WILL DON'T KNOW WHETHER WE LD BE DOING OR NOT...
THE THOUGHT GIVING CABLE FREE N OVER A NEW LIFE S...TEMPTING...
...BUT SO WERE THE APPLES IN THE GARDEN OF EDEN...
I'M TWO FLOORS DOWN AND I COULD HEAR THE KID SCREAM.
LOUD. DEEP. AN ADULT SCREAM. FROM SOMEONE WHO'S LIVED THROUGH A LOT OF PAIN.
I JUST WANTED FARMBOY AND RED TO FIND THIS BLACK BOX GUY SO THAT I COULD BE DEPROGRAMMED

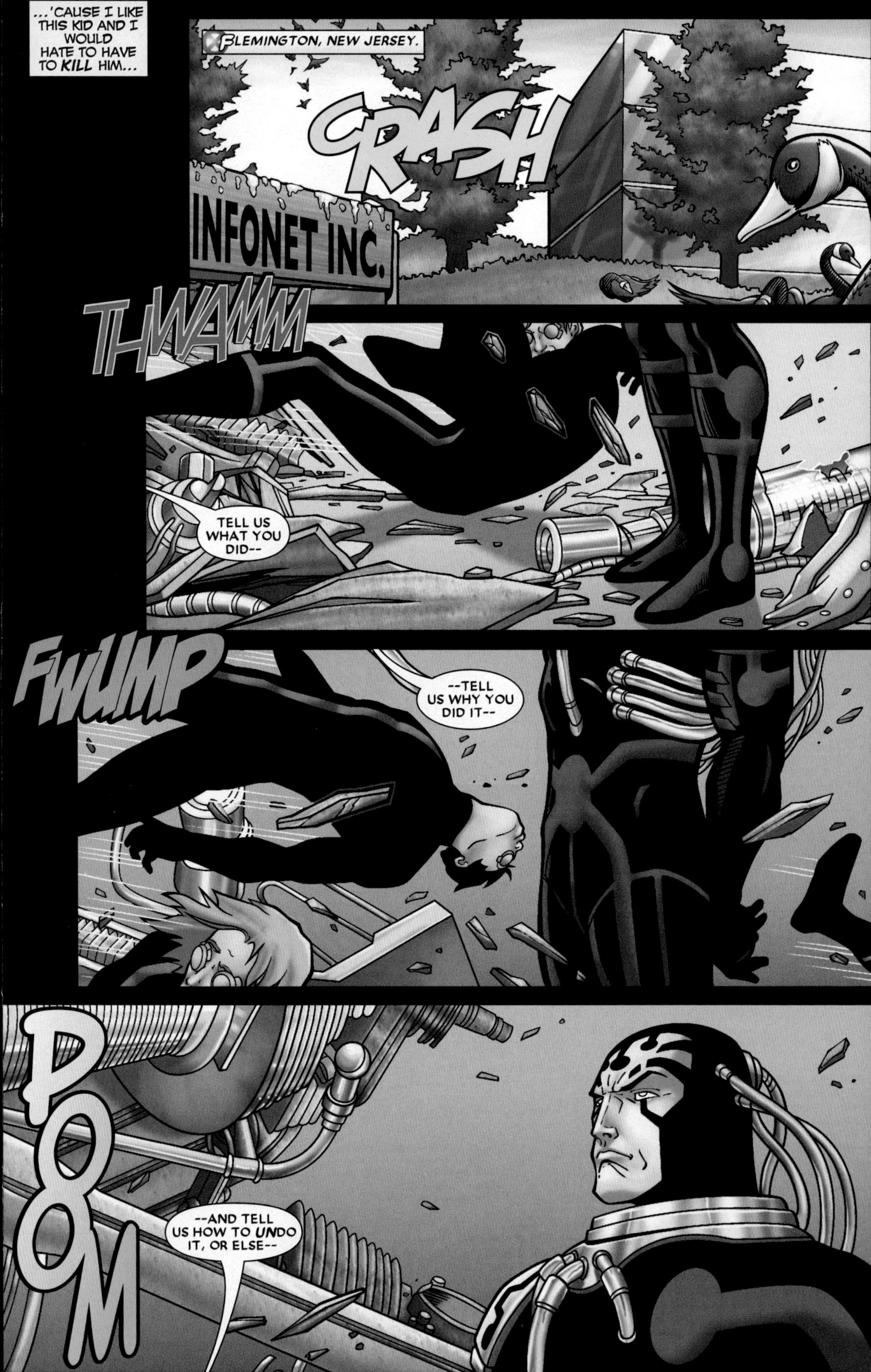
...'CAUSE I LIKE THIS KID AND I WOULD HATE TO HAVE TO KILL HIM...
FLEMINGTON, NEW JERSEY.
CRASH
INFONET INC.
THWAMM
TELL US WHAT YOU DID--
FWUMP
--TELL US WHY YOU DID IT--
POOM
--AND TELL US HOW TO UNDO IT, OR ELSE--

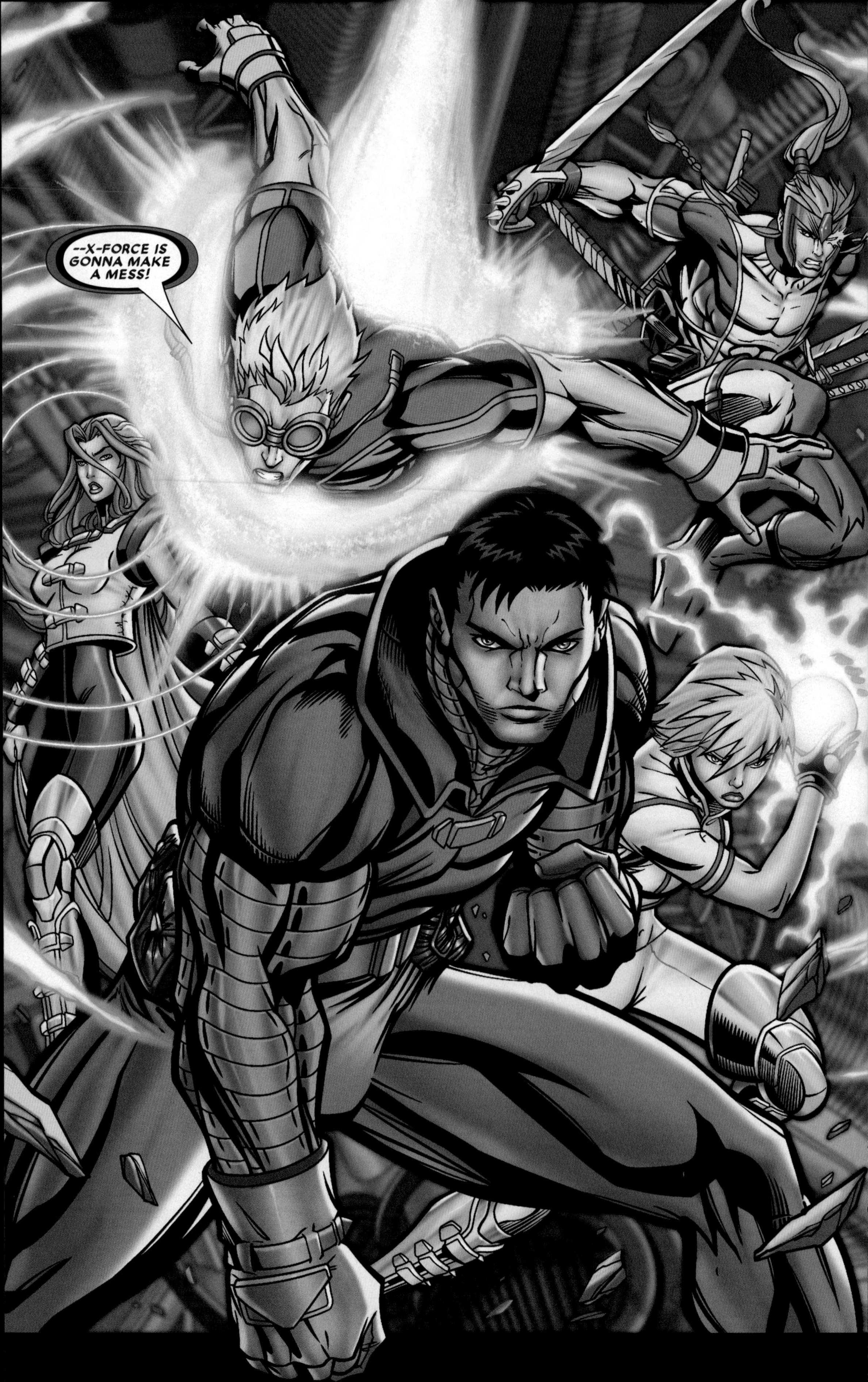
--X-FORCE IS GONNA MAKE A MESS!

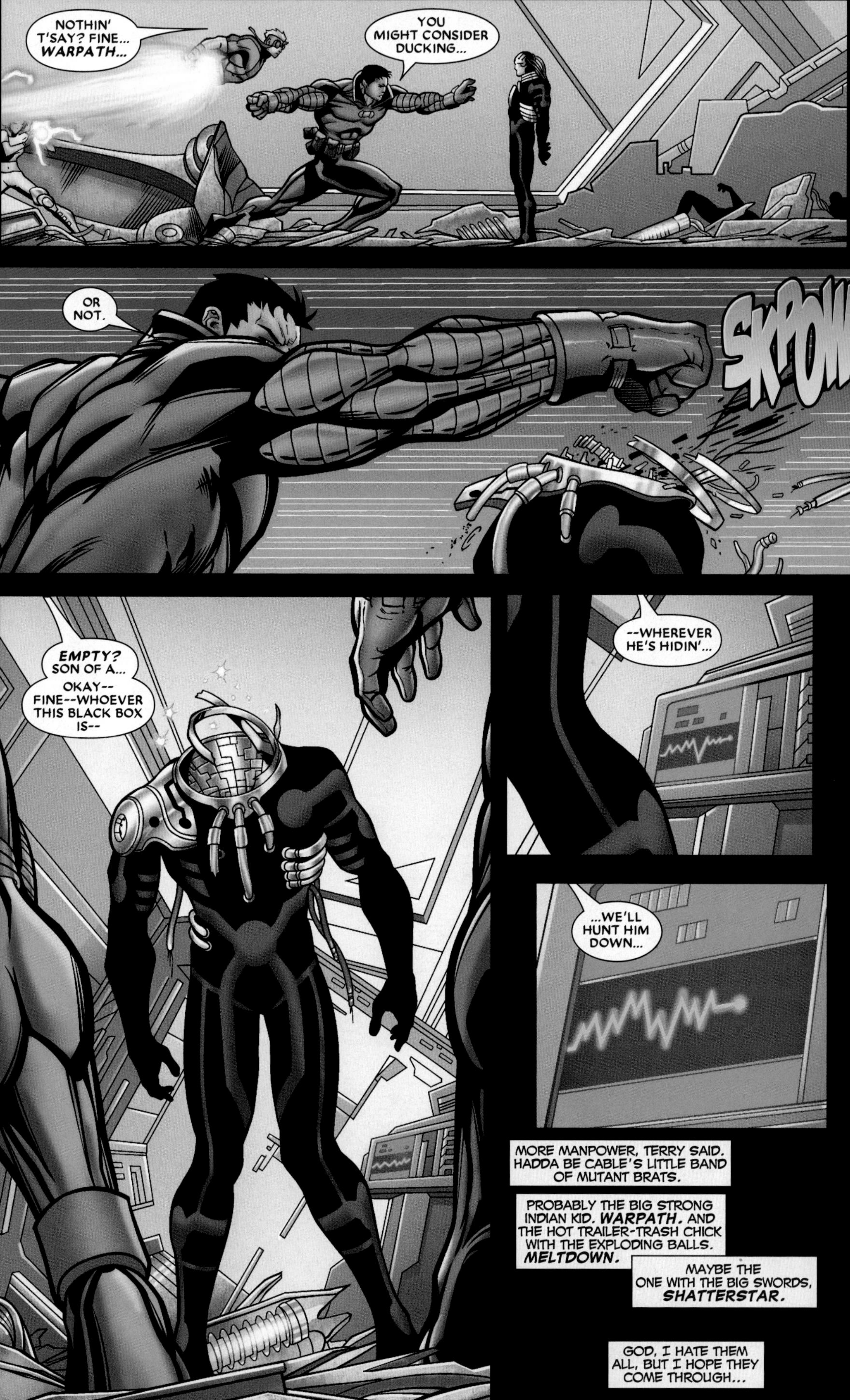
NOTHIN' T'SAY? FINE... WARPATH...
YOU MIGHT CONSIDER DUCKING...
OR NOT.
SKPOW!
EMPTY? SON OF A... OKAY-- FINE--WHOEVER THIS BLACK BOX IS--
--WHEREVER HE'S HIDIN'...
...WE'LL HUNT HIM DOWN...
MORE MANPOWER, TERRY SAID. HADDA BE CABLE'S LITTLE BAND OF MUTANT BRATS.
PROBABLY THE BIG STRONG INDIAN KID. WARPATH. AND THE HOT TRAILER-TRASH CHICK WITH THE EXPLODING BALLS. MELTDOWN.
MAYBE THE ONE WITH THE BIG SWORDS, SHATTERSTAR.
GOD, I HATE THEM ALL, BUT I HOPE THEY COME THROUGH...

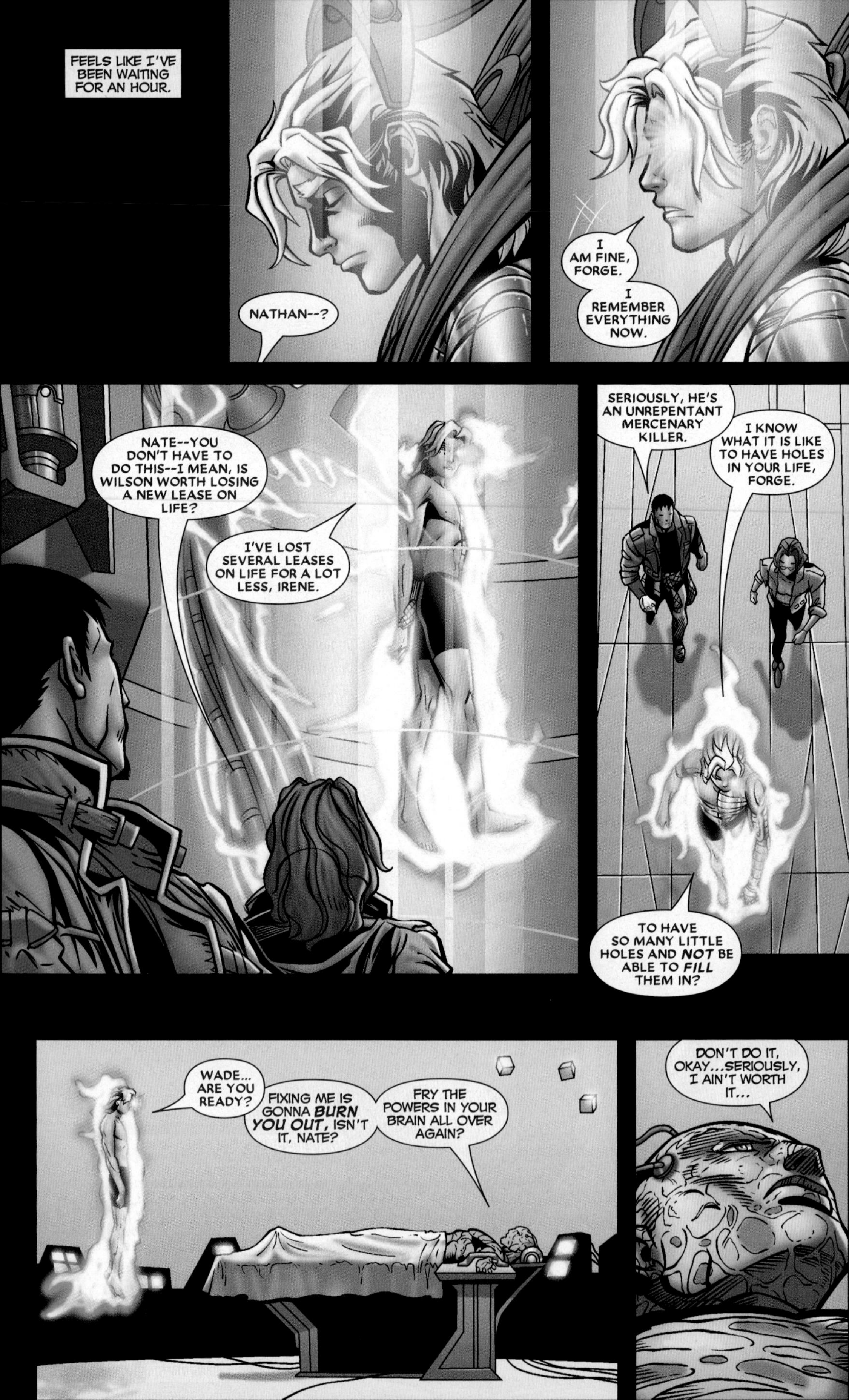

FEELS LIKE I'VE BEEN WAITING FOR AN HOUR.
NATHAN--?
I AM FINE, FORGE.
I REMEMBER EVERYTHING NOW.
NATE--YOU DON'T HAVE TO DO THIS--I MEAN, IS WILSON WORTH LOSING A NEW LEASE ON LIFE?
I'VE LOST SEVERAL LEASES ON LIFE FOR A LOT LESS, IRENE.
SERIOUSLY, HE'S AN UNREPENTANT MERCENARY KILLER.
I KNOW WHAT IT IS LIKE TO HAVE HOLES IN YOUR LIFE, FORGE.
TO HAVE SO MANY LITTLE HOLES AND NOT BE ABLE TO FILL THEM IN?
WADE... ARE YOU READY?
FIXING ME IS GONNA BURN YOU OUT, ISN'T IT, NATE?
FRY THE POWERS IN YOUR BRAIN ALL OVER AGAIN?
DON'T DO IT, OKAY...SERIOUSLY, I AIN'T WORTH IT...

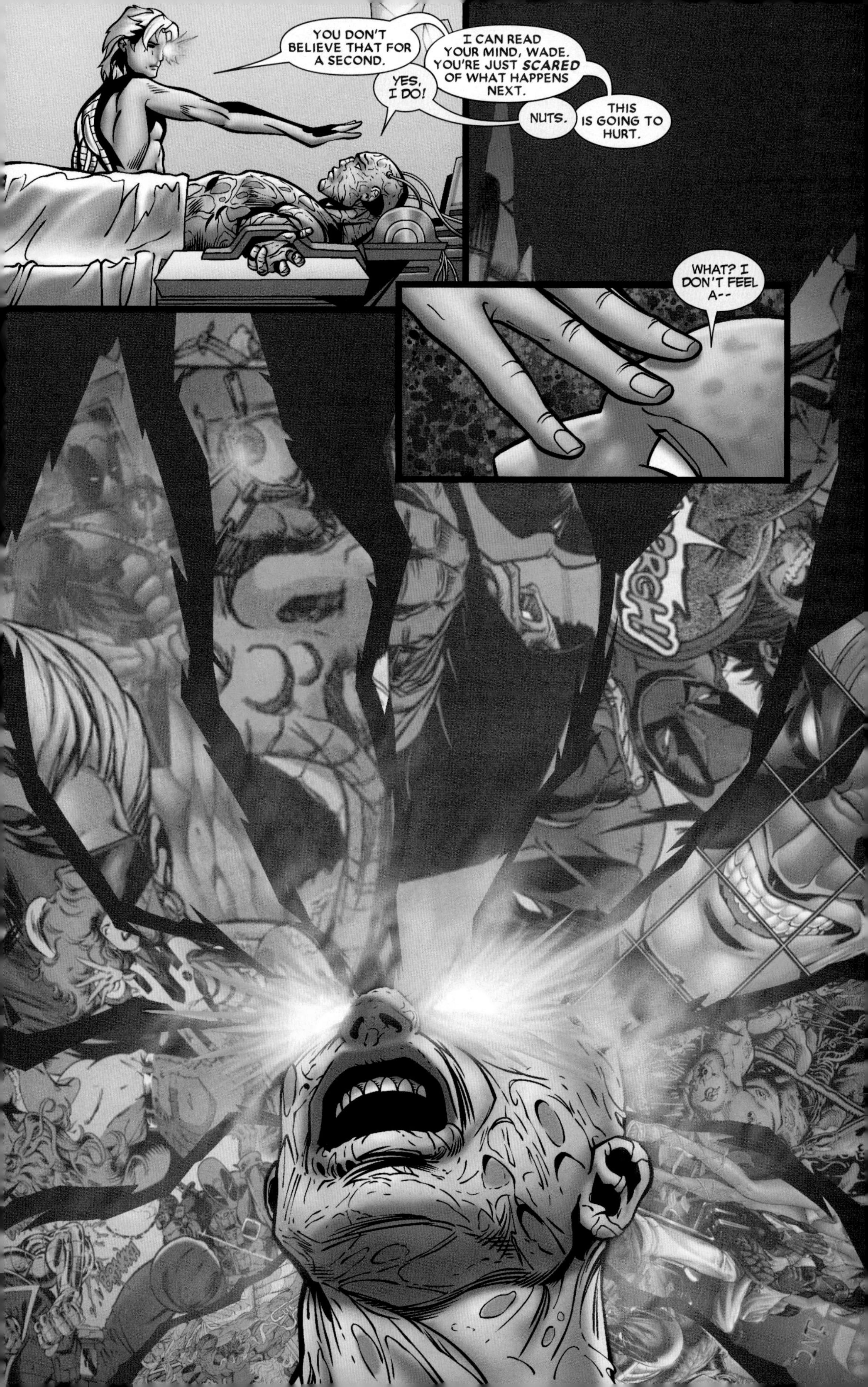
YOU DON'T BELIEVE THAT FOR A SECOND.
YES, I DO!
I CAN READ YOUR MIND, WADE. YOU'RE JUST *SCARED* OF WHAT HAPPENS NEXT.
NUTS.
THIS IS GOING TO HURT.
WHAT? I DON'T FEEL A--

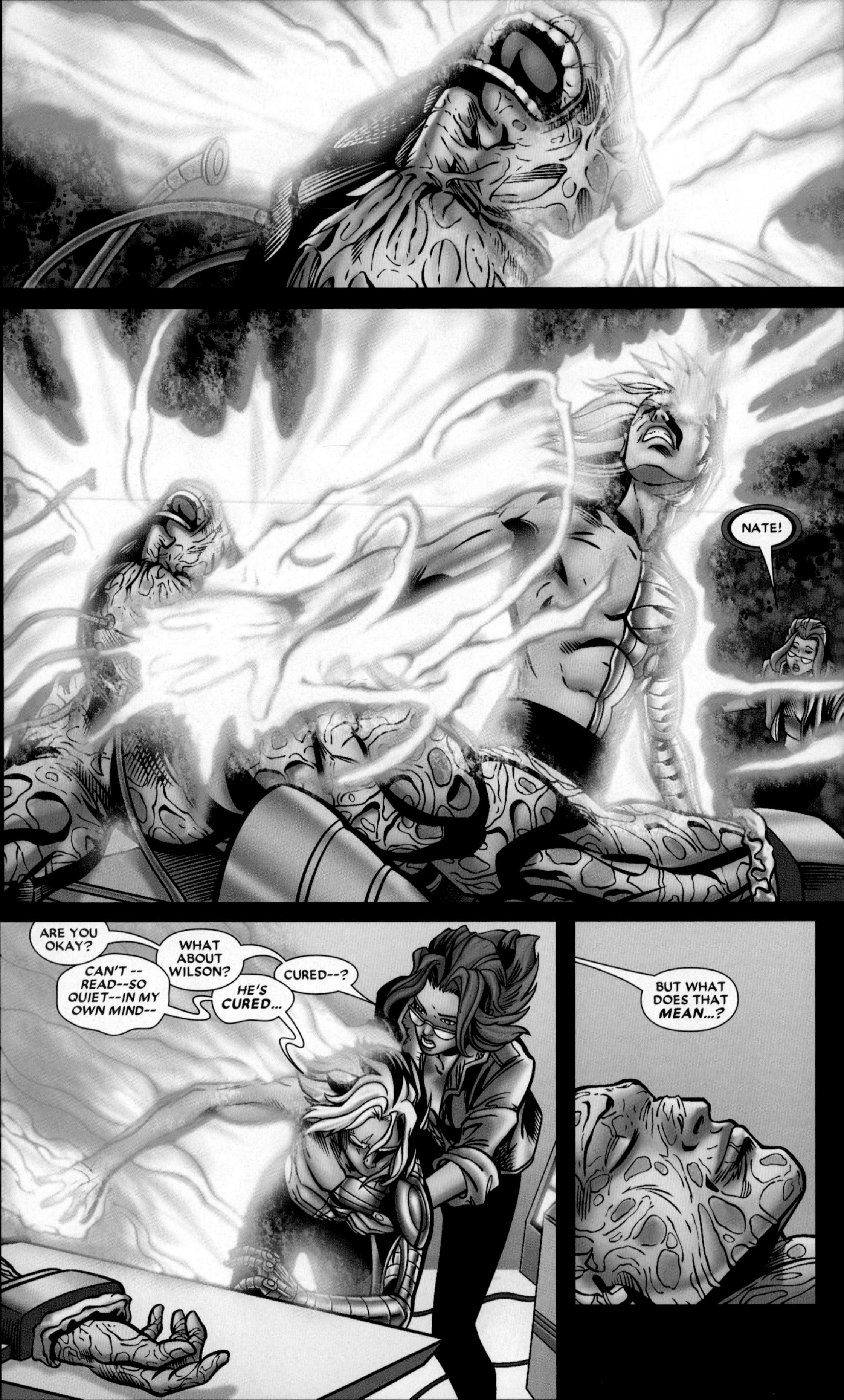
NATE!
ARE YOU OKAY?
CAN'T -- READ--SO QUIET--IN MY OWN MIND--
WHAT ABOUT WILSON?
HE'S CURED...
CURED--?
BUT WHAT DOES THAT MEAN...?

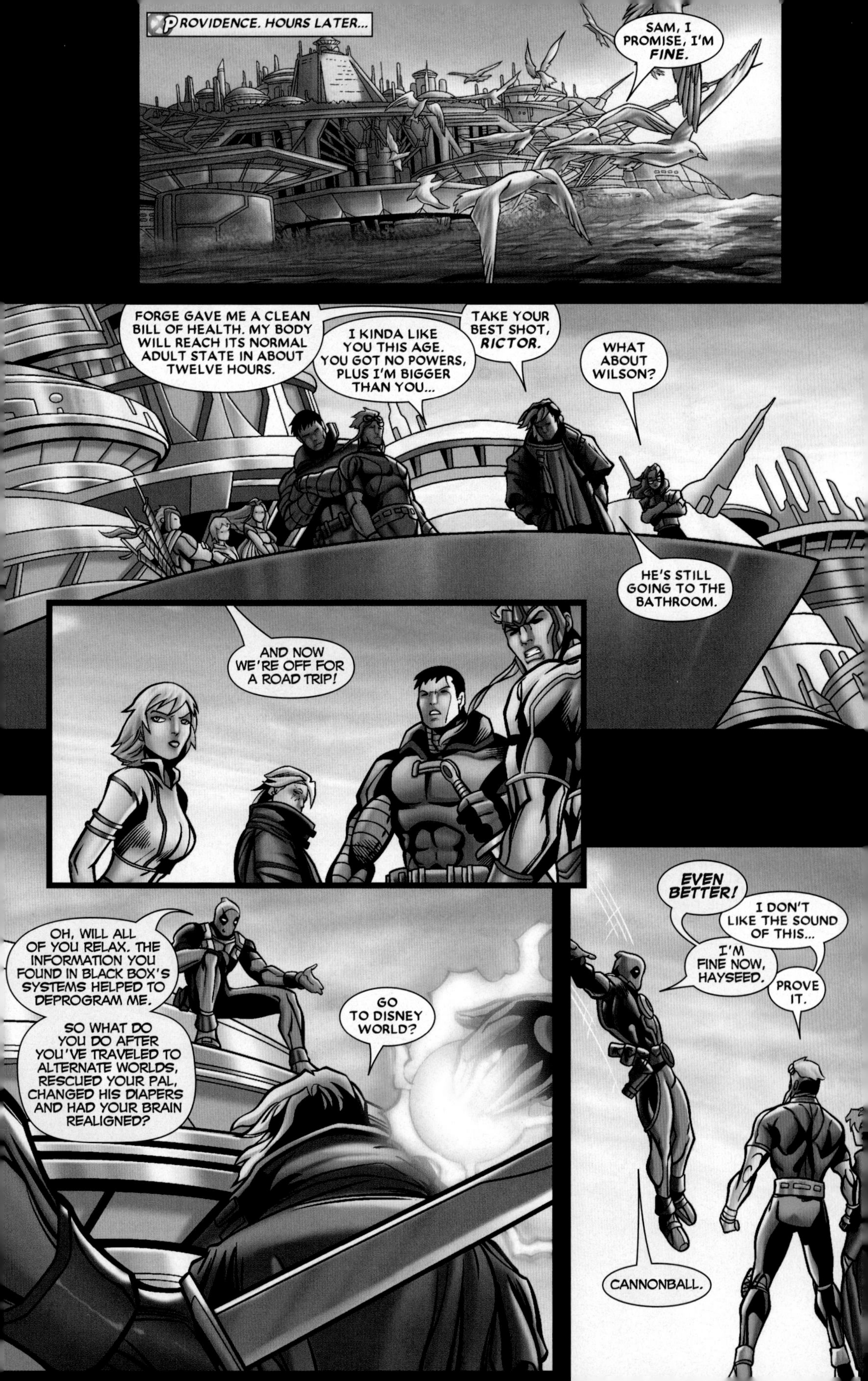
PROVIDENCE. HOURS LATER...
SAM, I PROMISE, I'M FINE.
FORGE GAVE ME A CLEAN BILL OF HEALTH. MY BODY WILL REACH ITS NORMAL ADULT STATE IN ABOUT TWELVE HOURS.
I KINDA LIKE YOU THIS AGE. YOU GOT NO POWERS, PLUS I'M BIGGER THAN YOU...
TAKE YOUR BEST SHOT, RICTOR.
WHAT ABOUT WILSON?
HE'S STILL GOING TO THE BATHROOM.
AND NOW WE'RE OFF FOR A ROAD TRIP!
OH, WILL ALL OF YOU RELAX. THE INFORMATION YOU FOUND IN BLACK BOX'S SYSTEMS HELPED TO DEPROGRAM ME.
SO WHAT DO YOU DO AFTER YOU'VE TRAVELED TO ALTERNATE WORLDS, RESCUED YOUR PAL, CHANGED HIS DIAPERS AND HAD YOUR BRAIN REALIGNED?
GO TO DISNEY WORLD?
EVEN BETTER!
I DON'T LIKE THE SOUND OF THIS...
I'M FINE NOW, HAYSEED.
PROVE IT.
CANNONBALL.

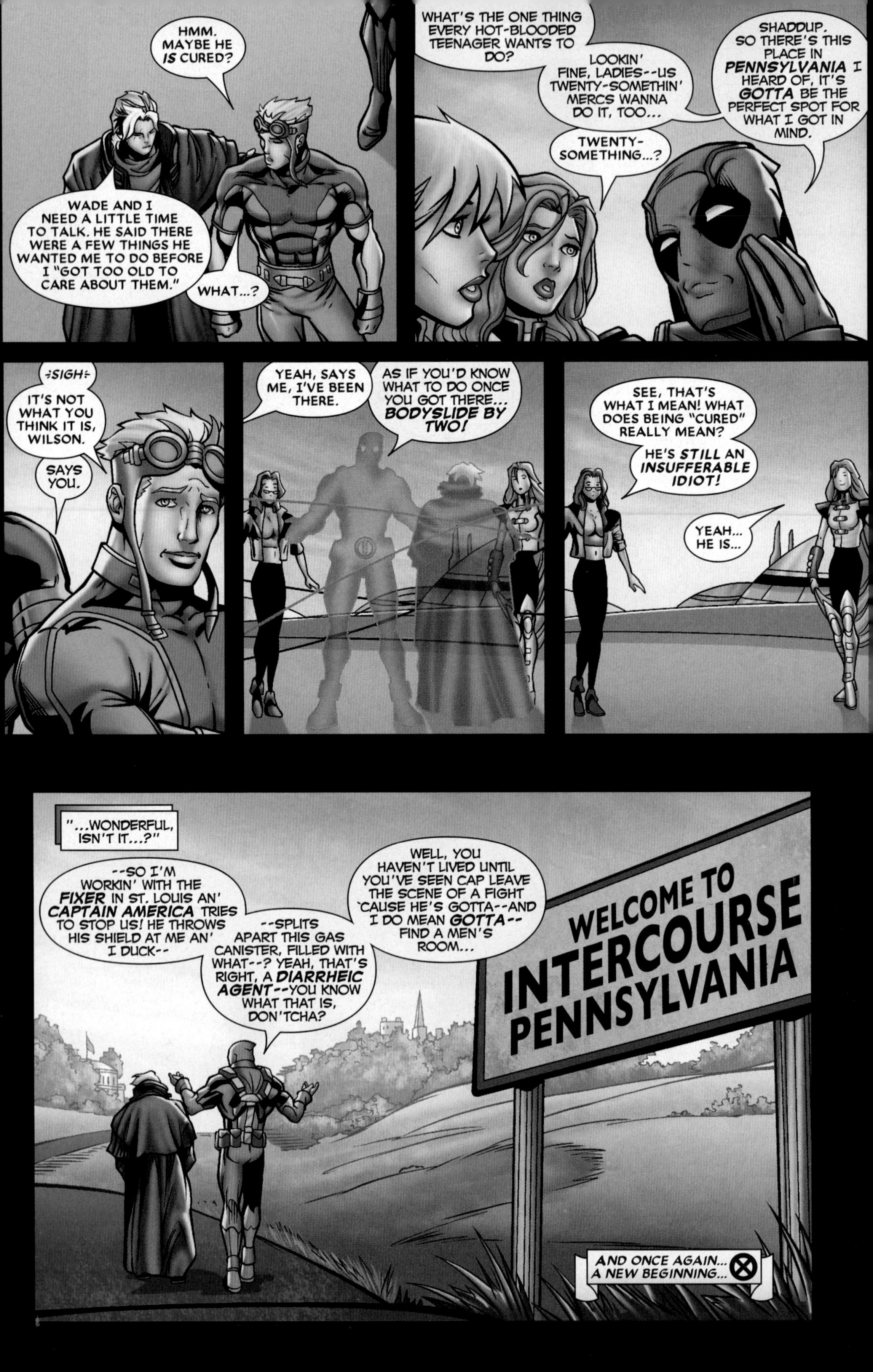
HMM. MAYBE HE *IS* CURED?
WADE AND I NEED A LITTLE TIME TO TALK. HE SAID THERE WERE A FEW THINGS HE WANTED ME TO DO BEFORE I "GOT TOO OLD TO CARE ABOUT THEM."
WHAT...?
WHAT'S THE ONE THING EVERY HOT-BLOODED TEENAGER WANTS TO DO?
LOOKIN' FINE, LADIES--US TWENTY-SOMETHIN' MERCS WANNA DO IT, TOO...
TWENTY-SOMETHING...?
SHADDUP. SO THERE'S THIS PLACE IN *PENNSYLVANIA* I HEARD OF, IT'S *GOTTA* BE THE PERFECT SPOT FOR WHAT I GOT IN MIND.
SIGH
IT'S NOT WHAT YOU THINK IT IS, WILSON.
SAYS YOU.
YEAH, SAYS ME, I'VE BEEN THERE.
AS IF YOU'D KNOW WHAT TO DO ONCE YOU GOT THERE... *BODYSLIDE BY TWO!*
SEE, THAT'S WHAT I MEAN! WHAT DOES BEING "CURED" REALLY MEAN?
HE'S *STILL* AN *INSUFFERABLE IDIOT!*
YEAH... HE IS...
"...WONDERFUL, ISN'T IT...?"
--SO I'M WORKIN' WITH THE *FIXER* IN ST. LOUIS AN' *CAPTAIN AMERICA* TRIES TO STOP US! HE THROWS HIS SHIELD AT ME AN' I DUCK--
--SPLITS APART THIS GAS CANISTER, FILLED WITH WHAT--? YEAH, THAT'S RIGHT, A *DIARRHEIC AGENT*--YOU KNOW WHAT THAT IS, DON'TCHA?
WELL, YOU HAVEN'T LIVED UNTIL YOU'VE SEEN CAP LEAVE THE SCENE OF A FIGHT 'CAUSE HE'S GOTTA--AND I DO MEAN *GOTTA*--FIND A MEN'S ROOM...
WELCOME TO INTERCOURSE PENNSYLVANIA
AND ONCE AGAIN... A NEW BEGINNING...